D0842815

GUANTÁNAMO, USA

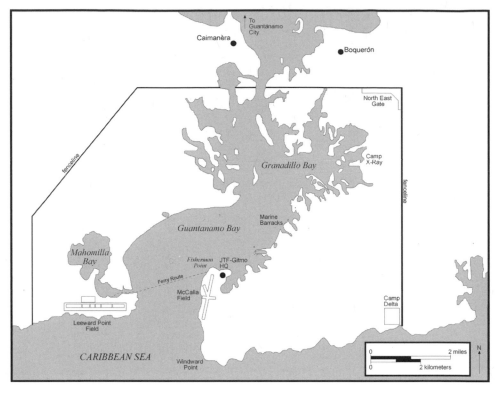

The Guantánamo Naval Base Fenceline. (Courtesy of the Cartography Laboratory, University of Alabama)

GUANTÁNAMO, USA

The Untold History of America's Cuban Outpost

Stephen Irving Max Schwab

University Press of Kansas

Published by the University Press of Kansas (Lawrence, Kansas 66045), which was organized by the Kansas Board of Regents and is operated and funded by Emporia State University, Fort Hays State University, Kansas State University, Pittsburg State University, the University of Kansas, and Wichita State University

Library of Congress Cataloging-in-Publication Data

Schwab, Stephen Irving Max.
Guantánamo, USA : the untold history of America's Cuban outpost / Stephen Irving Max Schwab.
p.   cm.
Includes bibliographical references and index.
ISBN 978-0-7006-1670-1 (cloth : alk. paper)
1. Guantánamo Bay Naval Base (Cuba)—History. 2. Navy-yards and naval stations, American—Cuba—History. 3. United States—Foreign relations—Cuba. 4. Cuba—Foreign relations—United States. 5. United States—History, Naval. I. Title.
VA68.G8S34 2009
359.7097291'67—dc22
2009024285

British Library Cataloguing-in-Publication Data is available.

Printed in the United States of America

10 9 8 7 6 5 4 3 2 1

The paper used in this publication is recycled and contains 30 percent postconsumer waste. It is acid free and meets the minimum requirements of the American National Standard for Permanence of Paper for Printed Library Materials Z39.48-1992.

For the two people who matter most in my life, Diana and David,
and in memory of my parents, Hope and Irving Schwab,
who gave me a love of learning

CONTENTS

An illustration section follows page 162

ACKNOWLEDGMENTS

I WAS SITTING IN THE TIMEWORN LIBRARY of the Carlos J. Finlay Museum of Sciences in Havana, Cuba, when I realized how important it is to acknowledge, or simply thank, the people who help you do research and write. For several hours, on two separate days, a young Cuban lady, Magolys Diago Sandoval, whom I had just met, sat next to me reading articles and books and alerting my attention to pertinent information. She would not accept compensation, and my experience with her was especially poignant because I know she earns a pittance working in a museum she loves, much of which is closed owing to lack of funds for repairs. On my next trip to Havana, I intend to give Magolys a copy of my book.

I especially thank Helen Delpar of the University of Alabama for helping me to decide that I should look at the history of Guantánamo. Both she and Tony Freyer complemented each other by giving excellent advice and expanding my knowledge of pertinent primary and secondary sources. I appreciate the guidance and encouragement provided by my other readers, Lawrence Clayton, Howard Jones, and Steven Ross. I also thank Howard Jones for sharing his research findings on U.S.-Cuban relations.

I feel certain that I would not have pursued historical studies at this stage of my life had it not been for the strong encouragement I received from James Corum, who is now dean of the Baltic Defense College in Tartu, Estonia. James was a student of mine in a Latin American area studies course at the Air War College in spring 1997. At that time, he was also a professor at the School of Advanced Air Power Studies at Maxwell Air Force Base, and, while he was in my course, he published his study *The Luftwaffe: Creating the Operational Air War, 1918–1945*. It was James more than anyone else who persuaded me that I could and should make scholarly contributions to historical literature. He insisted that I obtain a second M.A. degree in military history, publish an article in the *Journal of Military History*, and enter the Ph.D. program at the University of Alabama. He is a true friend and a valued colleague.

I thank my good and longtime friend Brian Latell for his wise counsel on various aspects of my work and his encouragement for me to complete my research. I acknowledge the frequent assistance and gentle kidding of my good friend Gary Maybarduk, who served in the U.S. Interest Section in Havana and shares my enthusiasm for Latin American studies. I appreciate the cooperation of the people whom I interviewed for this work: my former colleague Rear Admiral William Pendley, former assistant secretary of state Ambassador Viron "Pete" Vaky, former national security adviser for Latin America Robert Pastor; and Louis Perez Jr., who encouraged me to investigate the diplomacy involved in renewing the lease for Guantánamo in 1934.

I sincerely appreciate the conscientious help and wise guidance provided to me at all of the archives I visited, but special thanks are due to Glenn Helm at the Navy Department Library, Jim Leyerzapf at the Eisenhower Library, Rebecca Johnson Melvin at the Special Collections of the University of Delaware, and Stephen Plotkin at the Kennedy Library for the time and consideration they gave me.

I owe a debt of gratitude to those historians who have most influenced my approach to the complex and controversial history of Guantánamo. They are Richard Turk, Bradley Reynolds, and Donald Yerxa. I credit Donald Yerxa with introducing me to the analytical thinking of his mentor, the late Clark Reynolds, regarding the crucial role Guantánamo Naval Base has played in policing and protecting Caribbean sea lanes vital to U.S. commercial and security interests.

I am especially grateful for the cheerful assistance provided by the librarians and library assistants at the Gorgas Library at the University of Alabama, whom I have called upon repeatedly, and sometimes urgently, for help. Special thanks go to Pat Causey in Interlibrary Loan and to Betty Bryce, Barbara Dalhbach, Jonathan Darby, Jennifer McClure, Mary Ann Robbins, and Lisa Yuro in Government Documents and Reference Services. I could not have done this work without the resource skills of Brett Spencer, who has a superb ability to track down the most obscure references. I appreciate the responsiveness and quality of the maps prepared by the University of Alabama's cartography lab directed by Craig Remington.

The extensive field research that took me to West Branch, Iowa; Austin, Texas; Hyde Park, New York; Boston, Massachusetts; Independence, Missouri; Abilene, Kansas; New York City; Havana and Guantánamo Bay, Cuba; and four separate trips to Washington, D.C., would not have been possible without the generous financial support of both the Graduate School and the Department of History of the University of Alabama. I also owe a debt of gratitude to my dear friends Howard and Marie Claude Helman for inviting me to share their townhouse in Alexandria, Virginia; to Robert and Arax Terzian of Arlington, Virginia; and to Elliot Levine of the Bronx, New York, for similar acts of generosity. I must also thank my friend Raúl Mesa of the University of Havana for serving as an excellent guide and assisting my research during the week I spent in Havana, Cuba.

The University of Alabama provided resources and opportunity for my research with regard to Cuban history. Its "Cuba Initiative" program encourages an exchange of scholars between the University of Havana and the University of Alabama and hosts conferences for intellectual and cultural exchange. Professors and students from the university may travel to Cuba on a license from the U.S. government for purposes of research. This unique program, founded by Lawrence Clayton of the Department of History and supported by the Graduate School of the University of Alabama and by the University Library, coincided with the gestation of my research, which was one of the fruits of that remarkable program. I am profoundly grateful for the research opportunities afforded me by the Department of History and the Graduate School of the University of Alabama.

My wife, Diana, and son, David, deserve credit for the personal sacrifices they made for me to pursue my studies at the University of Alabama. I could not have written this work without the excellent editorial advice and creative inspiration provided by Diana, who serendipitously discovered this topic and insisted I write it.

GUANTÁNAMO, USA

Introduction
The Significance of Guantánamo

GUANTÁNAMO BAY LIES AT THE SOUTHEASTERN TIP of Cuba, facing the Caribbean. It encompasses a large naval base that occupies an area of approximately forty-five square miles of land and water. The bay itself is pouch-shaped. It is about twelve miles long in a northeast-southwest direction and six miles across at its greatest width. Ships enter and exit the bay between Leeward Point and Windward Point through a one-and-one-fourth-mile-wide channel with a forty-two-foot dredged depth. Because of its deep draft, length, and width, Guantánamo Bay historically has been able to accommodate a sizable portion of the U.S. Navy Fleet at any time. The geographical surrounding has its beautiful aspects—a broad stretch of blue water framed by crescent-shaped shores—but this is an arid section of Cuba, and the hills that hug the coastline are rocky and dotted with scrub trees and bushes.

The most compelling description of this tropical setting and its naval activity was written by Navy Officer K. C. McIntosh, who conceived the following word picture for the *American Mercury* during his seven-month assignment to Guantánamo Bay in 1926:

> On the steep shores of a ragged inlet, cut through the mangroves, is the naval station. Here are the target range and recreation field, the oil tanks, power plant, and storehouses. Along the cliff-top the low green bungalows of the quarters nestle in a tangle of palms and trumpet vines, a flowery oasis in a desert of scrub and thorn. . . . Then the fleet comes steaming in, a long gray line. The stolid battleships drop ponderous anchors near the naval station. Trim, lean cruisers in double row take position just beyond, and then come the clumsy, squat vessels of the train: store ships, repair ships, and tankers, their gray formation broken by the startling white of the floating hospital. . . . The glassy surface of the bay is crisscrossed with the droning wakes of a hundred busy motorboats. Gigs and barges speed back and forth carrying seniors on official visits. . . . "Bong! Bong! That's all we'll hear between now and April," yelps a turret officer. "Come on gang, let's go!"[1]

This evocative portrayal of a bustling but normal day between World Wars I and II at this naval station should suggest to the reader that imperialism viewed only as exploitation fails to capture certain essential qualities of Guantánamo. As the following history of this unique military outpost will illustrate, Guantánamo provides a useful prism through which to view U.S.-Cuban relations from the Spanish-American War to the present.

Today the primary missions of Guantánamo Bay are to serve as a strategic logistics base for the U.S. Navy's Atlantic Fleet, to support counterdrug operations in the Caribbean, to process undocumented aliens for U.S. refugee status or repatriation to their host country, and, since 2002, to incarcerate and interrogate international terrorist suspects. The prison called Camp Delta occupies a small portion of the base. The naval complex is located on the east side of the harbor. McCalla Airfield, on the east side of the harbor entrance, is inactive. Leeward Point Field on the west side is an active naval air station.

Before the 1959 revolution, thousands of Cuban workers commuted daily to the base, but President Lyndon Johnson authorized massive firings of workers who lived off base after Fidel Castro cut off the water supply from the Yateras water-pump station. Now only two elderly Cubans walk through the base's northeast gate daily to work. Under the terms of the 1934 U.S.-Cuban treaty concerning Guantánamo, the United States pays the Cuban government the equivalent of $2,000 in gold per year (now approximately $5,000) in monthly installments. The Castro government has not cashed a rent check since 1959.[2]

Guantánamo occupies a unique position among U.S. naval bases. It is our oldest overseas base, and the only one located in a hostile nation with which the United States has not had normal diplomatic ties for nearly fifty years. These facts alone should have prompted previous historical studies of Guantánamo, but the scholarly record has been surprisingly mute prior to Jana Lipman's publication of her valuable and well-researched *Guantánamo: A Working-Class History between Empire and Revolution*.[3] Many historians recall that Guantánamo was established after the Spanish-American War as a coaling station, and virtually all students of U.S.–Latin American relations know it has been a "finger in Fidel Castro's eye," but this is usually the full extent of their knowledge.[4] My argument here is that, within the context of U.S.-Cuban relations, Guantánamo since 1898 has been both a source of friction and a center for compromise. During the past century the significance of Guantánamo has changed from being central to peripheral. Ironically, it is at this periphery that Guantánamo has achieved its greatest notoriety as a prison/interrogation center for the detention of suspected international terrorists. At a much lower level of scrutiny because of its unique status as a U.S. naval base with a lease "in perpetuity" from the Cuban government, Guantánamo is the site of ongoing "fenceline talks," making it the only place in Cuba where regular dialogue between our two governments takes place.

Jana Lipman's book focuses on the men and women who worked at Guantánamo between 1939 and 1979. Her research in primary source materials is quite distinct from my work, with a strong emphasis on interviews with former Cuban workers, most of whom now live in Guantánamo City. Her work presents invaluable information and historical analysis of working conditions and U.S.-Cuban relations as they pertained to this unique naval base. Her thesis bears some similarity to mine in that she also argues that the Guantánamo Naval Station was a center for friction and compromise, as workers were expected to be both patriotic Cubans and trustworthy employees of the U.S. Navy. "In Guantánamo, base workers navigated the conflicts between U.S. colonialism and Cuban nationalism firsthand."[5] Of necessity, however, Lipman's study, and her only realistic research option, has resulted in conveying a largely one-sided picture simply because the people she interviewed have little or nothing good to say about the U.S. naval presence in Cuba.

Except for two unpublished dissertations, the history of Guantánamo until recently could be found only in fragmentary references in books and magazine articles, documents scattered throughout various archives, and M. E. Murphy's online work, *The History of Guantánamo*, published by the Public Affairs Office at Guantánamo in 1964, updated in 1982, and intended chiefly for base personnel and their families. His history does not purport to be official, authoritative, or scholarly. Now that Guantánamo has become a flashpoint for international criticism as a prison/interrogation center where suspected terrorists may be incarcerated indefinitely without "due process of law,"[6] there are some books that purport to be historical studies of the base. Most notable is *Guantánamo: A Critical History of the U.S. Base in Cuba* by David Deutschmann and Roger Ricardo. By the authors' own admission, this is "radical history," written from the perspective that "since 1959, the U.S. occupation has been challenged as a violation of Cuban sovereignty." Here one might ask, Why select 1959? Did not the Platt Amendment, which became part of the Cuban Constitution in 1902, constitute a violation of Cuban sovereignty by requiring that a U.S. naval station be established in Cuba? Or what about the signing of the lease later that same year that has enabled the U.S. Navy to occupy Guantánamo Bay continuously since December 1903? Connecticut Senator Orville Platt introduced his amendment as a rider to the Army Appropriations Bill when it was before the U.S. Senate early in 1901. The Congress approved the bill by a vote of forty-three to twenty, and President McKinley signed it into law on March 2, 1901. Although the Cuban Assembly initially rejected the measure, the Cuban legislators soon bowed to U.S. pressure and accepted it by a vote of sixteen to eleven, with four abstentions. On June 9, 1934, President Franklin Delano Roosevelt proclaimed a new Treaty of Relations between the United States and Cuba that abrogated the Platt Amendment, but stated that "stipulations with regard to the naval station at Guantánamo shall continue in effect." The U.S. Senate had given its advice that this treaty be ratified on May 31, 1934.

As for the dissertations, Bradley Reynolds's "Guantánamo Bay, Cuba: The History of an American Naval Base and Its Relationship to the Formulation of United States Foreign Policy and Military Strategy toward the Caribbean, 1895–1910" is a meticulously researched work. Reynolds's findings and extensive bibliography have been invaluable to my own research efforts. I agree completely with Reynolds's introductory observation that Guantánamo Naval Base was founded for "sound strategic and military" reasons,[7] and I also appreciate his attention to the important role exercised by the U.S. Navy's policy advisory group, the General Board, and foresighted naval officers, especially Admiral Royal B. Bradford, in advocating that the United States retain Guantánamo following the Spanish-American War.[8]

I have conducted my own extensive research of this period, however, because I believe that Reynolds's splendid work exaggerates the role of the navy's prestigious General Board as one of the key decisionmakers in the acquisition of Guantánamo. Certainly the board exercised great influence as the Navy Department's most senior advisory group, and its well-reasoned and equally well-documented recommendation that Guantánamo should be the site for a coaling station in Cuba found a receptive audience within the U.S. cabinet and in the White House. Nonetheless, the precedent-shattering move of requiring a newly independent foreign country, namely Cuba, to lease forty-five square miles of its territory for the establishment of a major naval base for an indeterminate period, which is precisely what happened at Guantánamo, was not merely the outcome of the formal deliberations of a naval advisory board or even a cabinet meeting. It was an executive decision made by President Theodore Roosevelt after consultations with his closest advisers including the secretary of war and, in this case, the military governor of Cuba.

Reynolds devotes insufficient attention to the importance of the evolving interaction between naval theorist Captain Alfred Thayer Mahan and naval activist Roosevelt as well as decisions taken by Roosevelt's trusted advisers—including Cuba's military governor, General Leonard Wood, and Secretary of

War Elihu Root—in charting U.S. naval policy in the Caribbean and Western Hemisphere and deciding that Guantánamo would be a key naval base in the region. As naval historian Thomas Buell has accurately noted, although the General Board had views on virtually everything from shipbuilding to strategy, "its advice was frequently rejected or ignored because those in authority in the Navy Department had their own ideas."[9] That the U.S. political and military elite made the decision to establish a naval base/coaling station in Cuba at the beginning of the twentieth century is significant. It leads us beyond Reynolds's thesis, which focuses only on strategic and military considerations, to a broader understanding of the powerful expansionist aims not merely of the Republican Party but indeed of the Progressive movement in the early twentieth century. Ultimately the decision to have a continuous U.S. naval presence in Cuba enjoyed broad bipartisan support that, especially during the Cold War, placed the indefinite retention of Guantánamo beyond the realm of political debate. In sharp contrast to Reynolds's work, the dissertation "Guantánamo Bay: The United States Naval Base and Its Relationship with Cuba" by Mary Ellene Chenevey McCoy is highly critical of the U.S. presence at Guantánamo. It purports to cover the entire period from 1494, when Christopher Columbus sailed into Guantánamo Bay and named it Puerto Grande, to the 1990s. Whereas McCoy devotes significant attention to the recurrent fresh water problems at Guantánamo, she avoids discussion of the base's key role in facilitating the transport of strategic materials from Latin America to the Allies during World War II by saying that her work "is not a military history."[10] My major difficulty with McCoy's approach, however, is her unqualified thesis that "the Guantánamo Bay Naval Base remains an illegal presence in Cuba, born of coercion and maintained by force."[11] The assertion that the U.S. leasing of Guantánamo was born of coercion and has been maintained by force can be substantiated by historical evidence and has long been the view of Cuban nationalists, even though this is a one-sided oversimplification of historical events.[12] McCoy's claim that the base is an *illegal presence,* however, echoes challenges Fidel Castro's government has made repeatedly but never substantiated. McCoy devotes inadequate attention to the overriding reality that there were two bilateral treaties, in 1903 and 1934, signed by the executives of both Cuba and the United States, that legally sanctioned the U.S. presence at Guantánamo. She fails to come to grips with the fact that under international law a treaty is a contract between nations that has binding obligations. The Vienna Convention on the Law of Treaties, adopted by the United Nations at The Hague in May 1969, now affirms that all treaties should act "as a means of developing peaceful cooperation among nations" and, therefore, be based on "principles of free consent and good faith." Article Four, however, states that the convention is not retroactive; instead it "applies only to treaties which are concluded by States after the entry into force of the present Convention with regard to such States." The Vienna Convention entered into force on January 27, 1980.[13]

McCoy also ignores the precedent that successive U.S. administrations from Theodore Roosevelt to George W. Bush have operated on the premise that these leases are valid. Moreover, all Cuban governments, including Fidel Castro's, have pledged to uphold Cuba's treaties and international obligations.[14] This pledge persists despite harsh international criticisms of Guantánamo's current use as a prison/interrogation center that has often denied fundamental U.S. constitutional rights—including due process of law—to suspected terrorists.[15]

In this regard, it is important to understand that Guantánamo's legal status as an overseas military base is unique. When President Theodore Roosevelt's administration negotiated an agreement with Cuba's first president, Tomás Estrada Palma, to lease Guantánamo for an unspecified period instead of purchasing it, Washington and Havana did not fully address, and left unresolved, the issue of the applicability of U.S. law and constitutional freedoms to Guantánamo. In the new millennium this issue of whether the Constitution follows the flag has become a subject of contentious debate. The U.S. attorney general's office under recent U.S. administrations, including those of George H. W. Bush, Bill Clinton, and George W. Bush, has argued before federal judges and the U.S. Supreme Court that Guantánamo is outside the confines of U.S. law and that constitutional provisions for due process do not apply. President George W. Bush signed into law the Military Commissions Act of 2006, which asserts Guantánamo is outside the jurisdiction of the U.S. legal system, including the Supreme Court. What is most surprising is that Cuba's Castro regime did not question this interpretation of Guantánamo as an autonomous and anomalous U.S. presence in Cuba.[16] On the contrary, Raúl Castro initially promised to capture and return to the naval base any suspected terrorist who might escape from Guantánamo. Similarly, Fidel Castro has never challenged Guantánamo's legal status in the International Court of Justice (ICJ). As criticism of harsh U.S. interrogation and detention practices grew, however, both Raúl and Fidel Castro added their voices to the international condemnations of Camp Delta (see page 232).

Jana Lipman's sociodiplomatic study of the multiple challenges and tensions Cuban workers confronted daily relies heavily on interviews she conducted in Guantánamo City from 2004 to 2005. Lipman states, "The city and people of Guantánamo are at the center of my analysis," and, to avoid linguistic confusion, she only refers to the confines of Guantánamo Bay by its military acronym "GTMO" (pronounced "Gitmo") or as the U.S. naval base. This is valuable research, but Lipman's readers should be mindful of the reality that her interviewees all knew they were speaking to a U.S. scholar whose work would be published in the United States. Living in a society where freedom of expression has not yet been achieved, it would be unwise as well as "impolitic" for such individuals to voice favorable opinions of their experiences at the U.S. naval base. The question persists, Why is there no dispassionate published history of Guantánamo Naval Base? There have been several distinguished scholars of Cuba in the United States, but as I have discovered, they do not try to analyze the anomaly of Guantánamo Naval Base in Cuban history and culture. Except for a generally applied Marxist critique of perceived U.S. imperialism, Guantánamo has truly been a blind spot for most Cuba scholars, who may have a political polemic or nationalist perspective but do not fully understand the reasons the United States has insisted on acquiring and retaining Guantánamo Bay. As for Cuban publications or broadcasts since Fidel Castro came to power, it would be impossible to hear or read any legitimate viewpoint other than Fidel's, his brother Raúl's, or that of the Cuban Communist Party.

Scholars have not had the only muffled voices. Before the Abu Ghraib Prison scandal focused worldwide attention on the existence of U.S. interrogation/incarceration centers for prisoners accused of being international terrorists—including Guantánamo—the U.S. public had not clamored for more news reporting from Guantánamo since Mike Wallace visited the base in 1972 to tape a segment for *60 Minutes*. The popular movie filmed in 1992, *A Few Good Men*, starring Jack Nicholson, Demi Moore, and Tom Cruise, reintroduced the topic of the base—and conveyed the image of a Marine Corps/U.S. Navy enclave in Cuba that operated as a law unto itself—but this image did not stay on the radar screen. Much of the explanation for the lack of scholarly attention to Guantánamo is attributable to the difficulty in ferreting out primary source documents in various archives. I personally have investigated every presidential library from Herbert Hoover through Lyndon Johnson, and, in each case, there have been at most one or two folders that specifically referred to Guantánamo. In the John F. Kennedy Library, for example, the solitary folder labeled "Guantánamo" contains virtually nothing of value because censors years ago blacked out the passages they deemed "classified." Of course, as the following chapters will show, I found materials pertinent to my study in other folders, but I have had to cast a wide research net.[17] I have found it particularly valuable, especially for studying the formative period of U.S.-Cuban relations prior to the acquisition of Guantánamo, to examine the private correspondence and memoranda written by such key figures as Theodore Roosevelt, Alfred T. Mahan, Henry Cabot Lodge, Leonard Wood, and Elihu Root. These were the elite decisionmakers who shaped U.S. naval and foreign policy with regard to Cuba and Guantánamo. Although these men probably knew subconsciously that their letters would be preserved as historical documents, it was often in these private moments that they most candidly revealed how global and regional considerations as well as their desire for the United States to become a "great power" influenced their thinking, intentions, and decisions. The determination to initiate such important and controversial policies and the strategic planning to execute them often evolved through more informal mechanisms such as conversations over dinner, chance encounters in corridors, and notes scribbled on pieces of paper that subsequently disappeared. Reading the preserved letters will tell only part of the story, but they may be the best clues we have. It is important to state at the outset that the U.S. acquisition of Guantánamo as an offshore, or forward, military base was the consequence of what one historian has called a "naval renaissance" that began in the early 1880s with the naming of a few determined individuals to the cabinet post of secretary of the navy.[18] The names of William Hunt, William Chandler, Benjamin Tracy, and Hilary Herbert probably are known to only a few students of U.S. naval history, but it was largely owing to their efforts that the U.S. Navy, whose weaknesses had become an object of domestic and international ridicule, revived, reformed itself, and, in less than twenty years, grew into one of the great navies of the world. As William Hunt wisely observed at the outset, naval regeneration was a needed auxiliary to protect the rapid expansion in U.S. foreign trade and investment occurring in the post–Civil War United States. He and the other individuals named above helped achieve this "naval renaissance." Without their initial efforts, it is safe to speculate that there would have been no U.S. Navy to fight and defeat the Spanish in the War of 1898, and Theodore Roosevelt probably would not have asked his good friend Senator Henry Cabot Lodge to urge President-Elect William McKinley to appoint Roosevelt assistant secretary of the navy. Guantánamo merits historical study from both the U.S. and Cuban perspectives. As an American who, apart from reading and research, has only a tourist's brief acquaintance with Havana, I cannot claim to fully appreciate or to represent unrequited feelings of nationalism with the passion or depth of feeling that Cubans, past and present, share. To the best of my ability, however, I have tried to present the "anti-imperialist" criticism leveled at the U.S. control of Guantánamo since 1898. In this context, it is worth noting that there have been and continue to be U.S. critics of the nation's efforts to dominate Cuba who see this interference as a major factor in Cuba's tragic inability to sustain economic prosperity or democratic rule. As this work will document, the United States has always treated Guantánamo in a broad international context. In the early 1900s, it was the U.S.

forward naval base intended to perform the multiple security functions of ensuring Cuba's independence, guarding U.S. maritime commerce transiting the Windward Passage, and protecting expansionist U.S. interests throughout the Caribbean Basin including the Panamanian Isthmus. During World War II, it served as the Caribbean's transshipment hub for the interlocking convoy system instituted to avert the destruction of strategic materials by Nazi submarines. In the Cold War, it became a symbol of the U.S. government's determination to fight communism by retaining a military presence in Cuba, face-to-face with the Soviet-backed government of Fidel Castro. Since the end of the Cold War, Guantánamo has provided detention camps for Haitian and Cuban refugees and maximum security/interrogation facilities for suspected terrorists. Throughout most of its history, it has also been a major naval, marine, and coast guard facility, serving a variety of training purposes.

Readers should understand that advocates for Guantánamo's continued existence as a forward naval base often have had to fight to obtain adequate congressional funding. Bradley Reynolds alludes to this problem in explaining the lack of start-up construction in the base's early years. For the most part, disagreements over funding issues were buried in congressional hearings, but occasionally they spilled into the open, as for example in 1911 when the contest was between enhancing Guantánamo's capabilities and closing bases at Pensacola and New Orleans.[19] The key point is that Guantánamo has no natural political constituency, or, to put it bluntly, there is no "pork barrel" on that base. Consequently, it has frequently taken the active intervention of the secretary of the navy or other senior cabinet officials to sustain Guantánamo financially as a major defense post.

Cuba's leaders generally have viewed Guantánamo within the confines of U.S.-Cuban relations. Prior to the Castro era, this could be attributed to Havana's recognition of the leverage the United States could and often did exert over Cuban affairs. This perspective occasionally has had its positive aspects—during World War II, Guantánamo helped ensure that Cuba and neighboring Caribbean states would not be threatened by Nazi invasion. For many decades, the base provided employment for Cuban nationals and served as an entry point for U.S. dollars. More frequently, however, Havana has perceived Guantánamo as a symbol of thwarted sovereignty. This negative interpretation is not unique to the Castro era; indeed, Fidel probably acquired his hostile attitude toward the U.S. presence at Guantánamo from the nationalist historians whose works he read and who taught him at the University of Havana in the late 1940s. There is much truth in British historian Hugh Thomas's stinging criticism that the terms of the Platt Amendment, which enabled the United States to establish Guantánamo, "were as severe on Cuba as were those that the treaties of Versailles and St. Germain imposed on defeated Germany and Austria in 1919, and were as strongly resented. The only difference was that Cuba ostensibly had won its war."[20] There was one distinguished Cuban, Cosme de la Torriente, who would have objected to the sweeping nature of Thomas's condemnation of the Platt Amendment. Torriente, who had fought for Cuban independence and would later serve as Cuba's ambassador to the United States and as its foreign minister, was one of Cuba's primary negotiators in abrogating the Platt Amendment, but he viewed the U.S. naval base at Guantánamo as an essential defensive outpost for Cuba and the United States. After Fidel Castro forged his alliance with the Soviet Union, he and his brother Raúl, of course, manipulated Guantánamo as a symbol of U.S. imperialism. Yet throughout its history, as this book will document, Guantánamo has also served Cuban purposes as a site for mediation and compromise. Prior to the Castro era, critics of the Platt Amendment and Cuban advocates for independence from any foreign domination were fighting a deepening U.S. commercial and investment interest in Cuba that long predated the Spanish-American War. Intermittently throughout the nineteenth century, senior U.S. policymakers voiced the desire to acquire Cuba or at least to establish a permanent physical presence in the Caribbean, but they were unable to transform their dreams into reality. In 1823, Secretary of State John Quincy Adams informed his minister in Madrid, Hugh Nelson, that Cuba and Puerto Rico "are natural appendages of the North American Continent, and one of them—almost in sight of our shores—has become an object of transcendent importance to the commercial and political interests of our Union." Obviously, Adams's primary interest was Cuba, as he made clear to Nelson: "Its commanding position with reference to the Gulf of Mexico and the West Indian seas . . . give[s] it an importance in the sum of our national interests with which that of no other foreign territory can be compared." He then went so far as to suggest that, in the event of a struggle for independence, Cuba should be annexed to the United States. "Cuba, forcibly disjointed from its own unnatural connection with Spain, and incapable of self-support, can gravitate only toward the North American Union, which . . . cannot cast her off from her bosom."[21] The next great expansionist to dominate the State Department was William H. Seward, who, like Adams, was often frustrated by political opposition.[22] In the Caribbean, Seward bypassed Cuba to seek a coaling station in the Dominican Republic. He negotiated a draft treaty with Denmark to purchase the Virgin Islands, and he obtained Colombia's tentative approval to build a canal through the Panamanian Isthmus.[23] He also probed possibilities of acquiring Cuba, Haiti, Culebra Island,[24] French Guiana, Puerto Rico, and St. Bartholomew. None of these ventures succeeded, largely because the U.S. Senate was angered by Seward's loyalty to increasingly unpopular President Andrew Johnson.[25] Nonetheless, as diplomatic historian Walter LaFeber perceptively discerned, Seward "wanted to hold islands in the Caribbean which would serve as strategic bases to protect an isthmian route to the Pacific and prevent European powers from dabbling in the area of the North American coastline."[26] As with Adams, Seward's expansionist thinking would influence subsequent strategic planners, including Alfred Mahan, Theodore Roosevelt, and Henry Cabot Lodge. All these men were avid students of U.S. diplomatic history and close friends of historian Henry Adams, who had attributed Seward's failures to "a fixed policy, which, under his active direction, went too far and too fast for the public."[27] A central argument of this book is that the acquisition of Guantánamo in December 1903 was an important first step by the United States to establish a military presence in the Caribbean that persisted and has become especially controversial in today's international environment. As Donald Yerxa asserted in *Admirals and Empire* (1991), the use of the terms *empire* and *imperialism* can evoke a strong emotional response in a reader and enmesh a historian in unproductive arguments. In hopes of avoiding such pitfalls, I would say at the outset that, like Yerxa, I view the creation of a U.S. naval station in southeastern Cuba as part of a broad strategy that encompassed annexations, the establishment of protectorates, and limited but forceful interventions of which the cumulative effect was to create "an exclusive sphere of influence and an unquestioned U.S. hegemony" throughout the western Atlantic and Caribbean regions.[28] Policymakers Theodore Roosevelt and Secretary of War Elihu Root certainly would have bristled at being labeled "imperialists" or "empire builders," but it was their decisive moves in the Caribbean that persuaded their British counterparts, Foreign Secretary Lord Landsdowne and Admiral of the Fleet Sir John Fisher, to dismantle the North American and West Indies Squadrons of the Royal Navy in 1904 and 1905 and thus permit the United States to safeguard its imperial interests.[29]

The United States has occupied Guantánamo continuously for more than a century. Over time, the base's functions have evolved dramatically from its origins as a coaling station. It has served as an emergency repair facility for ships at sea, been used as a deployment center to provide relief from hurricane damage to other islands in the Caribbean, and facilitated shakedowns, gunnery exercises, and amphibious warfare training. During World War II, it acted as the Caribbean hub for the interlocking convoy system to transport strategic materials to the Allies through U-boat-infested waters. Since 2002, it has acquired worldwide notoriety as the best-known U.S. incarceration/ interrogation center for suspected international terrorists. It also continues to serve as a U.S. naval station with a coast guard detachment and a migrant operations center. The question, Is Guantánamo a necessary outpost for American security? is in contention today, but as this work will demonstrate, this question was also being argued inconclusively by admirals in 1916. Many modern strategists could easily dismiss the justifications of Alfred Mahan and Theodore Roosevelt for acquiring Guantánamo as outdated and irrelevant, but it would be folly for them to ignore the truth that Mahan's and Roosevelt's views and prescriptions emphasized the need to incorporate evolving technologies, to adapt to new political realities, and, above all, to comprehend the importance of geography in making operational and strategic decisions. That may explain why the U.S. government still publishes Mahan's writings as "essential reading for professional marine and naval officers" and why policymakers could still find wisdom in the collected works of Theodore Roosevelt.[30]

The chapters that follow are arranged chronologically with the exception of my discussion of the works of Cuban historians concerning Guantánamo. I have chosen to place these works in the context of the periods when they were written.[31] Chapter 1 covers the late nineteenth century, focusing on the buildup of the U.S. Navy from the early 1880s to the Spanish-American War, which was an essential prerequisite to U.S. participation and victory in that conflict, and the important relationships of Theodore Roosevelt that shaped his thinking with regard to his establishment of Guantánamo as the first overseas U.S. naval base. Chapter 2 analyzes Guantánamo's role in the defeat of the Spanish Navy in Cuba. Chapter 3 covers the period from 1898 to 1903, during which the U.S. government, for various reasons, decided to override Cuban objections to its obtaining Guantánamo Bay under an open-ended lease arrangement. Chapter 4 examines the expanding role of the U.S. Navy in the Caribbean and Guantánamo's importance as a naval and marine training center and logistical support base from 1904 to 1932. Chapter 5 discusses President Franklin D. Roosevelt's decision to abrogate the Platt Amendment and to renew the lease for Guantánamo by repeating the exact language of the 1903 treaty. This chapter analyzes the various reactions of Cuban historians and diplomats writing in the 1930s and 1940s to the U.S. military possession of Guantánamo. It also examines the crucial defensive role Guantánamo played as the hub of a vast convoy system that transported strategic goods through the Caribbean Basin and Atlantic region to the Allies during World War II. Chapters 6 and 7 look at Guantánamo during the height of the Cold War, during the Eisenhower, Kennedy, and Johnson administrations, examining the recurrent clashes between Cuba, the Soviet Union, and the United States over the U.S. presence at Guantánamo that culminated in President Johnson's decision to make the base independent of Cuba by firing hundreds of commuter workers—especially those suspected of being disloyal or spies for Castro's revolutionary government—and building a desalinization water plant. Chapter 8 is a postscript that examines Guantánamo's continuing role as a naval training facility and its increasingly controversial function of serving as a refugee relocation center and as an offshore U.S. prison/interrogation center for suspected international terrorists. It is ironic that, even though the Castro government persistently argues that the U.S. occupation of Guantánamo is illegal, this is the only place in Cuba where monthly diplomatic exchanges occur between U.S. and Cuban officials to resolve problems such as the repatriation of undocumented aliens.

It is appropriate to view Guantánamo's past within the conceptual framework of Atlantic history, especially the interactive aspects of distinct cultures within the Atlantic region. Years before the McKinley administration decided to intervene in Cuba's war for independence from Spain, Theodore Roosevelt grasped the significance of Alfred Mahan's advocacy that the United States be alert to any opportunity to transform the Caribbean Sea—then dotted with European imperialistic outposts—into an American Mediterranean. Roosevelt worked with Mahan to make this theory a reality, and Roosevelt, as a military strategist and man of action, moved decisively to free Cuba from Spanish rule. After that was accomplished, Roosevelt, as governor, vice president, and president, worked closely with senior military advisers to secure Guantánamo as a U.S. naval base. He clearly saw Guantánamo as a strategically positioned fortress in the Caribbean-Atlantic region—an American Gibraltar—that would protect the Americas from further European imperialistic incursions and guard the canal route he intended to build through the Panamanian Isthmus. From June 10, 1898, when U.S. marines landed at Guantánamo, until now, this Cuban bay has functioned as an important base for deployments to other Caribbean islands. It facilitated and protected Allied shipping in two world wars, and it has frequently been a point of encounter involving friction and accommodation between the United States, Germany, the Soviet Union, the nations of origin of suspected international terrorists, and always between the United States and Cuba.[32]

As you read the following chapters, it is also important to keep in mind the sharp contrasts between daily life at Guantánamo Naval Base and in the nearby Cuban towns, especially Guantánamo City, which under normal conditions would be half an hour away by automobile. At its prime, let us say from the 1950s to the early 1990s, Guantánamo Naval Base resembled other U.S. military communities with an added tropical flavor. Writer-traveler Tom Miller visited it in 1990 and called it "the Navy's Club Med," with its five outdoor movie theaters, health club, scuba diving, horseback riding, golf course, comfortable housing for officers, base exchange, nearly four hundred miles of paved roads, and the only McDonald's and Starbuck's in Cuba. What made it uniquely Guantánamo, according to Miller, was the base library museum with its Spanish-American War photos, a collection of old bottles—one from the 1890s—and another of seashells. A rock monument at Fisherman's Point (just north of McCalla Airfield) marks the spot where Columbus is said to have landed.

On the same trip, Miller visited Guantánamo City, where, as one of his Cuban hosts remarked, "the potholes have streets"—often named for Cuban heroes like Máximo Gómez. Its large buildings, such as the Cuban Writers Union, have high ceilings, windows covered with iron grillwork, and small wooden porches that almost reach the street. In the 1940s and 1950s, before Castro, much of Guantánamo City's commercial life depended on the naval base, and local hostelries proudly bore the names Roosevelt Hotel, Kentucky House, and Washington Hotel. Today the Cuban and American worlds may intersect only in a television set in the Hotel Guantánamo, where a tourist can tune in to *CNN Headline News*, David Letterman, or the World Series, and even get full-length movies direct from Guantánamo Naval Base, as alternatives to Televisión Martí. A guantanamero, or local, told Miller, "Some of us learn English this way."[33]

1

The Rise of the U.S. Navy and Theodore Roosevelt

The Spanish-American War of 1898 developed from American desires to free Cuba from Spanish rule and from the big-navy expansionism of Captain Mahan and Assistant Secretary of the Navy Theodore Roosevelt.
—Clark G. Reynolds[1]

Mahan and Roosevelt were the closest of friends and could often be found in the company of Brooks Adams, John Hay, and [Henry Cabot] Lodge.
—Walter LaFeber[2]

WITHOUT QUESTION, the single most important figure in establishing Guantánamo as the first overseas U.S. naval base was Theodore Roosevelt. President William McKinley's administration determined that the United States would have a naval station in Cuba, and Roosevelt selected Guantánamo to be that station. The historical process that led to the creation of that naval base began in the early 1880s with the modernization and strengthening of the U.S. Navy as the nation made the necessary military preparations to step onto the world stage as a recognized great power. As this chapter will document, Theodore Roosevelt played an increasingly significant role in this formative process.

In 1882, at age twenty-three, Roosevelt published his first book, *The Naval War of 1812,* which critics on both sides of the Atlantic praised for bringing a fresh and balanced perspective to that historic conflict. Throughout the work, Roosevelt used the past to criticize contemporary weaknesses in U.S. naval affairs. On page two of the Preface, he set the tone: "At present people are beginning to realize that it is folly for the great English-speaking Republic to rely for defense upon a navy composed partly of antiquated hulks and partly of new vessels rather more useless than the old."[3]

Roosevelt's criticism was justified. By the early 1880s, the U.S. Navy was in wretched shape. Part of the problem was that in the post–Civil War period, the Navy Department was an easy target for graft and corruption. As naval historians Harold and Margaret Sprout accurately wrote, "The Navy department spent millions of dollars for materials and labors, with little in the end to show for it save a collection of worthless ships, an army of enriched contractors, a host of political retainers, and partisan strength at the polls in the favored constituencies."[4] Another important aspect of the U.S. Navy's decline was that the United States had failed to keep pace with the rapid changes in naval technology occurring in Great Britain, France, Germany, and elsewhere—including Chile. As naval historian Kurt Hackemer has found, after the Civil War, "Americans lost interest in the fleet, asking only that it serve in its traditional roles of coastal defense and commerce protection." By the late 1870s, "European observers no longer took the American fleet seriously." Neither did Chile. When the United States tried to act as peacemaker in the War of the Pacific (1879–1884) by sending its obsolete wooden vessels of the Pacific Squadron into the war zone, the Chileans, from the decks of their British-built armored war ships, impolitely told the Americans to mind their own business.[5]

The deterioration in U.S. naval power since 1865 had occurred, in large measure, because the chain of navy secretaries stretching from President Andrew Johnson's administration to that of President James A. Garfield was weak and contained several incompetents. The most useless was Richard Thompson from Terre Haute, Indiana, who served from March 13, 1877, to December 20, 1880, and was so ignorant of naval affairs that, upon seeing his first ship, he reportedly exclaimed, "Why the durned thing's hollow. I always thought they were solid."[6] Probably more accurate, but equally damning were Thompson's formal remarks to Congress that emphasized the advantages of having a strong merchant marine, from which we could "improvise a navy in . . . an unexpected emergency."[7] Late in the term of President Rutherford B. Hayes, Thompson accepted a bribe from an agent of French impresario Ferdinand de Lesseps. When President Hayes—who had forcefully opposed de Lesseps's initiative to dig a canal through the Panamanian Isthmus—learned of the transaction from Secretary of State William Evarts, he instructed Evarts to dismiss Thompson with the tactful words, "The President decided to accept [your resignation] to relieve you of all embarrassment on the subject."[8] Thus, Thompson became the only secretary of the navy to be "fired," and this sordid matter was an appropriate prelude to reform in the department and a new era for the U.S. Navy.[9]

Building a Better Navy: Hunt, Chandler, Whitney, Tracy, and Herbert

By 1881, the United States as a commercial society had largely recovered from the depredations of the Civil War, and, in a word, its exports were on the verge of "booming."[10] As business leaders demanded overseas markets, they also clamored to rebuild the U.S. Merchant Marine, and these pressures gave impetus to widening efforts to reform and strengthen the U.S. Navy. Just before President James Garfield was assassinated, he appointed Louisiana judge William Hunt secretary of the navy. Hunt may have had a personal stake in strengthening the navy because one of his sons was a naval officer, and he also had the insight, energy, and managerial skills requisite to making progress. He quickly grasped the enormity of the challenge that confronted him. Of the 140 navy vessels in commission, only 52 were considered "effective," and none of the "effectives" had modern armaments.

Hunt sounded the claxon for reform in the opening sentences of his first annual report: "The condition of the Navy imperatively demands the prompt and earnest attention of Congress. Unless some action be had in its behalf it must soon dwindle into insignificance." He then observed that U.S. mercantile interests ranged over "all quarters of the globe," and that those engaged in foreign commerce "look to the Navy for the supervisory protection of their persons and property." Admitting the navy's inability to respond to calls for protection, Hunt forcefully asserted that "these things ought not to be." He did not propose that the United States build a formidable fleet, but that its navy "should at all times afford a nucleus for enlargement upon an emergency. . . . It should be sufficiently powerful to assure the navigator that in whatsoever sea he shall sail his ship he is protected by the stars and stripes."[11]

As secretary, Hunt sought the best professional advice available by establishing a board of senior officers called the Naval Affairs Committee to address the specific needs of the U.S. Fleet. When the board's report was completed, he sent it to Congress accompanied by his own strong plea for immediate action. He also convened a group of selected senators and representatives and naval officers to discuss general issues of naval policy in an effort to facilitate communication between Congress and the service.

One of Hunt's lesser-noticed but more significant achievements was convincing President Chester Arthur to issue an executive order in March 1882 that created the Office of Naval Intelligence (ONI), to be attached to the Bureau of Navigation. Initially a tiny staff, the ONI would post naval attachés to major foreign capitals and become the U.S. government's primary source of information on military developments worldwide. It would also expand its responsibilities from overt data collection and analysis into war planning and espionage activities.[12]

In personnel matters, Hunt sought to impose a sense of discipline on a service that had become lax in its practices. One of his measures that produced unexpected consequences was an order that "women shall not be allowed to reside onboard vessels of the United States Navy . . . nor shall they be taken as passengers on such vessels." A few months later, when Hunt made an unannounced visit to the U.S.S. *Tallapoosa*, he found that the commander's wife was living onboard the ship in violation of his directive. His severe, public chastisement of this officer attracted widespread attention when the New York humorous weekly *Puck* satirized the incident in a brief caricature titled "The Lord of the Seas," in which William Hunt commands an armada composed of "three mud scows supplemented by a superannuated canal boat."[13]

Hunt served as secretary of the navy for just over one year, from March 7, 1881, to April 16, 1882. On April 7, President Chester Arthur had put pressure on Hunt to accept a diplomatic posting as minister to Russia in order to appoint William Chandler as secretary of the navy, thus fulfilling a political promise he had made to his predecessor, President Garfield. Arthur may also have picked Chandler because he considered him a more experienced political manager than Hunt had proved to be. Nevertheless, Hunt may justly be regarded as the first in a series of powerful navy chiefs who built the armored battle fleet that would see action in the Spanish-American War.[14]

William Chandler, a cunning Republican politician, has been derided as a "hack politician" but also lauded as the "founder of the modern navy." Indeed, he was both. In 1876, he played a prominent role as counsel to the Florida electors in fixing the closely contested election of President Hayes, and in 1880 at the Republican convention, he persuaded key delegates to cast the crucial swing votes to nominate Garfield. President Garfield had sought to reward Chandler with the post of solicitor-general, but the Senate refused to confirm him. In April 1882, President Arthur named Chandler to be Hunt's successor as secretary of the navy, and the Senate confirmed him by a margin of twenty-eight to sixteen.

Shortly after Chandler took office, the Naval Affairs Committee recommended that expenditures for repairs of old ships be limited to 30 percent of the cost of their replacement. Chandler, realizing that many of the vessels still in service needed to be discarded in order to build a modern fleet, asked Congress to cap the cost of repairs at 20 percent of replacement value. His decision to have the first four modern steel warships all built by Morgan Ironworks provoked heated accusations that Chandler had played favorites in awarding the contract because the shipyard's owner, John Roach, was a well-known contributor to the Republican Party. The ships, named *Atlanta*, *Boston*, *Chicago*, and *Dolphin*, became collectively and infamously known as the ABCD ships. Only the smallest ship, the dispatch boat U.S.S. *Dolphin*, had been completed by the end of President Arthur's administration. Chandler faced down mounting criticism in his annual report for 1884, stating that the Naval Affairs Committee had endorsed the designs, that the ships possessed all the necessary qualities for unarmored warships, and that being of "moderate size and cost," they would constitute "useful and important parts of a modern naval force."[15] Even with their defects, the well-publicized fact that these ships, known as the "White Squadron," constituted the beginning of a modern navy evoked the popular support necessary to permit additional naval construction.

According to naval historian Walter Herrick Jr., Chandler often ignored political criticism of his forceful measures to reduce wasteful administrative costs and to make sea duty the criterion for advancement. He shut down naval yards at Pensacola, Florida, and New London, Connecticut, and he frequently resisted pressures from within his own party to reinstate incompetent officers. His greatest single achievement was to establish the Naval War College at Newport, Rhode Island.

To call Chandler the founder of the modern navy may be excessive praise, but he made important contributions. With his encouragement, naval technology advanced, especially with the innovation of new high velocity guns and successful experiments in the use of liquid fuel for marine engines. Equally important, the atmosphere within the Navy Department improved under Chandler as "apathy yielded to enthusiasm, and drift to direction."

In addition to Chandler's tangible achievements, he communicated a new vision for the navy in his formal statements to Congress. He asserted that establishing coaling stations abroad was an increasingly pressing issue of naval defense. He renewed the recommendation he had made in his annual report of 1883 that a line of U.S. naval defense be constructed "from the Gulf of Mexico to the Massachusetts coast," and specified that "additional coaling and naval stations be established at some or all of the following points: Samaná Bay, or some port in Hayti [sic]; Curacao, in the Caribbean Sea . . . one at the best point on the Atlantic side of the Isthmus of Panama, and another . . . on the Pacific side."[16]

As diplomatic historian David Pletcher has found, in the latter part of the nineteenth century, U.S. expansionists (a catchall term for commercial interests, venture capitalists, and political/military strategists such as Mahan, Roosevelt, and Lodge) increasingly viewed control of the Caribbean Sea as strategically necessary "to protect American trade lanes to South America and the Pacific against European domination." The Caribbean region was also an enticing target for investment. Pletcher quotes various enthusiasts: "Cuba possesses every advantage . . . that nature could bestow upon so small a portion of the globe." "Santo Domingo is one of the garden spots of the earth." "The resources of Venezuela are immense." And finally, "Why should we not have our naval stations in every sea and harbors of our own? Why not have our own Hong Kongs and Singapores?"[17]

As an astute politician, Chandler obviously listened to and responded positively to such siren calls. Like his predecessor, Hunt, he commented on the requisite interdependent relationship between growing U.S. overseas commercial interests and a watchdog navy: "The germ of a maritime force may exist, but it must remain undeveloped while there is no commercial fleet and no maritime population upon which to draw as a naval reserve." In ringing words, he implored, "Can it be supposed that in the event of war fifty vessels of all sizes and 8,000 men will fight our naval battles, transport our troops, maintain blockades, and cut off the enemy's commerce? Yet almost within such narrow limits are we now confined by the deplorable condition of our commercial marines."[18]

Many of these pleas, of course, did not receive immediate attention, but over time, they would constitute a litany for naval expansion that progressive Republican leaders would recall and to which they would add their own voices. Also, William Chandler continued to exert considerable influence after retiring as navy secretary at the end of President Arthur's term in 1885. In 1887, he was elected to the U.S. Senate, where he served until 1901. As a member of the Naval Affairs Committee, his advice and support were frequently solicited by Assistant Secretary of the Navy Theodore Roosevelt.[19]

To forge a world-class navy in the late nineteenth century, as Chandler had tried to do, was an enormous challenge and commitment for the United States, given that in the mid-1880s there were no furnaces, mills, or foundries capable of producing nickel steel hull plates or forging the heavy guns and propeller shafts required by the armored cruisers specified in the ABCD contracts with Roach.[20] John Beeler's analysis regarding the modernization of the British Navy is pertinent to the similar, but subsequent transformations in the U.S. Navy:

> The construction of a steam battlefleet was but the opening chapter of a technological revolution. . . . Iron supplanted wood and steel supplanted iron for the construction of ships' hulls. Armor was incorporated and modern, breech-loading rifled ordnance firing explosive or armor-piercing shells replaced smoothbore muzzle-loading cannon. . . . In addition to the physical makeover of the battlefleet, the technological revolution had far-reaching ramifications in such spheres as naval architecture and tactics.[21]

This technological revolution would necessitate changes in the requirements for navy yards and naval stations with regard to maintenance, repairs, and coaling. From the U.S. perspective, Theodore Roosevelt attested to the need for naval officers and sailors alike to possess engineering skills. In a letter supporting a bill for personnel changes, Roosevelt observed that "steam, with its attendant complicated machinery, has been made the motive power of war vessels, and there is a tendency now everywhere visible to add electricity to steam and to multiply the number of engines in every great warship, so as to furnish not only the motive power, but the power by which the turrets, guns, and hoists are hauled."[22]

The first administration of President Grover Cleveland, from 1885 to 1889, subjected the Navy Department to political turbulence, but Cleveland's navy secretary, William Whitney, also made important reforms that strengthened the U.S. Navy. When Cleveland took office as the first Democratic president since the Civil War, he signaled that he intended to eliminate spoils and bureaucratic waste in the Navy Department by appointing William C. Whitney as its secretary. Whitney, who was an able corporate lawyer and a reform-minded politician, made some administrative changes by centralizing auditing and purchasing procedures and attacking corrupt practices in various navy yards. He also built on the efforts of his Republican predecessor, Chandler, to increase the size of the fleet by adding about thirty new ships. According to Herrick, Whitney, however, "clung to the old strategy of coastal defense and commerce destruction . . . and failed to perceive the strategic advantage [of] a unified battle fleet having offensive capability."[23]

Whitney not only failed to credit Chandler's initiatives to jump-start the construction of modern battleships in U.S. shipyards, he castigated his predecessor's association with shipbuilder John Roach as evidence of corruption within the Navy Department. In particular, he criticized the workmanship on the dispatch boat *Dolphin,* which would later play a significant role in the Battle of Guantánamo. When the *Dolphin* managed to pass every one of its acceptance trials, Whitney ordered Captain Richard Meade "to drive her into the first storm he could find." Encountering a gale off Cape Hatteras, the *Dolphin* performed satisfactorily, and Whitney subsequently abandoned his vendetta. The U.S.S. *Dolphin* went on to have a noteworthy period of service. It cruised around the world before it was assigned to blockade duty in Cuba and participated in the taking of Guantánamo Bay in 1898. From 1899 until World War I, it served as a special dispatch ship for the secretary of the navy and frequently transported dignitaries, including President Theodore Roosevelt. It also surveyed the mouth of the Orinoco River. In 1905, it carried Japanese diplomats from Oyster Bay to Portsmouth, New Hampshire, to negotiate the settlement of the Russo-Japanese War. During World War I, it became the flagship of the Third Squadron, Atlantic Fleet, where it participated in the occupation of Santo Domingo in 1916. It subsequently operated in the Gulf of Mexico and the Caribbean to protect merchant shipping until the end of the war. The *Dolphin* remained in commission until December 8, 1921.

Important technological advances occurred during Whitney's administration. He persuaded Congress to authorize the construction of seven additional man-of-war ships, some of which, notably *Baltimore, Charleston,* and *New York,* set new precedents in speed and firepower. Whitney also encouraged technological advances that enabled domestic heavy industries to produce the machinery, ordnance, and armor plate to equip powerful battleships. The Navy Department also acquired the Austrian-developed "automobile torpedo," which soon became its most deadly weapon. In a short-sighted move, Whitney sought to undermine the Naval War College as a war planning institution, in particular by reassigning its presidents, Stephen Luce and Alfred Mahan, to sea duty.

The next assertive secretary of the navy was Benjamin Tracy, whose administration marked a new era of forceful naval leadership. General Tracy, as he was popularly known, had previously distinguished himself as a senior officer in the Union Army and as a prominent New York attorney and judge.[24] Known as a person of integrity and initiative, Tracy took office under propitious circumstances. Naval reconstruction had made steady progress throughout the 1880s.

Domestic political conditions were favorable for Tracy to put his stamp on the navy's future. A Republican majority controlled both houses of Congress, and Speaker of the House Thomas Reed was an open advocate of naval expansion. Most important, Tracy enjoyed the confidence and close friendship of President Benjamin Harrison. In February 1890, Harrison brought Tracy to the White House to heal from burns from a fire that had destroyed his home and killed his wife and daughter.[25]

For the first time, strategic planning became the basis for the Navy Department's major policy recommendations as Tracy looked primarily to Captain Alfred T. Mahan at the Naval War College as his primary source of inspiration and guidance. The two men apparently became close friends in summer 1889 when Mahan was making the final revisions to his forthcoming book, *The Influence of Sea Power upon History.* At the same time, his continued tenure at the War College had been called into jeopardy by recent negative fitness reports. According to a doctoral study by Herrick, Tracy intervened on Mahan's behalf with his superior officers by arguing the significance of Mahan's "literary efforts."[26]

Tracy's first and blistering annual report of 1889 clearly bears the imprint of Mahan's ideas, and has been celebrated as "one of the most forceful documents in the entire history of American naval policy."[27] It opens with a ranked order listing of the world's top eleven navies based on each country's number of effective warships. England was at the top with 367 vessels, and Austria was last with 54. The United States, with 42 vessels, Tracy then states, "cannot take rank as a naval power." He maintained that defense, not conquest, is the objective of U.S. naval policy, but, to be effective, "the defense of the United States requires a fighting force." Unarmored vessels—which constituted the bulk of the U.S. fleet—might function as "commerce raiders," according to Tracy, but they did not constitute a "fighting force." "We must have armored battleships" with the capacity "to raise blockades" and "to beat off an enemy's fleet on its approach," and, if needed, "to divert an enemy's force from our coast by threatening his own."[28] In this first report, Tracy was not ready to advocate that the United States build bases offshore, but he did note great U.S. cities on both the Atlantic and Pacific coasts that were either defenseless or could not be effectively protected by land fortifications. He therefore recommended the immediate construction "of two fleets of battleships," eight for the Pacific and twelve for the Atlantic and Gulf regions.[29]

Almost immediately, Tracy's recommendation was followed by the even more ambitious proposals made by the "policy board" Tracy had created to design a program of naval expansion. The board's report, published in January 1890, advocated the construction of more than 200 modern warships that would include a fleet of battleships with a cruising range of 15,000 miles. Not surprisingly, this report evoked widespread protest, including the condemnation of "fanaticism" by the pronavy *New York Herald,* and Secretary Tracy quickly distanced himself from the board's plan.[30] The House Naval Affairs Committee, however, with the guidance of Representative Charles Boutelle of Maine, took these various recommendations seriously enough to propose the construction of "three sea-going, coastline battleships . . . with a coal endurance of about five thousand knots."[31] In congressional debate, Boutelle argued for a fighting fleet "powerful enough . . . to break the blockade of any of our great maritime ports . . . to drive off foreign aggression from our shores, *and to seize and hold bases of supply in the immediate vicinity of the American coast.*" Boutelle added special emphasis to the last point, stating that, in the event of war, *"possession would be absolutely essential to the safety of our coastline."*[32]

Boutelle's remarks resonated with Secretary Tracy and other senior members of the Harrison administration. Tracy was especially intent on establishing effective control over a coaling station on the Samoan Island of Pago Pago, which lay astride the main shipping lane between California and Japan. In these South Pacific islands, U.S. expansionist ambitions vied with those of Germany and Great Britain under a condominium (or joint) agreement that, in the words of one historian, "acted to safeguard the equality of

American, German, and British interests, but not to guarantee the autonomy of the native government."[33]

The Harrison administration explored various possibilities of acquiring naval bases in the West Indies, but preliminary negotiations proved inconclusive. Tracy favored the acquisition of the Danish West Indies, and there was some talk of establishing a joint naval protectorate with the Portuguese over the Azores, but Secretary of State Blaine's objections to both initiatives prevailed. Writing to President Harrison while summering in Bar Harbor on August 10, 1891, Blaine outlined his own expansionist vision:

> In regard to the purchase of the Danish Colonies, St. Thomas, and St. John, my prepossessions are all against it, until we are by fate in possession of the larger West Indies. They are very small, of no great commercial value, and in case of war we would be required to defend them and to defend them at great cost. At the same time they lack strategic value. They are destined to become ours, but among the last of the West Indies that would be taken. . . . I think there are only three places that are of value enough to be taken. . . . Cuba and Porto [*sic*] Rico are not now imminent and will not be for a generation. Hawaii may come up for decision any unexpected hour, and I hope we shall be prepared to decide it in the affirmative.[34]

The issue of acquiring naval bases was also linked to the growing interest in building an interoceanic canal through the Isthmus of Panama. Secretary Tracy was an enthusiastic advocate of such an undertaking because, as he repeatedly argued in his annual reports, a canal would enable the United States to defend its Atlantic and Pacific coasts with a one-ocean navy. On this point, Tracy's views closely reflected Mahan's strategic thinking, but he and Mahan differed as to which Caribbean islands should be asked to provide outposts to guard the approaches to the canal. Mahan had suggested establishing a base in Cuba, but Tracy vetoed this as "impracticable" and chose to focus instead on acquiring Mole St. Nicolas in Haiti and Samaná Bay in Santo Domingo. According to Herrick's extensive research on this topic, Tracy and President Harrison assumed that they could easily persuade Haiti and the Dominican Republic to lease naval stations because they reasoned that both governments were weak and their leaders susceptible to manipulation. To their astonished disappointment, both island nations rejected their diplomatic proposals. When Tracy (with the approval of President Harrison) subsequently resorted to heavy-handed tactics that included the dispatch of U.S. warships, he antagonized the island regimes into intransigence, and he also became the target of angry editorial criticism from leading U.S. newspapers.[35]

In spite of these setbacks, Tracy achieved many of his goals as secretary of the navy. In November 1892, he summarized the progress in battleship construction during his tenure as follows: nineteen steel warships had joined the fleet and an additional nineteen vessels had been laid down. These ships collectively provided greater tonnage and firepower for deep-sea offensive operations than any that had preceded them. Tracy then recommended additional construction, and concluded his final annual report with the warning that although much progress had been made, "other nations have not been idle, and the United States is not yet in a condition of adequate defense."[36]

Viewed in perspective, Tracy's influence on the Navy Department consisted of more than battleship construction. He had elevated the prestige of the Naval War College as a center for developing naval strategic planning and doctrine. His hard work, strong personality, and close relationship with President Harrison had all served to elevate the importance of the position of navy secretary within the cabinet, for at times his influence was at least commensurate with that of Secretary of State Blaine. Tracy's failure to achieve his goal of establishing naval stations in the Caribbean also provided lessons learned for subsequent naval secretaries, including Secretary John Long and Assistant Secretary Theodore Roosevelt. Perhaps Tracy's chief adviser and propagandist, Captain Mahan aptly summarized the most important lesson in his 1893 article "The Isthmus and Sea Power" the year Tracy resigned his post. Mahan advised U.S. naval policymakers to exercise wisdom and patience: "Control of a maritime region is insured primarily by a navy; secondarily, by positions upon which as bases the navy rests. At present the positions of the Caribbean are occupied by foreign powers, nor may we, however disposed to acquisition, obtain them by means other than righteous."[37] Mahan's syntax and the use of the word "righteous" may seem antiquated to today's reader, but the message is clear. The acquisition of foreign naval stations must be handled at the right time, deftly, and with popular support. This is a lesson for his global strategy that Theodore Roosevelt in turn would learn from Mahan and apply during his presidency.

When Grover Cleveland returned to the White House in 1893, he named Alabama lawyer and longtime member of the House of Representatives Hilary A. Herbert to head the Navy Department. Since Herbert had served for three terms as a member of the Naval Affairs Committee, plus one term as its chair, he was well qualified for the post. Initially, it appeared that Herbert, like William Whitney, would try to undo some of the accomplishments of his immediate Republican predecessor. Herbert had criticized Secretary Tracy's ambitious battleship program in 1890, and he had also opposed the creation of the Naval War College. Soon after becoming navy secretary, however, Herbert emerged as a vigorous advocate of more battleship construction and a strong supporter of the War College. The most important factors that influenced this change in perspective were the insights Herbert gained from comparing U.S. warships with the finest warships of eight foreign fleets at the Columbian Naval Review held in New York Harbor on April 26, 1893, an eye-opening visit to the college in Newport in summer 1893, and his growing enthusiasm for Captain Mahan's major works on the influence of sea power.[38]

Herbert's annual report for 1894 clearly reflected his new thinking in candid language. With regard to the War College, he admitted:

> For some years I was not inclined to believe that the advantages to be derived from a war college . . . were sufficient to justify the expenditure. A visit, however, to that institution at Newport . . . sufficed to change my conviction on the subject. . . . Its proper purpose is the study of strategy and tactics, the solution of war problems as affected by modern naval applications, questions which can only be taken up with advantage by officers of experience. My careful examination of this whole question greatly impressed me with the importance of at once establishing the institution upon a firm and substantial basis.[39]

Later in the same report, when Herbert addressed the issue of what U.S. naval policy should be, he asserted that "if our government in the future is to command the peace . . . it must have more battleships and more torpedo boats."[40] His vision of the future role for the U.S. Navy looked to the Pacific, where he noted that our interests with China, Japan, and the Pacific islands are now closely linked by "powerful lines of fast steamships," but his main focus was on Latin America and its surrounding oceans, which he asserted "now demand the presence of American ships of war to a greater extent than ever before, and this demand will steadily increase."[41]

Throughout his term of office, despite lingering problems of economic recession, Herbert would lobby Congress, with varying degrees of success, to build more armored battleships, torpedo boats, and light-draft gunboats. Under his guidance, the United States Navy had advanced from seventh to sixth place among the great nations in naval strength, ahead of Spain but lagging behind Germany, Italy, Russia, France, and Great Britain. In his final report of 1896, he took special note of the growing U.S. interest in the Caribbean and addressed the need to establish a naval station on the Gulf coast. As a valedictory warning, he stated, "Our obligations and duties on this hemisphere are recognized by the world, and cannot be met unless we are possessed of naval strength. If our merchant marine increases . . . as it no doubt will, the present naval strength will be very far from what it should be."[42]

What was the goal for U.S. naval strength to which Secretary Herbert alluded but did not specify? The question is important, but unanswered, because no one ever clarified the goal. From 1881 to 1896, or from William Hunt to Hilary Herbert, the security emphasis within the Navy Department had shifted from guarding the U.S. coastlines to protecting our expanding commercial interests to asserting the U.S. presence in the Caribbean, the South Atlantic, and the Pacific Ocean. Or as Mark Shulman has succinctly described these changes: "The emphasis of naval construction shifted from protected cruisers to armored cruisers and then to battleships." Moreover, the philosophy of naval strategy had shifted from "the best defense is a defense" to "the best defense is an offense."[43] These changes in naval security, construction of warships, and strategy occurred well before the United States intervened in the Spanish-Cuban war or even thought seriously about establishing Guantánamo Naval Base in Cuba, but these changes prepared the United States to be ready and willing to go to war. The only plausible answer to the question that began this paragraph is that the United States was using its navy to achieve and proclaim its great power status. That this was the ultimate goal is suggested in Hilary Herbert's impressionistic essay on the great naval review of 1893. He thrilled to the sight of thirty warships at anchor in "this beautiful sheet of water" where "each one seemed hung with rainbows of many colors." "But the crowning feature" for Herbert was the parade of the sailors through the streets of New York—a "unique body of men drilled and disciplined into fighting machines." "Never was such a sight witnessed before as the sailors of nine different nations marching together, and never was anything better calculated to impress upon those who saw them the lesson that the American sailor can keep his place upon the seas only when his Government is behind him." Herbert concluded his report with the prediction that "if America would maintain her place in the vanguard of civilization, she must at all times be prepared for war." No other U.S. nationalist of this era, not Theodore Roosevelt or Henry Cabot Lodge, could have linked the yearning for "great power" status with the future of the U.S. Navy more effectively.[44]

Roosevelt's Circle of Influence: Mahan and Roosevelt

President Theodore Roosevelt's determination to have a U.S. naval station at Guantánamo, Cuba, was an important piece in his plan to forge a modern, powerful navy and to assert a lasting U.S. presence in the Caribbean and Gulf of Mexico. It was also the culmination of his wide-ranging reading and thinking about the role he believed the United States was destined to play as a great power of the twentieth century. Roosevelt counted philosophers, historians, fellow politicians, former secretaries of the navy, and senior naval officers—including his brother-in-law William S. Cowles—among his close associates, and with all of them he carried on a lively correspondence that frequently touched on naval matters and the destiny of the United States as a maritime power. Among those who influenced his thinking on both subjects, none played a more formative role than a senior professor at the Naval War College, Captain Alfred Thayer Mahan.

The friendship between Roosevelt and Mahan rested on a mutual belief in the value of lessons taught by naval history and a shared perception that a modern maritime nation had to have a powerful navy that included strategically placed naval fortifications as well as battleships. Of course, they did not always agree on some important issues, but argument and discussion often drew them closer.[45] Indeed, the inception of their relationship stemmed from their independent research and writing of scholarly works, for both were accomplished naval historians.

In *The Naval War of 1812*, Roosevelt argued that training and advance preparations combined with courage had enabled the United States to win the war. Emphasizing the importance of accurate gunnery, swift ships, and precision in joint maneuvers, Roosevelt concluded, "The American prepared himself in every possible way; the Briton tried to cope with courage alone."[46] Prior to launching his political career, Roosevelt's publication of *The Naval War of 1812* had established his reputation as a naval historian and as a critical thinker on naval preparedness. As biographer H. W. Brands correctly observes, "Before long Roosevelt would ally himself with such prominent writers and public figures as Alfred Thayer Mahan and Henry Cabot Lodge in pressing for a large policy . . . premised on the construction of a modern battleship fleet that could project American power far beyond American shores; it came including the acquisition of naval bases and coaling stations overseas, an American Empire in the Caribbean, and the Panama Canal."[47]

We do not know if Mahan ever read *The Naval War of 1812*, or when Roosevelt first read anything by Mahan, but in the summer of 1887, as Roosevelt was doing his research for *The Winning of the West*, he responded to a request from Admiral Stephen Luce to support the newly founded Naval War College, saying, "I know Captain Mahan by reputation very well; it is needless to say that I shall be delighted to do anything in my power to help along the Naval college."[48] On May 6, 1890, Captain Mahan published his first great work, *The Influence of Sea Power upon History, 1660–1783*, which predicted that if a Panama canal route were built, the Caribbean would be transformed into "one of the great highways of the world," and "the position of the United States with reference to this route will resemble that of England to the Channel and of the Mediterranean countries to the Suez route."[49] Within days of this book's appearance, Mahan had sent complimentary copies to Secretary of the Navy John Long and to the influential Congressman Henry Cabot Lodge,[50] informing them that he hoped the work would "lay a broad foundation for the study of naval warfare" and that "the experience of the past [would] shape the policy of the future." Because Roosevelt was then serving as chair of the Civil Service Commission, it is understandable that Mahan did not include him on his mailing list, but Roosevelt bought and read the entire work between May 11 and 12, whereupon he wrote to Mahan, "I think it very much the clearest and most instructive general work of its kind," and "I am greatly in error if it does not become a naval classic."[51]

Roosevelt subsequently submitted his laudatory review of Mahan's *Sea Power* to Horace Elisha Scudder, editor of the *Atlantic Monthly,* and it appeared in the October 1890 issue.[52] The high points of this piece are worth discussing because it was much more than a book review; in effect, Roosevelt adopted Mahan's ideas to write his own polemic that there was a pressing need for the United States to create a "fighting fleet" to ensure its defense. He opened by stating that "Captain Mahan has written distinctively the best and most important book on naval history which has been produced on either side of the water for many a long year." Roosevelt praised Mahan's Introduction for "showing the practical importance of studying naval history to those who would use aright the navies of the present." He took account of Mahan's sensitivity to the country's circumstances, including "the need of adequate fortifications and navy yards" and "the necessity of a large commercial marine." Surprisingly, Roosevelt did not call the reader's attention to Mahan's intriguing speculation as to how dominance of the Caribbean could advance U.S. commercial interests, but he made clear that Mahan's reasoning was not lost on him when he wrote, "From the time when Gibraltar was taken, to the beginning of the war for American independence, England possessed the undisputed supremacy of the ocean." He then showed how Mahan's work called attention to U.S. naval vulnerabilities in the event of war with a European power, warning that the United States lacked any forward base for "commerce destroying"[53] or "a line of battle to fall back upon." Toward the end of his review, Roosevelt made his own forceful argument: "We need a large navy, composed not merely of cruisers, but containing a full proportion of powerful battleships. . . . It is not economy, it is niggardly and foolish short-sightedness to cramp our naval expenditures while squandering money right and left on everything else from pensions to public buildings."[54]

In his analysis of Roosevelt's commentary, historian Richard Turk called the reader's attention to one sentence he believes stood out as Roosevelt's highest praise of Mahan's work: "Hitherto, historians of naval matters, at least as far as English and American writers are concerned, have completely ignored the general strategic bearing of the struggles which they chronicle; they have been for the most part mere annalists, who limited themselves to describing the actual battles and the forces on each side." Turk then asked rhetorically, "Did Roosevelt demean his own work in this negative assessment?"[55] It is doubtful that Mahan took this particular sentence as a concession of intellectual superiority on Roosevelt's part, but it did set the tone for their subsequent dialogue and collaboration on issues of naval strategy and global balance of power, in which each thinker knew his views would be taken seriously by the other.

From the early to mid-1890s, Roosevelt's professional commitments with the Civil Service Commission and as Police Commissioner of New York allowed him occasional brief periods to indulge his interest in naval matters, and his relationship with Mahan continued to evolve. In April 1893 he reviewed Mahan's next major work, *The Influence of Sea Power upon the French Revolution and Empire*. In his commentary, Roosevelt noted Mahan's emphasis on the "folly" of relying on "privateering or commerce-destroying to cripple a resolute enemy." Roosevelt then forcefully asserted, "The only way to make headway against sea power is by sea power itself . . . having a thoroughly first-class navy, able to hold its own with the navy of any European nation."[56]

In October 1893, the *Atlantic Monthly* published Mahan's aforementioned article, "The Isthmus and Sea Power."[57] After advocating the construction of a U.S. canal through Nicaragua, he forcefully asserted that "freedom of inter-oceanic transit depends upon predominance in a maritime region—the Caribbean Sea—through which pass all approaches to the Isthmus." He also observed that "control of a maritime region is insured primarily by a navy" and that, for the United States, "defense" will eventually have "application at points far away from our own coast."[58] When this article appeared, Mahan was again at sea, having been reassigned from the Naval War College to command the flagship *Chicago* in European waters.

We have no written record of Roosevelt's response to Mahan's advocacy of a U.S. canal and strategic positioning in the Caribbean, but he almost certainly read the article and applauded its message. On May 20, 1894, he confided to his older sister, Anna, "It is a great misfortune that we have not annexed Hawaii; gone on with our navy, and started an inter-oceanic canal at Nicaragua." Later, he wrote to Lodge, "I do wish our Republicans would go in avowedly to build an oceanic canal with the money of Uncle Sam."[59]

It was during this time that Roosevelt and Mahan became personal friends. Twice Roosevelt sought to help Mahan overcome obstacles in his naval career. In early 1893 he tried but failed to prevent Mahan from being recalled to sea duty.[60] Subsequently, Roosevelt together with Lodge had greater success in persuading Navy Secretary Hilary Herbert to ignore an extremely negative fitness report by Mahan's commanding officer, thus allowing Mahan to retire with honor in 1896 and devote his energies full time to writing as a naval historian, theorist, and publicist.[61]

Other Major Figures Enter the Picture: Lodge, Cowles, McKinley, and Long

Henry Cabot Lodge was for many decades Theodore Roosevelt's most important political ally, and, like Roosevelt, he was eager to transform Mahan's advocacy of U.S. sea power into a reality. Lodge and Roosevelt became friends in spring 1884, when they tried unsuccessfully to prevent the Republican nomination of James Blaine for president. Years later, Roosevelt wrote in a memorandum that "from that time on, he [Lodge] was my closest friend, personally, politically, and in every other way, and occupied toward me a relation that no other man has ever occupied or will ever occupy. . . . For the past twenty-four years I have discussed almost every move I have made in politics with him."[62]

What drew these men together was a shared belief in the great destiny of the United States and a common concern that to ensure that destiny, the federal government had to strengthen its defenses. In 1879, Lodge had publicly proclaimed, "We are in the very prime of life as a nation. . . . We are vigorous, powerful, rich, and masters of a continent. . . . We have built up an empire so great that . . . it is a chief factor in the affairs of civilized men." Within a few years he would begin to agitate for a more vigorous foreign policy and a more powerful navy.[63]

In the early 1880s, Roosevelt, Mahan, and Lodge would have agreed completely that the U.S. Navy was in deplorable shape. It consisted mainly of wooden cruisers and outdated monitors left over from the Civil War. Captain Mahan had lamented in 1882 that the navy had reached its nadir: "We have not six ships that would be kept at sea in war by any maritime power." The following year, Mahan was assigned to sea duty in South America, where the War of the Pacific was raging between Chile and Peru. After he took command of the *Wachusett* in Callao, Peru, he described the ship as "an old war-horse, not yet turned out to grass or slaughter." In Mahan's view, the three foreign ships in the harbor—German, Chilean, and Italian—were all superior to the *Wachusett*.[64]

We have no record of Mahan communicating his views about the wretched state of U.S. warships in the 1880s to Lodge or Roosevelt, even though his blunt description of the *Wachusett*'s multiple defects quickly earned him a reputation as a "chronic complainer" within the Navy Department. Almost certainly, it did not advance his career for him to plead directly to the secretary of the navy on May 15, 1885, to be relieved of command in a furious letter that protested, "The *Wachusett* is probably the worst commander's command in the service. . . . I have borne it long enough."[65] In time, invidious comparisons between the U.S. Navy and its South American counterparts did surface in high-level political discussions. In January 1888, Roosevelt sent Lodge a copy of a speech he had earlier delivered to the Union League Club, in which he had trumpeted, "It is a disgrace to us as a nation that we should have no warships worthy of the name. We are actually at the mercy of a tenth-rate country like Chili [*sic*]."[66]

In summer 1895, Theodore Roosevelt's older sister, Anna (whom Roosevelt affectionately called "Bamie" or "Bye") married Navy Captain William Sheffield Cowles, and soon Roosevelt and Cowles were writing to each other on naval history and related topics. On November 14, 1895, Roosevelt thanked Cowles for sending him James Froude's *The Spanish Story of the Armada,* saying, "I have managed to read a good deal of the 'Armada' usually when alone at breakfast."[67] A month later, Roosevelt again wrote to Cowles in regard to President Cleveland's protest that the British were violating the Monroe Doctrine in their efforts to assert control over oil-rich territory on the disputed border between Venezuela and British Guiana. Roosevelt confided, "I earnestly hope our government does not back down. If there is a muss, I shall try to have a hand in it myself!"[68] By April 5, 1896, Roosevelt's desire to uphold the Monroe Doctrine extended to Cuba. In one of his most revealing letters, he told Cowles, "I think we ought to interfere in Cuba and indeed I believe it would be well were we sufficiently farsighted steadily to shape our policy with the view to the ultimate removal of all European powers from the colonies they hold in the Western Hemisphere." Roosevelt then abruptly changed the subject to probe Cowles's technical opinion on naval gunnery issues, asking why newly built U.S. battleships did not have the "6-inch quick-firer guns" that were then commonplace in British battleships.[69]

Other letters by Roosevelt in 1895 and 1896 showed his growing concern with Cuba's second struggle for independence and his willingness to fight for a "Cuba Libre." On March 19, 1895, he wrote New York governor Levi Morton to request that "in the improbable event of a war with Spain, I beg you with all of my power . . . get me a position in New York's quota of the force sent out. . . . I must have a commission in the force that goes to

Cuba!"[70] One year later, at the same time he wrote Cowles, he also groused to his "Darling Bye," "I wish our people would really interfere in Cuba, but the President [Grover Cleveland] shies off from anything but Venezuela. We ought to drive the Spanish out of Cuba, and it would be a good thing in more ways than one."[71]

What Roosevelt meant by his enigmatic phrase "more ways than one" can be discerned from his correspondence with Lodge and with Lodge's expansionist pronouncements that conjoined the need for a "great" navy with his view that U.S. intervention in Cuba would soon become a "necessity." In March 1895, Lodge published "Our Blundering Foreign Policy" in *Forum,* in which he asserted that "England has studded the West Indies with strong places which are a standing menace to our Atlantic seaboard. *We should have among those islands at least one strong naval station, and when the Nicaraguan canal is built, the island of Cuba . . . will become to us a necessity."*[72] Roosevelt almost certainly read Lodge's article—both men frequently contributed to the *Forum*—and indeed this article may have prompted Roosevelt's impassioned plea to Morton a few days later. On February 25, 1896, Roosevelt wrote Lodge of the "infinite obstacles" he was encountering in his efforts to rebuild New York City's Police Department, predicted that he would eventually "be legislated out," and concluded by praising Lodge's public advocacy of an independent Cuba, saying, "It is one of the best things you have done."[73]

If this letter suggests that Roosevelt was tiring of his current assignment as police commissioner, that was indeed the reality. On December 6, 1896, he complained to Cowles, "I should welcome being legislated out of office; the law hampers us terribly and of my three colleagues, one, Parker, is a thorough knave, and another, Grant, a fool." Then, choosing to end on a revelatory upbeat note, Roosevelt wrote, "I dined with Mahan the other night; and it was very pleasant."[74]

The 1896 presidential election of William McKinley provided Lodge the opportunity to seek a subcabinet post for his dear friend and expansionist ally Theodore Roosevelt. On November 29 of that year, Lodge met with the president-elect in Canton, Ohio, and during their wide-ranging discussion of foreign policy issues that touched on Hawaii and Cuba, Lodge proposed that McKinley appoint Roosevelt assistant secretary of the navy. As Lodge subsequently informed Roosevelt, McKinley "spoke of you with great regard for your character and your services and he would like to have you in Washington." Lodge then said that McKinley had voiced one concern: "I hope he has no conceived plans which he would wish to drive through the moment he got in."[75]

McKinley was not the first senior U.S. government official to fear Roosevelt would exceed his authority and ignore bureaucratic channels if he were appointed to high office. In 1888, Secretary of State James Blaine had denied a request by Henry Cabot Lodge to make Roosevelt assistant secretary of state. Noting that he liked to take his summer vacations in Maine, Blaine wrote to Lodge's wife, " I do somehow fear that my sleep at Augusta or Bar Harbor would not be quite so easy and refreshing if so brilliant and aggressive a man had hold of the helm. Matters are constantly occurring which require the most thoughtful concentration and the most stubborn inaction. Do *you* think that Mr. T.R.'s temperament would give guaranty of that course?"

Even though Lodge managed to persuade McKinley that Roosevelt would not be insubordinate and would seek only to advance naval development policies already under way, McKinley's qualms were well-founded.[76] The truth was that McKinley had Roosevelt's number, and Roosevelt had also taken McKinley's measure. Shortly before the election, Roosevelt told Anna, "McKinley himself is an upright and honorable man. . . . He is not a strong man, however, and unless he is well backed, I should feel uneasy about him in a serious crisis."[77] According to career diplomat and scholar Warren Zimmermann, Roosevelt also quickly and accurately assessed his own ability to exert influence on the formation of naval policy within the new administration. In his view, Secretary of State John Sherman was senile, Secretary of War Russell Alger incompetent, and his own boss, John Long, an affable politician who, by his own admission, had "no special aptitude for the Navy."[78]

On April 17, 1897, Roosevelt formally resigned his post as New York police commissioner, and two days later he entered his new office in the White House's War Department. He quickly gained direct access to President McKinley. At the end of his first week, on April 26, he was advising President McKinley that "we should keep the battleships on our own coast and in readiness for action should any complications arise in Cuba."[79]

Between May 1 and May 6, 1897, Mahan and Roosevelt engaged in a significant policy planning exchange. On May 1, Mahan wrote, "I would suggest that the real significance of the Nicaragua canal now is that it advances our Atlantic frontier by so much to the Pacific & that in Asia, not in Europe, is now the greatest danger to our proximate interests." On May 3, Roosevelt replied, "My dear Captain Mahan: I fully realize the importance of the Pacific coast . . . but there are big problems in the West Indies also. Until we definitely turn Spain out of those islands (and if I had my way that would be done tomorrow) we will always be menaced by trouble there." On May 6, Mahan completed the exchange: "My Dear Roosevelt, Your letter has been read and destroyed. You will believe that when I write to you it is only to suggest thoughts, or give information. . . . I have known myself too long not to know that I am the man of thought, not of action."[80]

In their discussions of naval strategy, Roosevelt and Mahan would have known and had direct access to the war gaming scenarios being developed at the Naval War College. In 1894, the War College recommended that, in the event of a war with Spain, the U.S. Navy should focus its offensive operations on Cuba. The following year, another scenario discussed, but ultimately rejected, the option of attacking the Philippines on the grounds that success there "would not be of great value to us" and that it would prove "more costly than an attack on Spain's West Indies possessions." In 1896, however, a staffer at the Office of Naval Intelligence, Lieutenant William Kimball, developed a more complex and ambitious war plan that involved a simultaneous blockade of Cuba, an attack on Manila—which would suspend Spanish access to Philippine revenues—and the dispatch of other U.S. vessels to harass the Spanish coast.[81]

As Roosevelt began his rise to national prominence, he would keep his eyes focused on opportunities to advance U.S. naval interests in both the Pacific and the Caribbean. It is well known that on February 25, 1898, when Secretary Long was out of the office, Roosevelt ordered Commodore George Dewey to Hong Kong to block the Spanish Fleet and, in the event of war with Spain, to attack the Philippines.[82] What is not well known is that, also on February 25, Secretary Long, knowing Roosevelt's intent, had scribbled the following message to his deputy: "Dear Mr. Roosevelt, Revoke your order for moving guns till you can consult the President. Do not take any such step affecting the policy . . . without consulting him or me."[83] Roosevelt chose to disobey Long's instruction, and Long reportedly was furious—confiding to his diary that Roosevelt "has gone at things like a bull in a china shop."[84]

In reality, both McKinley and Long had prior knowledge of Roosevelt's strongly held desire to seize the Philippines, and they knew that from the assistant secretary himself. Roosevelt had given serious consideration to war-planner Kimball's 1896 recommendation that, in the event of a war with Spain, the U.S. Navy should occupy Manila and turn it into a base of further operations. As early as mid-September 1897, Roosevelt told President McKinley, "If things look menacing about Spain . . . our Asiatic Squadron should blockade and, if possible, take Manila." On September 21, Roosevelt made the same recommendation to Senator Lodge. It was also in September that President McKinley placed Dewey in command of the Asiatic Squadron and in October that he approved orders that placed the squadron on a war footing. It is inconceivable that McKinley or Roosevelt would have excluded Navy Secretary Long from such crucial recommendations and decisions.[85]

Why then had Long scribbled his admonishing note before leaving the office on February 25 or penned the anguished entry in his diary on the following day? Here the historical record is silent, and we can only assume that Long had suffered a moment of panic when he thought of the potentially negative consequences of Roosevelt's independent action. In any case, neither Long nor President McKinley would reverse Roosevelt's command. A full two months would elapse before the United States declared war on Spain on April 25, 1898. Dewey steamed from Hong Kong three days later and took Manila on May 1, 1898. Roosevelt unilaterally had charted U.S. naval policy by extending the scope of the Spanish-American War to the Philippines at the outset of hostilities.

Roosevelt submitted his resignation as assistant secretary of the navy to President McKinley on May 6, 1898. The following day, Secretary Long communicated his utmost regret: "Let me assure you how profoundly I feel the loss I sustain in your going, for your energy, industry, and great knowledge of naval interests."[86] Roosevelt, of course, left the War Department to join his new friend Colonel Leonard Wood in raising the First Volunteer Cavalry Regiment, the Rough Riders, to fight in Cuba.[87] When Roosevelt left Washington, Captain Mahan, who had accepted an appointment to the Naval War Board, moved to occupy Roosevelt's house. As Roosevelt had reasoned to his brother-in-law Douglas Robinson on April 2, 1898, "My usefulness in my present position is mainly a usefulness in peace . . . but in time of war, the naval officers will take their proper position as military advisers and my usefulness would be at an end." He further explained to Robinson that, having advocated war with Spain, he felt honor-bound to go to the front to fight in Cuba. "I have a horror of the people who bark but don't bite."[88]

Roosevelt's correspondence with his close friends and extended family prior to joining the fight in the Spanish-American-Cuban War is also instructive for what it did not say. He never mentioned Spanish general Valeriano Weyler, whose brutal policies of military occupation in Cuba attracted so much negative attention from the press. He also ignored the "leaking" of the De Lome letter that characterized President McKinley as "weak and catering to the rabble." He did mention the "terrible tragedy" of the explosion and sinking of the *Maine* in two brief letters to his sister Bamie, but he also said that "no one can tell what the cause of the disaster was," and "even if it were due to Spanish treachery, it might be impossible ever to find out." Roosevelt admitted that he was preoccupied with the fact that his second wife, Edith, was suffering from an illness her doctors could not diagnose or treat. "I have not felt the loss of the *Maine* nearly as much as I would if I had not had so much to worry over in my own home."[89] On March 9, 1898, Roosevelt told his friend, seasoned U.S. diplomat Henry White, that "our feeling of grief at the loss of the *Maine* in this Department has been sunk in a very eager desire to find out the cause of the disaster and to avenge it if it is due to outside work." Roosevelt then said he hoped the U.S. government would regard the *Maine* incident as a part of the "whole Cuban business," and that the only permanent solution "is Cuban independence."[90] Clearly, Roosevelt's reasons for warring with Spain had everything to do with carving out a global role for the United States and its navy and establishing a permanent presence in both the Caribbean and Pacific Oceans and virtually nothing to do with the emotional issues that persuaded many idealistic young men, including Carl Sandburg, who enlisted in the Sixtieth Illinois Infantry and participated in the invasion of Puerto Rico.

Unlike Lodge and other close associates, including Leonard Wood, Roosevelt never wanted to annex Cuba.[91] From his military barracks in San Antonio, Texas, and onboard the U.S. transport *Yucatan,* Roosevelt wrote separate letters to Lodge that emphasized the importance he placed on the United States retaining Puerto Rico, the Philippines, and Hawaii and securing the "independence of Cuba."[92] He would not change his mind on that subject, but when it eventually came to the issue of situating offshore bases, Guantánamo Bay would feature as the one spoil of war he would never relinquish.

It is ironic that, decades later, one of Cuba's most distinguished diplomats, Cosme de la Torriente, and one of its most outspoken nationalist historians, Herminio Portell Vilá, would portray Roosevelt's involvement in Cuba in uncritical, heroic terms, speaking only of his efforts to make Cuba independent, stable, and prosperous, and completely ignoring Roosevelt's determination to establish at least one permanent U.S. naval station there. In a talk at Havana's Veterans Center on October 27, 1935, Torriente spoke of the profound admiration and "devotion without limits" the men of his generation who had fought in the Spanish-American War felt toward this "dynamic man of excellence." He recalled that Roosevelt never lost interest in the problems of the Cuban people or the welfare of their nation, and he mentioned a letter he had received from Roosevelt, written shortly before his death, in which Roosevelt had expressed great satisfaction for Cuba's assistance to the United States upon entering World War I.[93] In the same wide-ranging talk, Torriente also briefly mentioned his personal role as secretary of state in negotiating in 1934 the end of the Platt Amendment and in converting into a more equitable agreement between the two nations "the imposition that had made the naval station at Guantánamo a bilateral problem."[94]

Sixteen years later, in 1950, Portell Vilá delivered his in-depth review of Roosevelt's role in the history of Cuba to the Club San Carlos in Santiago, Cuba. Portell Vilá clearly saw Roosevelt as an imperialist but not as an annexationist insofar as Cuba was concerned. He said:

> There is no doubt that Theodore Roosevelt was an imperialist, but [Leonard] Wood's imperialistic plan did not interest him in the least. . . . The inauguration of the Republic of Cuba constituted for Roosevelt, as the liberty of a people should always do to every man of honor and of liberal conviction, a motive for great and legitimate satisfaction. . . . As far as Cuba is concerned, more were his good accomplishments than his errors. . . . When Theodore Roosevelt died, the Cuban people expressed their deep grief over the loss of the best friend they had among the Americans.[95]

2

The Battle for Guantánamo in 1898

"A SPRUCE YOUNG SERGEANT OF MARINES, erect, his back to the showering bullets, solemnly and intently wigwagging to the distant *Dolphin*!"[1] This is how novelist and Spanish-American War correspondent Stephen Crane captured the heroic actions of Sergeant John H. Quick in redirecting the gunfire of the offshore U.S.S. *Dolphin* from friendly to enemy positions at Cuzco Well, the only potable water supply in Guantánamo Bay. Overwhelmed, the Spaniards began to retreat, and U.S. marines quickly secured the high ground surrounding the large natural harbor in southeastern Cuba that they intended to use as the primary coaling station and naval outpost. Sergeant Quick was awarded the Congressional Medal of Honor, and Guantánamo became a symbol of lasting pride for both the U.S. Navy and Marine Corps.

The year 1898 was not the first time foreigners invaded Guantánamo Bay. The largest harbor on the south side of Cuba, approximately two and one half miles wide, it has been a magnet for sailors since Christopher Columbus, on his second voyage to the Caribbean, aptly identified it as Puerto Grande in 1494. Spanish settlers began to arrive shortly thereafter to populate the future Oriente Province and to found the nearby settlements of Caimanéra and Guantánamo City. In the era of the Spanish Main, the bay often served as a base of operations for pirates who preyed on treasure-laden ships transiting the Windward Passage, and, at other times, it protected ships riding out the frequent hurricanes in the West Indies.[2]

It was during the eighteenth-century struggle between England and Spain for control of Caribbean trade routes, known as the War of Jenkins' Ear (1739–1748), that Admiral Edward Vernon sailed into Guantánamo Bay with a sizable but debilitated invasion force and renamed it Cumberland Bay in honor of King George II's younger son. Vernon and Army General Thomas Wentworth had previously attempted to take Cartagena (in New Granada, later Colombia) from the Spanish, but Wentworth, who lacked prior military campaign experience, squandered both time and resources, allowing the Spanish to strengthen their defenses. At the conclusion of his disastrous assault, Wentworth had lost 654 men to death and wounds, and he reported to Vernon that he had 3,569 men left, many of whom were sick with yellow fever and others of whom were too exhausted to be of service.

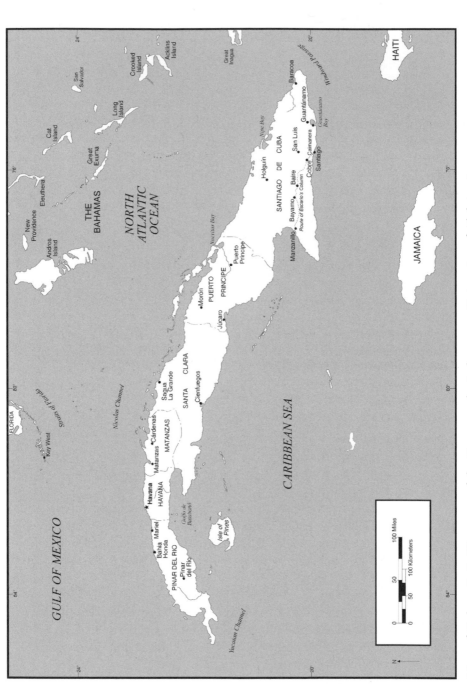

Map of Cuba, 1898. (Courtesy of the Cartography Laboratory, University of Alabama)

This, according to Charles Nowell's well-documented study, was the sad state of Wentworth's troops before they attempted to march from Guantánamo to Santiago de Cuba.[3]

Upon their arrival in "Cumberland Bay," Vernon and Wentworth hoped to use the harbor as the base from which British troops could advance by land forty miles west to Santiago, but obstacles imposed by the Cuban jungle, lack of food, and yellow fever quickly thwarted their plans. The British expeditionary force lost approximately two thousand men and abandoned its march sixteen miles from Santiago. According to historian Forrest Sherman, more than one hundred men died of sickness in one week. One member of the expedition wrote, "Our men are very sickly and die fast, more from want of necessities than the inclemencies of the climate I fear. Some die from their own excesses in drink." The force had not encountered a single Spanish soldier. Within the year, Vernon's expedition retreated to Jamaica.[4]

This unhappy, short-term episode had various long-term consequences. George Washington's elder half-brother Lawrence, who served as a captain in "Gooch's Marines" under Vernon, would name his Virginia estate on the banks of the Potomac River in his honor.[5] Novelist Tobias Smollett, who participated in the ill-fated expedition as a British naval surgeon, subsequently wrote a thinly veiled and picaresque account of Vernon and Wentworth's misadventures in *The Adventures of Roderick Random,* in which he noted that England had not risked its best troops nor had "colonels and field officers of the old corps" embarked on this "dangerous and precarious undertaking, for which they are much to be commended." Finally, and more importantly, U.S. Army General Rufus Shafter, who would command the army invading Cuba, studied military accounts of Vernon's and Wentworth's mistakes as he sailed from Florida to Cuba on June 20, 1898.[6]

The pressures that impelled President McKinley to ask Congress on April 11, 1898, to grant him the authority to intervene militarily in Cuba had more to do with a breakdown in U.S. diplomatic efforts to persuade Madrid to grant Cuba its independence than with military provocations or the desire for territorial aggrandizement, although these elements, too, were present.[7] When McKinley entered the White House in 1897, Cuba had been engaged in armed rebellion since February 1895. Like his predecessor, President Grover Cleveland, McKinley had wanted to avoid being drawn militarily into this conflict. The fundamental difference between Cleveland and McKinley, according to historian Lewis Gould, was that whereas Cleveland had pursued a fundamentally pro-Spanish diplomacy, McKinley was more sympathetic to the Cuban rebels.[8] Gould's assessment, however, tends to overlook the racial prejudices McKinley, Roosevelt, and other U.S. expansionists shared. As political scientist Bartholomew Sparrow has observed, the McKinley administration feared the possibility of an independent Cuba more than it did the perpetuation of Spanish rule. "The president and his advisers did not . . . consult [with] Cuban leaders Estrada Palma and General Máximo Gómez. . . . Given that Cuban independence was unacceptable, [they] decided on military intervention." According to Sparrow, anti-imperialist critic Booker T. Washington identified the hypocrisy in the thinking of U.S. leaders when he asked, "What will this country do for the millions of dark-skinned inhabitants of Cuba, Porto Rico [*sic*], Hawaii, and the Philippine Islands that it has been unwilling to do for nearly 10,000,000 Negroes and Indians in the United States?"[9] Sparrow fundamentally accepts Pérez's thesis that Cuban independence was unacceptable to the United States.

Gradually the pressures increased for McKinley to act decisively; valuable U.S. property in Cuba was being destroyed, and many residents there from the United States believed their lives were in jeopardy. On February 9, 1898, the *New York Journal,* which had been reporting sensationalist accounts of Spanish atrocities in Cuba, published a provocative letter that had been intercepted by a Cuban agent. The letter, written by Spanish Minister Enrique DeLome and intended for Madrid, denounced McKinley as a "weak and low politician." Less than a week later, on February 15, the U.S. battleship *Maine,* which McKinley had sent to Cuba to protect U.S. interests and citizens and to confront Spain with an example of U.S. battleship strength, mysteriously exploded and sank in Havana's harbor.[10] McKinley made a final effort to conduct diplomatic negotiations with Spain, but when Madrid refused to discuss Cuban independence, McKinley asked Congress for authorization to use force. Even then, as Gould has found, McKinley's message to Congress left open the possibility for further negotiations with Spain—at least in theory.[11] He did not ask for a declaration of war; instead he asked lawmakers "to authorize and empower" him to secure an end to hostilities between "the government of Spain and the peoples of Cuba." He also sought the authority to establish a stable government in Cuba and "to use the military and naval forces of the United States as may be necessary for these purposes." In other words, the United States intervened to prevent the independence that Cuba had already won. By obtaining this broad authorization from Congress, McKinley expanded his presidential powers and laid the groundwork for the United States to establish a protectorate over Cuba.[12]

In April 1898, the United States was in a poor state of military readiness, especially the U.S. Army, whose units were largely scattered along the western frontier fighting Indians. McKinley did not believe the United States capable of defeating Spain. He confided to his friend H. H. Kohlsaat, editor of the Chicago *Times-Herald,* "Congress is trying to drive us into war with

Spain. The Spanish fleet is in Cuban waters, and we haven't enough ammunition on the Atlantic seacoast to fire a salute."[13] Another, perhaps more perceptive, observer was the youthful Winston Churchill, who, as a foreign correspondent in Cuba, reported:

> We did not see how they [the Spanish] could win. . . . We knew that Spain was not a rich country [and] by what immense efforts and sacrifices she maintained more than a quarter of a million men across 5,000 miles of salt water. . . . And what of the enemy? In these forests and mountains were bands of ragged men not ill-supplied with rifles and ammunition and armed above all with a formidable chopper-sword called a machete. . . . Here were the Spaniards out-guerrilla-ed in their turn.[14]

The official *History of U.S. Marine Corps Operations in World War II*, in its introductory chapter, "Origins of a Mission," observes that, as early as 1880, farsighted naval officers realized that they would likely be ordered to enforce the Monroe Doctrine in Caribbean or South Atlantic waters in order to counter intrusions by imperialist European powers intent on acquiring new bases or colonies and to protect rapidly expanding U.S. commercial interests. This mission would necessitate the development of ground troops assigned to the fleet for the purpose of securing advanced bases where the fleet could coal, replenish food and drinking water, and make emergency repairs.[15] This had not been a problem for the British Empire, which had an abundance of overseas bases, but it would be a challenge for the United States with its few outlying possessions.[16]

In the mid-1890s, professors at Newport's Naval War College devised various scenarios that explored likely outcomes of potential conflicts in the Caribbean including the possibility of U.S. intervention in a Cuban insurrection. Several studies projected a war between the United States and Spain over Cuba, which, to win, the United States would have to blockade Cuban ports and defeat Spanish naval forces in the area. Nevertheless, the entry of the United States into the Spanish-Cuban conflict found the U.S. Navy "unprepared to cope with the advanced base problem." In retrospect, it seems obvious that the Marine Corps would have been the logical choice for this assignment, but in 1898 the corps was a small unit that had not previously exercised such major responsibilities. That is why the creation of the U.S. Marines First Battalion was such a precedent-making event.[17]

On April 15, 1898, five days before Congress officially declared war against Spain, the Navy Department ordered the Marine Corps to organize a battalion in Brooklyn, New York, for "possible service in Cuba." The vagueness of this wording suggested that Navy Secretary John Long had not yet decided precisely how to use these marines, but the order did specify that the battalion would consist of five rifle companies (each with its own drummer and fifer) and an artillery company to be armed with the 1895 Colt machine gun—the latest in automatic weaponry—and three-inch rapid-fire guns. This is the firepower that would be brought to bear at Guantánamo.[18]

The First Battalion would eventually consist of 21 marine officers and 615 enlisted men, thus constituting more than one-fifth of the entire corps. Also serving with this battalion were 2 navy officers and 2 enlisted men.[19] To command the battalion, Marine Commandant Colonel Charles Heywood chose Lieutenant Colonel Robert W. Huntington, whose military career dated back to the first battle of Bull Run. In the 1870s, he had obtained a temporary assignment to the cavalry to fight Indians on the frontier. By the late 1890s, Huntington had a well-earned reputation for being one of the corps' most demanding officers. On April 22, 1898, the First Battalion sailed from Brooklyn bound for Key West in a former banana boat, the *Venezuela,* which had been converted into a transport ship and renamed the U.S.S. *Panther.* The ship's skipper, Commander George C. Reiter, resented his assignment and treated the marines as mere "cargo." When he reached Key West, he requested permission to order the marines ashore, without their gear, until they received further orders.[20] This action prompted Heywood to complain to the commander of the naval base at Key West that there was no logical explanation that the battalion had been unloaded when the *Panther*'s only assignment was to transport the marines.[21] Meanwhile, Huntington wasted no time and began to drill his men in tactical exercises and musketry.

All through May, the marines trained in Key West. As they awaited further instructions, they learned of Commodore George Dewey's victory at Manila and of the battleship *Oregon*'s ten-week "dash" of 13,000 miles from San Francisco around Cape Horn to Florida. Meanwhile, the U.S. Navy's Atlantic Squadron was encountering a mix of successes and failures in Cuban waters. Its commander, Admiral William Sampson, who was based in Key West, had multiple orders to blockade Havana, the northeastern ports between Cárdenas and Bahía Honda, and Cienfuegos on the south side of the island. As historian Bradley Reynolds notes, "McKinley and the Congress would have preferred a full blockade of the island but such a plan was impractical."[22] Two major obstacles were that Sampson had a scant twenty warships to patrol 2,000 miles of Cuban coast, and the only major coaling station was at Key West, more than 600 miles from Cienfuegos.

From the onset of hostilities, the lack of a coaling station in or near the south of Cuba hampered U.S. naval operations in various ways. The first ship to arrive off Cienfuegos on April 29 had to abandon its position because of lack of coal. Admiral Sampson's efforts to move warships toward southeastern Cuba were slowed by colliers, which had to be towed. On May

19, the U.S.S. *St. Louis* tried to cut the telegraph cable at Guantánamo, but finding the cable station well guarded, Captain Casper Goodrich first sailed toward Haiti's Mole St. Nicolas and then notified the Navy Department that he was heading for New York to recoal.[23]

Finally, on May 28, after learning that Spanish Admiral Pasqual Cervera had sailed into Santiago Harbor and could conceivably be bottled there, Secretary Long made his fateful decision with regard to Guantánamo.[24] In response to several urgent pleas from Commodore Winfield Scott Schley—who was near Santiago—that, because his Flying Squadron[25] was running low on coal and having problems with the collier, he be allowed to return to Key West to obtain 10,000 tons of coal, Long bluntly told Schley, "Unless it is unsafe for your squadron, Department wishes you to remain off Santiago, so can you not take possession of Guantánamo, occupy as a coaling station?"[26] Long then ordered Sampson to leave for Cuba immediately and asked three questions: How soon can you reach Santiago de Cuba? How long can you blockade there? Can you seize Guantánamo? On May 29, Sampson replied, "Answering first question, three days. I can blockade indefinitely; think that I can occupy Guantánamo."[27]

Long's suggestion to Sampson that he take Guantánamo and make it into a coaling station was obviously a well-considered move despite the lack of historical documentation. As Reynolds's meticulously researched dissertation reveals, on May 26, the same day Long received Schley's first message regarding his coaling difficulties, a top-level operational strategy planning session had taken place at the White House between President McKinley, Secretary of War Russell Alger, Secretary of the Navy Long, Army Commander General Nelson Miles, and the senior member of the Naval War Board, Captain Alfred Thayer Mahan (retired). It is not surprising that there is no written record of the specific topics covered at this meeting, which could only be described as a war council concerned with the most urgent and sensitive matters. Given the makeup of this group, however, it is virtually certain that it was Mahan, the only naval strategist present, who recommended the occupation of Guantánamo.

With Sampson preparing to steam toward Santiago, Schley reconsidered his earlier decision to depart temporarily from Cuban waters, especially after receiving Sampson's order that he "blockade the Spanish squadron at all hazards." Early in the morning of May 29, Schley informed Sampson that he had partially repaired the collier and would coal the warships *Marblehead* and *Texas* at sea. At 10 A.M., off Santiago de Cuba, Schley telegraphed Long, "Enemy in port. Recognized *Cristobal Colon, Infanta Maria*, and two torpedo-boat destroyers moored inside Morro, behind point. Doubtless the others are here."[28]

Sampson quickly congratulated Schley on his discovery, repeated his

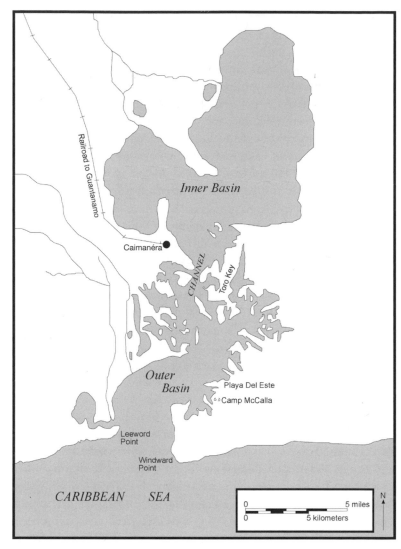

Map of Port of Guantánamo, 1898. (Based on information in
Notes on the Spanish War, Office of Naval Intelligence, 1899;
and William T. Sampson, "The Atlantic Fleet in the Spanish War,"
Century Illustrated Magazine, 57 no. 6. [April 1899]: 886–914.
Courtesy of the Cartography Laboratory, University of Alabama)

order to "maintain a close blockade," and commanded him to "send a ship to examine Guantánamo with view to occupying it as a base, coaling one heavy ship at a time."[29] Schley, however, did not send a ship to evaluate Guantánamo's capabilities as a coaling station, nor—according to one independent observer—did he maintain a particularly "close blockade." Years later, Ralph Paine, who had gone to Cuba as a reporter for the *Philadelphia Press,* criticized Schley for his "dilatory and stupid tactics" in keeping his Flying Squadron "ten to twenty miles offshore instead of closing it to bar [Cervera's] exit." As soon as Sampson arrived at Santiago, however, Paine reported that he "promptly established a masterly blockade."[30]

Schley's decision not to make a reconnaissance of Guantánamo was also called into question by Captain Charles Sigsbee, who had previously commanded the ill-fated *Maine* and was now in charge of the *St. Paul.* On May 31, Sigsbee cabled Long that he had advised Schley that "Guantánamo should be seized. . . . In that case, United States vessels would have a fine base for operating against Santiago." Sigsbee added that he had discussed Guantánamo's assets with Sampson and "was much pleased to find that my views regarding that bay were about the same as his own."[31] As U.S. journalist and military historian Walter Millis would later write, "The Navy had discovered that in Guantánamo Bay they had a nearby and ample harbor, sufficient for all their needs of shelter, coaling, and repair." The only potential drawback was that, lying forty-five miles east of Santiago, Guantánamo would be "too far away to cover it with certainty if a hurricane should come."[32]

With Cervera blockaded in Santiago, Navy Secretary Long, knowing that nearby Spanish forces might come to his aid, asked War Secretary Russell Alger if the army had plans to land U.S. forces near the port. On May 31, Long informed Sampson that approximately twenty-five thousand U.S. Army troops commanded by General Rufus Shafter and accompanied by cavalry, siege guns, and mortars were embarking from Tampa for Santiago de Cuba. Inquiring about potential landing sites near Santiago, Long asked, "Will not Guantánamo, Cuba, be the best site for landing the cavalry?"[33]

Shafter, however, had his own ideas about where U.S. forces should land. Having read a historic account of Lord Vernon's calamitous failure to capture Santiago via Guantánamo, he knew that he might encounter similar obstacles, and thus was determined to establish a base much closer to his target. Arriving on the transport *Seguranca* off Santiago on June 20, he soon met with Sampson and the Cuban insurgent leader Calixto García to discuss possible landing sites. According to one colorful account of this meeting, subsequently known as the El Aserradero conference, the three leaders gathered around a map of Santiago and the surrounding Cuban coast. Sampson

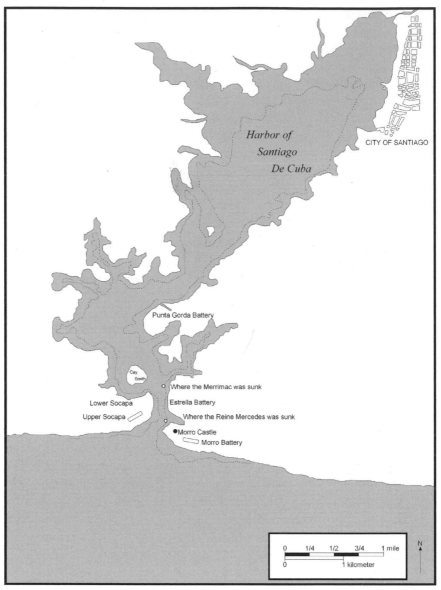

Map of Harbor of Santiago de Cuba, 1898. (Based on information in *Notes on the Spanish War*, Office of Naval Intelligence, 1899; and William T. Sampson, "The Atlantic Fleet in the Spanish War," *Century Illustrated Magazine*, 57 no. 6. [April 1899]: 886–914. Courtesy of the Cartography Laboratory, University of Alabama)

put his finger on Morro Point at the entrance to the harbor, but Shafter shook his head and pointed instead to the city of Santiago, on the northeast side of the harbor, five miles from the well-fortified Morro Point. Looking for a nearby beach, he focused both on the town of Siboney, eleven miles east of Santiago, and seven miles beyond that, the village of Daiquirí. At that point, General García estimated that there might be approximately fifteen hundred Spanish troops guarding Siboney, but probably only three hundred at Daiquirí. Taking García's advice, Shafter decided to land U.S. Army forces at Daiquirí.[34]

Weeks before Shafter arrived at Santiago, however, Long and Sampson had made their own moves to secure Guantánamo as a U.S. naval facility. Irritated by the repeated delays of the army's departure from Tampa—it was originally scheduled to leave for Cuba on June 4, but did not depart until June 14—Sampson decided it was imperative to establish a nearby coaling station in order to sustain the blockade at Santiago. Accordingly, on June 4, he ordered Captain Bowman McCalla, who was commanding the U.S.S. *Marblehead* (one of the ships blockading Santiago), to proceed to Guantánamo.

Sampson probably could not have selected a better or more qualified officer to command the seizure of Guantánamo. In the first place, McCalla had prior experience in scouting for advanced bases. In 1885, as an agent of the Office of Naval Intelligence (ONI), he had been assigned to identify islands in the Bay of Panama that might serve to defend the isthmus.[35] While assigned to ONI, McCalla had also worked under Theodorus B. M. Mason, who was a pioneer in the development of amphibious doctrine, and McCalla had participated in the preparation of a study of the amphibious capabilities of the world's major navies. In its conclusion, the study recommended that a landing force should consist of expert riflemen backed by naval artillery. This work did not develop a landing force doctrine per se, but in 1891, ONI published a landing force manual titled *Instructions for Infantry and Artillery, United States Navy and Marine Application*. In 1898, Captain McCalla would refer to this manual aboard the *Marblehead*.[36]

Upon receiving Sampson's order, McCalla telegraphed Huntington in Key West to request that the First Battalion assist his efforts to seize the bay. Sampson followed with his own cable to Huntington on June 6.[37] In his own article published in the *Century Illustrated Magazine* in April 1899, Sampson wrote, "After the establishment of the blockade, my first thought was to find a harbor which could serve as a coaling station and as a base for the operations of the fleet pending a decisive action. The most available one was that of Guantánamo, forty miles to the east."[38]

In 1898, Guantánamo Bay's chief commercial function was to serve as the entrance to the sugar port of Caimanéra, located on the western shore of the inner bay, approximately five miles from the sea. On the eastern side of the entrance to the bay lay Fisherman's Point, a small fishing village on a flat beach below thirty-foot cliffs. After three years of renewed insurgency throughout Cuba's Oriente Province,[39] Spanish regulars and guerrillas occupied Guantánamo City, and Cuban insurgents controlled coastal outposts on the Yateras River and the western point of entrance to Guantánamo Bay.

The light cruiser *Marblehead,* the armed liner *Yankee,* and the auxiliary cruiser *St. Louis* left the blockade for Guantánamo around midnight on June 6. Arriving at Guantánamo in early daylight, the ships entered the harbor and immediately took possession of the lower bay, forcing the lone Spanish gunboat *Sandoval* to find refuge in the upper bay, where it began to transport Spanish troops from the town of Caimanéra across the channel to Toro Key.[40] The Spanish general guarding Guantánamo City, Félix Pareja, communicated the bad news to his commander at Santiago: "The 7th day at dawn brought seven ships before the port of Caimanéra. They fired grapeshot and all kinds of projectiles on the Playa del Este and Cavo Toro. . . . The American squadron in possession of the outer bay has taken it for a harbor of rest, they being anchored as if in one of their own ports."[41] The U.S. Navy had also shelled the cable station, and McCalla was able to report to Long that "all communication between Cuba and the outside world has been cut off."[42] After conducting its reconnaissance, the *Marblehead* rejoined the blockading fleet, but it now carried two Cuban guerrilla leaders who had come aboard from the Leeward Point of Guantánamo Bay. They had been sent by General Calixto García to assist Sampson in his offensive operations, and through them McCalla would establish liaison with General Pedro "Periquito" Pérez, who commanded insurgent forces in the outlying areas of Guantánamo City, and his chief of staff, Colonel G. García Vieta. Together they would provide valuable intelligence and military assistance to the U.S. forces.[43]

The marines left Key West onboard the *Panther* on June 7, 1898, arriving in Santiago de Cuba early in the morning of June 10, and within a few hours they reached Guantánamo ready to do battle. One of the young correspondents onboard the dispatch boat *Three Friends,* Ralph Paine, described the efficiency of the amphibious assault: "The *Marblehead* and the *Dolphin* raked the wooded hills and valley with shrapnel to drive back any lurking Spanish forces. Swiftly the marines filled the whaleboats and cutters from the naval vessels and were towed to the beaches by steam launches. It was done with order and precision. Within an hour the battalion was disembarked with its tents and supplies."[44]

Coming ashore proved the easiest part of the operation. While makeshift bands played ragtime and such popular tunes as "A Hot Time in the Old Town Tonight," sweating members of the artillery company offloaded the ships, and marines on the beach set fire to shanties and the remains of a blockhouse in the hope of preventing yellow fever. Twenty-three "leathernecks" (marines) succumbed to heat stroke. Despite the nearby presence of thousands of Spanish troops in Guantánamo City and several hundred even closer at Cuzco Hill, they did not initially fire on the marines, who had decided to pitch their tents on the hill overlooking the bay, but had done little to protect themselves by digging trenches. Correspondent Paine later recalled that it was around midnight when Spanish guerrillas crept near enough to begin "snap-shooting at the embers of the campfires," a tactic of psychological warfare "cunningly calculated to rasp the nerves of these detestable *Marinos Americanos* and rob them of sleep."[45]

The following afternoon, Colonel Huntington learned about Cuzco Hill and its adjacent well—the only source of potable water within two miles—from the Cuban guerrilla leader Laborde, who had helped McCalla pilot the *Marblehead*. As the two men talked, Spanish snipers killed two marines guarding the outlying thicket, making privates William Dumphy and Charles McColgan the first U.S. soldiers to die in Cuba.[46] This ambush in the late afternoon was the prelude to a concentrated and sustained attack by Spanish gunners that began that night. The most famous correspondent at Guantánamo, Stephen Hart Crane, recreated the scene for his readers of *McClure's Magazine*, "with a thousand rifles rattling; with the field guns booming in your ears; with the diabolic Colt automatics clacking; with the roar of the *Marblehead* coming from the bay; and with the Mauser bullets sneering a few inches over one's head."[47] In spite of the din, there were only six U.S. casualties—one of them, Assistant Surgeon Dr. John B. Gibbs, fatally shot through the lung. Crane had befriended Gibbs and was at his side when he died. "He was dying hard. Hard. He was long past groaning. There was only the bitter strife for air which pulsed out into the night in a clear penetrating whistle. . . . I thought this man would never die. I wanted him to die."[48]

The Battle of Guantánamo was Crane's first real war, and Gibbs the first real casualty of war he had ever observed. His *The Red Badge of Courage*, for all of its graphic realism, had been an imaginative recreation of the Battle of Chancellorsville. Huntington's after-action report of these events was less vivid than Crane's prose, but it was succinct and persuasive: "On the 11th [of June] the camp was attacked by a much superior force of Spaniards, and from that time until the 14th the battalion was constantly under fire and repulsed the enemy on every attack."[49]

Huntington, however, did not mention the repeated failed efforts of his men to find the enemy's hiding places—efforts thwarted by torrential rains, the thickness of the surrounding brush, and the adroitness with which the Spanish soldiers made their presence almost invisible, using brush and palm leaf to camouflage their bodies and smokeless powder to conceal their guns.[50] Welcome assistance arrived on June 12, when fifty Cuban officers and men arrived under the command of Lieutenant Colonel Enrique Thomas. These men, who knew guerrilla tactics, quickly deployed in pairs to slash and burn the brush and undergrowth that had allowed the enemy to penetrate the perimeter defenses.[51]

The recurrent attacks on the marines' exposed campsite persuaded Huntington to move the camp to lower ground and use the hill for defense. Correspondent George Kennan of *Outlook* magazine best described Huntington's contingency planning:

> There was some danger that the enemy would assemble in force on slopes of the eastern hills and then overwhelm the marines in a sudden rush-assault. . . . To provide for this contingency, Lieutenant Colonel Huntington withdrew his men from the eastern slope of the hill and posted them on the crest and upper part of the western slope, where they would be nearer the fleet and better protected by its guns.[52]

There was a more pressing problem—as a consequence of fending off the Spanish assaults, the marines were running out of ammunition. When Huntington requested that the *Panther* furnish more ammunition, he was rebuffed by Reiter, who informed him that the ammunition was needed for the ship's ballast and that if the marines wanted to salvage their gear, they had better retrieve it. When McCalla learned of Reiter's response, he became furious and ordered him immediately to unload 50,000 rounds of 6-millimeter ammunition. "In the future do not require Colonel Huntington to break out or land his stores or ammo. Use your own officers and crew." Shortly thereafter Huntington named his outpost Camp McCalla, but nothing at Guantánamo is named for Reiter.[53]

On the evening of June 13, after three days of almost constant harassment, Huntington decided to take decisive action against the Spanish. Acting on the advice of Lt. Col. Thomas, Huntington issued the order to destroy the well used by Spanish troops at Cuzco Hill, which was the only available fresh water supply within twelve miles. Huntington coordinated his plan of attack with McCalla. They agreed that two companies of marines, numbering about one hundred sixty men, accompanied by fifty Cubans, under the command of Captain George F. Elliott, would approach Cuzco from the sea cliffs, and a smaller marine contingent would proceed via an inland valley in an effort to close off a possible escape route. Before leaving camp, Elliott requested that Stephen Crane accompany him as an aide when needed. Elliott later reported to Huntington that Crane "was of material aid during the action, carrying messages to fire volleys, etc. to the different company commanders."[54]

As the marines and their Cuban auxiliaries assembled to move out of camp, Crane described their contrasting appearances. He saw the Cubans, on the one hand, as "a hard-bitten undersized lot . . . in short, peasants—hardy, tireless, uncomplaining peasants." The marines, on the other hand, appeared "businesslike and soldierly" in their "linen suits and black-corded accoutrements." Unlike the Cubans, their "bronze faces were not stolid at all." Instead, they appeared to be engaged in a realistic version of chess and had simply "come to wonder which wins—black or red."[55] As the combined forces marched eastward along jungle trails and over the cliffs, their movements were shadowed from the water by the U.S.S. *Dolphin*. Colonel Laborde served as guide for the main force, and another Cuban named Polycarpio led the smaller group. The rough terrain and tropical heat slowed their movement, and it was nearly 11 A.M. when the main force reached the horseshoe hill surrounding Cuzco Valley.

As they approached the well, the Cubans in front encountered the Spanish troops, resulting in a mad dash between the opposing forces for the crest of the hill, which the marines and Cubans won. Although the Spanish sought cover in a cluster of sea grape trees, volleys of shots quickly forced them into retreat. Huntington had sent Second Lieutenant Lewis Magill with fifty marines and ten Cubans to reinforce Elliott and to intercept the retreating Spaniards, but Magill's advance was blocked by gunfire from the *Dolphin*. At that point, according to Crane's eyewitness account, "Sergeant Quick arose and . . . produced a blue polka-dot neckerchief as large as a quilt. He tied it on a long, crooked stick. Then he went to the top of the ridge and, turning his back to the Spanish fire, began to signal to the *Dolphin*."[56] Quick's spontaneous action was at once a magnificent display of bravery and a significant military intervention. To be effective, he had to expose himself to both friendly and hostile fire. His use of the makeshift flag to advise the *Dolphin* via Morse Code of the whereabouts of Magill and his men saved their lives and enabled the ship to redirect its volleys against the Spaniards. Later Huntington sent First Lieutenant Mahoney and First Lieutenant Ingate with fifty men each to help Elliott, but they arrived too late to join the battle.[57]

Besieged from land and sea, most of the Spanish forces managed to escape, but the U.S. and Cuban soldiers had won a decisive victory with remarkably few casualties. According to after-action assessments, the enemy had sixty to sixty-eight men killed and more than one hundred fifty wounded out of about eight hundred troops. By contrast, the U.S.-Cuban losses were two Cubans killed and two Cubans and three U.S. privates wounded; twenty-three marines were temporarily overcome by heat, but all were treated onboard the *Dolphin* and recovered. The mission was evaluated as a success because the Spanish fort was destroyed, the well at Cuzco was filled up (while fresh supplies of water were transported daily from the *Panther, Resolute,* and *Vulcan*), and the Spanish retreated to Guantánamo City. They never again posed a serious threat to the U.S. naval presence at Guantánamo Bay.

Admiral Sampson was pleased with how the operation at Guantánamo had gone thus far. On June 15, he telegraphed Secretary Long that the affairs there were "much more satisfactory." He also indicated that more operations would be required to make the bay fully secure. Reporting that fifty more Cubans had joined U.S. forces there and that McCalla viewed their participation as being "of the greatest assistance," Sampson said that about five hundred more were expected and that they would "need Springfield rifles." He then added, "Fleet needs supply of both."[58] The following day, Sampson sent the *Marblehead, Texas,* and *Yankee* to shell the Spanish fort at Caimanéra (or Cayo del Toro) on the western side of Guantánamo Bay. The volleys succeeded in destroying the fort and drove the Spanish from this position. As the U.S. ships steamed up the bay past Jicacal Point, however, one of the *Marblehead*'s propellers was fouled by a contact mine that did not detonate. After successfully disarming the mine, the ships conducted a thorough investigation of the area and discovered that they had passed repeatedly through a minefield without injury. A few days later, smaller boats lowered from the *Marblehead* and the *Dolphin* swept the channel and managed to recover and disarm fourteen mines, none of which had detonated because of mechanical problems and barnacle growths on the contact levers.[59]

During the minesweeping operations, Spanish infantry at Jicacal fired on the U.S. boats. No one was injured, but McCalla subsequently ordered Huntington to make a reconnaissance and possible assault on the area. On June 25, between 2 and 3 A.M., Huntington led a combined U.S. and Cuban force using fifteen boats launched from the *Annapolis, Bancroft,* and *Helena,* to cross the bay while the *Helena* and the *Marblehead* took supporting positions south and west of the point. According to one correspondent, everyone aboard the vessels had been ordered to keep silent to ensure a surprise attack, but the stillness was shattered when one of the steam launches had engine problems and began to "rattle, wheeze, and cough." Fortunately, the Spaniards had already left the area, and the landing force was able to secure it without further incident.[60] As the perceptive correspondent George Kennan observed, Admiral Sampson had achieved his objective in taking

Guantánamo: "A safe and sheltered coaling and repair station for the vessels of his fleet."[61]

Within a few days, Guantánamo was transformed into the primary U.S. coaling station and ship repair facility in the Caribbean. On June 22, Sampson informed Long that he was sending "each of [his] heavy ships to Guantánamo to complete their coaling" and that he had ordered the *Yosemite* to coal at Guantánamo in order to sustain "an active blockade at Cienfuegos." The same report also stated that the ships at Guantánamo were being used to provide "arms, clothing, and food" to the Cuban forces positioned east and west of Santiago. On June 26, Sampson told Long that nine ships were currently coaling at Guantánamo, and that others would have to coal there. He explained that "in smooth waters, ships can coal off Santiago with some difficulty," but that "the weather may compel us to coal at Guantánamo." By June 19, Cervera's second in command, Lieutenant José Müller y Tejeiro, had begun to notice the comings and goings of the *St. Louis* and other U.S. ships between the blockade off Santiago and Guantánamo, but his remarks indicate that he did not understand what was happening. "Why did the hostile ships which remained all day long in front of the mouth of the harbor disappear at night? I do not know."[62]

Guantánamo met other vital needs of the military campaign. As an important gathering place for ships near but outside the war zone, it quickly developed into a logistical support center for dispersing ammunition, medical supplies, clothing, and food both to U.S. naval forces and to Cuban insurgents. Guantánamo also served as a postal station, a base for the American Red Cross, and, after the telegraph cable was reconnected between Guantánamo and Mole St. Nicolas, Haiti, a central communications center for transmitting messages between Washington, D.C., and U.S. military forces in Cuba.[63]

On July 3, 1898, with Santiago about to be overrun by U.S. and Cuban land forces,[64] Cervera sailed out of the harbor in a frantic effort to avoid capture by U.S. troops. It was a suicidal maneuver: the Spanish Fleet ran headlong into Sampson's blockade, only to be attacked and destroyed. The Spanish-Cuban-American war was effectively over—brought to closure by the U.S. Navy with the assistance of the Marine Corps.

Despite the ultimate U.S. victory over the Spanish at Santiago, the preceding stalemate was largely attributable to a lack of coordination between U.S. Army and Navy commanders that precluded joint operations. Indeed, Shafter and Sampson had clashed bitterly. Neither officer had the authority to command the other, nor could they agree on joint tactics to defeat the trapped garrison at Santiago. In 1901, former secretary of war Russell Alger published his version of *The Spanish-American War*, which strongly criticized Sampson for his failure to comply with Shafter's request "to force" Santiago harbor and thereby attack the Spanish garrison from the rear, possibly compelling an immediate surrender. Alger's biased account dismissed Sampson's arguments that he could not risk losing his ships to mines planted in the narrow entrance to the harbor, and at the same time Alger ignored the fact that Shafter, pleading insufficient troops, also refused to attack the garrison. As military historian Graham Cosmas has observed, neither commander was willing to compromise his position; consequently the stalemate persisted. The campaign ended on a sour note with Shafter excluding Sampson along with the Cuban generals from the surrender negotiations as well as the final ceremony of entering Santiago.[65]

There is much truth in Bradley Reynolds's assessment that most historians have overlooked or understated the importance of the seizure of Guantánamo Bay to the outcome of the Spanish-Cuban-American War.[66] Indeed, Charles Brown's cynical remark that "the taking of Guantánamo was a sideshow in the big circus of war" might easily be misconstrued by some of his readers as a perceptive evaluation.[67] Philip Foner's two-volume study of the conflict, which provides valuable information and critical insights into the dependence of U.S. forces on Cuban intelligence and assistance, contains a vivid quotation from an Associated Press dispatch that "the insurgents know the ground [around Guantánamo] so well that it is impossible for the Spanish bushwhackers to get close enough to do any damage."[68] Yet, even though Foner discusses Guantánamo in his chapter "U.S.-Cuban Relations," he does not mention the historical significance of Bowman McCalla or Robert Huntington, and the names Guantánamo, Huntington, and McCalla do not appear in his ten-page index.

The failure to discuss McCalla's commanding influence at Guantánamo is a serious oversight, particularly in any work that places emphasis on the contributions of Cuban insurgents to their struggle for independence; indeed, McCalla was one of the few leaders who fully appreciated the invaluable assistance both Cuban officers and guerrilla fighters provided their U.S. counterparts in the fight for Guantánamo. After the taking of Cuzco Well, he proclaimed the expedition "most successful," and he could "not say too much in praise of the officers and men who took part in it." That this statement included the Cubans he made clear in his communication to Sampson on June 16 when he wrote, "I desire to call particular attention to the devotion of the Cubans to the cause of freeing their land, shown in so many ways, by stating that the last words of the Cuban who was shot through the heart and buried on the field were Viva Cuba Libre!"[69]

Neither Marine Captain Elliott nor Huntington fully shared McCalla's perceptive appreciation of the Cuban contributions to their efforts. On the contrary, both of them indicated that they were the sole commanders of their respective expeditions, and Elliott, at one point, said explicitly, "The word support is a military misnomer, for the marines numbered 225 and the Cubans 50 in the fight, and although the latter were brave enough, their quality as efficient fighting men was on a par with that of the enemy."[70] This is certainly damning with faint praise!

Of the U.S. correspondents covering the battle for Guantánamo, Stephen Crane and Howbert Billman, who reported for the *Chicago Record,* were particularly impressed with the Cubans as fighting men, and recognized the value of their assistance to naval and marine forces. Even though Crane contrasted the marines' discipline and efficiency with the Cubans' excitable and unpredictable behavior under fire, he had high praise for the Cubans "daring": "They paid no heed whatever to the Spaniards' volleys, but simply lashed themselves into a delirium that disdained everything."[71] Billman saw the Americans and Cubans as working together "in perfect harmony." He also viewed the Cubans as indispensable guides, and observed that "the Spanish soldier has a wholesome dread of them in the field."[72]

Despite the efforts of persuasive battlefield correspondents[73] and powerful military officers such as McCalla and Sampson to direct favorable attention to the essential participation of Cuban soldiers, they did not achieve the public recognition they merited. There were assiduous efforts to publish the names, to conduct funeral services, and to mark the graves of all fallen U.S. soldiers with headstones, but the unknown Cuban dead were buried without ceremony in unmarked plots.[74] Sergeant Quick received the Congressional Medal of Honor he deserved. The secretary of war honored Dr. John Gibbs, the assistant surgeon who had died at Guantánamo, by naming an army field hospital in Lexington, Kentucky, for him.[75] No U.S. medals were struck nor were honors bestowed on Cubans who served at Guantánamo. There apparently was no established procedure to record their heroic contributions or even to identify those killed in combat. The annual reports of the Navy Department do not mention them. It is equally certain that Cuban nationalists subsequently believed that the Americans did not fully appreciate the sacrifices their countrymen had made at Guantánamo or elsewhere in Cuba to help the Americans defeat the Spanish.[76]

The seizure of Guantánamo was clearly an important part of the operational strategy that enabled the U.S. Navy to sustain its blockade of Santiago Harbor. Salvatore Mercogliano is accurate when he writes, "The history of modern American military ocean transportation began with the Spanish-American War. . . . The logistical demands of maintaining squadrons of steam-propelled warships great distances from their operating bases for extended periods necessitated a massive organizational effort to keep coal, spare parts, and provisions on hand." This is precisely the key function performed by U.S.-occupied Guantánamo.[77]

Moreover, the U.S. Marine presence at Guantánamo almost certainly played a decisive role in preventing or at least intimidating Spanish General Pareja and his 6,000 troops from leaving Guantánamo City to reinforce Santiago or to create problems for U.S. and Cuban forces elsewhere in Oriente Province.[78] Reynolds records that after the war General Shafter asked the rhetorical question, Why did Pareja not ever attack him? The rhetorical answer may well have been that, unable to access the cable at Guantánamo and hemmed in by Cuban insurgents, Pareja was effectively blocked from communication with the outside world. Even if Pareja had known that Santiago needed to be relieved, his men were probably too weak to have made a forced march. McCalla wrote that after the war he learned that Pareja's men had been starving in Guantánamo City on rations of one can of sardines per man every two days. In his memoir, Spanish naval officer Lieutenant Müller y Tejeiro also recalled that Guantánamo City had been in desperate shape: "Where could reinforcements have come from? . . . From Guantánamo none could come for lack of provisions."[79] As Herbert McNeil succinctly summed up the situation, "The threat posed by U.S. naval forces and a battalion of marines at Guantánamo Bay, plus the stranglehold on land communications by 1,000 Cuban insurgents, effectively pinned down an army of 7,000 [Spanish] men, which might have changed the outcome of the fighting at Santiago and prolonged the war."[80]

On October 28, 1899, the U.S. Office of Naval Intelligence made public an official document published by the Superior Council of the Spanish Ministry of War regarding the capitulation at Santiago, Cuba. According to the *New York Times,* the document emphasized the importance of the blockade instituted by U.S. naval forces and declared that "without their cooperation, it would have been impossible for the American forces [on land] to have compelled the surrender of Santiago." The document further stated that no reinforcements could reach Santiago except by sea, and "this eventuality became a vain hope from the moment the American ships completely closed the harbor entrance."[81] In his memoir, *Battles and Capitulation of Santiago,* Cervera's second in command, Lt. Müller y Tejeiro, in attempting to explain how Spain lost Cuba, admitted, "I have never been able to understand the reason why a fleet was sent to Cuba that was in no manner able to cope with that of the United States and which therefore could in no wise [*sic*] prevent the ships of the latter from blockading our ports and controlling the sea."[82]

The U.S. Marine Corps had many reasons to be proud and grateful for the opportunity to fight and serve at Guantánamo. One of the battalion's most significant achievements was to keep its men healthy in a tropical climate. After the men returned to the United States on August 26, 1898, they received thorough medical examinations. The subsequent inspection report by Adjutant Major George Reid found that "from April 22, when they embarked onboard their transport in New York, to the present time, there has not been a single case of yellow fever nor death from disease of any kind." He considered this "remarkable," especially since these men were the first U.S. troops to land in Cuba and were potentially vulnerable to the same diseases as other U.S. troops, among whom "fever, diarrhea, dysentery, etc., caused so many casualties."[83]

One of the reasons the men had stayed healthy was that they had used only distilled water for drinking and cooking. Moreover, the battalion's quartermaster, Charles McCawley, had exercised the foresight to buy wine casks in Key West for use as additional water containers in camp. They practiced other health precautions such as burning garbage and changing their clothes frequently.[84] Their tents had mosquito netting. For the first time, during the Cuban campaign, the marines wore brown linen campaign suits instead of the woolen blue uniforms that had previously been regulation issue. They also wore new-style shoes and lightweight underwear. All of these innovations contributed to comfort and reduced the incidence of fatigue and susceptibility to heat stroke.[85]

Another noteworthy achievement of the marines at Guantánamo was their successful employment of the Winchester-Lee assault rifle. The advantages of this state-of-the-art weapon was that it was a semiautomatic weapon that could fire multiple shells (using five round clips), was easy to reload, and used smokeless powder. The disadvantages were that the guns could not be used to fire single shots while the magazine still had ammunition and that, over time, the powder caused the rifled bore to erode. Both the Winchester-Lee and the Spanish Mauser, when accurately aimed, proved deadly weapons.[86]

The greatest and most lasting significance of Guantánamo for the Marine Corps was that it gave them a new sense of mission. For the first time they had acted as a designated expeditionary force assigned to land on enemy beaches for the purpose of establishing a land base from which they could protect and defend nearby U.S. Fleet operations. They had also validated the prediction made by Captain Alfred Mahan in 1890 that the Marine Corps "will constitute a most important reinforcement, nay, backbone to any force landing on the enemy's coast."[87]

Their well-documented success in meeting all the challenges connected with this important assignment laid the basis for the Marine Corps' assumption of new tactical and operational responsibilities, its concomitant growth in size and in its budgetary requirements, and ultimately the development of amphibious assault and advanced base warfare. In the words of naval historian Ivan Musicant, "The little action at Guantánamo held enormous significance for the future of the Marine Corps. . . . [It] opened new vistas of actions to seize forward bases for the fleet, a mission that remained with the Marine Corps through World War II."[88]

Huntington's battalion did not fade away quickly. After leaving Cuba, it spent approximately three weeks in Portsmouth, New Hampshire, at a site Huntington named Camp Heywood in honor of the commandant. The ostensible reason for assigning the unit to this location was to enable the men to "rest and get malaria out of their system." It also gave Heywood time to attract more favorable publicity to the First Battalion to enhance its reputation and thus to elevate the corps' status within military circles.[89] Before the battalion disbanded, it had paraded through Portsmouth, and its detachments subsequently paraded in Boston, New York, and Philadelphia. On September 22, 1898, despite heavy rains, President McKinley reviewed remnants of the battalion led by the U.S. Marine Band. Two of the battalion's officers, Elliott and First Lieutenant Wendell C. Neville, went on to serve as commandants of the Marine Corps. Allan Millett has justly observed, "After the War with Spain, the American public would never again have to ask what a Marine did. Instead the word *marine* now evoked an image of bravery, discipline, competence, and devotion to duty."[90]

In its broadest sense the occupation of Guantánamo had certainly demonstrated the benefits of its geographical proximity to Santiago, and for geopolitical thinkers such as Alfred Mahan, Henry Cabot Lodge, and Theodore Roosevelt, it had provided fresh evidence for their advocacy of establishing a naval base that would perform the multiple functions of overlooking the Windward Passage, sitting astride the shortest route between the United States and the isthmus of Central America, and facilitating quick deployments when necessary to other islands in the Caribbean. That Guantánamo served as the primary base from which the U.S. Army launched its invasion of Puerto Rico on July 21, 1898, was further proof of its enhanced relevance to new and expanding U.S. strategic interests. Moreover, as Lieutenant Staunton, who had served as Admiral Sampson's assistant chief of staff, wrote, "After the surrender of Santiago, the heavy ships assembled at Guantánamo for overhauling and repairs preparatory to crossing the Atlantic."[91] Guantánamo was slowly becoming a centerpiece in what would be a new relationship between the United States and Cuba.

3

Cubans Resist U.S. Base Acquisition

MULTIPLE FACTORS AND SEVERAL KEY INDIVIDUALS, both Cuban and U.S. nationalists, were involved in the decisions both to retain Guantánamo after the war with Spain had ended and ultimately to establish it as the first U.S. naval base on foreign soil. A permanent U.S. military presence in Cuba was not the outcome Cuban rebels had fought for or even anticipated as the consequence of the U.S. intervention in summer 1898. Nor were all influential Americans united in a desire to see the United States embark on empire-building beyond its shores. In the end, the leasing of Guantánamo Bay would be the culmination of hard-fought negotiations between Cuba's first president, Tomás Estrada Palma, and the twenty-sixth president of the United States, Theodore Roosevelt.

One of the fundamental premises underlying U.S. imperialistic moves was the perception that the war had given the United States a new empire, much of it based in the Caribbean, and that it would be the primary responsibility of the U.S. Navy to police and protect it. As Rear Admiral Henry Clay Taylor wryly remarked from his perspective, "We look abroad and find that we have fallen into the possession of vast and rich territories. We did not want them."[1] Yet this is precisely the outcome strategist Alfred Thayer Mahan and policymaker Theodore Roosevelt had worked to achieve. It would be an oversimplification to say that Roosevelt was intimately involved in every move necessary to make Guantánamo a permanent naval station. He was, nevertheless, in many aspects, the principal architect. It was Roosevelt who urged McKinley to appoint Leonard Wood military governor-general of Cuba, and it was Wood, along with Secretary of War Elihu Root—in whom Roosevelt held great confidence—who pressured Cuban nationalists first into granting the United States the constitutional right to lease or buy naval stations, and, second, into choosing Guantánamo as the appropriate site. It was, of course, Roosevelt who as president wrote and signed the bilateral treaty that, in effect, granted the United States a permanent lease to Guantánamo Bay.

Indeed, the acquisition of Guantánamo became a central focus of strategic and diplomatic concern as U.S. leaders sought to stabilize Cuba and at the same time to acquire a naval base that would be well positioned to protect the now vulnerable island nation and other rapidly expanding U.S. interests in the Caribbean region. To Washington's surprise, it found that during the U.S. military occupation that followed the Spanish-American War, it had to deal with new Cuban leaders, many of whom wanted complete independence and strongly opposed selling or leasing any naval station to the United States.[2] This opposition strengthened the hand of anti-imperialists in the United States and other political leaders who opposed the annexation of Cuba. Even as Cuban nationalists grudgingly realized they would have to accept the terms dictated by the Platt Amendment, which would make Cuba a protectorate and grant the United States a perpetual lease to a naval station, they also hoped that, in return, the United States would grant favorable tariff concessions to Cuban products, especially sugar. Ultimately, President Roosevelt would make the decisions to acquire Guantánamo and to liberalize the tariff. Confronted with multiple challenges in the Caribbean and Pacific regions and seeking to achieve his own ambitious goals, Roosevelt chose to deal with the Cuban nationalists firmly, or as he would later justify his actions, to uphold "honor and expediency."

But before that, the armistice on August 12, 1898, and the subsequent Treaty of Paris concluded on December 10, 1898, meant that Spain recognized Cuba's independence and the U.S. military occupation of both Cuba and the Philippines. Spain also ceded the Philippines, Guam, and Puerto Rico to the United States. This sweeping victory, which in effect gave the United States an empire, confronted the McKinley administration with daunting administrative and military challenges in both the Caribbean and Pacific regions. Cuba needed to recover from the devastation of prolonged warfare. In the Philippines, McKinley faced an independence movement and subsequent insurgency led by the popular rebel leader Emilio Aguinaldo.[3] There were the questions of how to administer Puerto Rico and Guam.

Domestically, McKinley had to deal with criticism from the newly organized Anti-Imperialist League, including such notables as Andrew Carnegie, Mark Twain, Samuel Gompers, and William James. In short, it was not a propitious moment for the White House to advocate the establishment of a U.S. naval base on newly independent Cuban soil. As Bradley Reynolds rightly observes, in the aftermath of the Spanish-American War, the McKinley administration publicly proclaimed Cuba's right to independence and insisted that the United States had intervened for humanitarian reasons. Even Henry Cabot Lodge said nothing about the need to retain naval bases in Cuba.

This does not mean that the U.S. government dropped the issue. On the contrary, senior naval officials, whose careers were largely shielded from political criticism, now pressed forward with efforts to secure naval bases throughout the Caribbean.[4] As Richard Challener has found, after the war with Spain, the U.S. Navy was convinced that the most important requirement to defend U.S. interests was to maintain an effective watch on both the future canal and the Caribbean. To do this would necessitate the acquisition of naval bases and coaling stations throughout the Caribbean region.[5]

The fighting in Cuba had barely ended when, in mid-August 1898, the Naval War Board, in compliance with a directive from the Senate Naval Affairs Committee, prepared a report for Navy Secretary John Long that analyzed potential sites for offshore coaling stations. Drafted by the board's most distinguished member, Mahan, the report included several precedent-shattering recommendations. Taking into account the lengthy and time-consuming dash required of the battleship *Oregon* to join the U.S. Fleet, the report asserted that it was now a national necessity to dig a canal through the isthmus of Central America, with the substantiation that "the military significance of the Canal, to us, is rapid communication between our Atlantic and Pacific coasts."[6] To ensure the security of such a canal, the board recommended the establishment of a naval station in the Caribbean as near as possible to the canal's Atlantic terminus.[7]

Without referring directly to the blockade of Santiago or specifically mentioning Guantánamo's proven worth, Mahan took for granted the assumption that the United States could not afford the coaling problems it had encountered in the war with Spain. He simply stated, "It is obvious that the United States requires coaling stations outside its own territory from which coal can be freely and certainly obtained during war." Mahan then said it was the board's opinion that coaling stations should be established in both the northern Pacific and the Caribbean Sea. With regard to the Caribbean, Mahan reasoned that "the Windward Passage between Cuba and Haiti is the great direct commercial route between the whole North Atlantic coast and the isthmus," and that "no solution of the problem of coaling and naval stations can be considered satisfactory which does not provide for military safety on that route." Observing that "the two most available ports are Santiago and Guantánamo on the south shore of Cuba," Mahan compared the two ports and found that Santiago might provide a more defensible shelter from storms and hostile penetration, but its channel narrowed to a width of 330 feet, whereas the entrance to Guantánamo was never less than 2,550 feet wide. Indicating that the Naval War Board was divided on the issue of choosing between Santiago and Guantánamo, Mahan suggested that Long seek the advice of officers who had experience in navigating and using both harbors. However, he forcefully asserted, "When Cuba becomes independent, the United States should acquire, as a naval measure, one of these ports, with a portion of adjacent territory."[8] In its concluding paragraph, the

report, observing that oceanographic charts provided insufficient data, recommended that there should be "a speedy examination by naval vessels" to
determine which sites possessed the most advantages for establishing naval
or coaling stations. The report further recommended that the War Department make a comparative study of the military strength of alternative sites
and estimate the costs of fortifying them.

The navy began to implement Mahan's recommendations the following
year, when in June 1899, the gunboat *Eagle* arrived at Guantánamo to begin
surveying its wide harbor. In his subsequent contribution to the *Annual Report of the Navy Department for the Year 1899*, the chief of the Bureau of
Equipment, Commander Royal B. Bradford, recorded in persuasive detail
the *Eagle*'s findings to emphasize the potential value of Guantánamo as a
future naval station:

> The work at Guantánamo Bay was exceptionally extensive. There is in this
> bay more than one hundred miles of waterfront and twenty-five square miles
> of water area. The survey included the coast of Cuba running two miles to the
> westward of the entrance to the bay and seven miles to the eastward, as far as
> Escondido Bay, covering a total area of over one hundred square miles, within
> which all features of importance were fully developed. . . . An entirely new
> deep-water channel, hitherto unknown to the pilots or anyone in the vicinity
> was discovered leading from the lower bay to the port of Caimanéra, seven
> miles inland. Through this channel, vessels drawing twenty-six feet of water
> can be taken into the upper bay, while nineteen feet was the limit in the lower
> channel. This discovery adds greatly to the importance and value of Caimanéra
> as a seaport.[9]

Meanwhile, the gunboats *Vixen* and *Yankton* would survey other Cuban
harbors. Two years later the *New York Times* could report that most of the
large harbors along Cuba's northern and southern coasts had been surveyed
and charted, and that the harbors of Cienfuegos and Guantánamo were the
best on the southern coast.[10] In a similar article published the same day, the
Washington Post announced that intensive U.S. naval surveys had determined the most available harbors for coaling and naval stations in Cuba.[11]

Even before the *Eagle* had reported the results of its survey, Commander
Bradford had a strongly favorable impression of Guantánamo's merits. In
September 1898, he had written to Long urging him to press for the retention of Guantánamo as a naval base.[12] In his letter, Bradford emphasized the
merits of Guantánamo's geographic proximity to the Windward Passage;
indeed, he proclaimed it the "best site in the Caribbean." As the naval officer most responsible for U.S. colliers and coaling stations worldwide, his
recommendations carried added weight.[13]

Bradford had voiced similar views when he testified before the Senate Committee on Foreign Relations on March 30, 1898, regarding the explosion and sinking of the *Maine*. In response to a question regarding the length of time required for the *Oregon* to sail from Callao, Bradford seized the opportunity to change the subject to discuss coaling problems in a future Cuban war zone:

> You all understand the geographical situation of these islands. In the west the islands of Key West and Dry Tortugas, where we hope to keep coal enough, are only 90 miles from Havana, and ships operating around the west end of Cuba can coal there, but it is about 600 miles to the east end of Cuba, Cape Maysi on the Windward Channel, and on that route the navigation is difficult and the navigable waters are narrow and confined. . . . So it would be dangerous to pass to and from in order to get coal at Key West. . . . It is very important to have a coaling station at the east end of Cuba, and right across the Windward Channel is the very excellent harbor of St. Nicholas Mole, which belongs to Haiti. . . . I have urged on the Secretary, and I believe it has been communicated to the President, that that port be hired or leased, or obtained in some way, as a coaling station.[14]

Long did not act quickly on Bradford's recommendation, but he apparently took it to heart. On December 31, 1898, Long confided to his diary, "What an immense task it is to change our whole system of government in Cuba and Porto [sic] Rico . . . inasmuch as the Government of these colonies must be military for the present. The Navy is saddled with new responsibilities. We must establish naval stations at Porto [sic] Rico, Cuba, Guam, and Manila."[15]

Advocacy of Guantánamo and other potential sites for naval and coaling stations in the Caribbean was not restricted to government publications, official communications, and certainly not to diaries. Shortly after the signing of the Treaty of Paris in December 1898, three of the navy's most senior officers, Commander Bradford, Rear Admiral Taylor, and Captain Charles H. Stockton sought to inform the literate U.S. public with regard to important lessons learned from the war, to identify the challenges that confronted the U.S. Navy with its enhanced responsibilities to protect its new and far-flung island possessions, and to specify the requirements to meet those challenges.[16] Bradford and Taylor published their articles sequentially in the *Forum* in early 1899. Their purview was global, but Cuba and Guantánamo would figure prominently in their strategic calculations.

Bradford's article titled "Coaling-Stations for the Navy" focused on the challenges of coaling the U.S. Fleet in wartime. He began by observing that, under the "Laws of Nations," neutral countries may furnish only enough coal to enable a belligerent ship to reach a home port. Under peaceful conditions, most U.S. warships had a steaming radius from two thousand to four thousand miles without recoaling, but in wartime this radius would be much reduced because all of the engines were continually fired to prevent surprise, to chase, or to escape. This reality, of course, necessitated more frequent coaling. Coal was at least as important to a steaming warship as ammunition. "It should be borne in mind," Bradford wrote, "that our warships now have no sail-power. Without coal they are as helpless as a dismasted sailing-vessel in mid-ocean." Citing the recent example set by Commodore George Dewey in taking Manila, Bradford responded to critics who argued that Dewey should have sailed away after destroying the Spanish Fleet by asking:

> Where could he have gone? The nearest United States port was 7,000 miles from Manila. Honolulu, which did not belong to us at that time, is 5,000 miles from Manila. The public does not realize how much Dewey had at stake when he entered Manila Bay. He had to win, and further, to capture a base for his ships where they could receive supplies of coal, provisions, ammunition, etc. No retreat was open to him.[17]

Bradford also examined the coaling problems presented by maintaining the lengthy U.S. blockade at Santiago. Prior to the capture of Guantánamo, it was necessary to have the ships coaled at sea by steam colliers. "Rarely did a vessel of war have one alongside without some damage resulting, both to the war-vessel and to the colliers." Even after the coaling station was established at Guantánamo, forty miles from Santiago, Bradford recalled that, at the critical moment the Spanish Fleet left Santiago Harbor, one of the most powerful U.S. battleships, the *Massachusetts,* was coaling at Guantánamo and thus unable to participate in the decisive naval battle. "The point here made is the necessity of having coal near at hand at the immediate theater of war."[18]

Bradford foresaw the possibility that the United States would confront new naval challenges now that "the prestige of the United States has doubled at the courts of Europe since the naval battles of Manila and Santiago . . . [and] some of the European powers are becoming alarmed at the appearance of another Anglo-Saxon naval power." Looking southward, Bradford predicted that "the building of an isthmian canal in the near future is a certainty: it will be a highway between our Atlantic and Pacific coasts, and must be guarded as an army defends its line of communication." One of the immediate and lasting consequences of such a canal would be to magnify our maritime interest throughout the Caribbean region. "It is of paramount importance," Bradford asserted, "that we have coaling-stations and depots for supplies located near all the great strategic points in the West Indies." He then specified the "strategic points" as the Yucatan Channel, the old Bahama Channel, the Windward Passage between Cuba and Haiti, and the Mona Passage between the Dominican Republic and Puerto Rico. The United States, he wrote, will have "sufficient authority to insure stations in Cuba near these important places where coal may be obtained." In this article, Bradford did not mention Guantánamo or any other potential Cuban site— possibly to avoid arousing public sentiment on a sensitive issue under active policy consideration. However, we know from Bradford's other statements that he believed Guantánamo had the most to offer in terms of geographic location, excellent anchorage, and protection from hurricanes.[19]

Admiral Taylor considered the war with Spain too brief and the enemy too feeble to draw many lessons applicable to future warfare. However, he acknowledged that the war's primary result had been to transform the United States into the "imperial republic of the world." The war had also transformed the U.S. Navy into "a vital necessity" charged with protecting "vast and rich territories" for which the United States was now responsible.

Like Bradford, Taylor saw the West Indies and the Caribbean as a strategic zone in which the United States had acquired interests that would soon become "paramount and pressing." He did not mention Cuba or Guantánamo by name. Instead, he asserted more broadly that "Nature has so placed the Gulf of Mexico and the outlet of the Mississippi that the commercial and naval power which shall occupy this continent . . . must dominate those seas and islands, whether that domination be friendly and commercial or warlike." To drive home his perspective, he added with nationalistic fervor, "We find ourselves now in a position to dominate that great barrier ridge of the Antilles, the strong first line of defense for a future isthmian canal. The results of successful war have placed us in the position that naturally belongs to us."[20]

Taylor also imagined the creation of new naval bases consisting of dock-yards to provide "dry docks for heavy ships, coal in large quantities, stores of provisions and ammunition, machine-shops for all kinds of repairs, and defense-works on shore that could be counted on to hold out in the temporary absence of our fleet." He viewed the creation of such naval stations as essential because they would enable the United States to maintain an ongoing naval presence in strategic centers of operations. He further reasoned that these stations could compensate for problems in long-distance communications as well as deficiencies in the number of battleships. Indeed, he advocated that "in considering the future of our navy . . . the cost of a naval base should be figured; and when a certain number of battleships have been provided for, the outflow of money should be diverted to the establishment of an advanced but primary naval base."[21]

In his prescient article "The American Interoceanic Canal," published in the *Proceedings of the United States Naval Institute* in December 1899, Captain Stockton argued persuasively that a permanent naval station in Cuba would protect the new U.S. strategic interests in the Caribbean and guard the future canal. Stockton believed not only that the construction of such a canal was a certainty but also that its value to U.S. national interests would outweigh its commercial importance, which would still be "a matter of great moment, [but] not a vital one." He foresaw that the canal would tie U.S. interests more closely to both Europe and Asian/Pacific nations and that to protect the canal it would be imperative for the United States to establish offshore naval stations, in particular to guard the approaches to the Caribbean Basin, namely the Yucatan Channel and the Windward Passage. Stockton reasoned:

> In importance of geographical and strategical position with view to the Canal and the routes thereto from the United States, Cuba stands first in order of all the islands and countries of the West Indies. Its commanding position with respect to the Florida Straits and Yucatan Channel on the north and west is augmented by its position toward the Windward Passage and the channel north of Jamaica on the south and west.[22]

Noting the geographical position of Cuba in relation to the Mississippi River and its valley region, Stockton visualized the island nation as "an outer bar of the Mississippi" that would command the Yucatan Channel, the Florida Straits, and the Windward Passage, the "outlets of the Gulf of Mexico." His perception of the need for naval stations in Cuba was more expansive than anyone else's. Observing the "strategical" relationship of Havana to the Florida Straits, Cienfuegos to the Yucatan Channel, and both Santiago and Guantánamo to the Windward Passage, he advised: "These great military ports give Cuba its strategic value to the United States if it remains under the sovereignty of the United States. If it should pass to the control of a sovereignty other than that of our own, it should be one whose policy will be in unison with us."[23]

Stockton was especially concerned about protecting the Windward Passage because of what he foresaw as the chronic instability of Haiti. His argument with regard to the island of Hispaniola (now divided between Haiti and the Dominican Republic) had its obvious racist overtones, which unfortunately must have resonated with most of his readers:

The island is interposed between Cuba and Puerto Rico. . . . There is more reason to look for interference [there] than in any other country of the West Indies. In fact, the island with its two semi-civilized states forms the tinder box . . . of the Caribbean. In possession of a foreign power, Samaná Bay would leave open Puerto Rico and the Mona Passage and St. Nicolas Mole . . . to be used as a base of operations against Cuba and the Windward Passage.[24]

To add emphasis to his advice to the U.S. government to establish naval stations throughout the Caribbean, Stockton warned of the potential threat to the navigation of the future canal in wartime if the United States did not command the Caribbean sea lanes. He simply noted that a naval blockade of the east end of the canal would stop the transit of all ships—"one cork is alone necessary for this bottle." Given the outcome of the Spanish-American War, namely the new empire the United States would knit together, he saw building the canal as an inevitable consequence and a virtual necessity. He predicted:

The questions that will arise about the Canal will be almost exclusively maritime and with the great naval powers. . . . To perform the duty of protecting and keeping the Canal open to the commerce of the world, as well as the imperative duty of protecting our own trade, a competent naval force is essential. *In other words, a naval predominance in these waters is essential; for after all no matter what treaties exist or are made, the control of the Canal will rest with the nation having control of the Caribbean Sea. For this naval force there must be naval stations in the Gulf of Mexico and the Caribbean Sea to furnish facilities for coaling, docking, and extensive repairs to ships and machinery, and also to serve as depots for military and naval supplies of all kinds.*[25]

The United States was also interested in establishing a naval and coaling station on the Pacific coast of South America, in the large harbor of Chimbote on Peru's northern coast. U.S. Minister Stephen Hurlbut first broached the subject in 1881 during the War of the Pacific. Hurlbut seized the initiative by promising to support Peru's territorial claims in exchange for obtaining the use of Chimbote as a coaling station, but an outraged Secretary of State Blaine, who had not been previously consulted, halted the negotiations. Hurlbut died before any agreement could be concluded. Discussions resumed from 1888 to 1889, but Peru was unwilling to cede territorial jurisdiction over Chimbote to the United States, which would include the right to fly the U.S. flag over the base. In late 1901, knowing that the new administration of Theodore Roosevelt intended to build a transisthmian canal through

Panama, Peruvian vice president Isaac Alzamora informed Secretary of State John Hay and President Roosevelt that his government might be willing to lease Chimbote and possibly also the adjacent port of Samanco. Roosevelt was initially interested, but, once again, Peru's terms proved too high. They included a ninety-nine-year lease of Chimbote without any territorial concessions in return for U.S. support of Peru's claims in its lingering Tacna-Arica dispute with Chile, an outright gift of U.S. warships to Peru, and a loan sufficient to cover major improvements in the Port of Callao. When Peru tried to revive its proposal in 1909, the U.S. Navy was no longer interested in establishing a naval station on the Pacific coast south of Panama.

Bradford, Taylor, and Stockton, all advocating the establishment of new naval stations in the Caribbean, made their well-reasoned arguments in the most influential magazines and journals of the era and also appealed directly to senior policymakers. As senior naval officials, these men had earned reputations as naval planners and strategists, and they were frequently asked to give testimony and expert opinions before the increasingly powerful congressional committees concerned with naval affairs. The obvious similarity in their views helped create a basis of political and military support in the United States for the efforts of policymakers such as Wood and Root more intimately involved in planning Cuba's future and, in particular, the future of Guantánamo. Unfortunately, Wood came to power in Cuba only through a protracted contest with his superior officer, Major General John R. Brooke. Wood ultimately emerged the victor because of his administrative genius and the strong support of Roosevelt, and Brooke left in disgrace. Later, nationalist Cuban historians, especially in the era of Fidel Castro, would lump Wood together with Brooke as military imperialists. Antagonism to Brooke's incompetent and arbitrary administration spilled over into Wood's tenure and complicated arguments over the Platt Amendment and the retention of Guantánamo.

To understand the origins of Cuban resentment toward the retention of Guantánamo as a U.S. naval station, it is essential to keep in mind that the United States got off to a bad start with the military administration that began in December 1898 and lasted until May 20, 1902. The United States did not have any laws for governing colonies, and U.S. military officers had virtually no prior experience in running a foreign country.[26] Consequently most senior officers who were assigned to administer Cuba, and, in particular, its first military governor, Brooke, relied chiefly on what they had learned by serving in outposts on the U.S. western frontier. Brooke himself was a sixty-one-year-old U.S. Army officer who had fought at Gettysburg, briefly run a scandal-ridden training camp at Chickamauga, and, based on his seniority, had been selected by McKinley as the first governor of Puerto Rico and then governor-general of Cuba.[27]

By all accounts, Brooke failed to prepare the Cubans for self-government. Although he implemented emergency relief and sanitation measures, collected revenues, established schools, and improved conditions in prisons, he ignored the details of daily government by creating an elaborate departmental structure—with no effective oversight—that quickly degenerated into what was at best a laissez-faire administration.[28] He also offended Cuban nationalists by excluding the Cuban Army and its leader, General Máximo Gómez, from participating in the transfer of government ceremony in Havana that took place on January 1, 1899. Brooke then further antagonized the Cubans by restoring Spanish laws in their entirety.

In the United States, the Brooke debacle would draw together the proponents of the future Platt Amendment to form a powerful coalition of professional naval officers, senior policymakers, and commercial interests whose collective interests would be served by an amendment that would make Cuba a protectorate of the United States. Roosevelt was the first prominent figure to suggest by transparent innuendo that his friend and recent comrade in arms, Wood, now military governor of Santiago, replace Brooke in Havana. As governor of New York, on January 7, 1899, Roosevelt broadcast his views in "General Leonard Wood: A Model American Military Administrator" in the *Outlook*. He opened with the assertions that the United States had a responsibility to secure good government in the newly acquired territories and that the achievement of that goal depended largely on the efforts of the men Washington designated to administer the provinces. It was essential, Roosevelt maintained, "to have first-class men . . . to administer these provinces," and to give them "the widest possible latitude . . . to solve the exceedingly difficult problems set before them." Roosevelt gave detailed examples of Wood's boundless energy, competence, and resourcefulness. He attested that he had frequently observed Wood in Santiago following the surrender and that whenever he saw Wood, he was engaged in one of his multitudinous duties. Roosevelt warned that "all conditions are ripe for a period of utter anarchy, and under a weak, a foolish, or a violent man, this anarchy would certainly have come." Wood, however, through energy, firmness, common sense, and moderation, had made great improvements. "By degrees, he has substituted the best Cubans he can find in the places both of the old Spanish officials and of the Americans who were put in temporary control."[29] Taking a broad view of the new U.S. responsibilities, Roosevelt cautioned that "the inhabitants of the islands are not at this moment fit to govern themselves. In some places they may speedily become fit. . . . Until the moment arrives, they have got to be governed by men carefully chosen who are on the ground, who know what the needs really are, and who have the power given them to meet these needs."[30]

Roosevelt did not criticize Brooke directly. In fact, Brooke's photograph and a wry description of him as being "of massive build and over six feet high—a man built for big undertakings" preceded Roosevelt's article. Nonetheless, the message in Roosevelt's article was direct: colonial administrators of Wood's ability merited full support by Washington and Havana. If Brooke in Havana should prove unequal to the challenges confronting him or obstruct the constructive efforts of Cuba's regional military governors, Wood was waiting in the wings and should replace him.

In May 1899, Wood provided his own perspective of "The Existing Conditions and Needs of Cuba" in the *North American Review.* His first paragraph began, "What is needed in Cuba at present is a firm but liberal and just government of the people, for the people, and by the people, under American military supervision for the time being." Without attacking Brooke by name, Wood condemned his administration, or lack thereof, by stating, "What is to be avoided above all things is militarism, military pedantry, unelastic methods, and any continuance of the old Spanish system of multitudinous officeholders filling unnecessary offices and rendering practically no return for the salaries paid them."[31]

On July 1, 1899, Roosevelt once again sought to replace Brooke with Wood. This time he wrote Secretary of State John Hay, making the plaintive request, "If you think it worthwhile after reading this letter, pray show it to the President. I have written on somewhat the same lines to Attorney General [John] Griggs." He began by noting that he was "uneasy about the way things seem to be going both in the Philippines and in Cuba, and also at the mutterings of discontent with what we have done in these islands." He warned that potential disasters in U.S. colonial policy would not only shake the McKinley administration but could have other profound effects, including "the definite abandonment of the course upon which we have embarked." Roosevelt then urged that McKinley immediately place Wood in command of all of Cuba with the authority to do whatever "he deems wisest in shaping our policy for the island." Without mentioning Brooke's name, Roosevelt emphasized the need for tact and judgment, and praised Wood as being as much "a born diplomat as he is a born soldier." He observed that Wood had the facility to get along with both Spaniards and Cubans, noting that "they like him, trust him, and down in their hearts are afraid of him." He ended his letter by asking Hay once again to show the letter to McKinley, saying "if he cares to talk with me, I should like to come on."[32]

If this plea by Roosevelt did not have the immediate impact he wanted, subsequent developments helped to force Brooke's replacement. On August 9, 1899, the *New York Times* reported that the U.S. War Department was calling Brooke to account in response to complaints from Cubans "not of the professional agitator class" who had criticized Brooke for his failure to promote civil government and to address the needs of public education.[33] It was the new secretary of war, Root, who on December 13, 1899, appointed Wood governor-general of Cuba.[34] Five days later Root wrote Roosevelt: "I know you were pleased by the appointment of Wood in Cuba. The situation there is exceedingly delicate and difficult. Anything which the thoughtless and uninstructed would consider absolute success is practically impossible, but I think Wood is competent to secure a greater degree of success there than anyone else."[35]

McKinley had appointed Root, a prominent corporate attorney, as his secretary of war in August 1899. Root had no experience in military or diplomatic affairs, but he was well grounded in judicial procedure and believed that most diplomatic problems could be solved through arbitration. One of the reasons McKinley appointed him was that Root had previously written that "the Cuban cause is just [and] the Cubans are exercising their inalienable rights in their rebellion." Root agreed with McKinley that Cuba should be a sovereign nation and that it should be protected by the United States until it was ready for the responsibilities of independence. On December 20, Brooke issued his final report, stating that it had been difficult for him to work "in a foreign country . . . among strangers, a strange people, speaking a foreign language." He concluded, "Progress may have seemed slow to others, but the foundations of a future government were being laid."[36]

Not everyone accepted Brooke's defense at face value. It was after he had been reassigned to another command post in the United States that his prior administration received the criticism it merited from U.S. Army Major J. E. Runcie in "American Misconduct in Cuba," published in the *North American Review* in February 1900. Runcie gave full voice to the concerns that had animated Roosevelt when he wrote, "The history of the American occupation since the day the entire island passed into American hands is simply the story of what has been done at Havana. It is a record of error and neglect, of folly, ending necessarily in failure, and, possibly, in shame and disgrace." Runcie underscored many of the same criticisms made earlier by the *New York Times*. With regard to the judicial system, he found that "corruption exists everywhere." He directed specific attention to the efforts made to organize and improve public education by the military governor of Santiago, Wood, which had been undone by the Cuban secretary appointed by Brooke. Runcie found that "judges of all grades, civil governors in every province," and almost all civilian officeholders had been selected from the former Cuban Army, with the result being "a political machine . . . constructed under the cover of American authority, but bitterly hostile to every American influence." Runcie concluded his essay with a sweeping indictment of the Cubans whom Brooke and his hand-picked subordinates had placed in positions of responsibility: "Wherever Cubans, under nominal American control, have been trusted to exercise the functions of government, the result has been worse than failure." The only progress Runcie could discern had been the increase in the receipts from customs houses and the dramatic reductions in the death rate through improvements in public health and sanitation. These were departments where Americans had been fully in charge. Runcie warned, "There exists throughout the island a condition of tame anarchy, which awaits only the withdrawal of the American forces to burst out into anarchy of another type. . . . If no change occurs soon, the last state of Cuba bids fair to be far worse than the first."[37] Runcie's observations ring true insofar as the problems and animosity engendered by Brooke's incompetent administration had created an atmosphere of antagonism and mistrust that did not completely abate in spite of Wood's best efforts to prepare Cuba for self-government.

At first glance, the story of Brooke's failed administration of Cuba may seem irrelevant to the establishment of a naval station at Guantánamo. In at least two respects, however, it provided the administrative basis and helped forge the personal ties that made Guantánamo possible. When Root replaced Brooke with Wood, he became the cabinet member most directly involved in Cuban affairs. On the personal level, Brooke's missteps, which threatened to sabotage Roosevelt's earlier efforts to make Cuba a viable and independent nation, forced the former Rough Rider to pay close, ongoing attention to Cuban developments even from Albany. Moreover, Roosevelt's recognition of Wood's administrative genius and his ultimately successful efforts to persuade Root to appoint him governor-general of Cuba created the durable bond between these three policymakers that facilitated their collective efforts to provide for the defense of Cuba and the Caribbean.[38]

Roosevelt, Root, and Wood shared serious qualms about the ability of the Cubans to govern or to defend themselves. Each in moments of frustration voiced opinions that reflected his racial prejudices and the insensitive arrogance characteristic of the social elite of the era. In his angry moments Roosevelt could dismiss Cubans, Colombians, and other Latin Americans as "dagos." During the war, Roosevelt had grumbled, "We should have been better off if there had not been a single Cuban within the army. . . . They accomplished literally nothing, . . . were a source of trouble and embarrassment, and consumed much provisions."[39] Root, who had visited Cuba briefly during Brooke's administration in 1899, confided to his friend Paul

Dana, the editor of the *New York Sun,* on January 16, 1900, "I do not believe any people, three-fourths of whom are contented to remain unable to read and write, can for any very long period maintain a free government."[40] Even Wood, who generally was upbeat in his written communications to his superiors about Cuban aptitudes, at one point lamented to Root that Cuban politicians were "doctors without patients, lawyers without practices, and demagogues living on the subscriptions of the people and their friends."[41]

On December 5, 1899, McKinley in his state of the union address said, "The new Cuba yet to arise from the ashes of the past must needs be bound to us by ties of singular intimacy and strength if its enduring welfare is to be assured. . . . Our mission . . . is not to be fulfilled by turning adrift any loosely framed commonwealth to face the vicissitudes which too often attend weaker states." Privately, McKinley had bluntly instructed Wood "to get the [Cuban] people ready for a republican form of government. . . . Give them a good school system. . . . Put them on their feet as best you can. We want to do all we can for them and to get out of the island as soon as we safely can."[42]

Wood took command of Cuba's military government on the morning of December 20, and immediately went to work. According to one account, he walked into the Hotel Inglaterra, dropped off his luggage, and then left for his first meeting with Gonzalo de Quesada, Cuba's unofficial chargé d'affaires. His work habits never varied—he was up by 5:30 A.M. and worked until midnight. He inspected prisons, hospitals, courts, public works projects, and schools throughout Cuba, usually going by boat since the sea lanes were much faster than rural roads. In this way, he quickly became familiar with the topography and the harbors of Cuba.[43]

Wood's administrative scope is most evident in the *Civil Reports* published under his direction. They are incredibly comprehensive and detailed. Examples include exact descriptions of the conditions of gardens and streets—accompanied by photographs—of Havana and other Cuban cities. There is a list of every item to be included in the meals served to prisoners in Cuban for breakfast, lunch, and dinner. Wood sent a Cuban representative, Falco, to the Fifth Congress of Criminal Anthropology in Amsterdam instructions to collect documents and to write a comprehensive mono- of his findings. Wood's most significant achievement, however, was his siastic support for the work of the U.S. Army Yellow Fever Commis- popularly known as the "Reed Commission" after its leader, Dr. Walter With the benefit of martial law, Wood and his aides Major Jefferson R. nd Major William C. Gorgas worked to destroy the breeding grounds "Aedes aegypi" mosquito, which produces yellow fever, throughout Then, when a vaccine was developed, Wood decreed that vaccination was obligatory for all Cubans. It is worth noting that, in the subsequent report, the Cuban secretary of state and government wrote, "En su Movimiento de avance indiscutible necesario y por último en primer línea, el Honorable Gobernador Militar Leonard Wood [fué el] generoso iniciador de esa idea bienhechora para la Isla de Cuba, mejor dicho para la humanidad entera" ("for his firm backing of an indisputable necessity, the honorable Military Governor Leonard Wood was the generous initiator of this well-achieved idea for the island of Cuba, or, better said, for all humanity").[44]

Beginning in 1900, the United States moved to secure its new strategic interests in Cuba. Root knew that he was obligated to uphold the Teller Amendment, which granted sovereignty and promised to prepare Cuba for full independence.[45] At the same time, from the outset of his tenure as secretary of war, Root thought that an enduring special relationship had to be established between the United States and Cuba for their mutual interest and protection. According to Patrick De Froscia's dissertation on Root's diplomacy, Root, like Roosevelt, was "an ardent nationalist [and] a vocal Monroeist" who believed "the Caribbean was an American lake and directed policy within that context."[46] In April 1900, at a dinner honoring the memory of Ulysses S. Grant, Root predicted that the United States would soon be called upon to uphold the Monroe Doctrine, and forcefully declared, "We are not going to abandon it. If necessary we will fight for it." This statement was widely interpreted, both in Europe and the United States, as a thinly veiled warning aimed at imperial Germany. Indeed, there was some evidence of German war plans to invade the Caribbean and attack the eastern U.S. seaboard.[47]

Root believed, almost instinctively, that Germany was jealous of the new U.S. territorial acquisitions in the Caribbean and Pacific regions, and had little, if any, respect for the Monroe Doctrine. In October 1897, in an interview, Germany's former chancellor Prince Otto von Bismarck had denounced the "extraordinary insolence" of the Monroe Doctrine, and, one year later, he referred to the doctrine as a "presumptuous idea" that Washington had been unable consistently to interpret and apply.[48]

Great Britain was finding it increasingly difficult to assign major naval assets to protect its Caribbean interests and, at the same time, to maintain naval supremacy in its own waters. The signing of the Hay-Pauncefote Treaty, in which Britain acknowledged the unilateral right of the United States to build an isthmian canal, was a major step toward establishing a regional partnership with the United States in the Caribbean. By late 1902, British Foreign Secretary Lord Lansdowne had persuaded his government to openly endorse the Monroe Doctrine.[49]

Roosevelt shared some of Root's concern regarding Germany's potential threat to the Caribbean and the Western Hemisphere. Roosevelt, who spoke German fluently, had top level access to the Kaiser's circle through his close friend Count Hermann von Sternberg, and knew the Germans far better than Root. Nonetheless, Roosevelt confided his concern to Henry Cabot Lodge on March 27, 1901: "The Germans regard our failure to go forward in building up the navy this year as a sign that our spasm of preparation . . . has come to an end; that we shall sink back, so that in a few years, they will be in a position to take some step in the West Indies or South America which will make us either put up or shut up on the Monroe Doctrine."[50]

To guard against this eventuality, efforts to acquire Guantánamo were already under way. On April 17, 1900, the members of the newly constituted U.S. Navy General Board voted unanimously to inform their civilian superiors that Guantánamo was their first choice for a naval base in the West Indies.[51] On May 14, 1900, Root forwarded to Wood a letter he had received three days earlier from Long, which opened with the statement:

> Since the termination of the war with Spain, the Department has had under consideration the selection of a site for a naval coal deposit somewhere near the east end of Cuba. In view of the probable construction of a trans-isthmian canal, the possession of Porto Rico [*sic*], and the necessity for protecting the island of Cuba from foreign aggression, it is necessary that the United States should control the windward passage through which commerce and our transports and warships must pass on the way to the canal from northern ports. The strategic value of this passage is very great.[52]

Drawing on detailed information Bradford had prepared, Long advised Root that the Navy Department "has decided that Guantánamo Bay possesses the most advantages" to control the passage. After specifying where the coal deposit should be located within the entrance to the bay and voicing the hope that "the land can be acquired at a small cost per acre," Long concluded his letter by requesting that Root bring the letter to Wood's attention so that he could initiate discussions with the Cubans. In his letter of transmittal, Root advised that the matter should be treated as confidential and urged Wood to take "early action."[53] True to form, Wood quickly found and began negotiating with the Cuban property owners around Guantánamo.[54]

In June 1900, Captain Asa Walker, who was a member of the Navy General Board, sought to spur on Root and Wood's efforts to secure Guantánamo with his own advocacy in "Notes on Cuban Ports," published in the *Proceedings of the United States Naval Institute*. It began with the statement, "Cuba from its size and situation may well be considered the most important of the West Indian islands." Walker described Cuba as the "natural sentry-box to the Gulf of Mexico and to the waters washing the shores of Yucatan and Honduras." Cuba's harbors could either provide "bases for hostile operations against the United States" or, alternatively, "locations from which to meet and ward off such attacks." Walker's emphasis throughout his brief article was on geographic location. He wrote, "It seems self-evident that any attack made on the United States in the future will have for its objective our possessions and dependencies in the West Indies, and it is in those waters that the Navy will be called upon to defend the national rights and honor."[55]

Making a survey of nineteen Cuban ports, Walker found many harbors suitable for commercial use, but only a few that had "the requirements demanded of a naval base." He described the military merits of four ports—Havana, Nipe, Cienfuegos, and Guantánamo—and advocated that all of them should become defensive outposts of the United States, but he argued that Guantánamo should function as the "main base for naval operations connected with the islands and waters lying to the southward and eastward of Cuba."[56]

On June 20, 1900, Root wrote Wood to request a reduction of infantry troops in Cuba to be reassigned to the Philippines—"leaving only such troops as are absolutely necessary to preserve order." Indicating that the United States would still have to defend Cuba after "we turn the government over to Cuban hands," Root said that Bradford had asked him "to say something more to you about the purchase of land for a naval station at Guantánamo." Root added his own emphatic thoughts that the United States must be able to guarantee Cuba's security:

> I think it is very important that the United States should become the actual owner of the waterfront for naval stations, not only at Guantánamo, but at Havana, and, probably, at some other points in the island. . . . Someone will have to decide what means the United States shall retain to require that government [Cuba] to fulfill all the obligations for protection of life and property for which we will continue to stand as practically a guarantor to the other civilized powers.[57]

Even though Wood and Root were Republicans and, therefore, at least nominally committed to black suffrage in the United States, their separate remarks indicated that both feared disastrous consequences if illiterate blacks in Cuba were allowed to vote. Wood wrote, "The individual who on reaching twenty-one has not shown enough energy to accumulate $250, nor learned to read and write . . . is a social element unworthy to be counted on for collective purposes. Let him not vote!" In a similar vein, Root commented, "When the history of the new Cuba comes to be written, the establishment of popular self-government based on a limited suffrage, excluding so great a proportion of the elements which have brought ruin to Haiti and San Domingo, will be regarded as an event of the first importance."[58]

On July 18, 1900, Wood attended a formal dinner given by Root for McKinley, and, according to the private account of one of the guests, when the conversation turned to Cuba, the president remarked, "Cuba will have an early opportunity to experiment with self-government."[59] Over the next few days, the three men met several more times to plan the conditions necessary for a U.S. withdrawal from the island. The discussions were secret, with only sketchy details released to the press. An article published in the *New York Times* on July 21, based on comments by Wood, reported that the date of September 15 had been set for an election of Cuban delegates to a constitutional convention. It also announced that U.S. troops probably would withdraw from Cuba in less than nine months, but did not specify the conditions for the withdrawal.[60] The Minneapolis *Tribune* accurately predicted that Washington would insist on having naval stations in Cuba.[61] E. L. Godkin, editor of the often polemical journal of political opinion the *Nation,* had the greatest critical insight into the secret discussions. He reported that the administration had prepared a plan under which the United States would manage Cuba's foreign relations and retain control of fortifications "for a period of years, if not indefinitely, which command the port of Havana and other important cities." Godkin then asserted, "Unless we are prepared to take Cuba, for better, for worse, and forever, we ought to take no portion of her duties and responsibilities. What we promised her was independence, not suzerainty."[62]

On July 25, 1900, McKinley directed that the military governor of Cuba promulgate an order for holding a constitutional convention in Cuba. Civil Order 301 specified that a general election would take place throughout Cuba in September to elect delegates to a convention in Havana on the first Monday in November 1900 to frame and adopt a constitution for the people of Cuba. The order also specified that the convention would "provide for and agree with the Government of the United States upon the relations to exist between the Government and the Government of Cuba."[63]

On September 26, Wood informed Root of the outcome of the elections. Only two of the thirty-one delegates elected to the Cuban Constitutional Convention, by Wood's reckoning, could be called true conservatives. The others ranged from conservative former revolutionaries to extreme radicals. Wood clearly was worried about what kind of constitution these future delegates would write. He confided to Root, "I hoped they would send their very best men. They have done so in many instances, but they have also sent some of the worst agitators and political rascals in Cuba."[64]

Wood opened the Cuban Constitutional Convention on November 5,

1900. He instructed the delegates that their first duty was "to frame and adopt a Constitution for Cuba." Then, they were "to formulate what . . . ought to be the relations between Cuba and the United States." From November 9 to 27, 1900, Root visited Cuba for the second time, traveling throughout the island with Wood and meeting with several Cuban leaders. He purposely did not attend any sessions of the Constitutional Convention.[65]

On December 3, 1900, in his annual message to Congress, McKinley recalled his earlier directive of July 25 that the Cubans elect delegates to a convention to frame a constitution as a basis for a stable and independent government in Cuba. He then informed Congress, the nation, and Cuba, "We have in Cuba between 5,000 and 6,000 troops. For the present our troops in that island can not be withdrawn or materially diminished, and certainly not until the conclusion of the labors of the constitutional convention now in session and a government provided by the new constitution shall have been established and its stability assured."[66]

In early January, Wood met with the convention's president, Domingo Méndez Capote, who told him the subject of naval stations was a "touchy" one for many Cubans, but that a lower U.S. tariff on Cuban imports might change their minds. Wood dutifully reported this conversation to Root, and, in his letter dated January 4, 1901, he also mentioned that Méndez Capote and the radicals would oppose any control by the United States over Cuba's relations with other foreign governments. On January 9, 1901, Root wrote a lengthy and stern reply to Wood. He observed that it was "exceedingly doubtful" under any circumstances that Congress would grant tariff concessions on Cuban sugar and tobacco. He warned, "I hope that the convention will not take it into their heads to present any such proposition as a part of a scheme under which they will consent to such rights and powers as we think we ought to have in Cuba."[67] In a tone of exasperation, Root advised Wood that "the sooner the convention finishes its labors and sends its conclusion to the President the better. . . . We desire as soon as possible to be relieved from the burden and annoyance of their government and the expense of maintaining troops there, which must be about a half million dollars a month."[68]

Root then made explicit his chief concern:

We now have by virtue of our occupation of Cuba and the terms under which sovereignty was yielded by Spain, a right to protect her which all foreign nations recognize. It is of great importance to Cuba that that right . . . should never be terminated but should be continued by a [naval] reservation. . . . If we should simply turn the government over to the Cuban administration, retire from the island, and then turn round to make a treaty with the new government

. . . no foreign State would recognize any longer a right on our part to interfere in any quarrel which she might have with Cuba, unless that interference were based upon an assertion of the Monroe Doctrine. But the Monroe Doctrine is not a part of international law and has never been recognized by European nations.[69]

After further reflection on these important matters that, in his mind, involved not only the future of U.S.-Cuban relations but also the new, enlarged security concerns of the United States, Root wrote a letter to Secretary of State Hay on January 11, 1901, in which he outlined the conditions under which the U.S. military would withdraw from Cuba that would ultimately form the basis of the Platt Amendment. He asked Hay "to turn over in his mind the advisability of requiring the incorporation into the fundamental law of Cuba" provisions including:

[The] United States reserves and retains the right of intervention for the preservation of Cuban independence and the maintenance of a stable government, adequately protecting life, property, and individual liberty. . . . To facilitate the United States in the performance of such duties . . . and for her own defense, the United States may acquire and hold the title to land and maintain naval stations at certain specified points.[70]

Root then recalled that Great Britain had preserved the right to intervene in Egypt after it ceased to be a crown colony, so that England could still maintain "moral control and prevent the backsliding of the Egyptian Government." He suggested that Hay consult his State Department experts on this subject, adding, "It is important to reach sound conclusions upon the scope and effect which the reservation of a right of intervention in Cuba would have."[71] Root, of course, was seeking to find out how Britain had acquired its continuing authority over the Suez Canal in order to establish a similar and lasting control over naval stations established in Cuba.

Over the next few weeks, Root met with Connecticut senator Orville Platt, who proposed incorporating Root's demands into the Cuban Constitution. Platt then met with the other Republican members of the Committee on Relations with Cuba on February 3, 1901, at the home of former navy secretary, now Senator William E. Chandler, and they all agreed that the United States should insist on having naval stations in Cuba. Platt subsequently communicated the views of his fellow committee members to Root, and on February 7, Platt and Root discussed their joint recommendations with McKinley. Following that meeting, Root drafted a memorandum in which he enumerated eight demands he, Platt, and McKinley had designated as conditions for a U.S. withdrawal from Cuba. Second on the list was the demand for naval bases.[72] On February 9, 1901, Root sent a formal letter to Wood in which he stated:

> It would be a most lame and impotent conclusion, if, after all the expenditure of blood and treasure by the people of the United States for the freedom of Cuba, and by the people of Cuba for the same object, we should, through the constitution of the new government . . . be placed in a worse condition in regard to our vital interests than we were while Spain was in possession, and the people of Cuba should be deprived of that protection and aid from the United States which is necessary to the maintenance of their independence.

He then enumerated five provisions that "the people of Cuba should desire to have incorporated into their fundamental law." Provision Five specified that "the United States may acquire and hold title to land for naval stations."[73]

The informal way in which Wood chose to communicate Root's provisions to leading members of the Constitutional Convention backfired. The timing of the arrival of the U.S. demands could not have been worse. On February 11, the Cubans had agreed on a draft constitution, and had also created the Committee on Relations, consisting of one delegate from each province, to discuss the future of U.S.-Cuban relations.[74] On February 15, Wood received Root's instructions as he was getting ready to leave Havana to take U.S. humorist John Kendrick Bangs on a crocodile hunt in the Zapata Swamp of Matanzas Province.[75] At the last minute, Wood decided to invite the members of the convention's Committee on Relations to join him, apparently thinking that having a conference onboard his comfortable yacht would be more productive of good relations than in the confines of government buildings in Havana. Indeed, the discussion there was amicable. But Wood had misjudged the Latin temperament and its unstated belief that ceremony and formal decorum should attend the decisions of matters of state. When he returned to Havana, he confronted hostile delegates who told him that he had insulted the convention by the way in which he had "pitched" some of its members. Moreover, they found Root's provisions at odds with their conception of a free Cuba and were especially offended by the U.S. insistence on having naval stations in Cuba.[76] In reality, Wood had demonstrated that he was indifferent to the aspirations of Cuban nationalists. As a perceptive editorial correspondent of the *New York Times* would subsequently write, "The Cubans do not fear unfair treatment or criminal aggression from the United States. They simply look upon its terms [the Platt Amendment] as an assertion, to which they are asked to adhere, of their incapacity to govern themselves. . . . Several of the delegates have said to me, with pleading earnestness: 'We do not want to be treated like children.'"[77]

Wood underestimated the intensity of Cuban hostility to the Platt Amendment, or he assumed it would be short-lived. In either case, he informed Root on February 19 that the only serious objection was the "reference to naval stations," which was the seventh article in the Platt Amendment, and that there also was "some apparent objection" to the third article, which gave the United States the right of intervention.[78] Wood then revealed that he was more upset by the Cuban reaction than his earlier words had suggested by stating, "The objection to [the naval stations] seems to be a matter principally of sentiment combined with a certain amount of selfishness. Among the elements now dominating the politics of the island there is little or no gratitude for what has been done by the United States."[79]

The members of the Cuban Constitutional Convention made no serious objection to the other provisions that specified the Cuban government would not enter into treaties with foreign powers that could impair its independence or permit foreign powers to obtain lodgment in or control over any part of Cuba or incur public debts it could not discharge. It would ratify and validate all of the acts of the United States in Cuba under military occupation, and execute and extend as necessary all plans for the sanitation of cities so as to prevent the recurrence of epidemics and the spread of infectious diseases.[80] The Platt Amendment also stated that the Isle of Pines would be omitted from the proposed constitutional boundaries of Cuba with its title to be left to future adjustment by treaty.[81]

On February 21, Wood formally communicated the terms under which the United States would grant "independence" to Cuba to Representative Diego Tamayo. Three days later, a celebration in Havana commemorating the sixth anniversary of the 1895 revolution quickly turned into an anti-American demonstration. There were angry speeches attacking the U.S. proposals—especially the insistence on having naval stations. Some Cubans waved banners proclaiming "Nada de Carboneras!"[82]

The Cuban Constitutional Convention also objected vociferously to the third article of the proposed amendment, which stated: "The government of Cuba consents that the United States may exercise the right to intervene for the preservation of Cuban independence, the maintenance of a government adequate for the protection of life, property, and individual liberty, and for discharging the obligations with respect to Cuba imposed by the Treaty of Paris on the United States, now to be assumed and undertaken by the government of Cuba."

The Cuban delegates tried to avoid having this provision inserted into their constitution by declaring that Cuba would assume the obligations specified in the Treaty of Paris that would not allow any foreign government to use Cuba as a base of operations. From the U.S. government's perspective, this article was central to U.S. efforts to stabilize Cuba. Root's original language (contained in both his letter to Hay on January 11 and his formal communication to Wood on February 9) that the United States would "reserve and retain the right of intervention" might have given the article greater weight by borrowing language from the Treaty of Paris, but Platt's rewording to "Cuba consents that the United States may exercise the right to intervene" made it more acceptable to the members of the convention.[83]

Meanwhile, in Washington, D.C., the McKinley administration decided to press forward with its own agenda for Cuba without waiting to hear from the convention. On February 25, 1901, Senator Platt, with the obvious backing of Root and McKinley, formally introduced the resolution to become known as the Platt Amendment as an amendment to the Army Appropriations Bill.[84] Among the demands that the Cubans would have to accept before the U.S. Army would withdraw from the island was the requirement specified in Article Seven that "the Government of Cuba will sell or lease to the United States land necessary for coaling or naval stations at certain specified points, to be agreed upon with the President of the United States."[85]

A minority of prominent Americans opposed what they viewed as the imperialistic aims of policymakers Roosevelt and Lodge and their associates. These critics of U.S. expansionism in the late nineteenth century included such diverse figures as diplomat Charles Francis Adams, educator Booker T. Washington, labor leader Samuel Gompers, Progressive reformer Jane Addams, Senators George Hoar of Massachusetts and John Morgan of Alabama, and writers William Dean Howells and Mark Twain. Although they became known as the "anti-imperialists," they formed more of a loose collectivity than a well-organized movement, and they ultimately failed to change the course of U.S. foreign policy. Nevertheless, they established a moral precedent for the recurring criticism of the justice of the new U.S. policies in Cuba, Puerto Rico, and the Philippines, where rights promised by the U.S. Constitution did not necessarily accompany the "Stars and Stripes." Diplomatic historian Walter McDougal makes the persuasive argument that "the United States went off the rails in terms of its honored traditions when it went to war with Spain," and the most important consequence of this military intervention in terms of foreign policy was that "a newly prideful United States began to measure its holiness by what it did, not just by what it was."[86]

One of the most trenchant critics was Mark Twain, who initially had applauded U.S. intervention in both Cuba and the Philippines, believing that the United States was fighting exclusively to free these island nations from Spanish oppression. That had in essence been the officially stated goal, with McKinley proclaiming that any annexation of foreign territory would constitute "criminal aggression," and with Congress guaranteeing Cuban independence in the Teller Amendment. Twain, however, became quickly disillusioned after he read the terms of the Treaty of Paris, which gave the U.S. control over Cuba, Puerto Rico, Guam, and the Philippines. Although he directed his most biting criticism against U.S. actions in the Philippines, he also satirized the new U.S. policies in Cuba in a talk at Princeton University in 1902:

> Training made us nobly anxious to free Cuba; training made us give her a noble promise; training has enabled us to take it back. Long training made us revolt at the idea of wantonly taking any weak nation's country and liberties away from it, a short training has made us glad to do it, and proud of having done it. . . . There is nothing that training cannot do. . . . It can turn bad morals to good, good morals to bad, it can destroy principles, it can re-create them, it can debase angels to men and lift men to angels. And it can do any one of these miracles in a year—even six months.[87]

Another prominent U.S. humorist and fellow anti-imperialist, George Ade, wrote:

> We haven't the appearance, goodness knows,
> Of plain commercial men;
> From a hasty glance, you might suppose
> We are fractious now and then.
> But though we come in warlike guise
> And battle-front arrayed,
> It's all a business enterprise;
> We're seeking foreign trade.[88]

One of the outspoken opponents of the Platt Amendment was Senate Minority Leader John T. Morgan of Alabama. Ironically, Morgan had been one of the most committed activists in expanding the U.S. role in hemispheric affairs. In 1898, he had advocated that the United States acquire "military outposts and harbors of refuge for the protection of our commerce" in the West Indies. His hard-fought efforts to persuade the U.S. government to build a canal through Nicaragua had earned him the fond tribute of "Canal Morgan."[89] Morgan's objection to the Platt Amendment was that he rightly believed it was being imposed on Cuba without the consent of the members of the Constitutional Convention. Believing that the acquisition of naval stations should be negotiated with the Cubans through diplomatic channels, Morgan denounced the Platt Amendment as "a piece of arrogant hypocrisy" in view of McKinley's prior promise that "Cuba shall be free and sovereign," and he called on his colleagues to withhold their votes until they had heard from the Cubans.[90] Despite Morgan's fervent plea, both the Senate and House quickly passed the Platt Amendment, and on March 2, 1901, McKinley signed it into law.

Meanwhile in Havana, the Cuban Committee on Relations on February 27 prepared a formal document titled "Report on the Relations Which Should Exist between Cuba and the United States." It stated that if Cuba granted the United States the right to acquire title to land for naval stations at designated places along the coast, "in reality [Cuba] never would be independent of the United States." As an alternative that they hoped would end the U.S. demand for naval bases, the Cuban delegates proposed that "the Government of the Republic of Cuba should not enter into any treaty with a foreign power which would tend to impair Cuban independence. . . . Cuba should never permit her territory to be used as a hostile base against the United States or any other foreign nation."[91]

As soon as Wood learned of the Cubans' counterproposal, he informed Root:

> The danger which confronts us is the moral cowardice of all these men. . . . They are emotional and hysterical. . . . They will individually assure me that the relations are just, with the possible exception of naval stations. . . . Collectively they are timid. They are unwilling to be responsible for anything, but say they are willing to accept pretty much whatever we propose, if the United States insists on it.[92]

There can be no doubt that, on occasion, Wood manipulated and tried to browbeat the Cuban delegates into submission. For example, on February 26 he summoned General Máximo Gómez to the governor's palace, after which he quoted the Cuban hero as having said that if the U.S. forces left, "within sixty days the Cubans would be fighting among themselves." Gómez denied ever making such a statement, but it was widely reported in U.S. newspapers. Much later, Wood told reporters for Havana newspapers that he had been "misquoted."[93]

Root stiffly informed Wood on March 2 that if the Cubans did not cooperate, the United States would convene another constitutional convention. He insisted that "no constitution can be put into effect in Cuba and no government can be elected under it until they [Cubans] have acted upon the question of relations in conformity with this act of Congress." In other words, the military occupation would continue until the Cubans had accepted and complied with the Platt Amendment, which was now law. The United States was determined to acquire naval stations and to fulfill the other requirements of the Platt Amendment.[94]

Angry Cubans began demonstrating in the streets of Havana against the U.S. demands on the night of March 2. Even though Wood told Root that 90 percent of the Cubans supported the United States, he also suggested that Washington consider sending the naval squadron based at Key West to Havana to prevent riots. On March 6, he again wrote Root to warn him that the Cubans might reject the Platt Amendment. On March 29, Root advised Wood:

> I hope you have been able to disabuse the members of the Convention of the idea that the intervention described in the Platt Amendment is synonymous with intermeddling in the affairs of a Cuban Government. . . . It gives to the United States no right which she does not already possess . . . but it gives her, for the benefit of Cuba, a standing as between herself and foreign nations in the exercise of that right which may be of immense value in enabling the United States to protect the independence of Cuba.[95]

Root was saying that the intent of the Platt Amendment was to strengthen the Monroe Doctrine. It was to inform the outside world that the United States would install naval bases in Cuba to protect Cuba and to fortify the expanding interests of the United States in the Caribbean region. In spite of Wood's subsequent efforts to mollify Cuban leaders, they persisted in their condemnation of Article Seven, denouncing it as "a constant menace to our internal and external peace and a deep wound to the feeling of our people." On April 12, the convention rejected the Platt Amendment by a vote of eighteen to ten, and requested a meeting with McKinley.

This act of negation by the Cuban Constitutional Convention served to fortify the determination of top U.S. naval officials and senior policymakers to make no concessions to the Cubans until after they had incorporated the verbatim language of the Platt Amendment into their own constitution. More important for Guantánamo's subsequent history, what followed established the precedent that major disagreements between the United States and Cuba over Guantánamo would quickly move up the chain of command to be resolved at the highest levels of both governments. From April 25 to May 5, five Cuban representatives met with senior U.S. officials including President McKinley, Secretary Root, Senator Platt, and Admiral Bradford, who represented Long and the General Board. According to the Cubans' version of their meeting with Root, he had informed them that the Monroe

Doctrine was not recognized in international law, but that the Platt Amendment would be.[96] When the Cubans raised the possibility of U.S. trade concessions, McKinley replied that they must first ratify the Platt Amendment, but promised that his administration would consider a tariff reduction. U.S. leaders, however, rebuffed all requests to change the wording of the Platt Amendment, and the Cubans returned home believing they had accomplished nothing.

The Constitutional Convention spent the rest of May debating the provisions of the amendment. On May 17, Wood telegraphed Root that Méndez Capote had assured him the amendment would pass by a large majority, but that the Cubans would interpret Article Seven to mean that their government would sell or lease the necessary lands for coaling or naval stations provided that "they will only serve the military or naval purposes to which they shall be applied." Root cabled back, "It would be better for the Convention to use the exact words of the Platt Amendment."[97]

On May 28, the convention voted fifteen to fourteen—with Méndez Capote breaking the tie—to approve the Platt Amendment with such minor changes as saying that "the naval stations . . . are established with the sole purpose of protecting American waters from foreign invasion directed against Cuba or the United States."[98] According to the *New York Times,* several Cuban "radicals" denounced the actions of the "conservatives." The paper reported that Tamayo was especially vindictive and declared that everyone who had voted in favor of the Platt Amendment "was a traitor to his country." He was ultimately persuaded to retract his statement, but Gómez, who derided those who voted with the majority as "perjurers," refused to have his remarks stricken from the record.[99]

Root was furious that the Cubans had added their own interpretation to the amendment, and, after consulting with McKinley and other senior U.S. officials, he told Wood that "the Cuban acceptance of the Platt Amendment is surrounded by such a cloud of words . . . that it is difficult to tell what the real meaning is." Wood dutifully conveyed Root's message to the Cubans and explicitly told them, "No one can interpret the scope of the Platt Amendment except Congress."[100] On June 4, Root wrote Vice President Roosevelt, who was summering at Oyster Bay, that he believed "the Cuban situation will eventually come out all right."[101] Root's optimism was well founded. On June 12, 1901, the Cuban Constitutional Convention, by a vote of sixteen to eleven, adopted the Platt Amendment exactly as written as an appendix to the Cuban Constitution. Nine of the eleven delegates who voted no were from Oriente Province, where the Guantánamo Naval Base would be built.[102]

With the struggle for Cuban acceptance of the Platt Amendment behind them, U.S. policymakers began to move forward with their plans to establish naval stations in Cuba. They knew from recent experience, however, that the issue was a sensitive one, and so moved at a measured pace to avoid needlessly antagonizing Cuban nationalists. In late July 1901, Bradford prepared a new report for Long and the General Board that emphasized the need to expedite the acquisition of Guantánamo. Long forwarded Bradford's memorandum to Secretary of State Hay to request that the department seek broader support for Caribbean bases at the Pan-American Conference in Mexico City.[103]

On September 14, 1901, with McKinley dead from an assassin's bullet, Roosevelt took the oath of office as the twenty-sixth president of the United States. He had served as vice president for little more than six months, but despite his prior interest in acquiring naval stations in Cuba, the historical record is silent as to what extent, if any, in that role he may have influenced the administration's position on the Platt Amendment, especially with regard to its firm insistence on retaining Article Seven. This is not surprising. Vice presidents in that era often were shadow figures, and Roosevelt spent most of the time from mid-March to late August at his home in Oyster Bay. Yet, it would have been most uncharacteristic of Roosevelt to be wholly disengaged from a policy initiative that profoundly interested him, and in which the two key players, Elihu Root and Leonard Wood, were among his closest friends. The only documentary evidence that presents itself to date are two letters that illustrate Roosevelt's profound interest in and encouragement for their work.[104] As Frederick Marks has found in his scholarly investigation of Roosevelt's style, "In the realm of diplomacy, Roosevelt was more apt to communicate vital information on the tennis court or on a strenuous hike through Rock Creek Park than he was to commit it to writing."[105] It can easily be imagined that he would converse with Root or Wood on horseback or send them notes with the instruction "destroy after reading." What cannot be said authoritatively is that he played a key role in the drafting of Article Seven or insisting that the Cubans incorporate it into their constitution.

On November 1, 1901, Dewey, as head of the Navy General Board, forwarded to Long the board's unanimous recommendation that the United States immediately obtain and develop Guantánamo into a repair and coaling facility. The recommendation argued that the navy now required a base at Guantánamo to monitor the waters around Cuba, guard the future canal, and protect other U.S. interests in the Caribbean. A base at Guantánamo Bay would help "in resisting demonstrations . . . aimed against Puerto Rico, Haiti, or eastern Cuba." It would also dominate the Windward Passage, "the main thoroughfare for fleets, either of war or commerce, between the

North Atlantic Ocean and the Spanish Main, and the isthmus and Central America." The board also indicated that Guantánamo's capacious harbor could serve as a haven for the U.S. Atlantic Fleet, "there being no harbors for large vessels on our own coast from the Chesapeake to Pensacola, a distance of 1,350 miles." The board wanted Long to ask Roosevelt and Hay to initiate efforts to acquire Guantánamo before the United States relinquished its control of Cuba. Long subsequently notified the board that the president generally approved of their recommendations.[106]

Nevertheless, even with the Platt Amendment in place, U.S. efforts to acquire Guantánamo, or any naval station in Cuba, moved forward at a measured pace. Any assassination of a president of the United States, of course, has highly disruptive consequences for the formulation of national policy. Few men may have been better prepared or more willing to confront presidential responsibilities than Roosevelt in mid-September 1901. Still, he had to establish his own working relationship with the cabinet, build his own constituency within Congress, and, even though honoring the uncompleted promises of the martyred McKinley, he had to offer new themes that would establish his own administration.

One of those themes was to create his own positive relationship with Cuba. In his first annual message to Congress, Roosevelt sought to put recent acrimonious negotiations far behind him by noting simply that "such progress has been made toward putting the independent government of the island upon a firm footing that [soon] . . . this will be an accomplished fact." In lofty but not insincere language, Roosevelt extended the nation's "heartiest greeting and good wishes to the beautiful Queen of the Antilles as she unfolds this new page of her destiny." He then directed Congress's attention to what he termed "the vital need" to make a substantial reduction in U.S. tariffs on Cuban imports into the United States. Observing that the Cuban Constitution had "affirmed what we desired," he boldly proclaimed that, in international matters, Cuba "should stand in closer and more friendly relations with us than with any other power." In Roosevelt's view, this meant that the United States was bound by "honor and expediency to pass commercial measures in the interest of her material well-being."[107] He wisely made no mention of the requirement for naval stations.[108]

On May 20, 1902, Wood formally turned the government of Cuba over to its first elected president, Tomás Estrada Palma.[109] Estrada Palma had fought as a revolutionary in Cuba's Ten Years War (1868–1878), after which he had worked in exile with José Martí in New York, where he had become a U.S. citizen. His political aspirations for Cuba were, in many respects, similar to those of Roosevelt, but Estrada Palma advocated leasing, not selling, naval stations to the United States. He also insisted on limiting the number of U.S. bases to no more than two, neither of which would be Havana.[110]

President-Elect Palma had formally communicated these views to the United States in March 1902 in a meeting with Rear Admiral Taylor—who represented the General Board—Secretary of State Hay, and new Secretary of the Navy William H. Moody. Shortly after this meeting, the General Board sent Moody a letter stating that "in view of the fact that the settlement of affairs between the United States and Cuba seems likely to take place soon, the General Board desires to put itself on record . . . as being strongly in favor of the selection of Guantánamo as the best position for our chief naval base in Cuba."[111]

President Roosevelt, however, had not yet committed himself solely to Guantánamo and wanted to keep his options open to select other bases as well.[112] On October 23, Roosevelt wrote in a somewhat impatient tone to Secretary Hay:

Would it not be just as well to let the Cubans know at once and definitely that, whatever is done about reciprocity, the naval stations are to be ceded and in the near future? There is no intention of placing a naval station at Havana or at Santiago, but the question itself is not a matter open to discussion by the Cubans. It is already contained in their constitution, and no discussion concerning it will be entertained.[113]

On October 27, Roosevelt communicated his views directly to President Estrada Palma in response to a letter he had received on September 12. He agreed to the Cuban president's suggestion that U.S. artillerymen should withdraw from coastal fortifications, including Havana, to which they had been assigned by Governor-General Wood, but Roosevelt made the counter-proposal that these artillerymen should be transferred to the proposed naval stations instead of being recalled to the United States.[114] He expressed the hope that future communication on the subject of naval stations could be handled through normal diplomatic channels by the secretary of state. He then pointedly but politely told President Estrada Palma:

The places where our naval officers think that the stations would be most useful for the common defense of the two countries have long been well understood in a general way, and I have an impression that your people do not object to the locations proposed. As we do not ask for a station at Havana, the arrangements which I now suggest would lead to an immediate withdrawal of all the artillery-men in the neighborhood of that city and this, I suppose, would meet the main difficulty of public sentiment to which you refer in your letter.[115]

On February 16, 1903, President Estrada Palma formally agreed to lease to the United States, for coaling and naval purposes, two sites: Bahía Honda

on the north side of Cuba (near Havana), and Guantánamo Bay.[116] The
lease gave the United States the right to use and occupy the waters adjacent
to the naval stations, but also specified that "vessels engaged in the Cuban
trade shall have free passage through the waters provided in this grant."
The length of the lease was not specified and the agreement only stated that
"the United States of America agrees and covenants to pay to the Republic
of Cuba the annual sum of two thousand dollars . . . as long as the former
shall occupy and use said areas of land by virtue of the agreement."[117]

The wording regarding the issue of sovereignty in Article Three was somewhat ambiguous and, over time, Guantánamo's status would become the
subject of legal controversy and adjudication. It stated:

> While on the one hand the United States recognizes the continuance of the ulti-
> mate sovereignty of the Republic of Cuba over the above described areas of land
> and water, on the other hand the Republic of Cuba consents that during the
> period of the occupation by the United States of said areas under the terms of
> this agreement the United States shall exercise complete jurisdiction and control
> over and within said areas.[118]

In other words, even though Guantánamo would be leased and not purchased, it could remain under U.S. military control indefinitely. This meant
that its legal status as a naval base would be unique and somewhat ill-
defined. Strictly speaking, it did not belong to the United States, yet the U.S.
government could use it for whatever military purpose it deemed necessary.
What this might mean in terms of legal issues that could arise at Guantánamo, in particular those involving the extension of U.S. constitutional
remedies including due process and the writ of habeas corpus, was not addressed. Thus, from the outset, Guantánamo would be autonomous and
anomalous.

Using his power of executive order, President Roosevelt cosigned the lease
on February 23, 1903. The terms of the lease agreement specified that the
United States would pay to the Republic of Cuba the annual sum of $2,000
in gold coin. In return, Cuba granted the United States 19,621 acres of land
at Guantánamo, with 11,058 on the windward side of the bay and 8,563 on
the leeward side. The water area comprised an additional 9,196 acres, making a total acreage of 28,817 acres or 45 square miles. Within twenty-four
hours after President Estrada Palma had signed the lease, Moody wrote to
Senator Eugene Hale, chair of the Committee on Naval Affairs, to request
that Congress appropriate "not less than $100,000" to begin the develop-
ment of Guantánamo Naval Station.[119] The congressional groundwork for
Moody's request had been well prepared—several members of the Naval
Affairs Committee had recently toured Guantánamo with him and were in

a receptive mood. Consequently, the Naval Act of March 3, 1903, granted the funds requested. Indeed, the naval appropriations for 1903 were the largest Congress had ever granted and would not be equaled or surpassed until 1916.[120]

On March 24, 1903, Moody, accompanied by a congressional delegation onboard the U.S.S. *Dolphin,* announced after a formal inspection that Guantánamo would become the principal U.S. naval station in the West Indies.[121] On May 6, a joint U.S.-Cuban survey team was established to survey the bay, set the boundaries, and update maps and records. During the course of this work, the commander of the U.S.S. *Nashville* learned from Cuban engineers that a terrible water shortage existed in and around the vicinity of the bay and that previous attempts to dig successful wells had failed.[122]

Meanwhile, Estrada Palma had specified new conditions that meant additional delay in implementing the lease. He now insisted, for his own political reasons, that both the United States and Cuba obtain ratification from their respective legislative assemblies of a "permanent treaty" that would incorporate the Platt Amendment and another treaty providing for the leasing of certain areas of land and water for the Cuban naval stations. For his part, Roosevelt considered these unnecessary delaying procedures. He was also disturbed by rumors that the Cuban Congress planned to adjourn without ratifying the lease. On March 15, 1903, he asked Root, "What do you think of this? Would it not be a good plan to put our troops thus peaceably on the lands we intend to take as coaling stations?"[123]

In his public appearances during this period, however, Roosevelt presented a positive outlook for U.S.-Cuban relations, and, at the same time, put pressure on President Estrada Palma and the Cuban legislature to cooperate. Speaking in Minneapolis on April 4, Roosevelt focused his remarks on the Cuban reciprocity treaty, which the U.S. Senate had just approved. He observed that by lowering the tariff on Cuban imports, the United States was offering Cuba "her natural market," and, at the same time, widening the "market for our products."[124] He then linked Cuba to the expansion of U.S. defense requirements, saying:

> We must occupy a preponderant position in the waters and along the coasts in the region south of us; not a position over the republics of the south, but of control of the military situation so as to avoid any possible complications in the future. Under the Platt Amendment, Cuba agreed to give us certain naval stations on her coast. The Navy Department decided that we needed but two and we have specified where these two are to be.

Noting that President Palma had concluded the agreement "giving them [the naval bases] to us—an agreement which the Cuban legislative body will doubtless soon ratify," Roosevelt affirmed that "the Republic of Cuba has assumed a special relationship to our international political system, under which she gives us outposts of defense, and we are morally bound to extend to her . . . the benefits of our own economic system."[125]

On May 13, after receiving disturbing news from Hay regarding opposition in Havana to signing the Permanent Treaty, Roosevelt advised him, "I wonder if it would be possible to let the Cuban people understand as delicately as possible that those coaling stations must be ours, and that they are laying up for themselves grave trouble in the future if they do not immediately put them in our possession."[126]

This focused campaign, combining diplomacy with public pressure and "Big Stick" initiatives, finally worked. The Permanent Treaty, which incorporates the Platt Amendment, was signed on May 22, 1903. The treaty agreeing to lease Guantánamo and Bahía Honda was signed in Havana on July 2 and approved by President Roosevelt in Washington on October 2.[127] The ratifications of the lease were exchanged between the two governments in Washington on October 6.[128]

On October 28, the U.S.S. *Dixie* sailed for Guantánamo with 400 marines to attend the formal transfer of the bay to the United States and to provide a garrison for the naval station. By early November several U.S. warships were in the waters near Guantánamo as preparations got under way for the first major winter naval maneuvers of the U.S. North Atlantic Squadron to be joined by a Caribbean Squadron. The plans as reported in the *Washington Post* stated that the maneuvers would commence in December in the vicinity of Culebra, Puerto Rico, and then continue in Guantánamo from late January until the end of February 1904.[129]

On November 12, the *New York Times* announced that "without any formality, the United States has come into formal possession of the coaling station at Guantánamo."[130] In reality, U.S. Minister Squiers in Havana had notified Hay on November 9 that President Estrada Palma had advised him that it would be best if Cuba did not participate in any public ceremony of transfer.[131] Neither Squiers nor any high-ranking Cubans were present at Guantánamo at noon on December 10, 1903, when the marine brigade and five navy companies, joined by a few local Cubans, watched the raising of the U.S. flag over McCalla Hill, accompanied by the customary twenty-one-gun salute. Without any additional fanfare, Guantánamo would now be under the full control of the United States for an indefinite period.

4

The First Overseas U.S. Base

Here we are ensconced in Guantánamo Bay for ten years, and we have not raised a finger to fortify what the Russians or the Japanese, or any other predatory people, would immediately convert into a great naval station and citadel, and proudly christen "Mistress of the Caribbean."

—Stephen Bonsal

THIS SCATHING COMMENT BY ONE OF the more perceptive correspondents who had covered the Spanish-Cuban-American War captures the frustration those who labored to establish the base must have felt after repeated failures to persuade Congress to fund Guantánamo sufficiently.[1] The years from 1903 to 1933 were often challenging ones for this particular naval base when it had to cope with inadequate funding to defend its facilities and to resolve its persistent water supply problems. Nonetheless, Guantánamo continued to justify its existence as a base for rapid deployment to other sectors of Cuba and the Caribbean in times of emergency and as a critical center for training and logistics. As the opposition to the Platt Amendment both in Cuba and the United States became stronger, so did the U.S. government's determination to retain Guantánamo under a new lease that would virtually replicate the language of the 1903 treaty.

Historians who view Guantánamo merely as an enduring vestige of U.S. imperialism in Cuba have overlooked the involvement of Cubans themselves in its growth and perpetuation. Cuban political leaders, diplomats, various commercial enterprises, and workers have all participated in the development and maintenance of this unique facility. In return, it has served their interests, tangible and intangible, by providing employment, requiring multiple goods and services, facilitating a steady inflow of foreign investment, protecting major U.S. and Cuban enterprises, and serving as a stage for political debate and diplomatic negotiation between two vastly unequal powers. The latter is especially true because it provided Cuba with a forum it otherwise would have lacked. As this chapter will show, there has been nothing static about this base. Like the Platt Amendment itself, it has often been the focal point of competing, even clashing interests, both Cuban and American. It is true that Cuba has never been given a free hand to determine Guantánamo's future nor has it been in a position to forcibly change the

95

status quo. In short, Guantánamo's endurance as an overseas U.S. fortress has often required Cuban acquiescence, but it has also enabled the two nations to address and even resolve bilateral frictions.

The navy secretary's report at the end of 1903 provides insight into the plans and hopes for the significant role the Guantánamo Naval Station would fulfill in the Caribbean region concurrent with the establishment of the U.S. Caribbean Squadron. Secretary of the Navy William Moody wrote that by 1902 the Navy Department had found it necessary to station ships constantly in the West Indies and the Caribbean to protect U.S. interests and "those of other nations committed to our care," maintain order, and fulfill the treaty obligations of the U.S. government. He recounted that the North Atlantic Fleet had conducted important maneuvers in Caribbean waters in 1902 and that, in recognition of the region's growing naval and commercial importance, the navy had now created a Caribbean division of the North Atlantic Fleet with the Caribbean Squadron as "a separate and permanent organization." This decision may have reflected the thinking of the newly created Joint Army and Navy Board, whose primary purpose was to serve as the military's final reviewing authority for U.S. war plans.[2]

> The squadron will have ultimately as its base the naval station at Guantánamo, and will be composed of swift cruisers and light vessels able to proceed speedily to points where the protection of American interests or the fulfillment of American duties is demanded. . . . The duty of this squadron is preeminently that of coast defense, but it will constitute a reserve force ready in case of need to cooperate with the principal fleet in the West Indies.[3]

This vision of Guantánamo's future role would often clash with the more parochial concerns of members of Congress whose decisions on naval appropriations would become law.

To comprehend the reasons for growing congressional opposition to granting the total amount requested by the secretary of the navy annually for Guantánamo, beginning with the 1904 hearings on naval appropriations, it is necessary to understand the dramatic growth of the naval budget that occurred under President Theodore Roosevelt. From 1901 to 1905, total naval appropriations rose from $85,000,000 to $118,000,000, an unprecedented record for a peacetime administration.[4] The requests for Guantánamo had to compete with those for other naval stations as well as the more exorbitant costs of building and equipping the new battleships Roosevelt wanted for his "Great White Fleet." As Bradley Reynolds argues in his comprehensive discussion of the 1904 naval budgetary debate as it applied to Guantánamo, the central issue for Congress was simply priorities.[5] It was not whether to grant the funds necessary to make it a functioning naval station but rather "how far and how quickly to proceed in Cuba" given other requests for significant outlays in the same budget. The competing demands were to fund other important bases such as Subic Bay and Pearl Harbor, to build first-class battleships and armored cruisers equipped with the most advanced ordnance, and to satisfy congressional constituents, particularly in districts that already had their own naval stations with unmet needs.[6]

The arguments against granting Guantánamo the full appropriation of $1,015,000 requested by Moody ranged from contentions that the United States should spend more money instead to develop Key West as the principal base in the Caribbean, or that money would be better spent on Subic Bay to secure the Philippines, to criticism of Guantánamo's vulnerability to attack from its surrounding hills and its lack of an adequate water supply. Guantánamo's ability to defend itself became more questionable following Japan's successful attack on the Russian naval base at Port Arthur on February 8, 1904. That Japanese guns had decimated the Russian squadron at anchor without invading the port was not lost on perceptive U.S. military leaders, including Governor-General Leonard Wood. In subsequent letters to the War Department, Wood pointed out the similar weaknesses in defenses between Port Arthur and Subic Bay and, by implication, Guantánamo. Hills surround all of these bases, from which enemy artillery could, and in Port Arthur's case did, command the harbor. The unanswered question raised by Wood and others was, Could forward bases ever be adequately fortified?[7]

Several senior naval officers now objected to spending money to develop Guantánamo. Some argued that a naval station closer to the future canal, perhaps on the isthmus at Chiriqui Lagoon or Almirante Bay, Colombia, would provide better protection for the most valuable future U.S. asset. Other influential officers, especially forceful proponent of naval modernization Lieutenant Commander William S. Sims, wanted budgetary emphasis placed instead on building larger battleships with more powerful ordnance.[8]

Ironically, the attack on Port Arthur and other Japanese naval victories also had some positive consequences for Guantánamo. One of the lessons learned by U.S. naval strategists was that a fatal weakness of the Russians had been the wide dispersion of their fleet. The War College joined with Alfred Thayer Mahan in calling for an Atlantic concentration of the U.S. Fleet, and later a subsequent navy secretary, Charles Bonaparte, ordered all battleships out of the Pacific.[9] This fleet would soon be conducting its winter maneuvers in Caribbean waters with gunnery and war-simulation exercises in the capacious harbor of Guantánamo.[10]

When Congress finally approved the naval bill on April 27, 1904, it allotted to Guantánamo $385,000, plus the $600,000 that Moody received in general funding for naval stations. Following a study of the base's construction needs, which had been requested by the General Board, civil engineer C. A. Wentworth estimated that a fully equipped station at Toro Cay would cost $4 to $6 million.[11] Alternatively, a station built at the southeast corner of the bay would be more accessible to the sea, but would also be more expensive because of the need to fortify it. Wentworth had also investigated the water supply problem, and doubted that drilling efforts around the base would be successful. He advised that the Navy Department investigate the possibilities of having water delivered by trains or by pipes from the Yateras River. Wentworth submitted construction plans for several buildings including a hospital, storehouses for coal and other supplies, and an estimate for clearing the area of dense tropical growth. He promised to develop plans for wharves and a dry dock, but was still undecided where to build them at the lowest expense and greatest efficiency. Obviously, labor costs could be kept lower by hiring nearby Cuban workers.[12]

In late February 1904, Admiral George Dewey, in his role as chair of the General Board, visited Guantánamo to get his own firsthand impression of the projected naval station. While there, he observed the winter maneuvers of the North Atlantic Fleet, including nighttime target practice of U.S. warships.[13] This experience inspired Dewey to become a forceful advocate for developing Guantánamo into a major facility. On May 2, Dewey, on behalf of the board, sent a long memorandum to Moody endorsing the plans to develop Guantánamo and arguing that the base could be effectively defended from an enemy attack by forts on both sides of the entrance to the bay. It also argued that, because of the proximity of the United States, adequate military reinforcement would arrive before any enemy could seize the naval station. On May 19, Dewey again wrote the navy secretary to inform him that the General Board strongly recommended that he expedite the development of the base beginning at Cay del Toro, noting that, in the event of war, Guantánamo would be important not merely as a supply depot but as an advanced base to facilitate the wartime operations of the Atlantic Fleet throughout the Caribbean region. In 1904, Dewey requested temporary leave from his duties at the General Board to direct the winter maneuvers of the combined fleet at Guantánamo, but illness subsequently prevented him from assuming this command.[14]

Dewey's recommendations persuaded Moody to organize a planning group, known as the Swift Board, on June 7, 1904, whose assignment was to design and designate locations for docks, repair shops, barracks and officers' quarters, and everything else that would enable Guantánamo to repair twelve naval vessels simultaneously. By July 11 the Swift Board had completed its report.[15] Plans called for a full naval station to be built at Toro Cay, with a dry dock that could accommodate first-class battleships and a fully equipped Marine Corps post with drill field and exercise facilities to be located near Granadillo Point. In response to notices of contracts being let and job opportunities, Cuban, Chinese, and American construction workers soon began arriving at Guantánamo. Their initial efforts, however, were slowed by the difficulty in clearing the land and a poor site selection for the dry dock.[16]

It is significant that the navy sidestepped the issue of providing for Guantánamo's outer defenses. Neither Dewey nor Navy Secretaries Moody or Paul Morton asked the Swift Board to address Guantánamo's defense needs. The Navy Department took the position that it was the army's responsibility to defend the base. Nonetheless, the debate continued over the defensibility of Guantánamo and other forward naval bases.

When the hearings on the proposed naval bill for 1905–1906 began in December 1904, congressional resistance to new funding for Guantánamo promised to be stronger than the year before, in part because of the heated, unresolved debate over the defensibility of forward bases, plus the fact that some of the monies appropriated the year before had not been spent. Obtaining sufficient funding for Guantánamo was further complicated by the reality that Roosevelt was trying to chart his ambitious and costly naval policy from the White House. Roosevelt tried in letters to Speaker of the House Joseph Cannon and to the chair of the House Naval Affairs Committee, George E. Foss, to persuade them that the defense of U.S. interests required a "thoroughly efficient fighting navy." On December 27, the president told Cannon, "I want to go on with building up the navy, not merely for the sake of building it up, but for the sake of letting other nations see that our policy is definite and permanent."[17] Two weeks later, after he had approved special funding for ordnance at Guantánamo, Roosevelt sent a similar message to Foss informing him that "heavy battleships are what we need," and "it would be a serious misfortune to the whole country if at this time there should be a halt in the work of upbuilding the Navy." When Foss replied that he did not want to halt naval appropriations but felt a "disposition to let the navy program go over for a year," he received a swift rebuke from the president, who told him that his obstructionist attitude was a violation of "the plighted faith of Republican Party principles and an attack upon the honor of the nation."[18] Realistically, however, Roosevelt knew there were limits to how far and fast he could push Congress to build up the U.S. Navy, and, given his other priorities and the demands of the presidency, those limits had been reached. On March 3, 1905, the Senate approved a naval appropriations bill that allocated $300,000 to be divided among U.S.

coaling deposits including Guantánamo. Roosevelt signed the bill into law. On March 9, he conveyed a tone both of pride and philosophical resignation to his good friend Leonard Wood:

> Take it on the whole I have gotten an astonishing proportion of what I set out to get. When I became President three years ago I made up my mind that I should try for a fleet with a minimum strength of forty armor-clads; and though the difficulty of getting what I wished has increased from year to year I have now reached my mark. . . . For some years now we can afford to rest and merely replace the ships that are worn out or become obsolete while we bring up the personnel.[19]

Roosevelt did not mention Guantánamo or any other naval base in this letter, but the message was clear: the president would not risk any more political capital during the rest of his administration to fight for increased funding for the construction or fortification of offshore naval bases. He would, however, continue to discuss these issues with his intimate and like-minded associates, in particular Admiral Dewey and his brother-in-law and future rear admiral William S. Cowles.

Having failed to achieve its funding objectives for Guantánamo, the navy high command began to seek alternative ways to strengthen the base.[20] On February 7, 1905, in response to a plaintive request from the General Board, Morton wrote all the captains of the Atlantic Fleet asking their views on the defensibility and possible uses of Guantánamo. One of the respondents, Captain William H. Southerland, who had considerable experience in Caribbean waters, listed Guantánamo's defensive weaknesses as "its openness to attack from all directions [and] the inability of the surrounding country to furnish necessary supplies." Nonetheless, Southland recommended that Guantánamo be used for naval exercises and drills as well as coaling "even though we will not have a reasonable feeling that this base can be defended from enemy attack."[21]

Other officers suggested that the United States enlarge Guantánamo. Cowles, who was commanding the U.S.S. *Missouri*, advised that to do something about Guantánamo's defenses, the United States should control "the back country and adjacent coasts" to Guantánamo Bay. He believed this would not only give the base more adequate defenses but also improve relations with Cuba by demonstrating "that our protectorate is not one merely on paper," but one that would defend Cuban as well as U.S. interests. The commandant of Guantánamo, Commander Charles Rogers, agreed with Cowles. He advocated that the State Department make every effort to secure the hills around the base, since this would be the only way the United States could protect the station.[22]

Taking these responses into account, on April 26, 1905, the General Board wrote Secretary Morton urging him to ask the State Department to reopen negotiations with the Cubans to enlarge the base's perimeter. In the board's words, "It should be impressed upon the Cuban authorities that it is imperative for the assurance of their own political integrity that Guantánamo be securely held by the United States."[23] Despite the board's repeated requests, neither Morton nor his immediate successor, Charles Bonaparte, undertook any initiative to enhance Guantánamo's natural defenses. It may be, as Bradley Reynolds has suggested, that Roosevelt and his new secretary of state, Elihu Root, were unwilling to reengage with the Cuban government in seeking to enlarge the base, especially since a similar request made in 1902 had been flatly rejected.

It was Commandant Rogers who first proposed that the United States seek to exchange its unwanted lease at Bahía Honda for an enlargement of the naval station at Guantánamo. In his lengthy memorandum to the secretary of the navy on May 2, 1906, Rogers said he believed, as the result of many conversations he had with Cubans, that they would be more willing to accept an extension of Guantánamo's perimeter than a large U.S. naval presence at Bahía Honda given its proximity to Havana. The General Board agreed with Commander Rogers, and, in an official statement on June 20, observed that Bahía Honda "is not and never will be of particular benefit to the United States," and recommended that "as the extension of the present boundary of Guantánamo would benefit the naval station . . . the Secretary of State be requested to take such steps as may be necessary to secure an exchange."[24]

Increasingly the major consideration involved in enlarging Guantánamo was the need for potable water. In spring 1907 there was such a severe drought that the city of Santiago made an appeal to the base for water, and, to maintain good relations, Commandant Albert Ackerman immediately sent 180,000 gallons to help alleviate the crisis at the expense of Guantánamo's own needs.[25]

Official requests from the Navy Department to the State Department to engage with the Cuban government to make specific changes in the boundaries of Guantánamo Naval Station were sent on April 4, 1907, and again on July 13. Diplomatic efforts to persuade the Cuban government to exchange Bahía Honda in return for an enlargement of Guantánamo commenced on July 17, when the State Department instructed the U.S. minister in Havana to open negotiations with the Cuban government. A tentative agreement was signed in Havana on December 27, 1912, but the Cuban Senate subsequently postponed indefinitely its ratification of the new treaty. [26]

Senior U.S. officials had considered using the Isle of Pines as a potential site for a U.S. naval base in Cuba because of its size—approximately eleven hundred square miles—and its location, which is due south of Havana. This issue, however, was complicated by the Isle of Pines' undefined territorial status. Because the Platt Amendment, which delimited Cuba's boundaries, had failed to mention the isle, it became an ongoing subject of bilateral contention, with both U.S. and Cuban diplomats claiming it. The U.S. Department of State prepared a draft treaty in 1904 renouncing any territorial claim to the Isle of Pines, but the U.S. Senate postponed taking any definitive action. Diplomatic historian Lester Langley has attributed this delay to the obstructionist influence of U.S. investors who had already begun to settle and invest in the isle. According to Langley, "The investors, of course, opposed the 1904 treaty and fought its ratification successfully for twenty years on the argument that, if Cuba resumed domination over the island, they would be taxed heavily."[27]

In January 1906, Senator Joseph B. Foraker, chair of the subcommittee of the Senate Foreign Relations Committee designated to determine the legal status of the Isle of Pines, published a report recommending that, since the United States had already leased Guantánamo and Bahía Honda, an additional naval base on the Isle of Pines was unnecessary.

The issue of the Isle of Pines' legal status was only resolved definitively on March 24, 1925, when the United States proclaimed a new treaty in which it formally relinquished to Cuba all claim of title to the Isle of Pines. As Janet D. Frost observed in her study of this historical issue, "This treaty had been awaiting ratification for over twenty years." Langley has also noted that the wording of the 1925 treaty protected the investments of isle property owners from the United States.[28]

In the early 1900s, U.S. expansionist moves in the Caribbean attracted favorable attention from Great Britain's redoubtable naval strategist, Admiral John Arbuthnot "Jackie" Fisher. He and other British leaders also saw recent improvements in Anglo-American relations, most notably the Hay-Pauncefote Treaty of 1901, as proof that Britain accepted the fact that the United States reigned supreme in the Panamanian Isthmus and neighboring Caribbean waters.[29] Far from viewing the enhanced U.S. naval presence in the region as constituting any threat to nearby British possessions, Fisher could not conceive of any justification for a future Anglo-American conflict. On the contrary, he predicted that, of all possible war scenarios, "a fight with our cousin across the Atlantic is perhaps the most improbable."[30]

As a man of action as well as a naval strategist, Fisher mounted efforts to persuade Britain's senior policymakers that it would serve their best interests to withdraw British warships from the Caribbean and thus permit the United States to safeguard both nations' interests in those waters. Fisher had long viewed the dispersal of the Royal Navy Fleet around the globe as costly and ill-advised.[31] In 1902, in a letter to Lord Charles Beresford, who served simultaneously as a rear admiral and member of Parliament, Fisher confided, "Just look at the mass of small craft we have in commission all over the world. They can neither fight nor run away. . . . Burn them all at once and damn the Consuls and Foreign Office! It can be proved absolutely that no necessity exists for isolated vessels on any station whatever. All vessels should be with the flag, or working in detached squadrons to give squadron leaders experience. The curse of the Navy are small non-fighting, isolated ships, absorbing valuable officers and men and all deteriorating."[32]

Beresford quickly accepted Fisher's reasoning, and together the two men began to press for closer Anglo-American naval cooperation. The strategic thinking of Fisher and Beresford almost certainly took into account the recent sizable expansion of both the German and Russian Navies, although some historians have cautioned that the German threat to British interests should not be overstated. According to Fisher's biographer, Richard Hough, in the early 1900s Britain's military leaders regarded France as their most likely adversary and based their war planning and maneuvers on this premise. Fisher, however, was more concerned about a potential challenge from Germany. In November 1901, he confided to the *Times* naval correspondent, James Thursfield, "I have always been an enthusiastic advocate for friendship and alliance with France. They never have and never will interfere with our trade. . . . The Germans are our natural enemies everywhere." In any case, Donald Yerxa is almost certainly justified in his observation that "by 1902, Fisher had concluded that the Royal Navy was unable to meet the plethora of potential challenges to its command of the world's oceans."[33]

On November 27, 1903, a *New York Herald* article proposed that U.S. and British squadrons engage in joint maneuvers in the Caribbean during the month of January. Both British and U.S. sources credited Beresford as the primary instigator of this initiative, which received stronger initial endorsement from U.S. naval officers than their British counterparts. Nevertheless, the *New York Herald* continued to keep the issue alive in leading articles and editorials.[34]

For his part, Fisher, as commander of Britain's powerful Mediterranean Fleet, had proposed in 1902 to his superiors that the North American and West Indies Squadron be abolished, with its warships to be reassigned to Gibraltar to act as a swing fleet between Great Britain and the Mediterranean. The Royal Navy did not adopt Fisher's proposal, however, until November

1904, one month after he had taken command as first sea lord. By that time, Fisher had built considerable government support for redistributing the fleet, and the admiralty stamped its final approval in early December. Moreover, as Jan Morris has revealed, an order in privy council had made Fisher, unlike any of his predecessors, solely responsible for ensuring the fighting effectiveness of the British Fleet, and ordered him specifically to cut its enormous costs. By the time he completed his reforms, "the Navy was no longer an imperial exhibition, but essentially a European weapon of war based upon the North Sea."[35] Accordingly, the Royal Navy began to withdraw warships from its bases at Halifax, Jamaica, St. Lucia, and Ascension Island, and to reduce its presence in Bermuda. As a sop to British interests in the West Indies, who had complained vociferously that U.S. influence in the Caribbean would escalate dramatically, the admiralty agreed to an annual visit by the Fourth Cruiser Squadron, based at Devonport, and also to retain one third-class cruiser in West Indian waters. Fisher did not doubt that the United States would move swiftly to fill any void caused by the departure of the British Fleet. In *Naval Necessities,* he predicted, "In the Western Hemisphere the United States are forming a navy the power and size of which will be limited only by the amount of money which the American people choose to spend on it."[36]

By the end of 1905, Britain no longer maintained a strategic naval presence in the Caribbean. In that same year, a U.S. marine visiting the British garrison on St. Lucia reported, "The Officer commanding the troops stated that he thought the island would be turned over to the United States. Even the small darkies on the streets greeted us with cries of 'The Yankees are coming.'"[37]

The United States, however, was reluctant to light the torch by intervening in Cuba in September 1906 to address issues of growing insurrection and political paralysis. Simply stated, the problems of governance had originated in the months prior to the scheduled presidential elections of 1905, when President Tomás Estrada Palma, now seventy years old and increasingly feeble, proved unwilling to risk the virtually certain election of Liberal opposition leader General José Miguel Gómez and his corrupt vice presidential running mate, Alfredo Zayas. Estrada Palma may have been unfit to continue to lead the nation, but he was known to be scrupulously honest. Both Estrada Palma and his Moderate followers feared that Gómez and Zayas, if allowed to take office, would loot the surplus in the treasury. Accordingly, Estrada Palma and his forceful secretary of the interior, Freyre de Andrade—who was in charge of domestic security—began systematically to fire all government employees who were not Moderates. The Liberals, realizing that they had no chance of winning an election, withdrew their candidates, and, on December

1, 1905, Estrada Palma won reelection without opposition. The Liberals then went into open armed rebellion, which included several pitched battles with police and rural guards along Cuban railway lines, and by early September 1906, Cuba appeared to be on the brink of civil war.[38]

On September 9, 1906, Roosevelt wrote his friend eminent British historian George Trevelyan that widespread revolt had broken out on the island and that the Cuban government had just notified him that it intended to ask the United States to intervene forcibly within the next week. He told Trevelyan in confidence that he had replied with "a most emphatic protest against their doing so." He then described his quandary: "On the one hand we cannot permanently see Cuba a prey to misrule and anarchy; on the other hand I loathe the thought of assuming any control over the island such as we have over Porto Rico [*sic*] and the Philippines. We emphatically do not want it."[39]

On September 8 the consul-general in Havana, Frank Steinhart, had cabled Washington that Estrada Palma wanted Roosevelt to send two vessels immediately—one to Havana and the other to Cienfuegos. Two days later, the White House agreed reluctantly to dispatch the ships, but did not assign them any specific mission. In his cable to Steinhart, Acting Secretary of State Robert Bacon indicated that Roosevelt had no intention of intervening until the Cuban government had "exhausted every effort to put down the insurrection and had made this fact evident to the world." Then on September 12 Steinhart notified Bacon that the rebellion had increased in several provinces, including Havana, and that the Cuban government had "no elements to contain it, to defend the towns and prevent the rebels from destroying property. President Estrada Palma asks for American intervention, and begs that Roosevelt send to Havana with rapidity two or three thousand men."[40] After conferring with Navy Secretary Bonaparte, Roosevelt authorized the U.S. Navy to send three battleships, a cruiser, and the transport *Dixie* with a marine battalion to Havana to protect U.S. interests and fulfill the nation's obligations to Cuba. He also dispatched Secretary of War William H. Taft and Bacon to restore order.

What Roosevelt and Taft feared most and worked assiduously to avoid was the outbreak of a guerrilla war in Cuba. As military historian Allan Millett rightly interprets the U.S. administration's concern, "Such a war [coming in the aftermath of the Philippine insurrection] would likely strip the United States of troops, become expensive in lives and money, and be enormously costly with the American voter."[41] In this context, neither Roosevelt nor Taft wanted to exacerbate nationalist tensions unnecessarily by making Guantánamo the port of U.S. naval intervention. Fortunately, such an action was unwarranted as most of the insurgent violence was confined to northern Cuba, and U.S.-owned sugar plantations near Guantánamo were never endangered. The marines at Guantánamo were in a state of readiness for possible action, and a train at nearby Caimanéra was made available for military transport if needed, which it was not.[42]

In Havana, however, events quickly forced Roosevelt's hand. Taft and Bacon sought repeatedly to patch together a compromise, but as it became apparent that they could not secure any modus vivendi between the contending factions, Roosevelt authorized Taft to land the marines and to take control if the Cuban government should fall. When Estrada Palma and his cabinet resigned in the late evening of September 28, Taft saw no alternative but to establish an administration under the authority of the president of the United States, and to name himself as provisional governor of Cuba. The proclamation that he issued on the following morning sought to make the U.S. occupation as palatable as possible. The provisional government would be maintained only long enough to restore order, peace, and public confidence; the Cuban flag would continue to fly over government buildings; and it would be a Cuban government "conforming as far as may be to the constitution of Cuba." There was, of course, no mention of the Platt Amendment in Taft's proclamation, but it was evident to everyone that the second U.S. military occupation of Cuba had begun.[43]

There is no evidence that Roosevelt, Taft, Bacon, or even Bonaparte foresaw any advantages to the U.S. Navy resulting from the new military occupation of Cuba, but approximately forty-eight hours before Taft issued his proclamation, the commander of the Atlantic Fleet, Admiral John Pillsbury, wrote the General Board to suggest: "If we gain temporary possession [of Cuba] once more, would it not be a fitting time for the General Board to urge upon the Department the absolute necessity of enlarging the present concession as including the summits of hills surrounding . . . Guantánamo Bay?"

The General Board obviously liked Pillsbury's suggestion. On October 2, 1906, the board, speaking through Admiral Dewey, replied that it believed the expansion of Guantánamo would be very desirable, and it would press the State Department to propose a possible exchange of Bahía Honda for an enlarged Guantánamo.[44]

Soon another high-ranking naval officer would add his voice to that of Pillsbury and Dewey in advocating that Guantánamo be strengthened. Having recently been promoted to rear admiral, Cowles communicated his views on the importance of developing Guantánamo into a first-class naval station to the House Naval Affairs Committee on December 13, 1906. Cowles, who succeeded Admiral Royal B. Bradford as chief of the Bureau of Equipment, was an influential naval spokesman in his own right, but it is virtually certain that his statement had the full support of the White House.[45] Cowles began by noting that a "very good beginning" had been made to render Guantánamo "an efficient repair and supply base," but he advocated that it become a "stronger fortified and equipped naval base" given its strategic location, which "is essential to the protection of the Panama Canal and our trade interests." Moreover, if a future war should take place in Atlantic waters, Cowles argued that the most probable theater would be in the Caribbean, where "our battle fleet must have a fortified base where ships can refuel with coal, stores, and ammunition and repair damages quickly." He observed that, in peacetime, ships could easily be repaired in home yards, but, if war came to the Caribbean, damaged ships would have to be repaired in the theater and quickly. "The absence of one or two ships might mean the loss of our control, and this cannot be risked."

Cowles clearly did not see modern battleships with powerful ordnance as being a more important budgetary concern than the strategically positioned Guantánamo. To him, both were essential components of an effective naval defense zone. He reasoned, "Control of a maritime region is insured primarily by a navy; secondly by positions, suitably chosen and spaced one from the other, upon which as bases the navy rests, and from which it exercises strength." He ended his request to make Guantánamo the key base in the region by asserting that it could equal the future canal in its strategic importance: "The entrance to the Caribbean, and its transit across the Caribbean to the Isthmus, are two prime essentials. . . . Therefore, in case of war, control of these two things becomes a military objective not second to the Isthmian canal itself, access to which depends on them. . . . The strategic center of interest for both the Gulf and the Caribbean is to be found in the Windward Passage."[46]

Despite Cowles's fine strategic reasoning, various members of Congress made strong arguments against enlarging or fortifying Guantánamo at that moment. As already mentioned, most of the political disturbances that had forced the U.S. intervention were near Havana. As a consequence, the War Department's top priorities had shifted from southeastern to northwestern Cuba. Second, the need to prepare outposts to defend the future canal or traffic passing through it was not a pressing one because construction at Panama had only begun. Finally, neither the War Department nor the State Department, nor even the White House, wanted to reawaken Cuban hostilities toward the U.S. naval presence at Guantánamo by exploiting the military/political intervention in Cuba as a pretext for enlarging the naval station. Certainly the Roosevelt administration did not want to risk inciting an insurrection in Cuba similar to the rebellion it had confronted in the Philippines.

Another important argument for developing Guantánamo was made by its new commandant, Albert Ackerman, whose assumption of command had coincided with the U.S. intervention. Ackerman recognized the potential value of Guantánamo City as a nearby resource to help fulfill the naval base's unmet needs, including its demands for a local workforce and its more pressing requirement for potable water.[47] He therefore asked the Navy Department for an appropriation of $85,000 for the fiscal year 1907–1908 to purchase water from Guantánamo City and to begin construction of a 200-million-gallon reservoir. He estimated that the base used 150,000 gallons of water per day, and he also mentioned that the station needed eventually to build a pipe to the Yateras River about eight miles away. Ackerman cautioned, however, that such a pipe would run through Cuban territory, which at the moment was "undesirable."[48]

Rear Admiral Robley D. Evans, the new commander of the Atlantic Fleet, shared Ackerman's concerns. When he was at Guantánamo in late December 1906 for the winter maneuvers, he observed that "the water supply was totally inadequate, though there was a fine river running through the country only a few miles away."[49] He subsequently pressed the matter with the Navy Department, and in early February 1907 received permission to survey the Yateras River to determine how much water it could supply to the naval station. The survey team, accompanied by Evans, estimated that the flow of water was 10 million gallons per day, and, having interviewed local inhabitants, reported that the river had not been dry for more than twenty years. Its report, recommending that the navy extend Guantánamo's boundary to encompass the Yateras, went to the General Board in mid-February, which in turn forwarded it to the joint Army-Navy Board, which recommended to the State Department that negotiations be reopened with the Cubans to resolve water and defense problems at Guantánamo.

Despite these various initiatives to provide for the needs of the naval base and enhance its capabilities, congressional opposition to granting the funds requested by the secretary of the navy remained firm. In the 1907–1908 proposed budget, the Navy Department asked for $704,800 for Guantánamo, but the House Naval Affairs Committee recommended $0. The committee made substantial cuts in the requests for all other bases, but Charleston received $239,000; Norfolk, $235,000; and Subic Bay obtained $115,000. The two subsequent years were equally dismal: in 1908–1909, the navy secretary requested $425,000 for Guantánamo; the committee again recommended $0. This time, Subic Bay also failed to get an appropriation, but Pearl Harbor received the full $1,000,000 requested. In 1909–1910, the navy asked for $450,000 for Guantánamo, and Congress approved $0. Subic

Bay was also bypassed, but once again Pearl Harbor garnered $900,000 of the $1,300,000 requested.[50]

The congressional arguments against funding Guantánamo during the annual hearings, described in detail by Bradley Reynolds, were fairly consistent over time. Objections focused on Guantánamo's proximity to coastal Gulf stations (Key West, Pensacola, and New Orleans), the carryover of unspent discretionary funding, the administration's pressure to build more battleships, and the objections of some to all increases in naval spending, particularly in peacetime. Additionally, by 1908 both Congress and naval policymakers had seen the Great White Fleet complete its sail around the world, coaled almost exclusively by colliers. In the minds of many observers, including Dewey, the future need for offshore coaling stations would be much reduced. This collective opposition forced Roosevelt to prioritize his administration's requests to fund naval stations, as illustrated in his communications with Cannon in 1908. On February 21, Roosevelt urged Cannon to pay attention to the "defenses of the naval base at Guantánamo, Cuba." He noted that "they are very far from completion" and that "Guantánamo will be the main naval base of the United States in the Caribbean and the principal guard of the Atlantic entrance of the Panama Canal." He emphasized that it would take approximately as long to complete these defenses as it would to build the canal. In the same letter, however, Roosevelt urgently called attention to the lack of defenses at Pearl Harbor, where "not a single gun is mounted to defend the harbor," and he placed even greater importance on the future role of Pearl Harbor in defending U.S. interests throughout the Pacific region. After receiving Cannon's strong objections (by letter and conversation) to his naval program, on February 29, Roosevelt restricted his requests to "the fortification of Hawaii and the establishment of a naval station at Pearl Harbor." The appropriations bill for Pearl Harbor subsequently passed the House by a vote of 246 to 1.[51]

Budgetary figures and debates over appropriations, however, tell only part of the story. Eyewitness impressions of Guantánamo by such different personalities as Admiral Evans and journalist-diplomat Stephen Bonsal provide unique insights into Guantánamo's deficiencies and its unrealized potential. During his inspection in late 1906 and early 1907, Evans found that "a few small frame houses had been built for the accommodation of the officers on duty there, and tents put up for the marines who guarded the property." He was most impressed by Guantánamo's small-arm target range, which he proclaimed "the finest to be found anywhere in the world," and he also foresaw that the base would become an important training station "from which, as a safe anchorage, our rapidly growing fleet may manoeuvre and drill with the greatest possible advantage." At the same time, he sadly reported with regard to its defenses, "The army engineers have selected sites for mortar batteries and twelve-inch guns . . . [but] Congress has refused to appropriate more money, and in consequence all work must stop."[52] In contrast, Bonsal, who as a correspondent before and during the War of 1898 had done as much as any journalist to sensitize his U.S. readers to the sufferings of the Cuban people, wrote bitterly on his subsequent visit in 1908: "Today Guantánamo, the Vladivostok of the American Mediterranean, is only defended by its high and ancient renown, by an unarmoured receiving-ship with rubber plants and other trees growing out of its deck, that looks as if it had come, not for a career of conquest, but to stick fast in the mud for all time."[53]

Meanwhile, Guantánamo was proving its value as a naval station in new, dramatic, and unanticipated ways. U.S. naval forces at Guantánamo demonstrated their ability to respond quickly to a natural disaster elsewhere in the Caribbean following the massive earthquake that struck Kingston, Jamaica, midafternoon on January 14, 1907. The following day, the British governor, Alexander Swettenham, wired G. W. E. Griffith, the British minister in Havana, "Kindly send immediately bandages, lint, and wool for those injured by earthquake at cost of Colony."[54] Griffith, in turn, appealed to Cuba's provisional governor, Charles Magoon, for help.[55] Magoon then instructed Evans to send needed supplies by torpedo boat from Guantánamo to Kingston. Evans ordered two battleships, the *Indiana* and the *Missouri,* and the destroyer *Whipple,* under the command of Admiral Charles Davis, to leave for Kingston shortly after noon on January 16. The *Whipple* had reached Kingston by midnight, with Davis onboard, and the two battleships arrived around 7:30 A.M. on January 17. Davis quickly dispatched forces to work as "wrecking parties" under Jamaican supervision, distribute provisions, protect the U.S. consulate, help suppress a mutiny at the penitentiary, police the streets, bury the dead, and establish a makeshift emergency hospital on the grounds of a U.S. Jesuit mission in Winchester Park.[56] Governor Swettenham, who resented the U.S. relief actions, asked Davis on January 18 to "re-embark [his] working parties." Davis ordered his working parties to return to their ships, but because he had made arrangements for the *Missouri* to be coaled, he did not set sail until 4:00 P.M. on January 19. In the meantime, because the emergency hospital was on U.S. property, the surgeons and support staff continued to treat injured patients until January 19. When Davis left Kingston, he reported that the city was "a complete ruin," with shocking sanitary conditions and an insufferable stench.

The incident generated a short-lived diplomatic uproar in London and Washington and, to some extent, in Jamaica as other British officials, including the mayor of Kingston and the British archbishop of the West Indies, rushed to apologize for Swettenham's ingratitude and unseemly behavior. Even Swettenham reconsidered his actions and wrote brief thank-you notes to Root and Davis after being persuaded by his superiors to accept a new and much-needed shipment of about one hundred U.S. army tents for destitute refugees.

What remains ignored, however, is the alacrity and purposeful nature of the emergency response out of Guantánamo.[57] Somewhat buried in the press reports was the gratitude expressed for the food, medicine, and care and assistance provided by U.S. medical personnel and well-trained blue jackets.[58] According to one report, although it was in operation for less than two days, the emergency hospital treated more than fifty patients, including people with broken bones, fractured skulls, and cases of blood poisoning.[59]

By comparison, it is worth recalling that one year prior to the establishment of the naval base at Guantánamo, the United States had received an urgent call to respond to the disastrous volcanic eruption of Mount Pelée on May 8, 1902, which destroyed the city of St. Pierre on the island of Martinique in the French West Indies. On May 12, Roosevelt informed Congress that 30,000 had died and 50,000 were left homeless and in desperate need. He requested an immediate appropriation of $500,000, and he also directed the Navy Department and War Department to undertake relief efforts for the benefit of these stricken people.[60] On May 14, the U.S.S. *Dixie,* loaded with provisions, military officers, reporters, and scientists, sailed from New York. The voyage took seven days, and according to the *New York Times,* when the *Dixie* arrived in Fort de France it was met by local boats loaded with bread, fruit, and milk for sale. "There were already enough provisions on hand to provide for the refugees for about six months." The *Dixie* then sailed to nearby St. Vincent, where it discovered that the eruption of La Soufriere—also on May 8—had created widespread distress and that the need for relief was greater there than on Martinique.[61]

In the last year of the Roosevelt administration, the long-term funding prospects for Guantánamo brightened. Even though major funding for the base was not forthcoming, a definite and favorable shift in the attitude of Congress was evident in naval budgetary discussions in which Guantánamo's proponents made convincing arguments regarding its proven attributes as a training facility and its strategic value. They also made invidious comparisons with the inefficiency and waste evident in many domestic naval yards that had received more favorable consideration because of their political and economic influence. New advocates for increased spending at selected naval stations began to emerge, particularly in the U.S. Senate. Senator Eugene Hale, who was both chair of the Naval Affairs Committee and majority leader, made the point that, in a naval budget that had reached almost $137 million, less than $5 million would go to naval yards and stations. He also compared the total amount of $51 million that the United States had invested in all its yards and stations with the nearly $127 million Great Britain had allocated to three yards.[62]

Hale's advocacy of increased spending for U.S. naval yards evoked criticism from two senators, Joseph Dixon from Montana and Robert La Follette from Wisconsin. Dixon favored an overall reduction in spending for domestic navy yards, and called attention to the fact that most members of the Naval Affairs Committee had navy yards in their states—he accused them of serving their own interests. La Follette agreed with Dixon, but he also pointed to Guantánamo, which he said every naval authority agreed was of great strategic value but was "going to destruction" without any funding because it was not in any particular district or state. He supported his criticism with figures from the Navy Department's annual reports showing that the expenses at many navy yards greatly exceeded the value of the work done there. La Follette's arguments made telling distinctions between Guantánamo and other naval yards upon which naval policymakers would soon build.[63]

The election of Roosevelt's hand-picked successor, William H. Taft, in 1909 brought to the White House a president who, as secretary of war, had intervened directly in the Cuban turmoil of 1906 and also knew the arguments for and against the retention of Guantánamo as a naval station. Although Taft may have viewed the isolated and arid base as an undesirable assignment, he generally agreed with Roosevelt and senior naval officers that Guantánamo and other U.S. bases in the Caribbean were essential to the protection of expanding U.S. interests in the region. Both Taft's secretary of the navy, George von Lengerke Meyer, and his secretary of state, Philander Knox, shared and promoted this strategic perspective.[64]

Meyer, a successful Bostonian businessman and politician, had previously served as U.S. ambassador to Italy and Russia and as postmaster general under Roosevelt. He would lead the Navy Department throughout Taft's four-year term to provide sustained leadership and guidance. He also quickly formed a close friendship with Dewey, and became a strong proponent for the development of Guantánamo.[65]

Secretary Meyer provided a preview of the approach he would take toward Guantánamo in his brief remarks in the *Annual Report of the Navy Department for the Year 1909*:

The department desires to invite your favorable attention to the extreme desirability of developing the naval station partly established at Guantánamo,

Cuba. Certain facilities exist there, and a dry dock has been partly excavated, but funds are lacking to continue the building up of this important insular station. With the opening of the Panama Canal, the Caribbean Sea will become the scene of great commercial activity, and our responsibility as to the policing and maintenance of the canal and our interest in the whole Caribbean region urgently call for an adequate naval repair base in that locality.[66]

Meyer had chosen his words carefully. Neither he nor President Taft had the political skill or backing to continue naval expansion at the dramatic pace set by Roosevelt, but incremental advancements would be possible.[67]

The following year, Meyer began to lay the groundwork for strengthening Guantánamo by personally inspecting all navy yards with the intention of closing those that did not actively serve the needs of the U.S. Fleet. He also consulted the members of the General Board, Mahan, and other senior naval officers both active and retired. On September 24, 1910, Mahan, at Meyer's request, wrote the General Board that "a fleet pivoted at Guantánamo covers effectively the whole Gulf coast. . . . Precisely the same remark applies to the lines of communication from the Gulf ports to the isthmus. . . . Guantánamo covers them all. For these reasons, Guantánamo appears to rank next in importance as a naval station to the Chesapeake and New York."[68]

In the *Annual Reports of the Navy Department for the Year 1910*, Meyer recommended closing the navy yards at New Orleans and Pensacola and transferring their expensive equipment, including a floating dock, modern shop buildings, and excellent machine tools, to Guantánamo. His arguments were based on unalterable geographical (or strategic positioning) conditions. He reasoned:

The New Orleans yard lies about 100 miles up the Mississippi River . . . behind a levee, which must be relied upon at high water or flood of the river to prevent the navy yard from being flooded. Its position is such that in time of war . . . no large vessels should be sent there. The Pensacola yard lies on a large sheet of water, but it and Pensacola Bay could probably be bombarded by an enemy's vessels in spite of the fortifications at that place.[69]

Because of these geographical defects, Meyer concluded that both navy yards were strategically useless.

However, Meyer had determined that in the event of a war in the South Atlantic, U.S. defensive interests could best be served by positioning the U.S. Fleet in the Caribbean within easy access of Guantánamo for emergency repair and docking services. He considered it "inconceivable that an enemy's battleships will ever penetrate the Gulf of Mexico, unless our fleet

in the Caribbean has been defeated." He had also determined from his inspection of Guantánamo that the bay's broad harbor and deep water could
accommodate "a fleet of 35 battleships, with 16 more in the outer harbor, if
necessary." He therefore recommended that the floating dock be transferred
from New Orleans to a suitable location at Guantánamo, where the water
depth was at least forty-four feet, and that machine tools and the necessary
shop buildings be obtained from New Orleans and Pensacola. By taking
these measures, he estimated that the total cost of converting the naval station into a "small, but efficient" emergency repair facility would be between
$300,000 and $400,000.[70]

Meyer emphasized the cost benefits of transferring equipment in discussing
the future use of Guantánamo with President Taft, who justified his decision
to support the base largely on that basis. In his annual report to Congress
on December 6, 1910, Taft defended Meyer's controversial decision to close
New Orleans and Pensacola and to strengthen Guantánamo by stating:

> The Secretary of the Navy had personally examined every shipyard [and found
> that] there are several of these shipyards expensively equipped with modern ma-
> chinery which [are] entirely useless for naval purposes. . . . The Secretary points
> out that the most important naval base in the West Indies is Guantánamo, in
> the southeastern part of Cuba. Its geographical situation is admirably adapted
> to protect the Panama Canal, and he shows that by the expenditure of less than
> half a million dollars, with the machinery he shall take from other navy-yards,
> he can create a naval station at Guantánamo of sufficient size and equipment
> to serve the purpose of an emergency naval base. I earnestly join in the recom-
> mendation that he be given the authority he asks.[71]

With this endorsement from President Taft, plus his own extensive investigation, Meyer succeeded in persuading a congressional majority to upgrade the facilities at Guantánamo even though it would be designated as an
emergency repair facility. He had achieved the outcome that was politically
feasible, but it was not the outcome he, Mahan, Roosevelt, Dewey, or the
General Board had desired. He had briefly sketched his vision for Guantánamo in a letter written to his wife from onboard the *Dolphin* on November 3, 1910: "Here is another extraordinary harbor, only not so picturesque
as Santiago, but well adapted for the entire battlefleet to anchor within its
sheltered confines, with great natural advantages and greater possibilities as
a future naval base for the defense of the Panama Canal."[72]

Concurrent with Meyer's efforts to strengthen Guantánamo, Secretary
of State Knox had been seeking to enlarge the base to make it more secure.
This diplomatic process was even more time-consuming. Indeed, the decision to begin negotiations with the Cubans was delayed until the end of

the U.S. occupation. The U.S. proposal to exchange Bahía Honda in return for an expansion of Guantánamo was initially rebuffed by the Cuban diplomats in July 1909, who deemed the issue too politically sensitive, but Knox persisted. In August 1910, the U.S. minister to Cuba, John Jackson, received instructions to emphasize the importance of enlarging the base at Guantánamo in order to maintain Cuba's independence, and, if necessary, to remind the Cubans that the Platt Amendment states, "The Cubans *will* [State Department's emphasis] sell or lease the lands necessary for coaling or naval stations." Nine days later, Jackson responded that unless he received further instructions, he would wait until after the November elections in Cuba to raise the subject of an enlargement of the naval station.[73]

On January 7, 1911, Knox reopened the subject by advising Jackson that to obtain permission to enlarge the naval station at Guantánamo, the United States was willing, if necessary, to relinquish the tract at Bahía Honda. One week later, Jackson replied, indicating that the Cuban government was interested in negotiating an exchange, but that it was especially concerned whether Cuban vessels could pass freely through the waters of Guantánamo Bay. This issue threatened to become a sticking point for the U.S. Navy, which had insisted that the entire entrance to Guantánamo Bay—including the western shore of the harbor and the waters at the opening to the Bay—remain under U.S. control. However, when Jackson reported that Cuban vessels entering a Cuban port in the area wanted "to be spared the mortification of passing through American waters," Meyer replied that, in recognition of ultimate Cuban sovereignty, it would not be difficult for his department to issue appropriate instructions to the commandant at Guantánamo "that will effectively prevent all friction with the Cuban authorities." For their part, the Cubans insisted on an increase in the annual rent and the United States agreed to an increase in the fee of $5,000, but they balked on subsequent negotiations.

A tentative agreement to enlarge the boundaries of Guantánamo that gave the United States access to water from the Yateras River in exchange for the renunciation of Bahía Honda was subsequently signed in Havana on December 27, 1912, by U.S. minister Arthur M. Beaupré and the Cuban secretary of state, Manuel Sanguily.[74] Further complications, however, ensued. On January 22, 1913, Beaupré learned from Sanguily that some Cuban senators objected to ceding more Cuban territory to the United States. Sanguily recommended that the issue be postponed until after the May 1913 Cuban congressional elections. Even then, the new Cuban Senate refused to ratify the treaty. When in 1914 Havana informed Washington that the Cuban Senate was ready to act on the treaty, the Navy Department announced that it was reconsidering the entire issue of expanding the base. The negotiating process came to a complete standstill until 1921, when a formal inquiry conducted by Assistant Secretary of the Navy Franklin Roosevelt revealed that the navy had lost interest in the subject.[75]

Beginning in mid-May 1912, scattered outbreaks of violence by poorly paid African Cuban workers erupted throughout rural Cuba, especially in Oriente Province. As these "Independientes de Color" seized rural guard-posts and their leaders threatened to destroy foreign property, they provoked fear both in Havana and in Washington that "la guerra racista," or race war, had begun. According to estimates obtained by historian Louis Pérez Jr., approximately ten thousand African Cubans participated in these uprisings.[76]

The urgent tone of the emergency messages sent by Minister Beaupré to the Department of State prompted a quick and decisive response from Knox.[77] On May 23 he informed Beaupré that the Navy Department had agreed to dispatch the *Prairie* with 500 marines as well as the *Paducah* and the *Nashville* to the naval station at Guantánamo, "near the center of the disturbance." On June 5 Knox cabled the U.S. Legation in Havana that because the Cuban authorities had failed to take effective action to protect U.S. lives and property, the commandant at Guantánamo had been compelled to land four companies of marines. Indeed, between May 23 and May 27, 2,008 enlisted men and 69 officers had embarked on 9 U.S. battleships and sailed to Guantánamo for "temporary foreign tropical shore service."[78]

Nonetheless, the U.S. intervention was restrained; naval commanders had orders to intervene only to protect U.S. lives and property. Small detachments of marines fanned out from Guantánamo to protect Guantánamo City, Soledad, San Antonio, and other small cities in interior Cuba. The Cuban government appreciated the U.S. intervention; Secretary Sanguily said his government welcomed the marines to Guantánamo City and that Cuban troops thus relieved from guard duty would be immediately put in the field. By the end of June the Cuban government had effectively suppressed the rebellion, killing approximately three thousand blacks. On July 11, 1912, the Navy Department recommended the gradual withdrawal of three companies of marines from the Guantánamo district to the base. On August 3 a letter from the Navy Department stated that a force of 250 marines would remain at Guantánamo.[79]

The presidential inauguration of Woodrow Wilson on March 4, 1913, signaled a more activist role for the United States in the Caribbean region because Wilson, even more than his immediate predecessors, was determined to maintain order and stability. His first secretary of state, William Jennings Bryan, had hoped to forge closer ties with Caribbean nations, especially by extending credit on favorable terms, but the outbreak of World War I and the opening of the Panama Canal in 1914 also persuaded him to pay more attention to the strategic importance of the region and the potential conversion of naval stations, including Guantánamo, into advanced bases. His successor, Robert Lansing, placed even more emphasis on national security considerations.[80]

In September 1913 a bright undergraduate at the U.S. Naval Academy, Midshipman Edward Ellsberg, published a persuasive article in the *Proceedings of the United States Naval Institute* titled "Naval Strength in Naval Bases," in which he made clear distinctions between naval yards and naval bases, and he also drew a direct link between the value of Gibraltar as a well-fortified naval base for the British and the potential value of such bases as Pearl Harbor and Guantánamo to the United States if they were properly fortified. Ellsberg began by asserting that the key difference between a naval yard and a naval base was its position or geographical location: "A naval base must be so situated that what it has to offer—shops, docks, and fuel—can be utilized by the fleet without the necessity of leaving the theater of war. . . . It must dominate the situation by its location." The best illustration of this principle for Ellsberg was Gibraltar, a fortress whose name is synonymous with strength. As he observed, the base protected by Gibraltar consisted of a few dry docks and repair shops, but it protected them in a strategic location with powerful guns, not guns that could block or control the straits—which were thirteen miles wide—but guns that made the naval base at Gibraltar impregnable. "It is the fleet whose base that fortress makes secure that gives England her control of the Mediterranean, and England, realizing this, has spent $200,000,000 upon the defenses."

Ellsberg then called the reader's attention to Guantánamo: "This bay, without doubt the best location for naval purposes within a thousand miles of Panama, was acquired by treaty for the sole object of establishing a base there. Yet, outside of a Y.M.C.A. building there no improvements have been made."

Ellsberg concluded his essay by making the criticism that the United States had a large number of navy yards that were worthless in a strategic sense, and it also had a number of sites for bases that in lacking the necessary improvements and defenses were also worthless. "To enable our fleet to take the sea and fight in whatever quarter threatened interests may make it necessary, we must develop the bases from which that fleet may operate. . . . Newport, Norfolk, Key West, Guantánamo, Magdalena Bay, Mare Island, Bremerton, Pearl Harbor, Guam, and Corregidor are the links in the chain that we must forge."

In his brief essay, Ellsberg had said nothing new, but he had said it more succinctly and directly than Roosevelt, Mahan, or probably anyone else. Moreover, he had published it in a publication that was widely read by senior naval officials and policymakers on the eve of World War I. The timing for it to exert influence could not have been better.[81]

A likely reader was the young assistant secretary of the navy, Franklin D. Roosevelt. Now occupying the same position earlier held by his distant cousin Theodore, Franklin was also a great admirer of Mahan, whose major works he had studied when he was a student at Groton.[82] Believing, like Theodore, that it would be unwise to divide the U.S. Fleet between the Atlantic and Pacific coasts, Franklin begged both his cousin and Mahan to publish magazine articles on this topic, saying, "These would bring more results than if a hundred other officers and men in public life were to say the same thing." Theodore Roosevelt replied, "All right! I will do that. . . . I should of course regard it as a calamity not to keep the Fleet together."[83] The ex-president, however, did not follow through on this pledge, possibly because the outbreak of war in Europe two weeks later completely diverted his attention. Mahan, however, responded enthusiastically to Franklin's request and, after a lively exchange of ideas, wrote "The Panama Canal and the Distribution of the Fleet," in which he argued, "Halve the fleet and it is inferior in both oceans." Instead, he believed that upon completion of the Panama Canal, U.S. leaders should see the canal and the Caribbean as forming one great centralized defensive position: "The Canal, therefore, assures the communications of the fleet, and in this respect is to be considered as a highway, as a means of transit. The fleet assures the communications, the line of supplies to the Canal and its defenses, which from this point of view, are an advanced base of operations."[84] It would be Mahan's final written statement. He died on December 1, 1914.[85]

In 1913, the General Board developed an elaborate contingency plan for a war against Germany in the Caribbean that was named War Plan Black.[86] All scenarios played by the strategists strongly suggested that if relations with Germany deteriorated to the breaking point, the United States should concentrate its fleet in the western Atlantic, ready to move into the Caribbean as soon as war began. In March 1914, the General Board approved another contingency plan for a war against Japan, known as War Plan Orange. Although the primary focus of War Plan Orange was the Pacific region, the Caribbean also became important because the Caribbean canal route was vital to the rapid movement of Atlantic Fleet battleships into the Pacific theater of operations. Thus, prior to the completion of the Panama Canal and the emergence of a two-ocean U.S. Navy, the Caribbean was considered a pivotal region in both of these major war plans.[87] But which naval base in the Caribbean was deemed most important to support the fleet?

In attempting to answer this question, naval experts disagreed. Some, including Rear Admiral Charles Badger and Sims, favored Culebra over

Guantánamo as a forward, or advanced, base to support naval operations because they believed that its occupation would deny an enemy access to such places as St. Thomas in the Virgin Islands or Samaná Bay in the Dominican Republic. Others extolled the virtues of Guantánamo, and Badger even wrote a personal letter to Navy Secretary Josephus Daniels stating that Guantánamo was "a splendid place for fleet training . . . the like of which is possessed by no other nation in the world." A few even preferred Colón in Panama, even though it is on the periphery of the Caribbean Basin, because of its proximity to the canal and the fact that it was already well fortified.[88]

During this prewar period, the base at Guantánamo managed to improve its military capabilities. The navy sent a handful of aviators from Annapolis to conduct operations out of an aviation camp established at Fisherman's Point in Guantánamo Bay.[89] In his *Annual Report of the Navy Department for the Year 1913*, Daniels mentioned that instruction was being given in aeronautics at both Annapolis and Guantánamo, and at Guantánamo, the Navy Aviation Corps, acting in conjunction with the Atlantic Fleet, had solved "many useful and important problems [to secure] the future usefulness of the aeroplane in naval warfare." In fact, their operations demonstrated that aircraft could locate mines and submarines in shallow waters and coordinate other joint operations with the fleet.[90]

In reality, however, little was actually done in the early years of World War I to enhance the capabilities or the defenses of any of the Caribbean U.S. bases. In mid-1914, a frustrated Franklin Roosevelt wrote a memorandum to Daniels in which he proposed that a policy decision be made with regard to Guantánamo. In Franklin's view, the Navy Department had three options: (1) abandon base development; (2) continue to use Guantánamo for winter fleet exercises; (3) make definite plans to develop and fortify the base. At the bottom of the memorandum, Franklin had penned "no action taken."[91] The lack of attention to Guantánamo's needs was corroborated in a letter written by George Reeder, one of the secretaries of the Army and Navy YMCA Headquarters, to Daniels in April 1914 that described the quarters for enlisted men as extremely spartan, consisting of "conical tents without floors . . . [and] provided with no other light than that afforded by tallow candles."[92]

Despite the validity of Franklin's exasperated conclusion, senior naval strategists persisted in their efforts to identify bases in the Caribbean that would best serve U.S. security interests in wartime. On March 4, 1916, the General Board presented Daniels a well-argued memorandum titled "A Permanent Naval Base in the Caribbean." Their collective view was that the Caribbean should function as a new frontier or a first line of naval defense that an enemy would have to breach before it could threaten the continental United States. In the board's view, the most important considerations in establishing a permanent naval base that would have the capability to wage war were position, strength, and available resources. It then evaluated Guantánamo, Puerto Rico, and Colón on the basis of these criteria. It found that Puerto Rico's geographic location was the most favorable for shielding the region from an enemy fleet approaching from European waters, but that Guantánamo had more secure communications than those of either Puerto Rico or Colón. In terms of comparative strength, the board observed that Guantánamo had excellent sites for the emplacement of heavy guns, but that it would be necessary to establish a land defense in the rear of the base, as it would be for similar sites at both Puerto Rico and Colón. With regard to resources, the board believed that both Guantánamo and Colón had comparative advantages over Puerto Rico because of Guantánamo's proximity to U.S. markets and Colón's nearness to the Panama Canal. After weighing these factors, the General Board concluded that Colón's location "at the lower extremity of the Caribbean with the whole Sea in front" effectively disqualified it for consideration as a permanent base. The board could not, however, make a definitive choice between Cuba and Puerto Rico, and therefore advocated that both Guantánamo and Puerto Rico (including Culebra) should be "fully developed and amply protected."[93]

Even though the Navy Department once again failed to implement the well-reasoned recommendations of the General Board, this does not mean that its efforts were without consequences. In a federal bureaucracy where high-level papers are rarely destroyed, such important studies usually find their way into reference and background files that are reviewed and occasionally reconsidered by incoming administrations. That Guantánamo and Roosevelt Roads (in Puerto Rico) eventually emerged as key U.S. bases in the Caribbean region suggests that this memorandum of the General Board may ultimately have had greater impact than can be documented.

The marines stationed at Guantánamo were sent with battleships to suppress uprisings and protect U.S. interests in Haiti in 1915 and in the Dominican Republic in 1916. Marines entered Cuba through Guantánamo in February 1917 as they had in 1906 and 1912. These recurrent exercises in "gunboat diplomacy" had multiple unfortunate consequences. The stabilizing influence exerted by naval vessels and armed marines was almost inevitably short-lived and often began to erode as quickly as U.S. forces departed. The interventions engendered lingering animosity, even hatred, not only among suppressed revolutionary elements but also among nationalistic and perceptive citizens who believed their independence had been violated. At the same time, the United States, particularly under the paternalistic leadership of President Wilson, felt morally justified in these pursuits. Moreover, the official position taken by the U.S. State Department was that interventions (or interpositions) by one nation in the internal affairs of another nation for the purpose of providing adequate protection to the citizens of one resident in the other and to protect their property was not improper, but "a right recognized by international law."[94] Perhaps the most unfortunate and lingering consequence of the Wilson administration's frequent use of naval power was that its multiple failed attempts to promote political stability only strengthened the U.S. hold on the Caribbean region. In this context, Guantánamo was frequently seen as a convenient tool of this form of imperialism.

In early 1917, as the United States was preparing to enter World War I, political turmoil in southeastern Cuba once again prompted a U.S. military intervention in which Guantánamo and its commandant became centrally involved. The crisis originated in the decision of Conservative president Mario Menocal to seek reelection in 1916, disavowing an earlier promise that he would not run. When elections were held in early November, Liberal candidate Alfredo Zayas was predicted to win because of his party's widespread popularity. Both parties probably committed electoral fraud: about eight hundred thousand votes were counted out of an electorate that probably consisted of approximately four hundred fifty thousand.[95] Menocal won by a slim majority. The Liberal Party then appealed to the Cuban Supreme Court, which ordered new elections set for February 14, 1917, in disputed districts of Santa Clara and Oriente Provinces where violent partisan clashes had already occurred.[96] On February 12, antigovernment revolts broke out in Camaguey, Santa Clara, and Oriente Provinces, and rebellion quickly spread throughout Cuba. Most Liberal leaders joined the rebellion and some took up arms. In response, President Menocal ordered his armed forces to make widespread arrests. He also rejected last-minute requests from Washington to postpone the partial elections.[97]

To this point, telegrams from the State Department indicated that Lansing had been impartial and had tried to end the dispute by emphasizing the importance of adhering to legal procedures. After fighting broke out, however, the United States openly sided with the Menocal government. On February 13, Lansing laid the diplomatic groundwork for U.S. armed intervention by reminding both Cuban parties that Washington retained the right to restore political stability and that it would support only those "governments established through legal and constitutional methods."[98] A few days later the Wilson administration provided Menocal 10,000 rifles and 5,000,000 rounds of ammunition and also landed 220 marines to protect U.S. property. This aid enabled the Menocal government to hold off the rebels long enough to hold new elections and to declare victory in the contested districts despite overt instances of fraud.[99]

The crisis in Cuba was greatly exacerbated by events following the break in diplomatic relations between Germany and the United States on February 3, 1917, as well as growing concern in Washington that the Caribbean would soon become a new theater for the world war. Because of Cuba's geographic location along Caribbean lines of communication, the U.S. government became concerned that Germany might try to establish a secret U-boat base on the unstable island or launch a surprise attack on the fleet at Guantánamo.[100] In late February, Daniels recorded in his diary, "[President] W[ilson] said I am very free from G[erman] suspicions but so many things are happening we cannot afford to let Cuba be involved by G[erman] plots."[101]

Daniels would later write in his draft manuscript for *Our Navy in the World War:*

> The declaration of U-boat warfare was aimed at this country as well as at other nations. Germany might strike without warning, and our first consideration was the safety of the fleet. Only four months before Germany had sent the U-53 across the Atlantic, sinking a number of British vessels just off our coast . . . the air was full of reports of submarines in West Indies waters. We could not take any chances, and as it might be weeks before war was declared and the Navy be free to take offensive action, [so] the first thought was the protection of the fleet.[102]

As a preventive measure, on February 5 Daniels ordered that the virtually unknown Gulf of Guacanayabo become the temporary base, or as he put it, "the safe deposit vault" for the Atlantic Fleet. Under the cover of night, the fleet, commanded by Vice Admiral Henry T. Mayo, moved from Guantánamo to its new destination so quickly and secretly that Cubans residing near the bay "knew nothing of the change until they awoke to find that the battleships, destroyers, and other vessels were gone."[103]

According to Daniels, he had selected the Gulf of Guacanayabo as a harbor where U.S. battleships could rendezvous and continue their exercises chiefly because it was relatively unknown—not even listed on most maps of Cuba—yet it was a sizable body of water, extending approximately seventy miles from Santa Cruz del Sur to below Manzanillo and nearly to Cape Cruz. It was approximately fifteen miles wide at its broadest point, and the U.S. Navy Hydrographic Office had recently determined that its channel was deep enough to accommodate the largest battleships. It was also well protected from hostile attack, being surrounded by a chain of islands with many shoals.[104]

Early on February 14, Captain Dudley Knox, the commandant of the nearly empty Guantánamo Bay, was startled by the arrival of three Cuban gunboats just outside the harbor. The boats had fled from Santiago, which had been seized by rebel forces. Shortly after calling on the Cuban officers onboard the gunboats, Knox received a frantic message from the U.S. consul in Santiago asking him to send a warship to maintain radio communication. With the U.S. Fleet now in Guacanayabo Bay, only the aging but recently renovated U.S.S. *Petrel* was available for Knox to sail from Guantánamo to Santiago.[105] For the next four days, Knox functioned as a diplomatic negotiator with an agitated rebel commander who threatened to mine the harbor, sink ships, and bombard the city of Santiago if the gunboats returned. Trying to be objective, keep the harbor open, and protect the city of Santiago, Knox managed to mollify the rebel leader by keeping the Cuban gunboats at bay. On February 18, the U.S.S. *San Francisco* arrived to relieve Knox of any further responsibility in the matter and allow him to return to Guantánamo.[106]

The *San Francisco* landed additional marines who took control of the city until Cuban forces arrived to relieve them. Shortly thereafter gunboats arrived from Havana to land Cuban federal troops on the flanks and behind the rebel forces, eventually forcing them to retreat toward Guantánamo City. The fighting between government forces and rebels did not quickly abate, and the U.S. marines were supposed to act as a defensive force. The Cuban government throughout February and most of March seemed powerless to protect the sugar plantations, maintain communications, or protect U.S. lives and property; consequently, the State Department refused to respond to a formal request from the Cuban minister to withdraw the marines even after the Cuban troops began to subdue the rebels.[107]

It became evident that, apart from concern about protecting the U.S. Fleet in Cuban waters, Washington had been especially alarmed by reports that the rebels were burning nearby canefields and causing widespread destruction as they retreated into the countryside. On February 27, the naval station at Guantánamo reported that the systematic destruction of sugar plantations had begun and that it had dispatched marines to the affected areas to prevent further destruction and possible loss of life.[108] Historian Russell Fitzgibbons provided the following chronological account: "Coincident with reports of the burning of cane in Oriente, United States warships on February 26 had landed 220 marines at Guantánamo. Several hundred more were landed at Santiago on March 8, and a short time later several nearby strategic centers were occupied by small bodies of United States troops."[109] In an emergency session with his cabinet on February 27, President Wilson had decided to land troops at Santiago. To his diary, Daniels confided the following explanation for this particular deployment: "The Cabinet today decided to send a division to Santiago, Cuba, to make demonstration to help Government against revolutionists."[110]

In a concurrent eyewitness account, George Marvin described a meeting at a hotel in nearby Caimanéra between a sugar planter, a railroad manager, the consular agent, two marine majors, and the commandant at Guantánamo in which the sugar planter reported that "at least 2,500 of the revolutionaries had gone through his pasture lands yesterday, all but about 500 mounted and all well armed and draped with ammunition. They had threatened to burn his cane and they had promised to burn his million-dollar mill. . . . They had also made the naïve announcement that they had decided to cooperate with whatever German enterprise might develop in the island of Cuba." Marvin then reported that the commandant "could not allow a rabble, which had just expressly lined itself up with a submarine-operating nation, with which the United States was then at war, to take possession of territory, including a coastline, completely cutting off his naval station on the landward side."[111]

Lansing would later write in his memoirs that the United States had intervened "to protect the sugar plantations and to prevent interference with the grinding of the cane," as Cuban sugar exports were deemed vital to the U.S. war effort.[112] On May 18, the War Department complied with a request from the State Department to send two army regiments to Cuba to relieve the marines, who were needed in Haiti, and to assist the Cuban government in restoring order. This action constituted a death blow to the insurgency. On May 20, 1917, Menocal was inaugurated for a second term as president of Cuba.[113]

President Menocal demonstrated his appreciation for the U.S. intervention that sustained him in power in various ways. Cuba declared war on Germany on April 7, 1917, following the U.S. declaration by one day.[114] In return, the U.S. Navy sought to strengthen Cuba's capabilities to patrol its own waters by providing Havana wooden-hulled sub chasers and giving it access to U.S. shipyards so that Cuban ships and gunboats could be repaired and overhauled. Cuba also permitted U.S. warships to use all of its ports throughout the war. For the next few years, the Cubans made a concerted effort to fulfill the needs of the United States and the Allies for sugar.

The Caribbean did not become a major theater for armed conflict in World War I. Its shipping lines were nonetheless vital to U.S. and Allied economic security interests. Given the high volume of maritime shipping that transited the Gulf of Mexico and the Caribbean, it would have been negligent, even foolhardy, to have left the region devoid of naval patrols, especially given the demonstrated capability of imperial Germany to send its submarines into western Atlantic waters. Shortly after its entry into the war, the Navy Department created the Atlantic Fleet Patrol Force under the command of Rear Admiral Henry B. Wilson. He promptly assigned seventeen ships to patrol the Caribbean and Gulf regions. Although his commanders invariably reported "no enemy submarines or raiders observed," his decision reflected a realistic perception of the need to guard the Caribbean as well as a judicious use of naval power.[115] U.S. fears about the real possibility of German submarines invading Caribbean waters are evident in this official telegram sent to Sims on March 18, 1918, instructing him to take appropriate protective convoy countermeasures:

> Just received report which recommends if submarines be located in Western Atlantic: (A) Immediately close Florida Straits to traffic until measures for its defense are assured. (B) Trade from Gulf for European ports which now joins convoys to be diverted through Yucatan Channel to St. Thomas and proceed thence in one fast and one slow convoy per week under protection of French and United States cruisers. (C) Anchorage at St. Thomas to be prepared and protected by United States with aid of such patrol forces French Admiral and British Commodore can spare; coal stock to be provided by United States. (D) When defence of Florida Straits is assured present Convoy arrangements to be reverted to.[116]

For more than a decade following World War I, Guantánamo Naval Base changed little in size or function. In the late 1920s and early 1930s, Guantánamo's McCalla Field served as a base for testing dirigibles and seaplanes, and aircraft that patrolled the Caribbean region, including the Panama Canal, also used McCalla for basing and fueling purposes. In these years, more piers and buildings were constructed and a water distilling plant was installed.[117]

Pérez has provided an important perspective on the negative impact of Guantánamo Naval Base on the nearby squalid town of Caimanéra as well as on the provincial capital of Guantánamo City. For many years these urban centers were the primary destinations for sailors on leave and, in the course of events, they suffered the consequences of prostitution, venereal disease, and related problems.[118] Missing from Pérez's account, but equally valid, was the extensive Cuban complicity in this process of social degradation. This, of course, included the prostitutes, drug dealers, and bar and brothel owners, but also extended to local Cuban officials who profited from these activities in various ways, including what colloquial Spanish calls "la mordida" or the bribe.[119] In other words, as morally reprehensible as the situation might have been, the presence of U.S. sailors and marines was not necessarily unwelcome.[120]

In time, as a high number of U.S. troops remained stationed on Cuban soil, it mattered less how the United States had justified its intervention in Cuba in 1917.[121] Instead, this particular interposition of the U.S. military engendered new and lingering feelings of bitterness not only among Cuban Liberals but more broadly among anti-imperialist critics throughout the United States. They began to perceive that, as long as the Platt Amendment remained in force, Cuba could at any moment be reduced to the status of a temporary colony of the United States.

The 1920s were a time of rising Cuban nationalism in which virtually all local political groups voiced a common antipathy toward the Platt Amendment. On June 20, 1922, the Cuban Senate passed a series of resolutions protesting recurrent U.S. interference in the internal affairs of Cuba. In 1924, Geraldo Machado y Morales campaigned successfully for the presidency on the Liberal Party platform, committed to a "revision of the Permanent Treaty, eliminating the appendix to the Constitution, and winning Cuba an independent place in the world." On April 23, 1927, during a state visit to Washington, D.C., Machado told President Calvin Coolidge that the Platt Amendment "did a certain amount of moral damage to Cuba," and he voiced the hope that "someday some modification of the Platt Amendment could be brought about." President Coolidge blandly replied that the Platt Amendment was "as much Cuban as it was American," and he also said that the United States "had no desire to force anything on Cuba." Later that year, when Coolidge became the only U.S. president to visit Havana, on the occasion of the Sixth Pan-American Conference, Machado again raised the subject of the Platt Amendment and indicated there was some resentment in Cuba over the continuing U.S. occupation of Guantánamo Naval Base, to which Coolidge responded that there was "really nothing to talk about." In truth, Coolidge may have felt that he had been "blind-sided" because Machado had previously agreed to abide by Coolidge's selection of topics to be discussed.[122]

In 1928 economic historian Leland Jenks published his controversial study *Our Cuban Colony,* in which he wrote that the Platt Amendment had been devised to enable Cuba "to exist as an independent, sovereign republic," but as U.S. investments and enterprises in Cuba increased dramatically, "we became less concerned about the Republic of Cuba and . . . more concerned about 'interests' of the United States in that island." Consequently, in Jenks's view, we had misused the Platt Amendment "whenever possible to justify our conduct, distorting its meaning and intent grossly in so doing."[123] Over the next several years, two prominent diplomats, Cuba's experienced and well-reasoned diplomat Cosme de la Torriente and the U.S. ambassador to Cuba, Harry F. Guggenheim, would prepare the groundwork for the revocation of the Platt Amendment that would occur in the first term of President Franklin Roosevelt's administration.

On May 9, 1928, Torriente, speaking at the World Conference on International Justice in Cleveland, Ohio, called attention to the negative effect the Platt Amendment was having on U.S.-Cuban relations in an address titled "Dios Nos Hizo Vecinos."[124] He said, "Whenever you want to upset our people, you tell us that the Platt Amendment . . . converts the Cuban Republic into a protected nation, semi-sovereign [and] annexed." He then observed that "without [benefit of] the Platt Amendment, the government in Washington has intervened to protect its interests in various [Latin] American nations, whenever it has deemed it necessary. On the other hand, the said Amendment has only served as a constant object of criticism throughout the world."[125]

In April 1930, Torriente published his most incisive criticism of the Platt Amendment in *Foreign Affairs*. He began by recalling the emotional burden that had been placed upon the Cuban delegates to the Constitutional Convention by being forced by the U.S. government to choose between the "immediate establishment of the Cuban Republic and the indefinite postponement of the Constitution." Torriente then examined the articles of the Platt Amendment in light of subsequent history and found that some, such as Article Five requiring Cuba to take the necessary sanitation measures to eliminate infectious diseases, had been fully complied with and were no longer necessary. His most telling objection, once again, was to Article Three, which he found had been misused by the United States in 1906 to destroy a good government and in 1917 to keep in place a government that had been widely discredited. In defense of Cuba, Torriente argued that his government had wisely exercised its sovereignty (in violation of Article One, which prohibits Cuba from signing treaties with foreign powers) by entering the Great War on the side of the United States, ratifying the Versailles Treaty, joining the League of Nations, and by subscribing to the Statute of the Permanent Tribunal of Justice. Torriente concluded his appeal to the United States to abrogate the Platt Amendment by arguing that the right of the United States to intervene to defend Cuban independence should be replaced by "a pact whereby the United States would offer her support for the defense of Cuba against foreign attack." Finding that with the completion of the Panama Canal, "Cuba forms part of the natural defenses of the United States," he advocated that "Cuba would grant the privileges of the Naval Station at Guantánamo guaranteed in the present Article VII."[126]

The first U.S. diplomat who gave serious consideration to Torriente's arguments was Ambassador Guggenheim, who served as President Herbert Hoover's envoy to Cuba. On January 30, 1932, in the last year of that administration, Guggenheim addressed a memorandum to Secretary of State Henry L. Stimson titled "Reconsideration of Treaty Relations between the United States and Cuba." He began by describing his growing sense of frustration in failing to persuade Machado to implement political and economic reforms Guggenheim believed necessary to stabilize a government suffering the effects of the worldwide depression and a collapse in world prices for sugar. Guggenheim gloomily warned Stimson that "we confront the consequences of a government intent on perpetuating an unpopular grip on the country."

Guggenheim then reviewed the history of U.S.-Cuban relations from 1909 to 1929, and found that the Cuban government had followed the friendly advice of U.S. officials only when it (1) feared that failure to do so would prompt U.S. intervention under Article Three of the Permanent Treaty (Platt Amendment), (2) was seeking a foreign loan that depended on U.S. approval or acquiescence, or (3) believed that the Cuban opposition party would oust it from power if it did not adopt the recommended reforms. Guggenheim had also concluded from his own study of the U.S. military interventions of 1912 and 1917 that the United States had not been consistent in its application of Article Three.[127] Moreover, even though the Platt Amendment had been extremely unpopular in Cuba since its inception, in times of political upheaval contending Cuban factions had frequently sought to manipulate it as a political weapon that would prompt the U.S. government to intervene. Noting that the existence of Article Three "has led to requests for intervention on the part of both thoughtful and thoughtless Cuban leaders," Guggenheim warned Stimson of "an ever present threat of an intervention deliberately provoked"; it was conceivable that the opposition to President Machado, recognizing his control over the army and police, might conclude that only assassination or U.S. intervention could remove his government.[128]

Guggenheim proceeded to argue that the fundamental problem was Article Three of the Permanent Treaty. Citing the articles and addresses of Cosme de la Torriente that advocated abrogation of the Permanent Treaty, Guggenheim recommended that if the United States should have cause to intervene in Cuba, it should do so "only when such intervention would be justified and pursued under similar circumstances in other countries." He supported this recommendation with the reasoning that Article Three was "obnoxious to the Cuban people" and "impedes their political growth." Its elimination "would mean that we would treat Cuba as we treat the republics of South America . . . [and] that such a gesture would enhance the prestige of the United States throughout Latin America and increase the friendliness of the Latin American governments toward the United States."

Guggenheim did not advocate that the United States should do away with Article Seven of the Treaty, which provided for naval or coaling stations in Cuba. In 1930, the ambassador did not perceive the danger of foreign aggression to be "imminent or particularly applicable to Cuba." Nonetheless, he cautioned that any such danger "could be guarded against by the naval bases." Two years later he would write in a more polished and updated version of "Amending the Platt Amendment": "When Article VII was proposed . . . Cuba feared that the projected naval bases might be used as points for watching over the domestic actions of the Cuban government. This fear has been dispelled. There is general recognition in the light of the history of the past thirty years that the United States occupation of a Cuban naval station is only in the interest of protecting both the United States and Cuba."[129]

In 1934, Guggenheim would publicly advocate that whereas Article Three of the Permanent Treaty was "outworn and now inappropriate," Article Seven should be modified "to assure the United States perpetual use of adequate facilities at Guantánamo." These recommendations, obviously adapted to changing international circumstances, nevertheless had their origin in the memorandum drafted only for the eyes of Stimson in 1932. In preparing that memorandum, Guggenheim had recognized that any modification of the Permanent Treaty would constitute a "dramatic departure in our relationship with Cuba," and he told Stimson that he would understand it if the secretary accepted his advice in principle but did not consider the moment propitious to implement it. By April 1934, however, Guggenheim believed that the moment had arrived "to contribute to the development of Cuba's self-reliance."[130]

During the first thirty years of the naval station's existence, it had frequently facilitated U.S. military interventions in Cuba and the use of gunboat diplomacy elsewhere in the Caribbean. In performing this function, it incurred the animosity of Cuban nationalists and anti-imperialists throughout the hemisphere. At the same time, there was considerable merit in Guggenheim's statement that in moments of crisis, the naval base had functioned to protect both Cuban and U.S. interests. If nothing else, Captain Dudley Knox's four days as an untrained naval diplomat working without a fleet or a properly commissioned ship prevented Cuban rebels from destroying the port and city of Santiago. This incident, in the time of a world war, aptly illustrated Guggenheim's justification of Guantánamo's value to the hemisphere.

5

Peace and War
Franklin D. Roosevelt

THE ADMINISTRATION OF FRANKLIN DELANO ROOSEVELT (FDR) drew
the United States and Cuba closer in many ways as New Deal diplomacy
sought to strengthen economic and security ties throughout the Western
Hemisphere. With regard to Guantánamo, the policies of FDR echoed the
approach taken by his distant cousin Theodore Roosevelt. In 1934, at the
same time FDR abrogated the Platt Amendment to improve bilateral relations, he renewed the lease "in perpetuity" for Guantánamo, using the exact
language Theodore Roosevelt had dictated. Four years later, disturbed by
the growing militarism and aggressive moves of Germany, Italy, and Japan,
Roosevelt began to stress the U.S. naval presence in the Caribbean with
major fleet exercises, and shortly thereafter to expand Guantánamo's base
facilities. These and subsequent wartime developments would make Guantánamo once again a focal point for both friction and compromise in U.S.-
Cuban relations.

At the outset of the FDR administration, Cuba was mired with the United
States in the Great Depression. Shortly thereafter the island erupted in a
prolonged spasm of political turmoil that tested and often frustrated the
best efforts of senior U.S. diplomats to restore stability. This preoccupation
with Cuba added weight to public advocacy that the U.S. government terminate Cuba's protectorate status by abrogating the Platt Amendment, but
it did not lead U.S. officials to contemplate any changes with regard to U.S.
retention of Guantánamo. On May 29, 1934, the United States and Cuba
signed a new treaty that both abrogated the Platt Amendment and reasserted
the validity of the original agreements pertaining to Guantánamo signed in
1903. The only strident criticism of U.S. determination to retain the naval
base came from Cuban nationalists and leftists who continued to condemn
U.S. policies as "plattista" and from former provisional president Ramón
Grau San Martín, whose four-month administration the United States had
refused to recognize on the grounds that it failed to reestablish law and
order.[1]

The close economic and commercial ties between Cuba and the United
States in October 1929 meant that the onset of the Great Depression spread
almost immediately from Wall Street to Havana. The economic decline of

Cuba can be measured by the plummeting price of its chief export, sugar. In 1928, the price was 2.18 cents per pound. In late 1929, it had fallen to 1.72 cents per pound. In 1931, after the U.S. government imposed the restrictive Hawley-Smoot tariff, the price of Cuban sugar dropped to 1.09 cents per pound, and in 1933, it reached the all-time low of 0.57 cents per pound. This spelled disastrous consequences for the Cuban government and its people. As historian Luis Aguilar has perceptively noted, "The spread of misery throughout all sectors of the population was inevitable."[2]

The recurrent political spasms gripping Cuba in 1933 followed the downfall of President Geraldo Machado y Morales. Initially popular with both the Cuban electorate and U.S. interests, Machado's leadership skills proved inadequate to assuage the economic discontent engendered by the collapse of the Cuban economy. With the government's finances in disarray, Machado's response to insurrections and protest was to impose a brutal dictatorship under which the Cuban police became notorious for torture, and it was widely rumored that Machado fed his enemies to sharks by throwing them from El Morro castle into Havana Harbor. One student leader aptly characterized Machado as a "tropical Mussolini." His debacle finally came on August 12, 1933, when faced with a general strike and the defection of his own military, he realized that FDR's special U.S. envoy, Ambassador Sumner Welles, would take no action to rescue his administration.[3]

FDR was a longtime friend of Sumner Welles and trusted his expertise and judgment regarding U.S. relations with Latin America. On April 3, 1933, FDR had named Welles assistant secretary of state for Latin America, but on April 21, 1933, with tensions mounting in Havana, the president abruptly changed Welles's appointment to ambassador to Cuba. Obviously intending this assignment to be a temporary one, on May 6, 1934, Roosevelt notified U.S. Ambassador to Colombia Jefferson Caffery that he should be ready to relieve Welles "in about three months." The Cuban crisis, however, proved more prolonged. Not until November 24, 1934, did Roosevelt announce that Welles would soon resume his appointment as assistant secretary of state.

As soon as Machado had fled into exile, Welles sought to identify a Cuban leader who could restore public order. He quickly discovered that this challenge tested and frequently exceeded his considerable diplomatic skill. The following chronological account from August 1933 to January 1934 by Jane Franklin succinctly captures the difficulties in restoring national leadership.

August 12, 1933: Machado resigns and flees Cuba. With Ambassador Welles's approval, Carlos Manuel de Céspedes becomes provisional president. The military along with militant students and revolutionary groups oppose this U.S. choice.

September 5, 1933: The "Sergeants' Revolt" supported by students and led by Sergeant Fulgencio Batista y Zaldivar, overthrows President Céspedes.

September 5–10, 1933: A junta (the *Pentarquía*—Ramón Grau San Martín, Sergio Carbó, Porfirio Franco, José Miguel Irisarri, and Guillermo Portela) run the country. Ambassador Welles describes these rebels as having "communistic" ideas, and on September 7 he asks for U.S. military intervention. [FDR had already sent a few warships to Havana to reassure Americans, and, in response to Welles's request, he ordered additional ships ranging from battleships to coast guard vessels into Cuban waters, including Havana Harbor, but no troops disembarked.] According to Benjamin Welles's biography of his father, Sumner Welles recommended that the United States use limited force to restore Céspedes's constitutional government, but Secretary of State Cordell Hull and President Roosevelt rejected intervention on the grounds that it could lead to an indefinite military occupation.[4]

September 10, 1933: The rebels appoint Ramón Grau San Martín as president. The United States refuses to recognize his government and begins to pressure an overtly ambitious Batista to desert the rebels.

January 15, 1934: Batista, now a colonel, overthrows President Grau San Martín.

January 18, 1934: Manuel Márquez Sterling becomes president for less than a day until Colonel Batista replaces him with Colonel Carlos Mendieta Montefur. The United States recognizes the Mendieta government. Resistance persists. Batista continues to run the government as the "strongman" behind the scenes with U.S. approval.

May 29, 1934: Cuba and the United States sign the "Treaty on Relations between Cuba and the United States" abrogating the "Permanent Treaty" of 1903 and the Platt Amendment with the exception that the United States continues to occupy the naval base at Guantánamo.[5]

It can be argued that even if Cuba had been more stable, the Roosevelt administration was ready to repeal the Platt Amendment. Prior to the 1932 elections, in private talks in Albany and Hyde Park, New York, FDR and Welles had agreed on some basic principles for a new foreign policy approach toward Latin America. These included "no further armed intervention, equality between all American republics and . . . inter-American consultation if local disputes threatened neighboring republics or an outside threat imperiled the entire hemisphere."[6]

Following FDR's inauguration, public pressure mounted for the United States to terminate its protectorate in Cuba. The *New Republic* advocated, "If there is to be a New Deal in regard to Latin America . . . abrogation of the Platt Amendment should be the first card played." Hubert Herring, writing in *Current History,* observed, "The administration in Washington is as anxious to rid the United States of the Platt Amendment as Cuba is to be set free. The events of the six months since the fall of Machado have served to emphasize the futility of the present relationship."[7] Herring had not made explicit what would become increasingly evident—from the outset of his administration, FDR wanted to persuade all Latin American leaders to enter into what he called "a hemispheric partnership [with the United States] in which no Republic would obtain undue advantage."[8] The Platt Amendment had clearly become a hated symbol of U.S. hegemony over Cuba and thus an obstacle to achieving this goal.

All available evidence indicates that FDR and the State Department fully agreed with the points made by the *New Republic* and Herring. As Hull would later write in his memoir:

> By the so-called Platt Amendment to the treaty of 1903, the United States had the legal right to intervene in Cuba. . . . But the President and I were determined that we should not intervene in Cuba. Despite the legal right we possessed, such an act would further embitter our relations with all Latin America. . . . It would feed our traditional enemies whom I hoped to starve.[9]

Welles's approach to the interventionist authority granted to the United States by Article Three of the Platt Amendment was somewhat more complicated than the rationale given above by Hull. Welles had withheld recognition from the provisional government of Grau San Martín, he later claimed, only because the 1901 treaty was still in place. "Because of that fact, the United States would have been derelict in its obligations to the Cuban people . . . had it given official support to a de facto regime which was not approved by the great majority of the Cuban people and which had shown itself so disastrously incompetent."[10]

After the Platt Amendment was abrogated, however, Welles believed the U.S. government no longer had "any treaty right of intervention in any American republic," and advocated what he considered "the wisest inter-American policy in respect to recognition," namely the Estrada Doctrine, which would accord automatic recognition to any government when it took power.[11]

The intriguing question the FDR administration never addressed in the case of Cuba was, What specifically constituted "intervention"? As noted above, on September 7, 1933, FDR had sent a U.S. flotilla into Cuban waters, and, although no troops disembarked, at the end of January 1934 twenty-five warships were still assigned there. Even after the Platt Amendment was abrogated and FDR had sent the new treaty to the Senate, Welles's replacement as ambassador, Jefferson Caffery, requested that the cruiser U.S.S. *Richmond* remain off Havana Harbor, and reported that Mendieta and Foreign Minister Cosme de la Torriente agreed that the timing was inappropriate for the removal of the U.S. naval presence.[12]

Historian Irwin Gellman makes a telling point when he asks the rhetorical question, "If the United States had truly intended to end any possibility of intervention, why did it hold onto the Guantánamo Naval Station and encircle the island with warships?" Gellman's answer to his own question is equally instructive: "American troops remained on Cuban soil and the Cubans were painfully aware of the United States naval presence. Thus, the abrogation of the Platt Amendment was not a generous surrender of American rights, but simply the admission that intervention by treaty was no longer useful or desirable."[13]

The historical record makes it clear that the FDR administration had never entertained any thought of relinquishing Guantánamo. On May 21, 1934, Welles, who had resumed his appointment as assistant secretary of state, wrote a brief memorandum to the president that began:

> In my conversation with you yesterday regarding the projected treaty with Cuba you raised the two following points:
>
>   1. Whether Article II of the new treaty should contain a clause referring to the acts of the Second Military Occupation of Cuba in addition to the provision contained in Article II as now drafted covering the acts of the First Military occupation; and
>
>   2. Whether the Navy Department had given special consideration to the possibility of retaining the use of the waters of Bahía Honda for refueling or provisioning purposes in time of war between the United States and a non-American power.[14]

Welles responded to FDR, saying that the legal adviser to the State Department, Green H. Hackworth, had advised him that upon termination of the Second Military Occupation, which ended in 1909, "the acts of that occupation were validated by an exchange of notes between this Government and the Government of Cuba." To emphasize his point that no mention of the Second Occupation would be required in the new treaty, Welles stated that because "all acts of the American authorities during the Second Occupation were carried out by contractual right . . . [they] are not open to question." With regard to the president's question about retaining the use of the waters of Bahía Honda, Welles replied that Admiral William Standley, chief of naval operations, had assured him that the Navy Department had fully considered the matter, and in its judgment, "the rights we now possess at Guantánamo as well as the facilities afforded in Puerto Rico, the Virgin Islands, and continental ports, are so ample . . . as to make it unnecessary for us to consider utilizing the waters of Bahía Honda."[15]

Welles's account of his conversation with FDR prior to the signing of the new treaty concerning Guantánamo is especially noteworthy for its brevity and focus. Its content reveals the impressive grasp the president had not only of the history of U.S.-Cuban relations relating to Guantánamo but also of the hitherto unresolved diplomatic status of Bahía Honda and the possible value of retaining it for U.S. defensive purposes. FDR's query about Bahía Honda also indicates his vigilant concern about using Cuba to safeguard U.S. security interests should it be at war "with a non-American power." Having served as assistant secretary of the navy prior to and during World War I, he obviously had retained an active appreciation of Cuba's potential utility as a naval outpost.

The new Treaty of Relations between the United States and Cuba was signed into law with little ceremony in Washington, D.C., on May 29, 1934, by Hull, Welles, and Ambassador Manuel Márquez Sterling. The signing took place in Hull's office. In addition to the signatories named above, the only two living men who had witnessed the signature in Havana in 1903 of the original treaty—Sidney Smith of the State Department's treaty division and John Barrett, former director of the Pan-American Union—were also present. After the signing, Sterling gave a short address in which he informed Hull that "this treaty transforms the former pact . . . into a permanent and indestructible association to which Cuba brings the respect and admiration which the high virtues of the American people inspire in her." He also read a congratulatory telegram from Torriente that "last night the [Cuban] Cabinet put on record a vote of thanks to you." Hull recalled that in 1898, he had spent six months with his regiment in Cuba, and since then had "had a genuine personal interest in the Cuban people and have followed their progress with the greatest sympathy."[16]

The new treaty did not make any mention of the Platt Amendment. Its abrogation was effected by the replacement of the entire 1903 treaty. Article One of the new treaty simply stated: "The Treaty of Relations, which was concluded between the two contracting parties on May 22, 1903, shall cease to be in force and is abrogated, from the date on which the present Treaty goes into effect."

The purpose of Article Two was to revalidate the actions under the U.S. military occupation of Cuba "up to May 20, 1902, when the Republic of

Cuba was established." Article Three cited the original Lease of Coaling or Naval Stations to the United States signed by President Tomás Estrada Palma on February 16, 1903, and by President Theodore Roosevelt on February 23, 1903, and reaffirmed the language of that treaty pertaining to Guantánamo by stating: "Until the two contracting parties agree to the modification or abrogation of the stipulations of the agreement in regard to the lease to the United States of America of lands in Cuba for coaling and naval stations . . . the stipulations of that agreement with regard to the naval station of Guantánamo shall continue in effect."

The new agreement specifies that "so long as the United States of America shall not abandon the said naval station of Guantánamo or the two Governments shall not agree to a modification of its present limits, the station shall continue to have the territorial area that it now has, with the limits that it has on the date of the signature of the present Treaty."[17]

Article Four provided that should a contagious disease become widespread in either U.S. or Cuban territory, the government of the affected territory could suspend communications between designated ports for as long as it deemed advisable. In accordance with the advice given by Standley and Welles, the new agreement made no mention of Bahía Honda.

Hull would later record that, as soon as the new treaty had been signed, FDR sent it to the Senate with the accompanying message: "Our relations with Cuba have been and must always be especially close. They are based not only upon geographical proximity, but likewise upon the fact that American blood was shed as well as Cuban blood to gain the liberty of the Cuban people as an independent power in the family of nations."[18]

Two days later, on May 31, 1934, the U.S. Senate ratified the treaty. According to Hull's memoirs, the Cuban government subsequently "declared a three-day festival in celebration," and ratification by Cuba occurred on June 4, 1934.[19]

Not all Cubans, however, were rejoicing. Caffery reported to the State Department that Grau and many of his supporters had strongly objected to the new treaty by calling for a complete withdrawal of U.S. naval forces and insisting that all references to Guantánamo be eliminated from the text.[20] The State Department did not heed Caffery's warning of continuing Cuban nationalist opposition. It also responded to the few inquiries it received from U.S. citizens who had asked if the Platt Amendment had really been abrogated, given the U.S. determination to retain Guantánamo, with bland assurances that echoed the philosophy of Hull that "Cuba was to be the kernel of our new and positive policy toward Latin America."[21]

The sharpest criticism of the FDR administration's approach toward Cuba and Guantánamo came from a distinguished group of Americans handpicked by the Foreign Policy Association, in response to a formal invitation from Mendieta, to conduct an in-depth field study of political, social, and economic problems in Cuba and to recommend realistic solutions. After spending three months in Cuba, from mid-May to late July 1934, this blue-ribbon Commission on Cuban Affairs, headed by foreign policy expert Raymond Buell and including the distinguished journalist Ernest Gruening, published its findings in a book-length report titled *The Problems of New Cuba*.[22] In the first chapter, the report castigated the Platt Amendment for serving "indirectly to underwrite the worst features in Cuban political life." Its argument was that as a consequence of denying Cubans the right to revolt, corrupt and self-serving politicians had little reason to fear popular uprisings, which in the absence of democratic elections might have served as the only effective corrective to corrupt and irresponsible practices.[23]

Although the Commission on Cuban Affairs acknowledged that the recent abrogation of the Platt Amendment had "undoubtedly removed an outstanding obstacle" to the improvement of bilateral relations and the possibility of "better government in Cuba," the Summary and Conclusion of the report opened its discussion of bilateral relations by observing that "the Commission [had] found in Cuba numerous indications of antagonism regarding recent acts of the American government." It then recommended that the United States "consider the policy of surrendering its lease of Guantánamo." Reporting that "a number of Cubans find it difficult to reconcile . . . Guantánamo with an independent status for the Cuban Republic," it argued that the base's continuing "presence on Cuban soil," was not only "an anomaly" but, from the standpoint of U.S. self-defense, unnecessary because "there are a number of other harbors such as Vieques Sound [in Puerto Rico] which could be used as a base." The commission then recommended that "the United States . . . seriously consider whether the retention of Guantánamo will not cost more in political misunderstanding than it is worth in military strategy."[24]

Public reaction to the commission's comments regarding Guantánamo was, at most, muted. News coverage of the publication of its report appeared in the *Washington Post* and the *New York Times* on January 27, 1935, and both papers briefly mentioned the recommendation to relinquish the naval base, but without further comment. The following day a *Washington Post* editorial began by observing that the commission's report was "of special significance . . . because of its frank and constructive criticism of the relations between the State Department and the Cuban government." The rest of the piece lauded the commission for its efforts to conduct a careful investigation during a chaotic period and its success in producing a report "objective in its approach and impartial in its recommendations," but did not mention Guantánamo. A subsequent book review in the *New York Times* titled "New Light on Conditions in Cuba" limited its discussion of the commission's findings to agricultural reform.[25]

It may be that the lack of serious attention given to the commission's conclusion pertaining to Guantánamo was attributable to the fact that the report itself scarcely mentioned the subject. Instead, its 500 pages consisted of separate, in-depth chapters covering such topics as public health, education, social welfare, money and credit, soil and forestry, and, of course, several chapters on various aspects of the sugar industry and policy, but it only discussed Guantánamo in a single paragraph toward the end of the final chapter. There is no indication that FDR, Hull, or Welles took any of the commission's criticisms of recent U.S. diplomatic actions or initiatives toward Cuba seriously, and they certainly did not respond to criticism of the new lease for Guantánamo.

Instead, to strengthen diplomatic relations and commercial trade with Cuba, FDR initiated a series of economic moves that recalled the positive actions taken by his apparent role model Theodore Roosevelt in 1902 and 1903 to reduce the tariff on Cuban sugar. In March 1934, FDR created the second Export-Import Bank for the explicit purpose of financing U.S. exports to Cuba; in May, he reduced the tariff rate on Cuban sugar by 25 percent; and on August 24, 1934, a reciprocal trade agreement was signed that stated that all articles grown, manufactured, or produced in the United States or Cuba would be granted "exclusive and preferential reduction in duties."[26] The most important effect, as noted in the *New York Times,* was to reduce the rate on the importation of Cuban raw sugar from 1.5 cents per pound to 0.9 cent, "or approximately one-half our rate against the rest of the world, which is 1.875 cents."

In actuality, however, Congress had already set limits on the amount of refined sugar that could be imported from Cuba and other foreign producers with the passage of the Jones-Costigan Act of May 9, 1934. This act established a quota system based on an average of imports for the preceding three-year period from 1931 to 1933. Its critics noted that if a longer time frame had been chosen, Cuba's quota would have been higher. According to Robert F. Smith, these quota terms favored the interests of domestic beet producers more than FDR had intended when he proposed the legislation. The immediate result was that Cuba's quota for 1934 was about 28 percent, or 1,866,482 short tons.[27]

In spite of the FDR administration's efforts to sweeten its insistence on retaining Guantánamo, Cuba's most distinguished nationalist historians denounced the renewal of the indeterminate lease as a neo-imperialistic move. In 1935, Cuban archivist and historian Emilio Roig de Leuchsenring published his two-volume work *Historia de La Enmienda Platt: Una Interpretación de la Realidad Cubana*. As its subtitle honestly indicates, this was a reinterpretation of the history of the Platt Amendment, including its antecedents as well as its impact and consequences, written from a nationalistic and highly critical perspective. Indeed, Roig had never made any pretense of being objective. His overt intention was to shock and provoke his readers in hope of stimulating debate. As David Healy has written, "The tone of Roig's approach was evident in a 1923 speech . . . [when] he said it was ridiculous for ceremonial speakers to keep saying that Cuba owed the U.S. an eternal act of gratitude. . . . [Instead,] he jeered, 'It really is an eternal debt, because we are always paying it.'"[28]

In the first volume of the history, Roig recounted in fairly detailed, factual terms the history of the passage and application of the Platt Amendment, including, for example, the following description of how Cuban diplomatic negotiators managed to persuade their U.S. counterparts to limit their demands for Cuban naval or coaling stations to Guantánamo and Bahía Honda.

> Within the painful reality which, for Cuba, represented the surrender of part of its territory to a foreign power . . . the Cuban diplomats who negotiated this treaty proceeded intelligently and patriotically, obtaining, instead of a sale, what would become a rental agreement and . . . in place of the four stations—Guantánamo, Nipe, Cienfuegos, and Bahía Honda—which had been demanded officially on November 2, 1902—only two naval stations, Guantánamo and Bahía Honda.[29]

Roig, however, was both analytical and fair in his discussion of President Theodore Roosevelt's determination to have a naval station in Cuba, which ultimately was located at Guantánamo. He chose to view this topic much as Theodore Roosevelt had done—in terms of reciprocity—granting Cuba trading preferences in return for the concession of "certain naval stations on its coasts." Roig quoted from a speech Theodore Roosevelt had delivered in Minneapolis, Minnesota, on April 4, 1903, in which he had affirmed:

> Situated as Cuba is, it would not be possible for this country to permit the strategic abuse of this island by a foreign power. It is for this reason that certain limitations have been imposed on its financial politics and that naval stations have been conceded by it to the United States. They are so situated as to dispel any idea that the United States would ever misuse them against Cuba or in any other manner except to protect Cuba from assaults by a foreign enemy and to enhance the security of American interests in the waters to the south of us.

Roig then asked and answered the following rhetorical question: "What were those interests and what was their importance to the United States?" Paraphrasing Theodore Roosevelt's words, he replied, "These interests have been gradually increasing as the consequence of the war with Spain and will increase further with the construction of the Isthmian Canal. They are as much military as economic." Roig continued, "What value did Roosevelt place on the concessions that Cuba granted?" Roosevelt maintained that "The concession by Cuba of the naval stations is of the greatest importance from a military perspective." And finally, Roig asked, "How did Roosevelt judge Cuba's behavior toward the United States?" Roosevelt declared, "The concession of these naval stations is proof of Cuba's good faith in dealing with us. . . . She is honorably observing her obligations toward us."[30]

The most provocative aspect of this particular chapter may be found in the last phrase of its title: "The Treaty of Commercial Reciprocity between the United States and Cuba of 1903: Complement and Compensation for the Platt Amendment—Its Reduction in Benefits in Favor of Cuban Compensation Were Annulled by the Ill Treatment of the Yankee Tariff." Roig blames this "ill treatment" on actions taken by the U.S. government in 1930 under the Hoover administration to protect its domestic sugar interests by raising the tariff on Cuban sugar to 2 cents, which he says "completely annulled the limited benefits which had been granted to us by the Treaty of Reciprocity."[31] Despite Roig's bitter tone, his criticism is valid. As his compatriot Herminio Portell Vilá accurately judged in his positive but perceptive book review: "This is a mature book in which strident patriotism has no place. If Roig criticizes American diplomats and politicians . . . he does not fail to acknowledge and condemn with the utmost severity all Cuban political sins and sinners that have made possible the situation that he denounces."[32]

In Volume 2 of Roig's book, addressing the aftermath of FDR's reaffirming the indeterminate lease for Guantánamo and signing a new treaty, Roig condemned the United States in intemperate prose for what he obviously considered its attempts to mask imperialistic behavior by superficial protestations of being a "good neighbor" with a "New Deal" for Cuba.

> The naval station and [presence of] warships are nothing more than the dogs of prey placed by Yankee imperialism in Cuba to guard and preserve—compelling first and, if necessary, attacking—what is really profound, vital, and grave in the problem of our relations with the United States: the economic absorption and exploitation of Cuba and of Cubans. They have not abandoned this [absorption and exploitation] nor will they abandon it, carrying it out in accordance and in connivance with our politicians and governors, lackeys of imperialism, through the banks, public utilities, and providers of articles of prime necessity

(light, gas, telephones, trolleys, petroleum, etc.), the great sugar mills, and the one thousand, five hundred million [$1.5 billion] dollars of Yankee investment on the island.[33]

These words imply fury and profound disappointment. Roig may or may not have been a communist. What matters more is that, as a Cuban nationalist, he felt powerless to make his island nation truly independent of an economic dependency on the United States, which he saw as being maintained and enforced by such instruments as Guantánamo. He also probably believed that, over time, the honest intentions of Theodore Roosevelt, who had risked his own life to help achieve Cuba's independence, had been thoroughly corrupted.

The best-known Cuban revisionist historian was Portell Vilá, who, in addition to his scholarly attainments, was a political activist. He was a vocal opponent of the dictatorship of Machado in the early 1930s and a professor and confidant of Fidel Castro in the late 1940s and early 1950s. Hugh Thomas wrote that "in the early summer of 1953, Vilá was sitting in a bar in Havana when a young ex-pupil of his at the university, passing by, told him that he was planning an attack on a military installation [the Moncada barracks]." Brian Latell adds that, after explaining his plan of attack, Castro asked Portell Vilá if he thought the plan could succeed. When the professor said he considered success unlikely, Fidel responded: "Nevertheless, the plans have been laid. There is no turning back. We need a rallying point and if necessary we shall provide the martyrs." In 1960 Portell Vilá went into exile in the United States immediately after Fidel and Raúl Castro eliminated academic freedom from the University of Havana.[34] In his four-volume study, *Historia de Cuba en sus Relaciones con los Estados Unidos y España*, Portell Vilá's treatment of U.S.-Cuban relations is a well-sourced historical critique of what he views as U.S. imperialistic policies and attitudes toward Cuba. It documents, for example, Governor-General Leonard Wood's efforts to promote the annexation of Cuba.[35] It also cites Cuba's former minister to the United States Gonzalo de Quesada's observation that strong Cuban opposition to the granting of coaling stations had prompted some Americans to believe that the unresolved ownership of the Isle of Pines due south of Havana could be settled by making it "the basis of defense for American interests in the Caribbean Sea, or that if the Isle of Pines was found unsuitable—as it was afterwards shown to be—for coaling and naval purposes, it could be made the basis of negotiations for the acquisition of other sites."[36]

In his investigation of the period leading to the leasing of Guantánamo, Portell Vilá cites a memorandum prepared by the U.S. Navy General Board on December 7, 1900, that asserted the United States needed to occupy on a

permanent basis the bays of Guantánamo and Cienfuegos in order to defend
Cuba along with the interoceanic canal (construction of which had not yet
commenced), and enforce the Monroe Doctrine. At this point, Portell Vilá
editorializes:

> Of course the theory that the United States possessed the right of eminent do-
> main to occupy foreign territory was absurd and indefensible, and could have
> been extended to the occupation of Jamaica, Trinidad, Curaçao, and strategic
> points of Central America with more reason than to Cuba, but the Secretary of
> the Navy John Long, an anodyne personality whom Theodore Roosevelt had
> manipulated when he was his assistant, forwarded this recommendation of the
> General Board to the State Department.[37]

In this passage, Portell Vilá conveys his Cuban nationalist and anti-
imperialist sentiments in both his analysis and disparaging tone. At the same
time, his work is well documented, making effective use of both U.S. and
Cuban sources. In the introduction to his subsequent work, *Historia de la
Guerra de Cuba y los Estados Unidos contra España*, published in 1949,
Portell Vilá describes the U.S. intervention in Cuba as expansionist and
opportunistic:

> North American expansionism, which took advantage of the Cuban war in
> order to extend its influence through the Caribbean toward Panama, to cross
> the Pacific and arrive in the Philippines in order to create a first-class military
> force capable of confronting the European powers at Agadir and in World War
> I, had its origins in the Cuban war, which it [the United States] transformed into
> the foundation for a new phase of international rivalry.[38]

His most controversial assertions are that the United States would have
lost the Spanish-American War without Cuban assistance and that Cuba
eventually could have achieved its independence if the United States had
freely provided arms and ammunition to the Cuban rebels but had not intervened. Portell Vilá makes this argument in the *Historia de Cuba en sus
Relaciones con los Estados Unidos y España*, and develops it more fully
in *Historia de la Guerra de Cuba y los Estados Unidos contra España*, in
which he describes the various ways in which Cuban military leaders and
their troops made the difference between victory and defeat for the invading U.S. forces by covering the landing of U.S. forces and providing critical
intelligence pertaining to the size and location of Spanish troops. In *Historia
de la Guerra*, Portell Vilá mentions the taking of Guantánamo only in the
passing remark that "the Cubans were of much help at Guantánamo," and
he subsequently dismisses the impact of the devastating encounter between

Admiral Sampson's blockading force and Admiral Cervera's squadron by observing only that "the destruction of Cervera's squadron did not result immediately in the surrender of Santiago de Cuba."[39]

One of the most direct challenges to Portell Vilá's thesis was made by Cuba's "Grand Old Man" of diplomacy, Cosme de la Torriente. Torriente, who had served as General Calixto García's chief of staff during the war against Spain, voiced strong doubts about the ability of Cuba to free itself from Spanish rule without the decisive intervention of the U.S. Navy. In a paper he delivered before Cuba's Academia de Historia on August 12, 1948, Torriente proclaimed his view:

> For me, Cuba could consider itself free from the day that Americans and Cubans began to attack the Spanish fortification of Santiago, Cuba. Cervera's squadron was destroyed by that of Admiral Sampson. . . . Without the [U.S.] warships that destroyed the Spanish [Fleet], we Cubans would have required a very long time to achieve this nearly impossible goal, simply because a small collectivity such as ours, by itself, could not create a fleet of warships.[40]

All three of the writers mentioned above, two of whom were distinguished historians, the third a diplomat, statesman, and student of history, were prominent Cuban nationalists who believed the Platt Amendment had had a strong negative effect on the Cuban Republic and on U.S.-Cuban relations. Both Roig and Portell Vilá had penetrating criticisms of how the United States had intervened in Cuba's struggle for independence and had manipulated that intervention to advance U.S. interests in gaining dominance, even control, over Cuba. Of these two, Roig was the more bitter, but it was Portell Vilá who asserted that Cuba could have won its war without U.S. assistance—an assertion Torriente disputed by calling attention to the decisive naval victory at Santiago, facilitated and possibly ensured by the capture and use of Guantánamo as a coaling, provisioning, and repair naval facility. Yet what is most remarkable is that these three Cuban scholars shared a common positive perception of the role of Theodore Roosevelt—one of the men most responsible for the U.S. intervention in the Spanish-American War and the key figure in determining that the United States would have a naval base in Cuba for as long as it needed it. And this need would become more evident as the clouds of war in Europe began to advance across the Atlantic after France fell in mid-June 1940 and German U-boats began to attack merchant ships on July 1, 1940. Cosme de la Torriente would be one of the first to foresee that Guantánamo would provide mutual security for both Cuba and the United States.

In October 1940, Torriente published his article "Cuba, America, and the War" in *Foreign Affairs*, in which he asserted that should the United States be drawn into a war with the "totalitarian powers of Europe or Asia, Cuba's only course would be to render full and immediate aid." He reasoned that if the United States became engaged, Cuba would, too, because of its geographic proximity, but he also outlined the operational and strategic military advantages Cuba's location had to offer: "She is in a position to dominate both entrances to the Gulf of Mexico as well as one of the passages leading from the Atlantic Ocean into the Caribbean Sea. Cuba thus guards not only the southern coast of the United States but one of the principal routes to the Panama Canal."

Torriente then placed appropriate emphasis on the importance and value of Guantánamo to both U.S. and Cuban national security:

> Because of the disturbed state of the world, in particular because of Guantánamo's proximity to the Panama Canal, the United States could not give up the naval station. Furthermore, from the Cuban point of view the existence of the station is highly useful. In any war involving the United States, Cuba would run the risk of being occupied by enemy Powers, and in this event, the Guantánamo station would insure our receiving prompt help from the United States Army and Navy. . . . *If the United States Government should ever decide to abandon the Guantánamo station, Cuba might have to ask the United States to stay. Otherwise, enemy forces might occupy Cuban soil to the peril not only of Cuban independence but of the security of the United States.*[41]

This may be the clearest, most forthright statement by any writer of the value of having a U.S. military presence at Guantánamo in a perilous time. What makes it remarkable is that its author had been in the forefront of U.S.-Cuban relations as an officer in the Spanish-American War. He had lobbied for and then negotiated the termination of the Platt Amendment, and ostensibly was now seeking to build popular support for joint military collaboration by citing Guantánamo as a unifying defensive outpost in case a major war should endanger Caribbean waters.[42]

In spite of Torriente's well-articulated concern for Cuba's safety, in 1940 the United States was still woefully unprepared to defend its interests in the Caribbean or even to protect its own shores. There is some truth to the harsh judgment made by U.S. Army Chief of Military History Major General R. W. Stephens in his foreword to *The Framework of Hemisphere Defense* that "self-preservation and military measures" to protect the United States and its territories from attack by foreign powers "ceased to be of serious concern . . . during the nineteenth century,"[43] but Stephens and many other military historians overlook in such condemnations the devastating impact of the Great Depression on military preparedness.[44]

In his book *The Regulars*, Edward Coffman finds that even in the Roaring Twenties, post–World War I disillusionment and antimilitary attitudes combined into public pressure to limit federal government expenditures and "to reduce the Army to the point that it was negligible as a world power."[45] As a result, from 1923 to 1935, Congress restricted the size of the army to 188,750 troops. The onset of the Depression necessitated more restrictions. In September 1930, President Herbert Hoover instructed the army to limit its total expenditures to $444 million, $65 million less than the budget Congress had already approved. Early in the New Deal, the FDR administration cut army pay by 15 percent (commensurate with reductions in other federal salaries), and soldiers were furloughed without compensation for one month each year.[46] As naval historian Steven Ross has discovered, in 1934 the United States did have a major navy, with a muster roll of 9,582 officers and 80,312 enlisted men. The fleet, on paper, was impressive. It consisted of 15 battleships, 4 aircraft carriers, 25 cruisers, 245 destroyers, and 84 submarines, but "many of the destroyers and submarines were nearing the end of their service lives."[47]

By late 1937, FDR was sufficiently alarmed by recent aggressive moves by Germany, Italy, and Japan that on October 5, in a dramatic appearance in Chicago, he called attention to the spread of international lawlessness in which,

> without a declaration of war . . . [or] warning or justification of any kind, civilians . . . are being ruthlessly murdered with bombs from the air . . . [and] ships are being attacked and sunk by submarines without cause or notice. . . . Innocent peoples, innocent nations are being cruelly sacrificed to a greed for power and supremacy which is devoid of all sense of justice and humane consideration.[48]

Given the still predominant spirit of isolationism in the United States as evinced in the Neutrality Acts of 1936 and 1937, FDR was not prepared in this "Quarantine Speech" to challenge these belligerent nations, but he did warn U.S. citizens, "Let no one imagine that America will escape, . . . that this Western Hemisphere will not be attacked."[49] The speech precipitated a torrent of angry letters and telegrams to the White House castigating the president for "warmongering and saber-rattling." The absence of public support from Democrats in Congress and from Hull stung FDR and forced him to backtrack publicly but failed to persuade him that his sense of foreboding was inaccurate.[50] A few days later, he wrote to his old headmaster at Groton, Endicott Peabody, "As you know, I am fighting against a public psychology of long standing—a psychology which comes very close to saying *Peace at any Price.*"[51]

U.S. naval historians generally date the preoccupation of the FDR administration with defenses in the Caribbean-Atlantic region from early 1939, after the appeasement at Munich, but the president was personally monitoring German naval movements in the region before then. On March 17, 1938, he sent the following memorandum to both Welles and Chief of Naval Operations Admiral William D. Leahy: "I note that German battleship and transport will visit Samaná Bay [in the Dominican Republic] March 18th to 23rd. Why not have an American destroyer or some other ship in Bay at same time? Please expedite."[52]

In compliance with FDR's directive, a U.S. battleship was quickly dispatched from Guantánamo to Samaná Bay to shadow the Germans, and early on March 23 the German ships left the area.[53] Roosevelt's response to this intrusion was not surprising given his appraisal of the Third Reich's potential threat to this hemisphere, but the proximity of Guantánamo enabled the U.S. Navy to execute the appropriate defensive maneuver promptly and effectively. The incident also was an early warning of German interest and intentions in the Caribbean region that the United States would counter by bringing Guantánamo into play as a strategic Atlantic and Caribbean hub by 1943.

The sinking by Japanese aircraft of the patrol gunboat U.S.S. *Panay* on December 12, 1937, off the coast of Nanking, China, awakened U.S. strategic planners to the possibility that the United States might eventually fight a two-front war in the Pacific and Atlantic against Japan and the German-Italian Axis. These same strategic planners were cognizant of the Treaty of Friendship signed between Nazi Germany and Fascist Italy on October 25, 1936. They had also witnessed the strengthening diplomatic ties between Germany, Italy, and Japan evidenced by the signing of the Anti-Comintern Pact by Germany and Japan on November 25, 1936, and Italy's adherence to this pact exactly one year later. These disturbing developments combined with the militaristic aggrandizement of all three nations persuaded the Joint Army-Navy Board to reevaluate its war plans.[54] Until then, the contingency plan for fighting the Japanese (War Plan Orange) had been based on the assumption that war was most likely to be restricted to the Pacific. Now, with Germany and Italy sending massive military aid to fascist rebels seeking to overturn the Republic of Spain, war strategists began to realize that the United States might be forced to fight simultaneously in the Pacific and Atlantic oceans. In this event, the Panama Canal and the Caribbean Sea would be called into play as key operational areas for the U.S. Fleet. This would of necessity enhance the importance of Guantánamo and dictate that it would need upgrading and strengthening as a military base.

In 1938, the Guantánamo Naval Station was still a small base with a complement of 17 navy officers, 153 blue jackets, 5 Marine Corps officers, and 129 enlisted men. As Bradley Reynolds has surmised, its physical plant, including its training facilities and small airfield, was "barely sufficient to accommodate the fleet's [annual] exercises from January through April." As a major war in Europe became increasingly likely, however, the U.S. Navy initiated studies to evaluate Guantánamo's defenses and its potential utility in warfare. The most influential study was conducted in 1938 by the naval commission headed by Rear Admiral A. J. Hepburn. Its findings, which were reported to the House Naval Affairs Committee, included recommendations to extend the runways at the existing McCalla Airfield, upgrade the facilities "to make a satisfactory operating field," and develop a second airfield "for emergency operations" at Leeward Point on the other side of Guantánamo Bay.[55]

In late May 1938, FDR decided to make a dramatic showing of U.S. naval strength in the Caribbean-Atlantic region in conjunction with the opening of the New York World's Fair in spring 1939. The White House instructed the Navy Department to announce that the U.S. Pacific Fleet would transit the Panama Canal in early 1939 and conduct a major naval exercise (Fleet Problem No. 20) in the West Indies and the Atlantic Ocean, to extend at least as far south as the Equator. During March and April, the fleet would engage in target practice and other exercises at Guantánamo; it would visit the New York World's Fair in May and then return to the Pacific. Reports in the *New York Times* and the *Washington Post* emphasized the fact that this would constitute the largest naval force to transit the Panama Canal or to assemble in the Atlantic Ocean, and both papers quoted the ranking minority member of the Foreign Relations Committee, Senator William F. Borah, who predicted that this would constitute a warning "to totalitarian states not to meddle in the Western Hemisphere."[56]

On September 6, 1938, FDR took the decisive step of creating an Atlantic Squadron, to consist initially of fourteen new ships—seven light cruisers and seven destroyers—whose designated mission would be to serve as a task force strong enough "to discover and to turn back a sudden raid into the Caribbean." With this move, the administration was signaling to both Latin American neighbors and European adversaries its resolve to defend the Caribbean region. It also revealed a departure from FDR's earlier resolve to concentrate naval strength, for it meant that he now accepted the realistic need to divide the U.S. Fleet.[57]

New U.S. war plans that began to take shape after the Munich crisis of September 1938 made more realistic assessments of the conjuncture of geography with global politics.[58] Viewed through this perspective, the Panama Canal and the Caribbean Sea would become pivotal regions for U.S. Fleet movement. On November 9, 1938, the Joint Army-Navy Board instructed its planning committee to design a new War Plan Orange that would establish a "position of readiness" along the line of Alaska-Hawaii-Panama. The directive specified that the underlying assumption would be that Germany, Italy, and Japan were allies and that War Plan Orange would be a U.S. response to a fascist invasion of the Western Hemisphere and a simultaneous effort by Japan to seize the Philippines. According to historian Robert Dallek, FDR "inspired" the shift in military planning from exclusively national concerns to hemispheric defense. Dallek records that all five Rainbow Plans of 1939 focused on the defense of the Western Hemisphere.[59]

On January 7, 1939, Secretary of the Navy Claude Swanson declared that Guantánamo and sixteen other bases would constitute a naval defense area (NDA). This directive, which had been recommended by the U.S. Navy General Board, also imposed security restrictions on visitors to Guantánamo as well as the airspace in the vicinity of the base. The name NDA was changed to Defensive Sea Area and Airspace Reservation in November 1939.[60]

In fulfillment of FDR's request, the U.S. Pacific Fleet demonstrated its mobility by making a mass transit of the Panama Canal on its way to Guantánamo Bay in mid-January 1939. There commenced the largest naval exercise to date of the fleet's ability to defend Caribbean bases and sea lanes of the Caribbean. FDR, who took the opportunity to inspect the facilities at Guantánamo onboard the U.S.S. *Houston,* along with Vice Admiral Ernest King, watched the final stages of the exercise.[61]

Fleet Problem 20, which simulated a major invasion by Germany of Caribbean and Atlantic waters in support of a fascist revolution in Brazil, along with a U.S. counteroffensive, resulted in a blistering lessons-learned critique.[62] Among the new realities the exercise revealed was that aviation was transforming naval warfare—neither side had attempted to employ its battleships until after the respective air forces had completed their scouting and bombing missions. At a more fundamental level, Fleet Problem 20 exposed the weaknesses and insufficient number of U.S. naval and air bases in the Caribbean. As the commander of the U.S. (Black) Fleet, Vice Admiral Adolphus Andrews subsequently emphasized that it would be folly for the U.S. Navy to send its forces into Caribbean waters "against a strong foe . . . unless suitable bases are provided." Andrews further warned, "In view of the present world conditions, the importance of the West Indian area to our national defense, . . . and the lack of bases therein, it is high time that corrective measures be taken."[63] Andrews's recommendations involved not only strengthening inadequate existing U.S. bases but also leasing bases in the Caribbean from foreign governments. According to naval historian

Patrick Abbazia, FDR, "for whom the absence of bases in the Caribbean [was becoming] a pressing matter," read Andrews's report.[64]

Following the recommendations made by the blue-ribbon commission known as the Hepburn Board, Congress approved and the president signed into law on June 14, 1940, a bill for the expansion of Caribbean naval bases in San Juan, Puerto Rico, the Panama Canal Zone, St. Thomas in the Virgin Islands, and at Guantánamo. Under this program, Guantánamo would have facilities for three patrol squadrons, eight carrier squadrons, and four additional patrol squadrons with tender support (a type of navy ship used either for nonspecific or uncommon support, e.g., destroyer tenders or seaplane tenders).[65] FDR again demonstrated the importance he placed on Guantánamo by making a one-day visit there in December 1940 on the U.S.S. *Tuscaloosa.* Over the next few years, the U.S. government would appropriate $34 million to enhance the station's capabilities. New facilities were to include a Marine Corps base at Deer Point to accommodate approximately two thousand men and the construction of aviation facilities for the marines. Construction of an underground hospital, a bomb-proof structure comprising four concrete arch-type units built into a hillside, with 192 beds and complete hospital equipment, would begin in September 1941.[66]

The military buildup at Guantánamo had negative side effects. Jana Lipman describes the escalation in prostitution in nearby Caimanéra and Guantánamo City during the 1940s. She quotes one Cuban journalist who admitted that "prostitution was practiced throughout the country, but the most frank and degrading exhibition was in Caimanéra."[67] This may be an accurate assessment, but other sources report thousands of prostitutes working in Santiago de Cuba and Havana in the 1940s and 1950s. This, after all, was the time when Meyer Lansky and other mobsters were seeking to transform Cuba into a Havana-based underworld empire of casinos and nightclubs, in which prostitution served as a source for bribery and payoffs. According to crime writer T. J. English, local and military Cuban police profited directly from bordello payoffs. However, many sailors and officers were too hard at work at such activities as shakedown cruises, gunnery exercises, and training for amphibious warfare to go into Caimanéra. A brief interview with Lawrence Clayton, who spent some time at Guantánamo in the early 1960s as a navy ensign, makes the point: "We were working twelve and fourteen hours per day making sure our ship was seaworthy. I had a few meals and drinks at the Officer's Club, but I didn't even see the golf course!"[68]

With the planned expansion of Guantánamo to meet wartime needs, a major consideration was the need for an adequate supply of potable water.

In 1934, Congress had authorized the Navy Department to negotiate a twenty-year contract with a Cuban firm to supply water from the Yateras River to the naval base via a ten-mile pipeline that was ten inches wide. This project was completed by July 1939. In view of this pipe's limited capacity, however, Congress in September 1941 approved a more ambitious project to furnish an additional 2 million gallons per day. This required the installation of a new plant at the Yateras River that would pump water through 50,000 feet of a fourteen-inch main to two treatment plants at the station. A 500,000-gallon concrete reservoir would also be built along with three steel tanks, with a total capacity of 2 million gallons of treated water.[69]

In summer 1940, FDR confronted the probability that without the immediate transfer of U.S. destroyers to Great Britain, England would be unable to prevent a German invasion, with devastating repercussions for the United States and the Western Hemisphere. On June 18, the same day Prime Minister Winston Churchill delivered his famous "This Was Their Finest Hour" speech to the House of Commons, he also sent an urgent message to FDR that described the collective threat to England posed by Germany's occupation of the European coastline from Norway to the English Channel, the recent enhancement of Germany's U-boat fleet by the addition of 100 Italian submarines, and Britain's loss of almost half of its destroyers in home waters. Churchill then made his urgent request for U.S. destroyers, emphasizing that it was "a matter of life or death." The timing of this message gave added emphasis to Churchill's public warning that if England fell, "the whole world including the United States, and all we have known or cared for, will sink into the abyss of a new Dark Age."[70]

On the same day, former secretary of state Henry L. Stimson, in a nationally broadcast radio speech, began by asserting that "the United States today faces probably the greatest crisis in its history." He then called attention to "an appalling prospect. Only one force remained between the Nazis and the Western Hemisphere—the British Fleet. . . . If it should be lost, America, almost unarmed, must stand alone against the world." The following afternoon, FDR offered Stimson the cabinet post of secretary of war, informing him that the publisher of the *Chicago Daily News*, Frank Knox—already a forceful advocate of naval preparedness, who placed particular emphasis on the Caribbean—had agreed to accept the position of secretary of the navy. Thus, in these two fateful days, June 18 and 19, 1940, Anglo-American cooperation in naval security was born.[71]

On July 2, 1940, the Military Intelligence Division of the U.S. War Department reinforced Churchill and Stimson's warnings by forwarding to General George C. Marshall a memorandum prepared by its assistant chief of staff, Sherman Miles, that argued persuasively that Britain must be sustained as an active combatant to safeguard the Western Hemisphere and prevent Latin American nations, "all [of which] are unstable and tend to be authoritarian," from eventually entering the Nazi orbit. An equally alarming memorandum sent by the War Plans Division of the Navy Department to the chief of operations, Admiral Harold Stark, on July 10, warned of the possibility of an airborne invasion of northeastern Brazil coupled with an attempt by the totalitarian powers to seize the Panama Canal.[72]

The exchange of notes between Churchill and FDR in late August 1940, which became known as the "destroyers for bases agreement," involved the exchange of fifty aging U.S. destroyers for ninety-nine-year basing rights at eight British bases—St. Lucia, Antigua, Trinidad, Bermuda, the Bahamas, British Guiana, Jamaica, and Newfoundland.[73] As Donald Yerxa has accurately portrayed this arrangement, Great Britain desperately needed the destroyers to compensate for its losses at Dunkirk, to face new threats posed by Italy's entry into the war, and to protect its vital maritime sea lanes; the United States needed these bases to defend the Western Hemisphere.[74]

The destroyer-base agreement clearly enjoyed widespread support in the United States. Public opinion polls reported that four-fifths of those asked were in favor of acquiring the British bases and nearly two-thirds approved of transferring the destroyers in return. The Republican presidential candidate, Wendell Willkie, and other leading Republicans in Congress publicly endorsed both decisions. Senior U.S. military leaders recognized the costs required to modernize the bases and were more restrained in their approval. At the same time, they realized that these new outposts would greatly extend U.S. defenses into the Atlantic and Caribbean and enhance the mobility of air defense operations. Moreover, the Caribbean bases would provide additional protection for the Atlantic approaches to the Panama Canal and possibly enable army airpower to guard the bulge of Brazil.[75]

At the time, a *New York Times* article described the acquisition of these British bases as constituting a "vital necessity" for the U.S. Navy. A similar article in *Time* magazine, "Strategy: What the Bases Mean," affirmed that "getting the bases means to the U.S. much the same thing as six inches' extra reach would mean to a boxer: they make it possible to keep an enemy from getting in close where he could do much damage."

Both articles also mentioned Guantánamo and Puerto Rico, indicating that transforming all these sites into effective naval bases for warships and airplanes would involve great expense—the *Time* article quoted Knox as stating that the United States would immediately begin spending $25 million on its new bases—whereas the *New York Times* provided the justification that these bases "would enable the United States to command the Caribbean and maintain a watchful eye over the north coast of South America

[Venezuela], whose great oil production makes it vital that we permit no enemy to gain a foothold."[76]

Knox's statement did not mean that Guantánamo's needs were being ignored. At FDR's insistence, in September 1940, the new chief of naval operations, Stark, instructed Rear Admiral John Greenslade to convene an ad hoc committee to recommend specific improvements at Guantánamo. In his directive, Stark placed emphasis on the Caribbean as one of the world's most strategic areas the United States needed to control and on developing Guantánamo Bay as the most important U.S. base in the West Indies.[77]

Since the 1st Battalion, led by Lt. Colonel Robert Huntington, came ashore to claim Guantánamo on June 10, 1898, this particular bay has been associated with the origins of amphibious warfare as a designated mission of the U.S. Marine Corps. Indeed, the official history of Marine Corps operations opens its discussion of modern amphibious warfare with the statement: "The success of the Guantánamo Bay operation and the very real possibility that the United States' new position in world affairs might lead to repetitions of essentially the same situation led high-level naval strategists to become interested in establishing a similar force on a permanent basis: a force capable of seizing and defending advanced bases which the fleet could utilize in the prosecution of naval warfare in distant waters."[78]

According to the same study, in winter 1922 a marine regiment participated in the annual maneuvers of the Atlantic Fleet, in which their assigned problems included attacking and defending Guantánamo Bay and the island of Culebra, Puerto Rico.[79] It was not until 1935, however, that the chief of naval operations officially adopted the *Tentative Landing Operations Manual* and amphibious operations became official doctrine. To put the theories of amphibious warfare into practice, major landing exercises resumed on an annual basis, held each winter from 1935 to 1941 in the broad waters of the Caribbean by using the islands of Culebra and Vieques in conjunction with the fleet training activities at Guantánamo.

In 1940, the first Marine Aviation Group, commanded by Lt. Colonel Field Harris, which was attached to the 1st Brigade of Brigadier General Holland M. (Howlin' Mad) Smith, arrived at Guantánamo, where it quickly began extensive training at McCalla Airfield, including support for ground forces, fixed and experimental gunnery, bombing exercises, and landing exercises on aircraft carriers. Shortly thereafter, Smith brought the First Brigade to conduct Force Landing Exercise 6 (FLEX 6), in which he discovered that the shortage of landing craft made it virtually impossible to get his men ashore quickly enough to establish a defensible beachhead. As he would later complain, "For six years we had been putting into practice the new Marine doctrine but still lacked adequate equipment. . . . We did not possess a single ramp boat, although the Japanese had been using ramp boats in China for years."[80]

As a partial solution, Smith seized upon the newly developed destroyer transports used in combination with the landing craft vehicle, personnel (LCVP), developed by Andrew Higgins of New Orleans, Louisiana. When Smith returned to the Caribbean in command of the First Marine Division in February 1941, he brought three destroyer assault transports to conduct amphibious assault exercises on Culebra jointly with the First Army Division (FLEX 7). Before embarking on the exercise of executing a massive amphibious landing on the island of Culebra, the marines and army "completed several months' intensive training at Guantánamo," including multiple beachhead landings. *Time* magazine captured the full effect Smith had on the marine encampment at Guantánamo:

> When the First Brigade got to Guantánamo, it debarked in a juicy mango swamp near the naval station. General Smith took one look at underbrush that no man could walk through, and began snapping peremptory messages to Washington. Soon building materials and half a dozen bulldozers arrived from the States. . . . Howlin' Mad worked his men from 5:30 A.M. to 6 P.M., seven days a week. . . . By Jan. 1, the First Brigade had all the mess halls, kitchens, and heads (Marine for latrines) that it needed. It also had a good-looking tent camp.[81]

As Smith would later write, "FLEX 7 was historic as the final prewar exercise in the Caribbean." General Smith and the commander of the Atlantic Fleet, King, had jointly directed the maneuvers intended to train army, navy, and marine troops to coordinate their landing efforts, to test the validity and efficacy of amphibious warfare doctrine, and to enable senior officers from separate services to work together.[82]

After the landings on Culebra the 1st Marine Division returned to its base camp at Guantánamo. The *Time* magazine feature article on Smith, the "Old Man of the Atolls," provided a word picture of the value and challenges of this Caribbean training: "To train some 5,000 men in amphibious landings, Holland Smith and the Atlantic Fleet Commander Ernest J. King had to make and mesh their own rules. Navy gun crews had to be taught how to fire at beaches instead of at ships; Marines had to learn to scamper down rope cargo nets, [and] what to do once they had waded ashore."[83]

Smith, who went on to command the V Amphibious Corps in the assaults on the Gilberts, the Marshalls, and Saipan and Tinian in the Marianas, would later credit the lessons learned from these exercises with enabling U.S. forces to make successful landings in both the Atlantic and Pacific. As he recalled in his memoir, *Coral and Brass*, "the finest commendation I ever received" was from Admiral King, who at the conclusion of FLEX 7 had written to General Smith: "At the close of the recent intensive landing force exercises, I wish to express to you and to the troops under your command my feeling of satisfaction that such well-trained troops . . . are an integral part of the Atlantic Fleet, and my confidence in their capacity to do their full part and to do us all credit in whatever active operation may come their way."[84]

There is no doubt that the amphibious warfare training in the Caribbean region of Guantánamo, Culebra, and Vieques, Puerto Rico, paid enormous dividends in enabling U.S. Army and Navy forces to win World War II. In August 1947, Henry Stimson acknowledged that, for the United States, this had been an amphibious war:

> No enemy forces reached our mainland, and five million American soldiers were required to be transported across various oceans in order to get at their enemies. Troop transport and assault landings are traditionally the most difficult and dangerous of all military operations. . . . Practically no losses of men occurred in the transocean voyages, and remarkably few which could have been prevented by naval action occurred on the landings.[85]

Soon after King took command of the Atlantic Fleet in February 1941, he determined that to monitor the vast stretch of ocean from Newfoundland to Brazil, he would subdivide the region into various patrols. Accordingly, he assigned Rear Admiral Jonas Ingram to command the Caribbean Patrol, which soon would be renamed Task Force Three, and then the Southern Patrol. Consisting of four light cruisers, four destroyers, a minesweeper division, and several PBY patrol seaplanes, Ingram's unit patrolled in search of German warships not only the Caribbean but also the vast geographic triangle formed by Trinidad, the Cape Verde Islands, and Brazil.[86]

Well before the attack on Pearl Harbor, the U.S. Navy anticipated that German submarines were preparing to threaten the Caribbean. On August 24, 1941, for example, Admiral King ordered both Caribbean and Southern Patrol units to police the approaches to the Dutch Antilles in response to a report from London that two U-boats were en route to attack tankers refueling at the oil refineries in Curaçao and Aruba. The report proved false, as King had suspected, but his precautionary action was indicative of the realistic perception that the Germans would soon menace merchant shipping throughout the Caribbean.[87]

After Germany declared war on the United States, Adolf Hitler reportedly said, "Now we will see what our submarines can do." In December 1941 and in early 1942, the United States was woefully unprepared to counter the attacks of German submarines against Allied shipping in the Caribbean, and the Germans knew it. Admiral Karl Dönitz quickly began to exploit U.S. decisions to transfer warships from Atlantic and Caribbean waters to bolster its naval defenses in the Pacific in the aftermath of Pearl Harbor. Outside of the forces assigned to defend the Panama Canal, the Caribbean Patrol consisted of two Wickes-class destroyers (*Barney* and *Blakely*) both built during World War I, two equally old Eagle-class patrol craft, a seaplane tender, three outmoded submarines, a Dutch light cruiser, and a small assortment of recently converted yachts. They would have to contend initially with six Type IX long-range German submarines, each equipped with multiple torpedoes, and seven Type VII medium-range U-boats. A second wave of Type IXs would arrive in U.S. waters about two weeks later, and a third wave of Type IXs would depart for the Caribbean shortly thereafter. Other Type IXs would follow.[88]

What the Germans called the "American turkey shoot" began in mid-January 1942 and was an unmitigated disaster. Writers Philip Wylie and Laurence Schwab graphically portrayed the chaos and devastation inflicted by the U-boat attacks: "By night there were sudden pillars of fire at sea and by day, clouds of smoke. Into every port were carried the charred victims of the U-boats. Oil and debris sullied a thousand miles of beaches, and by March a man with an ordinary rifle could have entered the war against the Nazis by firing his shots from the Florida coast."[89]

By the end of January 1942, U-boats had sunk thirty-five ships between Newfoundland and Bermuda. On February 16, a single submarine, *U-156*, sank two British tankers, damaged a U.S. tanker, and attempted to shell the San Nicolas refinery on Aruba. That same day, other U-boats sank three more tankers (two British and one Venezuelan) off the Aruba coast. By the end of February, U-boats had sunk seventeen ships, almost all of them tankers, in Caribbean waters.[90]

In March and April, most of the U-boats moved in closer to the U.S. coastline and the Gulf of Mexico, but by May, thirty-seven U-boats accompanied by some Italian submarines were back in Caribbean waters to begin a new campaign. By the end of June 1942, Axis submarines had sunk at least eighty-six Allied merchant ships in the Caribbean. Once again, their main target had been the tankers in the Aruba-Curaçao-Venezuela oil region, where, according to the commander of the Caribbean Sea Frontier, Admiral John Hoover, the Germans "had a field day."[91]

To counter the U-boat menace, the United States scrambled to refit whatever seagoing craft it could find. War correspondent Fletcher Pratt captured the frantic makeshift nature of this defense response in an article he wrote for *Harper's Magazine*:

She was a seventy-foot cabin cruiser, intended for polite parties down the bay with cocktails and light laughter under the awning on the fantail. The Philadelphia Navy Yard, to which she was turned over for conversion, was smothered in big jobs on battleships and cruisers . . . [so] they gave her to the second-string mechanics, who somewhat insecurely attached a .50-caliber machine gun forward, installed two depth charges (all she could carry) aft, and slapped a coat of warpaint on her. In April 1942, when submarines were sinking ships all down the coast against the loom of city lights and were beginning to sift through the Caribbean, she was commissioned a warship of the U.S. Navy and turned over to a very junior lieutenant with bright new insignia of rank.[92]

It was not until July 1942 that the United States began to put in place the interlocking convoy system that would prove the most effective defense against U-boat attacks. According to naval historian Captain S. W. Roskill, beginning in 1940 the British Admiralty had sought to persuade the U.S. Navy to organize a system of merchant shipping control and to develop an "escort-of-convoy strategy," but "the Americans had not heeded" this advice. Instead, according to Roskill, "Merchant ships continued to sail in peacetime fashion, showing lights and using their wireless freely . . . while the warships and aircraft were used on hunts and patrols, and not as convoy escorts."[93]

The official explanation for not convoying strategic materials sooner was the scarcity of a sufficient number of escort vessels to create effective convoys. Even though naval strategists in both England and the United States had long been pressing for the creation of convoys, King's stated belief was that "inadequately escorted convoys [were] worse than none." It must also be acknowledged that the prewar U.S. Navy had focused more on the construction of large warships than on smaller vessels and that the navy planners had not given much prior thought to charting convoy routes, organizing escorts, or antisubmarine warfare.[94]

The initial steps involved in creating the interlocking convoy consisted of a collaborative effort between the Atlantic Fleet and the British and Dutch Navies to provide the necessary escort vessels to create the Caribbean routes. Four tentative routes were inaugurated in July, and by early September a well-defined system was established that enabled merchant ships to move with protection according to precise timetables similar to those used by the railroads. Even though thousands of ships were moving through scores of routes, the Caribbean system, as naval historian Samuel Eliot Morison found, was based on two fundamental principles: (1) the northbound convoys were scheduled to arrive at New York just before a transatlantic convoy would leave for Great Britain; (2) two main convoy routes, to which all the

Map of the Interlocking Convoy System, 1942–1943. See text for
explanation of relevant route abbreviations. (Based on information in
Samuel Eliot Morison, *The Atlantic Battle Won, May 1943–May 1945*,
vol. 10, *History of U.S. Naval Operations in World War II* [Boston: Little,
Brown, 1968])

others fed, were Key West to New York and return (KN-NK) and the Guantánamo to New York and return (GN-NG). According to Morison, these two convoys might be compared to express trains, with all other convoys similar to local trains feeding freight into the two major southern terminals. If a local convoy arrived in the major terminus a day late, its ships would have to wait until the next express convoy came through.[95]

Guantánamo would quickly emerge as the Caribbean focal point because it would be fed by the Guantánamo-Aruba-Trinidad (GAT-TAG) convoy, which transported most of the petroleum and bauxite that came from the Dutch West Indies, plus cargo to and from South America after the Trinidad South (TS) convoy to and from Brazil had been established.[96] There would also be the Panama Canal Zone–Guantánamo (GZ-ZG) convoy as well as the shuttle convoy between Key West and Guantánamo (KG-GK). To facilitate handling ship movement and assigning escorts, the Escort Vessel Administration was created in July and August 1942 with offices in Guantánamo and Trinidad. Later that year, Harbor Entrance Control Posts were also established at these bases to direct ships in and out of the harbors and to arrange berthing.[97]

In the initial stages, the process of providing convoy escorts was often haphazard and makeshift, owing to the lack of available small naval ships. Some of the escorts were of the kind described by Fletcher Pratt, and there were also the yachtsmen, or "maritime minutemen," in seagoing twenty-five footers or forty footers, who lacked depth charges but had radios and could report the position of a German sub if they spotted one or possibly come to the rescue if a tanker or freighter had been hit. For example, in August 1942, a convoy of eighty-three ships that assembled at Trinidad had only the patrol gunboat *Surprise* (PG-63) and three sub chasers serving as escorts. Because of the obvious weaknesses in escort protection, Admiral Hoover instructed his commanders to stay with the convoy at all times, not to detach even to rescue survivors of torpedoed ships.[98]

During the next nine months, however, the patrol and escort resources available to Admiral Hoover steadily increased. By April 1943, he had nine destroyers, three patrol gunboats, nine coast guard cutters, twenty-four sub chasers, and about forty other small craft. He also commanded approximately one hundred army aircraft based in Trinidad and Guiana as well as the Fleet Air Wing Eleven, consisting of thirty-one Martin patrol bombers (PBMs), thirty-five Catalina (PBY) flying-boats, and blimp Squadron Thirty.[99]

Confronted by these defensive measures, U-boat raids in the Caribbean ceased in December 1942, but resumed episodically in March, April, and May 1943. Then in July and August, Dönitz sent ten U-boats into the Caribbean, but by this time the U.S. Navy was ready for them. The U-boats managed to sink a comparatively modest 16,231 tons of shipping before U.S. forces sank five of the German submarines in the Caribbean, and two more were lost before reaching their home ports. The entry in one German commander's diary for August 23 foretold the end of Dönitz's Caribbean campaign:

> Entire Caribbean area . . . strong to very strong air patrol, changing to continuous air activity on U-boat being observed. Convoy traffic as formerly. . . . Isolated traffic protected by air and surface escort. . . . Day and night [radar] location everywhere, especially strong radar in Trinidad area. Slight chances of success. . . . Strength of crews taxed to utmost by heat and moist atmosphere. On the other hand enemy conditions for defense are favorable. This is apparent from the losses.[100]

As Donald Yerxa and Fitzroy André Baptiste have perceptively found, the real success story of the Caribbean interlocking convoy was not how many U-boats were sunk or driven off, but that most of the strategic goods produced in the Western Hemisphere—including everything from oil, bauxite, and rubber to soap, flour, vegetable oils, and of course sugar and coffee—managed to reach the Allies.[101] It was in these critical months between August 1942 and December 1943 that Guantánamo played its most significant wartime role. Functioning as the Caribbean junction for eight regular convoys, it was second only to New York as the busiest port in the Western Hemisphere. For 1943 and 1944, Lloyd's Register recorded that Guantánamo handled 17,678 ships in convoy, the greatest percentage of which were involved in the Guantánamo to New York (GN-NG) routes (6,500 ships in 297 convoys). Axis submarines sank a total of 137 merchant ships in the Gulf of Paria–Trinidad between February 1942 and December 1943, but, according to Baptiste's calculations, an average of 3,500 merchantmen and 1,000 warships safely entered and exited that area each year of the war.[102]

Air coverage played a significant role in protecting convoy operations in the Guantánamo Sector. During periods of peak activity from 1942 to 1943, two twelve-plane PBM squadrons, one fifteen-plane SBD squadron, and two blimps were permanently stationed at Guantánamo. At different times, they were supplemented by other navy and army aircraft squadrons. In his data-rich, carefully researched *War, Cooperation, and Conflict*, Baptiste finds that from the inception of convoy operations, the combined effect of sea and air patrols proved "immediately effective in virtually eliminating ship sinkings in the Guantánamo Sector."[103]

Fletcher Pratt, however, conveys a different image of the operations and composition of these convoys and their air support. According to Pratt, the improvisational aspect of these wartime expediencies persisted. He describes Admiral Hoover as resisting the formal imposition of a war room with a regional map to pinpoint the location of ships and airplanes by claiming that he could keep track of every ship in the Caribbean in his head, until his staff pointed out that "he was the only magician in San Juan and in war there is always the chance that any one man may become a casualty."

> Most of the ships . . . had sailing orders to Trinidad only; even their captains were ignorant of their ultimate destination. . . . The officer in charge of supplies and repairs was British Navy. . . . There was little shop equipment and no labor but natives, who formed the interesting habit of breaking tools so they could be paid without having to work for it. Nobody knows how he did the job. . . . The officer directing the making up of convoys and the hours of their sailing was American Navy; escorts were furnished by another American Navy officer, who took anything available down to such fantastic combinations as a U.S. destroyer, a Dutch gunboat, and a couple of British motor-torpedo boats. . . . In the air the convoys were covered by equally strange mixtures: Army, Navy, and Marine Corps planes, sometimes all working under the orders of a coordinating officer who might belong to any of the three.[104]

For the men who served onboard a convoy escort, the experience was almost always extremely uncomfortable, and, in scouting for U-boats, both tense and tedious. Pratt, who rode on the converted cabin-cruiser "Yippee" (*YP219*), wrote that "everybody aboard . . . was violently seasick; they could keep no fire and cook no food. . . . Anyone who could slept on deck, lashed down." One sailor, on a tanker en route from Guantánamo to Curaçao in the GAT convoy, complained in his journal for the week of November 15, 1942, of "the monotony, lack of privacy, and the strain of broken sleep and constant vigil attendant upon plying the ocean in wartime. . . . I remembered going on watch unrested after many fitful nights of trying to sleep fully clothed, the jaded nerves, and the blank memory and tired aching eyes."[105]

With the final departure of U-boats from the Caribbean in late 1943, the frenetic activity at Guantánamo began to subside. By summer 1945, families from the United States had returned to the base and the station became a temporary training facility for foreign personnel who had purchased U.S. war supplies. In 1946, for example, Chinese naval officers and sailors participated in maneuvers aboard U.S. ships. The station also resumed its earlier functions as the winter base for the U.S. Fleet and as a site for training marines in amphibious warfare. Bradley Reynolds recorded that by the late 1940s, the population of Guantánamo was approximately five thousand, of whom fifteen hundred were military personnel. This was down from nearly fifty-five hundred military and five thousand civilians assigned there in January 1944.[106]

The two U.S. ambassadors to Cuba during World War II, George Messersmith and Spruille Braden, held very different views of U.S.- Cuban cooperation during wartime. The Cuban public's quick reaction to the Japanese attack on Pearl Harbor elated Messersmith. He reported that the Cuban Congress had unanimously passed its own resolution of war against the Japanese on December 8, 1941, the same day FDR called for war. Two days later, Cuba also declared war on Germany and Italy. On December 12, Messersmith wrote Hull: "Although Cuba is practically defenseless and open to attack, the Cuban Government and people did not for one moment hesitate to support us when larger and stronger of our neighbors have taken halfway measures or so far, none at all."[107]

In a subsequent message to Hull sent on December 20, Messersmith again praised the Cubans for their support: "I might state that, while I had always felt that the Cuban people would respond positively to any action we might take with respect to war, I had not anticipated that the public response would be as enthusiastic, general, and gratifying as had been the case."[108]

Braden, in contrast, was more critical of the Cuban war effort and also of the FDR administration's bland reaction to documented reports of official Cuban corruption. As historian Irwin Gellman found, Braden "repeatedly criticized the islanders for their apathetic or hostile attitudes toward the United States' wartime policies. Braden also objected that the Cubans failed to attend to their harbor defenses, forcing American troops to maintain them."[109]

Messersmith and Braden shared a concern regarding the extent of corruption in Batista's government. On July 12, 1942, Messersmith informed Undersecretary of State Welles that "the government here . . . is in the hands largely of unscrupulous politicians who are interested only in getting out of their positions what they can while they are in them." In the same message, he warned Welles that the U.S. government should not place too much confidence in Batista: "Basically I do not believe that he likes us or ever will. He has been difficult to deal with while ruling from behind the scenes."[110]

For his part, Braden composed the lengthy memorandum "Conditions in Cuba and Our Policies in Respect Thereto" on July 22, 1944, in which he predicted that Batista's corruption would eventually foment revolution, and warned his superiors in Washington: "I have repeatedly sounded the alarm that the continued control of the Cuban government by Batista and his disreputable camarilla . . . unless restrained, would inevitably entail . . .

the disintegration of the democratic system of government, . . . the deterioration of Cuban-American relations, . . . [and] eventually an explosion by the Cuban people into revolution and possible chaos."[111]

In fairness, Cuba's involvement in World War II may be described as both cooperative and opportunistic. In 1942, after diplomatic efforts to create a Cuban military zone adjacent to Guantánamo for joint defense purposes had proven inconclusive, Havana permitted the United States to construct and operate two air bases, several auxiliary landing fields to be used for training purposes, mobile coast artillery, and air patrols.[112] Although Cuba's active role was restricted by the limited capabilities of its armed forces, its navy participated in joint operations with its U.S. counterpart in patrolling Cuba's coastline. Some Cuban nationals enlisted in the U.S. Armed Services and even served at Guantánamo. In May 1943, a Cuban submarine chaser sank the German U-boat *U176*, the twenty-first U-boat sunk that month.[113]

CHILI:—SAY, DOES YOUR MUDDER KNOW YOU'RE OUT? "A 'Chili' Reception." (*Puck*, 10, no. 250 [December 21, 1881]: 248)

"The Fight at Guantánamo: Marines under Lt. Col. [Robert] Huntington Repelling an Attack." (In *The Story of the War of 1898*, ed. W. Nephew King [New York: Collier, 1898])

"GOOD GOVERNMENT VS. REVOLUTION; — AN EASY CHOICE." (By Joseph Keppler; *Puck* 49, no. 1259 [April 17, 1901])

Correspondent Stephen Crane with sidearm, May, 1897. (By
C. Boehringer, Stephen Crane Collection, Special Collections Research
Center, Syracuse University Library)

Naval strategist Alfred T. Mahan, c. 1904. (Library of
Congress, LC-USZ62-120219)

Master geopolitician, President Theodore Roosevelt with globe, 1903.
(By Rockwood, Theodore Roosevelt Collection, Harvard College Library,
Cambridge, Mass. Reproduced with permission)

The U.S. Fleet in Guantánamo Bay, 1917. (Naval Historical Foundation, Washington Navy Yard, Washington, D.C.)

Cuba's First President, Tómas Estrada Palma, in the Palace in Havana, c. 1902. (Library of Congress, LC-USZ62-74561)

Aerial View of Guantánamo, 1947. (Naval Historical Foundation,
Washington Navy Yard, Washington, D.C.)

U.S. Marine Corps insignia on a huge concrete slab in front of building where monthly fenceline negotiations are held, 1964. The insignia was placed by Commandant John Bulkeley in response to provocations by Fidel Castro. (Operational Archive at the Navy Yard, Breuer Papers, Washington, D.C.)

Commandant John Bulkeley showing U.S. Navy Secretary Paul Nitze the water cutoff at Guantánamo, 1964. (Operational Archive at the Navy Yard, Breuer Papers, Washington, D.C.)

"HE 'TOLD IT TO THE ADMIRAL.'" Fidel Castro encased in a section of water pipe, 1964. (By Tom Ellinwood, Operational Archive at the Navy Yard, Breuer Papers, Washington, D.C.)

U.S. Marine guarding the Guantánamo fenceline with Cuban sentry post in distant background, May 2007. (Photo by Stephen I. Schwab)

The northeast gate between Cuba and Guantánamo, May 2007. (Photo by Stephen I. Schwab)

Camp X-Ray, the open-air detention center for Haitian refugees and "enemy-combatants," May 2007. (Photo by Stephen I. Schwab.)

Camp Delta detention and interrogation center, August 2004. (© Mark Wilson/pool/Reuter's/Corbis)

6

The Cold War, Part 1
Dwight D. Eisenhower

CUBA IN GENERAL AND GUANTÁNAMO IN PARTICULAR attracted comparatively little scrutiny from top-level U.S. foreign policymakers in the early years of the Cold War as preventing Soviet gains in western Europe and Greece consumed their major attention. President Harry Truman's administration did lobby successfully for the enactment of a hemispheric defense pact, beginning with the Chapultepec Conference in late 1945 and concluding with the enactment of the Inter-American Treaty of Reciprocal Assistance, popularly known as the Rio Treaty, on December 20, 1948. Also in 1948, Truman, while vacationing at his "little White House" in Key West, briefly toured Guantánamo, Puerto Rico, and the U.S. Virgin Islands. Presidential records at the Truman Library, however, contain only scattered and few documents pertaining to Guantánamo.

The Truman administration may have deplored the coup d'etat by which former Cuban president Fulgencio Batista regained power on March 10, 1952, but it moved quickly to recognize his new government. In his memorandum to the president dated March 24, 1952, Secretary of State Dean Acheson first called attention to "our very special position in Cuba," which included "heavy capital investment, enormous international trade, the Nicaro nickel plant operation, the Guantánamo Naval Base, three armed service missions, and the recent signing of a bilateral military assistance agreement which requires implementation." Acheson then advised Truman, "It would be detrimental to the special relations that this country has with Cuba to hold up recognition any longer."[1] On March 27, 1952, a U.S. State Department spokesperson announced that recognition was based on bipartisan criteria established by Acheson: that the new government was in firm control, that the people of Cuba had "acquiesced," and that the new regime had pledged to fulfill its international obligations.[2]

In truth, Batista had ousted the increasingly unstable government of President Carlos Prío Socarrás, which, even though democratically elected, had earned widespread contempt as one of the most corrupt and violent administrations in republican Cuban history. The *Washington Post* editorial published the morning after the coup dismissed Prío's government as "probably the most corrupt in Cuban history." It also recalled that, in the 1930s

Batista had "ruled Cuba with a pretty heavy hand" and that his regime also had known corruption. The breezy cover story on Batista in *Time* magazine described him as a dictator with "limitless ambition, plenty of ability, and no respect for his fellow men." The article summarily dealt with the lack of opposition to Batista's coup, explaining that after "seven years of riotously rotten government," the average Cuban was "too cynical about democracy to fight in its behalf." There was no mention of Guantánamo in the text, but a map of Cuba that highlighted sugarcane, tobacco, and coffee had an anchor symbol above Guantánamo Bay, right next to a bottle of rum at Santiago de Cuba.[3]

What mattered most to Washington in the deepening Cold War environment was that Batista, albeit a Cuban nationalist, was certainly no communist.[4] Within the first two weeks of his "new revolutionary government," Batista provided fresh proof of his anti-Soviet credentials by refusing to allow two Russian diplomats to enter Cuba. Moscow promptly terminated its diplomatic relations with Havana.[5] Batista also moved quickly to buttress his prior reputation as a strongman who could provide political and economic stability. In rapid succession, he suspended the 1940 Constitution, replaced the Cuban Congress with an eighty-member consultative council, and dissolved all political parties.

Batista's seizure of power exposed the weaknesses of Cuba's two highly factionalized major parties, the Auténticos and the Ortodoxos, neither of which could mount an effective democratic challenge to the new dictatorship. As historian Louis Pérez Jr. has succinctly written, "The Ortodoxos were leaderless and the Auténticos could not lead."[6] This political vacuum enabled more radical Cuban nationalists to challenge both Batista and the close relationship between Cuban and U.S. elites that had existed since the early 1900s. The leader of these revolutionaries was Fidel Castro, who had run as an Ortodoxo candidate for Congress in the 1952 elections that Batista canceled, but Fidel had also attacked the party for the "cowardice of its leadership."[7] In his reflective study of Prío's government and its demise, Charles Ameringer credits Fidel Castro with one of the most balanced criticisms of Batista's coup. Castro said, "It was right to remove from office a government of murderers and thieves. . . . But by what right do the military do so, they who have murdered and stolen without limit in the past?"[8]

In his memoir, *Waging Peace,* former president Dwight D. Eisenhower admitted that he was surprised first by the strength and success of Fidel Castro's rise to power, and, second, by Castro's subsequent decision to embrace communism and to ally his government with the Soviet Union.[9] Guantánamo first emerged as a flashpoint between Washington and the Cuban rebels in the summer of 1958, and the U.S. naval base continued to be a focus of tension as bilateral relations spiraled toward the breaking point, which came on January 3, 1961. The emergence of Cuba as Moscow's foothold in the Western Hemisphere gave this island nation a political significance it otherwise would have never achieved, and it also transformed Guantánamo into a unique U.S. military outpost. The more Castro moved Cuba into the Soviet sphere, the more entrenched the U.S. position became on Guantánamo.

After being imprisoned for less than two years following his failed assault on the Moncada army barracks in 1953, Fidel devoted his major energies to building an effective guerrilla organization and to appealing to a broad spectrum of politically disaffected Cubans. During this period, he distanced himself from most of the communist friends of his student days, and, in his famous interview with veteran Latin American correspondent Herbert Matthews of the *New York Times* on February 17, 1957, Fidel emphasized that he was a nationalist whose main objectives were to overthrow Batista and restore the democratic guarantees of Cuba's 1940 Constitution. Although he admitted that he was angry with the U.S. government for supporting Batista, he told Matthews, "You can be sure that we have no animosity toward the United States and the American people." Fidel would not openly criticize the United States until after he had taken power.[10]

Fidel Castro and his closest collaborator, his brother Raúl, initially challenged the United States over Guantánamo in an ambivalent, almost tentative manner as if they were probing to see how firmly the United States would defend the interests of the base. As this chapter will illustrate, it was not until summer 1958, when Castro's insurgents were virtually in control of the surrounding Oriente Province, that Raúl made any provocative moves toward Guantánamo. Even then, Fidel claimed that Raúl was acting on his own initiative. In retrospect, it appears that Fidel's distancing of himself from Raúl's actions was calculated to reinforce foreign perceptions that, even though Raúl was a communist,[11] Fidel, though admittedly a leftist, was keeping all his political options open, including how he would deal with the U.S. military presence at Guantánamo.[12] It probably is also true that even at this early stage, Fidel realized it would jeopardize and probably undermine his ambitions as a political leader if he were to confront the Eisenhower administration or the U.S. military directly over Guantánamo.

Clandestinely, however, in the mid-1950s some workers at Guantánamo began to smuggle weapons and gasoline to Castro's guerrillas in the Sierra Maestra. According to Jana Lipman, Frank País, who had been the leading organizer of the 26th of July Movement (M-26-7) in Santiago de Cuba, established an M-26-7 cell in Guantánamo City that quickly attracted adherents among base workers.[13] Lipman finds that "by 1958 base workers became a critical source of information, material, and equipment for the anti-Batista movement. . . . Guantánamo's M-26-7 also organized attacks against Batista's Rural Guard and participated in acts of sabotage." Lipman cites the experience of Gustavo Fraga Jacobino, a base worker and self-proclaimed Trotskyite who literally blew himself up in a dynamite explosion while preparing for an M-26-7 attack.[14] Base employees who affiliated with the M-26-7, however, did not engage in direct confrontations with their U.S. Navy employers. Instead, "they continued to work on the base and cash their paychecks [while capitalizing] on their ability to travel with relative ease on and off the base." By so doing, Lipman concludes, "workers established a new revolutionary narrative whereby Cubans took advantage of the base rather than GTMO taking advantage of Guantánamo."[15]

Guantánamo became a point of friction between Cuba's Castro brothers and the United States only six months before Fidel Castro took power on New Year's Day of 1959. On the evening of June 27, 1958, Cuban rebels operating under the command of Raúl Castro kidnapped twenty-four U.S. naval personnel, including eleven marines, when they were returning by bus to the base from shore leave in Guantánamo City. On the day before, a rebel group had attacked the facilities of the Moa Bay Mining Company on the north coast of Oriente Province and carried off eleven U.S. and two Canadian technicians and supervisory personnel. These separate incidents were conjoined in two priority telegrams rushed to Washington by Ambassador Earl E. T. Smith. The first message was a garbled communiqué that quoted rebel sources as saying the raid on the mining company was a protest against U.S. use of "gasoline supplied from *Moa Naval Base*." The subsequent telegram attempted to clarify the situation by stating that the rebels had seized the Americans in protest against "Cuban planes they claim gassing at Guantánamo Naval Base."[16]

The second telegram communicated the rationale behind Military Order No. 30, which Raúl Castro had issued to his rebel followers a few days earlier, instructing them to kidnap U.S. citizens in retaliation for the intensive bombardments his forces had been receiving from Batista's military aircraft. Raúl justified his order by claiming that these aircraft had been fueling and obtaining arms at Guantánamo. The reality was more complex. In May 1958, two months after a U.S. arms embargo had been enacted against Cuba, two Cuban transports had landed at Guantánamo to obtain 300 operational small rockets and turn in defective ones the United States had mistakenly sold to Batista's government before the arms embargo was enforced at the base. During a conference on the Cuban missile crisis hosted by Fidel in Havana in 1992, former U.S. diplomat and Cuba expert Wayne Smith reflected that the U.S. decision to deliver weapons to Batista at Guantánamo after the imposition of the embargo was a serious mistake because the 26th of July rebels were certain to find out that Cuban air force planes at the naval base were loading bombs and rockets to be used against the Cuban people.[17]

This is precisely what ensued. One of the unarmed Cuban transports had refueled at Guantánamo, and a clandestine report that included photographs of that incident taken by a base worker had been communicated to Raúl's headquarters and was subsequently published in a M-26-7 broadside. Although rebel claims that Batista was using the base to wage civil war were untrue, according to Cuban scholar Jorge Domínguez, the facts were unclear at that time. On February 13, the *New York Times* reported that Batista's government had begun pouring troops into Oriente Province in response to increases in rebel attacks and sabotage.[18]

There were more reasons for the kidnappings than Raúl had mentioned in his military order. When he was interviewed in his hideout by Jules Dubois of the *Chicago Tribune,* Raúl listed three reasons for the kidnappings:

1. To attract world attention in general and that of the United States in particular to the crime being committed against our people with arms which the government of the United States had supplied to Batista for continental defense.

2. To deter the criminal bombardments—with incendiary bombs, rockets, and even napalm bombs—which were being carried out against our forces and above all against the defenseless towns of peasants.

3. Some equipment, like tractors and vehicles, of Moa and Nicaro were taken as strict war necessities and for the construction of strategic roads within our liberated territories.[19]

As diplomatic historian Thomas Paterson has accurately noted, Castro's revolutionaries frequently denounced the long-standing and close ties between Batista and the U.S. military, and held them largely responsible for much of the death and destruction, including the victimization of noncombatants, during the insurrection. Since Guantánamo had long held the potential of being attacked as a lingering symbol of U.S. imperialism, the Castro brothers made it so.[20]

Raúl Castro never mentioned Vice President Richard Nixon's just-completed tour of Latin America, where his motorcade had been attacked by a rock-throwing mob in Caracas, Venezuela. Nonetheless, the timing of the kidnapping of sailors from Guantánamo, one month after the Nixon visit, may have been calculated to refocus heightened anti-U.S. sentiment internationally and especially throughout Latin America on the struggle of the Cuban rebels against the misuse of this U.S. naval base. If true, the gambit, at least to some extent, backfired. On June 30, a *New York Times* editorial belittled the kidnappings as "dangerous and rather juvenile escapades," and evenhandedly asserted that although Cubans generally may feel bitter toward the U.S. government, "American engineers working a mine in Moa Bay and American sailors assigned to our naval base at Guantánamo Bay are entirely innocent of American policies." On July 1, at a news conference, Secretary of State John Foster Dulles condemned the kidnappings as "blackmail," and when asked what he meant specifically, Dulles replied, "We can only infer that the action is being taken to bring about United States intervention in the internal affairs of Cuba, which we do not intend to do."[21] Dulles's remarks were followed two days later by a State Department press announcement that, with the notable exception of the exchange of small rocketheads at Guantánamo in May, no U.S. arms deliveries had been made to Cuba since March 14, 1958. The formal statement acknowledged that one of the unarmed Cuban transports had been given sufficient fuel at Guantánamo to return to its base, but insisted that "allegations that the Cuban Armed Forces are using the base for their military operations or as a source of fuel and arms supplies are completely unfounded."[22]

For his part, Fidel publicly insisted that Raúl's decision to kidnap the Americans had been made without his knowledge or approval.[23] He said that the rebels had found rocket fragments containing U.S. serial numbers, but that U.S. citizens should not be blamed for the actions of their government. Fidel also promised his rebel contacts in the United States that the hostages would be released immediately and that no more Americans would be abducted. Fidel's denial of involvement is suspect even if his letter of July 7, 1958, to Raúl was an authentic communication of second thoughts:

> I have not received any direct information about the earlier and present situation of the North American citizens who are said to be in the hands of your forces. . . . We must consider the possibility that elements of the dictatorship [are] exploiting this incident. . . . This would turn international public opinion against us as it would react with indignation to the news, for example, that several of those North Americans had been murdered by the rebels.[24]

It is possible that Fidel was manipulating this incident to add credibility to the fiction that whereas Raúl was a communist agitator, Fidel could be trusted by the U.S. government. Fidel and Raúl maintained separate rebel camps in Oriente Province, but it is unlikely that a massive kidnapping of U.S. citizens—certain to grab international headlines and provoke a serious confrontation with top U.S. officials—would have taken place without Fidel's full support. As Brian Latell has found, when Fidel was in the Sierra

Maestra, he knew every detail, even knowing how many unspent bullets each of his men had.[25]

Contrary to Fidel Castro's assurances to his rebel contacts in the United States that the hostage crisis would end immediately, two more Americans working at sugar mills near Guantánamo were kidnapped, and the stalemate between the rebels and the U.S. government continued. On July 3, *New York Times* correspondent Peter Kihss reported that, according to Guantánamo's base commander, Rear Admiral Robert Ellis, the navy captives were widely scattered through the mountains of eastern and central Oriente Province, and it would take some time to gather them together for release. Kihss also reported that Raúl Castro intended to apologize for the kidnappings of U.S. and Canadian sailors and civilians, and to reassure their families that no North Americans would be harmed in any way. Through official channels, Central Intelligence Agency (CIA) Director Allen Dulles provided his own version of good news. At the 371st meeting of the National Security Council (NSC) on July 3, Dulles said he had information that the Americans would gradually be freed in groups until all had been released.[26] On July 6, another exclusive story from Kihss quoted Raúl as having said that the U.S. hostages were "good protection against bombings by Cuban Government planes."[27]

Under increasing pressure to end the crisis, Smith had the CIA provide a special operator and shortwave equipment to establish communications between Raúl Castro's rebel hideout and the U.S. Embassy in Havana. Senior embassy officials carried information between Havana, Santiago, and Guantánamo. In his memoir, *The Fourth Floor*, Smith recalled that because of its proximity to the U.S. Consulate in Santiago and to the area where the captives were being held, the Guantánamo Naval Base was able to provide valuable cooperation and aid throughout the crisis. Its most dramatic activity was to deploy U.S. fighter aircraft on reconnaissance flights over the Sierra Madre with the intention of intimidating the rebels.[28]

True to Dulles's prediction, the rebels began to release their navy prisoners on July 13, 1958. When the last group of fourteen was freed on July 18, several said a Cuban commandant had told them they were released because "the rebels did not want to interfere with the U.S. military effort in Lebanon." Raúl Castro provided his own confirmation in a letter to Ellis, stating:

> Because of the measures adopted by your nation in the face of the latest international events—taking into account the need your army has for each one of your members in these moments—the Military Commands of the 26th of July Revolutionary Army in the 'Frank País' second front have decided to order the immediate release of all the sailors who still remain in our liberated territories.[29]

The kidnapping crisis concerning Guantánamo was over, but, as Smith wryly observed, Raúl Castro enjoyed kidnapping. In October 1958, his men abducted two Americans and several Cuban employees of Texaco and held them for ransom. This time Smith sent U.S. Consul Park Wollam, who had been in direct contact with the rebels during the Moa and Guantánamo hostage crisis, to inform Raúl that unless the Americans were released immediately, Smith would recommend that Washington renew its shipments of arms to Batista. Smith knew it was a threat that would be ignored by the State Department, but it might prompt the rebels to free the Americans. The gambit worked: three days later the Americans were released unharmed. The Cuban rebels abandoned the tactic of kidnapping Americans and turned to hijacking airplanes with equally provocative consequences.

The recurrent kidnappings had provoked animosities in both Washington and the Sierra Maestra that would linger. In late October, the conservative *New York Journal American* spoke for many in the Eisenhower administration in the editorial "Sick and Tired":

> We are beginning to get the impression that Fidel Castro, the Cuban rebel leader, considers kidnapping American citizens an act of playful diplomacy. . . . He has another think coming. . . . State Department spokesman Lincoln White said that the United States might have to take action unless these outrages stopped. . . . Castro now calls [such] statements "aggressive declarations." . . . The Castro attitude is a combination of arrogance and stupidity. . . . When a Washington official said, "We're sick and tired of having Americans kidnapped," he was speaking for us all.[30]

At the same time, on the other side of the Florida straits, Fidel warned the U.S. government to stop interfering in Cuba's revolution. In a radio broadcast from his headquarters in the Sierra Maestra, Fidel responded angrily to a State Department official's claim that the rebel kidnappings were "uncivilized conduct." Fidel replied that the Cuban people, not the U.S. State Department, should judge his actions.[31]

At Guantánamo, Ellis reported that fallout from the kidnapping had eroded the goodwill the naval base had traditionally enjoyed among the population in the surrounding area. Ellis's comment was included in a Cuba policy paper drafted by senior U.S. Embassy officials that predicted Guantánamo "may become a domestic political whipping boy." The paper also warned that Cuban communists were taking every opportunity to exploit the political turbulence.[32]

In mid-1958, Guantánamo Naval Base faced a new crisis involving the security of its only potable water source, namely the Yateras water plant, located five miles outside the base's perimeter. This was Guantánamo's most vulnerable point. The base's normal water consumption was approximately 2,000,000 gallons per day and on-site storage capacity was 500,000 gallons, which meant that, without access to the Yateras aqueduct, the base had two days' water supply. On July 25, 1958, the Cuban Army notified Ellis that its troops could no longer guard the water plant. The Cubans provided no specific reason for withdrawing the guards, but U.S. officials reasoned that government troops were either retreating from an area that was increasingly controlled by Raúl's rebel forces or that Batista had decided to assign them elsewhere. Dulles had earlier agreed that in the event Cuban Army guards were withdrawn, U.S. marines would be assigned to protect this vital water system. Undersecretary Christian Herter and Deputy Assistant Secretary for Inter-American Affairs William Snow, however, were reluctant to assign marines or any U.S. troops to guard a facility that was so far from the base. They anticipated a hostile reaction not only from the rebels but from other Cuban nationalists. Despite these well-founded apprehensions, the Department of State cleared a press release to be used by Ellis on the morning of July 28, 1958, when fifteen marine guards arrived at the Yateras River. As the *New York Times* article "U.S. Troops Land in Cuba for Duty" reported the following day, "This is the first time an armed detachment of U.S. Marines has entered Cuban territory in more than fifty years."[33]

The negative reaction of various Cuban opposition factions was virtually immediate. By evening, State Department officers were taking telephone calls from angry Cuban exiles in Miami and Washington. Protest demonstrators marched outside the United Nations building in New York. A report filed by the U.S. Embassy in Caracas, where the Cuban rebels had a office, warned that strong, potentially violent protests by students and supporters of the M-26-7 would occur all over Latin America if U.S. marines continued to guard an installation on Cuban soil.[34]

During the next few days, senior U.S. officials in Washington and Havana discussed the alternative options of hiring private Cuban guards to replace the marines or trying to persuade Batista to assign another army unit to protect the Yateras plant. The chief of naval operations, Admiral Arleigh Burke, argued forcefully against assigning Cuban guards to the waterworks. He reasoned that the guards would either be pro-Batista, which would make them vulnerable to guerrilla attacks, or pro-rebel, which would force the U.S. government to employ and negotiate with Castro's insurrectionists, which it obviously did not want to do. In Burke's view, the choice was to leave the facility unguarded or to retain the marines.[35]

In Havana, Batista expressed concern during a meeting with Smith about keeping the marines at Yateras, stating that the rebels might cause an incident designed to put the United States in an embarrassing position. He offered to assign 1,000 men to guard the Moa mine and 1,000 to guard the Nicaro nickel plants if the United States would supply 2,000 rifles and supporting equipment, but he made no similar proposal regarding Yateras. On August 1 at 7:00 P.M., Smith informed the Cuban government that the United States was preparing to withdraw the marines from the Yateras facility. A few hours later the Cuban minister of state told Smith that a new unit of Cuban troops was being assigned to guard Yateras. A subsequent press announcement downplayed the crisis aspects of the situation by indicating that the marines had been a temporary expedient while Cuban Army units were being rotated, and the government intended to provide adequate protection to the water installation in view of the importance of that supply to Guantánamo and especially in these moments of international crisis. The Cuban Army guard resumed its duties at Yateras on August 3, 1958.[36]

The imbroglio over the security situation at Yateras illustrated the growing desperation of the Batista government as it struggled to provide protection to important installations and at the same time preserve its military strength by removing army units from exposed positions in the eastern region of the island, which was increasingly under rebel control. The incident also brought into focus the growing animosity toward the U.S. military installation at Guantánamo—fueled by rebel propaganda—and especially the hostility that stationing U.S. troops on Cuban soil aroused. In truth, Guantánamo was already a convenient political whipping boy for Fidel and his adherents.[37]

Mary McCoy's dissertation research, some of which she conducted at Guantánamo Bay, dovetails with Jana Lipman's later finding in revealing that, at the same time Fidel and Raúl were publicly denouncing the U.S. government for using Guantánamo to support Batista covertly, the rebels themselves were manipulating sympathizers or rebel agents among the Cuban workers on the base to steal fuel, bullets, spare parts, clothing, and other items and smuggle them through the gate. According to the written account of former rebel operative José "Pepe" Bahía:

> Cubans who were helping the rebels had connections in all the shops on base. Employees were bribed in advance of an operation and supplied with plenty of rum. While they were drunk, the rebel sympathizers would load supplies on trucks. . . . One of the favorite tricks of those who drove cars or trucks to the base from Guantánamo City or Caimanéra was to stop in the morning at Boqueron and drain their gas tanks into storage barrels, keeping only enough to reach the base. Before returning home in the evening, they would fill their tanks to capacity. In this manner they carried off hundreds of gallons of gasoline.[38]

Smith apparently knew that the Cuban rebels were stealing weapons from Guantánamo. When he later testified at a Senate Internal Security Subcommittee hearing made public on September 11, 1960, Smith said the revolutionaries obtained arms and ammunition through Cubans attached to the base.[39]

By mid-November 1958 the Cuban government had virtually no capability to provide security to the Yateras waterworks. On November 15, Batista informed Smith that approximately one hundred poorly equipped soldiers were guarding the isolated aqueduct and that they were bait for rebels who wanted to capture Yateras for propaganda purposes. Batista asked Smith if the U.S. government could sell adequate arms to the Cuban troops to defend Yateras, or if Washington would permit the soldiers to withdraw and leave civilian personnel equipped with radio equipment to communicate to the U.S. naval base and to Cuban Army headquarters in Guantánamo City. Batista said that if the United States would not agree to either of these proposals, he would keep the current number of soldiers at Yateras even though they would be a "sacrifice." The State Department found both of Batista's proposals unacceptable. On November 23, 25, and 27, Cuban rebels surrounding Yateras forced the plant operators to cut off the water supply to Guantánamo for varying periods of time. On November 29, following a discussion of the water security situation at the secretary of state's staff meeting, the department issued a warning to the Cuban rebels: "The United States Government has been exercising patience and forbearance while making it known in the affected area as well as to the Cuban government the gravity with which it views the events of the past week. The United States Government expects that these irresponsible acts will stop and will not be repeated." Obviously suggesting that U.S. marines might be reassigned to guard the Yateras aqueduct, this message had the desired effect—rebel harassment of the Yateras facility stopped as abruptly as it began.[40]

The kidnappings of U.S. naval personnel, the propaganda accusing Guantánamo of aiding Batista, and the manipulation of the base's water supply combined with reports of growing communist influence within Castro's rebel movement to have the cumulative effect of antagonizing and alarming senior U.S. policymakers. At the 392nd meeting of the NSC on December 23, 1958, Eisenhower asked if the Department of State had requested that the Department of Defense prepare a study of military action that might become necessary in Cuba. Herter replied that State-Defense conversations had centered on the possibility of evacuating U.S. personnel. CIA Director Allen Dulles then suggested that the U.S. government ought to prevent a Castro victory. Eisenhower said he thought this was the first time that suggestion had been made in the NSC. Dulles responded that the communists appeared to have penetrated the Castro movement, and if Castro took over, communist elements probably would participate in the government.[41]

The triumphant entry of revolutionary forces into Havana on January 1, 1959, not only marked the beginning of the Castro era but the continuation of friction between Cuba and the United States over Guantánamo.[42] Since 1959, Fidel has frequently pointed to Guantánamo as the lasting symbol of the first U.S. "intervention" and "an unwanted, illegal presence." In counterpoint, U.S. leaders have repeatedly cited the 1903 and 1934 Guantánamo treaties as legitimate and binding, and have found new ways to justify the naval station's relevance to U.S. security.

In an apparent effort to reduce bilateral tensions at the outset of the revolutionary government, the United States replaced Smith with Philip Bonsal, who had extensive diplomatic experience in Latin America.[43] Moreover, to avoid any possible misunderstanding of U.S. intentions, on January 15, 1959, the U.S. Navy diverted an Atlantic Fleet amphibious task force that included 3,000 marines from its intended stop at Guantánamo, ordering the fleet to proceed directly to its exercise area near Puerto Rico. According to the *New York Times*, Fidel Castro had warned he would take reprisals if U.S. marines landed in Cuba.[44] In his memoir, *Cuba, Castro, and the United States*, Bonsal wrote, "It was my hope that it might be possible eventually . . . to achieve a modification of the status of Guantánamo that would give Cuba a participation in its operation similar to that enjoyed by our NATO allies in the American bases on their soil. But unfortunately the Cuban-American alliance was to be destroyed, not modified."[45] As the rift widened between the Eisenhower administration and the Castro regime, Bonsal was recalled to Washington in late October 1960 to serve as U.S. ambassador to the Organization of American States (OAS).

There was one notable instance when Fidel Castro adopted a traditional diplomatic approach toward upholding Cuba's international obligations including the bilateral treaties concerning Guantánamo. The occasion was his appearance before the American Society of Newspaper Editors on April 15, 1959. According to Herter's evaluation, "The Castro who came to Washington was a man on his best behavior, who carefully followed the advice of his accompanying ministers and a public relations expert." Herter deduced that the United States would probably have increased problems with the new Cuban government regarding the U.S.-owned Nicaro nickel plant, but stated that "Castro made it clear that he has no desire to create any issue with regard to our Guantánamo Naval Base."[46] Herter did not take Fidel's assurances at face value. He observed that "Castro is much more concerned with ends than means and he does not have the same idea of law and legality as we have in the United States." Impressed with Fidel's force of personality,

Herter saw him as a "born leader," but he also warned, "Castro remains an enigma and we should await his decisions on specific matters before assuming a more optimistic view about developing a constructive relationship with him and his government."[47] During the same visit, Fidel met privately with Nixon, who summarized his initial impressions as follows: "The one fact we can be sure of is that he has those indefinable qualities which make him a leader of men. Whatever we may think of him he is going to be a great factor in the development of Cuba and very possibly in Latin American affairs generally. . . . He is either incredibly naïve about Communism or under Communist discipline."[48]

Neither Herter nor Nixon could foresee that Fidel would soon become the closest U.S. antagonist geographically, but, on the basis of only a few hours of direct exposure, both of these senior U.S. policymakers had gained remarkable insight into the new Cuban prime minister's personality.

On April 26, 1958, a feature article titled "Why Latin America Is Vital to Us" by Matthews was published in the *New York Times Sunday Magazine*. Matthews, who had been openly sympathetic toward Fidel Castro since first interviewing him in the Sierra Maestra in 1957, castigated both Smith and Eisenhower for their blundering policies in Cuba, which he believed had been largely responsible for antagonizing the new Castro regime.[49] At the same time, Matthews emphasized the importance of such naval outposts as Guantánamo to U.S. security: "Without bases in the Caribbean islands and without the Panama Canal, the United States would be wide open to invasion." In words of ominous prophesy, Matthews added, "If one could conceive of hostile missile bases in Mexico or Central America, the peril would be obvious."[50] Obvious to whom? It can be safely assumed that Fidel in Havana and probably Nikita Khrushchev in Moscow were among Matthews's most avid readers. It is speculative but possible that on that April Sunday in 1959, Matthews unwittingly planted the seed for the future installation of Soviet missiles on Cuban soil.

After returning to Cuba, Fidel frequently included Guantánamo in his inflammatory attacks on U.S. policies. At a mass rally on October 26, 1959, he whipped the crowd into a frenzy by accusing the United States of using Guantánamo to launch airplanes that dropped incendiary bombs and shrapnel on the houses of Cuban peasants and sugar mills. Many at the rally repeatedly shouted "Afuera!" (Out!). When the *New York Times* reported this story, the Pentagon immediately warned Cuba that the navy had no intention of relinquishing the base and that Cuba could not unilaterally abrogate the treaty signed on May 29, 1934, that reconfirmed the U.S. right to use Guantánamo Bay.

Meanwhile, at the State Department, Special Assistant Robert Hilton wrote a memorandum to his boss, Assistant Secretary for Inter-American Affairs Roy Rubottom, informing him that he had been peppered with questions by Bromley Smith, a senior official of the NSC, about contingency plans to protect Guantánamo if Fidel attempted to recover it for Cuba "by diplomatic demand, by physical occupation, by demonstrators and squatters, or by other means." Hilton suggested that the State Department maintain ongoing contact with other concerned agencies, especially the Defense Department, regarding this issue. He also thought that the United States should enlist support from other countries of the Caribbean littoral whose security interests would be harmed if Castro tried "to render Guantánamo inoperable."[51]

In late November 1959, correspondent Tad Szulc reported that Guantánamo had been effectively sealed off by a tall wire fence enclosing the perimeter, and Cuban territory had been off limits to U.S. Navy personnel and their families for more than a year. Most of the 3,000 Cubans who worked at Guantánamo but lived in Cuba commuted by bus or ferry. Szulc found that the base's water supply from the Yateras River was still its most vulnerable aspect. During the revolution, Castro's rebels had demonstrated they could shut off the water whenever they chose, and Szulc noted that this threat to the base persisted.[52]

As concern mounted within the Eisenhower administration over the rapidly deteriorating relations with Cuba, *U.S. News & World Report* pointed to Guantánamo as the new hot spot in the Caribbean and the "focal point of anti-American agitation in Cuba." In the article "Big Base under Fire," the popular newsmagazine listed the features that made Guantánamo a base of major importance to the United States:

> It is located nearly as close to the Panama Canal as it is to the Cuban capital of Havana, and is situated to guard easily the narrow sea-lane approaches to the canal. It also provides a natural anti-submarine base for the vital Caribbean area. At the present time, nearly every ship in the Atlantic Fleet puts in here each year for repairs and supplies, plus training and recreation for the crew. More American naval activity is centered here than at most naval bases within the United States.[53]

Half a year later, *Life* magazine would acknowledge: "If asked for an honest appraisal . . . most military men would concede that with the increased mobility and endurance of modern armament, Guantánamo was not absolutely essential to U.S. defense. But they would hate to lose it. The base furnishes excellent facilities for training and giving logistical support to the fleet, and in wartime, it would anchor the defense of the Caribbean and Panama Canal."[54]

As bilateral relations continued to deteriorate, the Eisenhower administration devoted increasing high-level attention to Guantánamo. At the NSC meeting on January 14, 1960, Eisenhower said that if the Cubans attacked Guantánamo, the U.S. government would need support from the rest of Latin America and should do everything possible through the OAS to educate member nations on the current situation in Cuba. Burke reported that the Joint Chiefs of Staff (JCS) were concerned about Cuba, but that he felt the communization of Cuba would most likely be accomplished before the OAS would recognize the gravity of the situation. Eisenhower then said he believed an attack on Guantánamo would justify taking decisive action against Cuba. Nixon suggested that one way to persuade other countries in the hemisphere to share Washington's view of Castro would be to discourage private U.S. investors from investing elsewhere in Latin America; Nixon reasoned that once the Latin Americans saw that Castro was frightening investment away from their countries, they would not be favorably inclined toward Cuba.[55]

On January 22, 1960, Burke informed the Senate Foreign Relations Committee that the navy intended to keep Guantánamo Bay indefinitely to preclude its falling into the hands of "a major enemy power," meaning the Soviet Union. Burke assured the committee that the Cuban government had not made any formal demands that the United States withdraw from the base, but the possibility of such a move had been discussed at all government levels, including by the joint chiefs. He did not anticipate an immediate problem, but believed that some crisis might arise in connection with the base within the next few years.[56]

At a subsequent meeting of the NSC on March 10, Burke said that the United States had a legal right to stay at Guantánamo, and it was a very useful training facility. He told NSC members that the only way Castro could attack Guantánamo would be to cut off its water supply, and if that happened, "we could continue to support the base by means of Navy tankers, perhaps even by installing plants that manufacture fresh water from sea water." Burke assured the NSC that the 230 marines assigned to Guantánamo could repel an armed attack by the Cubans without reinforcements. In late January, a Cuban radio broadcast alleged that ten thousand U.S. marine reinforcements had landed at Guantánamo. This erroneous information had provoked Cuban Justice Minister Alfredo Yabur to announce that Cubans would fight a U.S. invasion "even if it were backed up by atomic bombs," and to warn that if U.S. marines land, "there will be millions of cadavers."[57]

The escalating tensions and animosities between the Eisenhower administration and the Castro regime certainly were not limited to or even largely confined to disagreements over Guantánamo. By March 1960, Cuba had expropriated more than seventy thousand acres of property owned by U.S. sugar companies, and Castro had signed the first major Cuba-U.S.S.R. trade agreement, involving crude oil, sugar, and a wide variety of other products, with Soviet Deputy Prime Minister Anastas Mikoyan.[58] It must also be acknowledged that Guantánamo had been repeatedly attacked by Fidel and Raúl Castro by words and actions as an unwanted U.S. military presence in Cuba. As a consequence, senior U.S. civilian and military policymakers were alarmed about the future of Guantánamo and the safety of its base personnel.

On March 16, 1960, NSC staffer Samuel Belk sent a memorandum to Eisenhower's special assistant, Robert Gray, that began, "The subject of Guantánamo Naval Base has become an open point of friction between the U.S. and Cuba," and that "barring U.S. initiatives, the situation will become increasingly and rapidly worse." The memorandum then sought to address three major concerns: "How shall the U.S. respond if the Castro regime unilaterally abrogates the treaty concerning Guantánamo? How shall the U.S. respond if Cuban citizens attack Guantánamo? How shall the U.S. respond in the event of serious attacks against U.S. citizens (in Cuba)?"[59]

Also on March 16, 1960, the NSC's 5412 Committee prepared a paper titled "A Program of Covert Action against the Castro Regime."[60] The stated purpose of the program was "to bring about the replacement of the Castro regime with one more devoted to the true interests of the Cuban people and more acceptable to the U.S." The paper stated that preparations had already been made for the development of paramilitary forces outside of Cuba to work with a covert intelligence and action organization to be created in Cuba. The recommendation of the paper was that the CIA be authorized to undertake the outlined program. On March 17, 1960, Eisenhower approved this proposal, which constituted the basis for what would become known as the invasion of Playa de Girón ("Bay of Pigs").[61]

In late March, Guantánamo's commander, Admiral Frank Fenno, fired Cuban worker Federico Figueras Larrazabal for "slander" after he made unsubstantiated verbal accusations on Cuban radio and in the newspaper *Sierra Maestra* that base workers were constantly abused by navy officials and that the United States was just looking for an excuse to land the marines. Larrazábal's dismissal provoked a diplomatic protest by Cuban Foreign Minister Raúl Roa requesting Figueras Larrazabal's reinstatement and asking that Guantánamo stop hiring numerous ex-members of Batista's army and other counterrevolutionaries. Bonsal responded directly to Roa, stating that out of 3,700 Cubans employed at the base, only 8 had been identified as former members of Batista's army or navy and none had been accused by Castro's government of any crimes or counterrevolutionary activities.

When Fenno also denied Roa's charges, the Cuban newspaper *Revolución* made new accusations and claimed that working conditions at the base were deteriorating daily. What *Revolución* meant by deteriorating working conditions was not explained.[62] Pérez has found that in the 1950s, Guantánamo was probably the largest single employer of Cuban workers in the vicinity. "About two thousand residents of the city of Guantánamo worked on the base as carpenters, mechanics, electricians, plumbers, painters, welders, truck drivers, gardeners, seamstresses, cooks, and maids. The base generated a payroll of almost $4 million annually."[63]

These diplomatic exchanges did not resolve the issue as far as Fidel was concerned. He now cited the base as an example of "Yankee imperialism," and in a three-and-a-half-hour radio interview broadcast nationwide on April 23, 1960, he denounced Eisenhower, Herter, and Rubottom for their "fascist, Goebbels-like" policies toward Cuba. Fidel accused Guantánamo officials of using various counterrevolutionary elements to set up "a focus of opposition" to his government. He charged that base planes were making unauthorized overflights of Cuban territory, and painted a picture of possible military aggression from the base at any time.[64]

On May 13, 1960, Castro acknowledged that a Cuban naval craft had fired on a U.S. submarine off Cuba's coast. He made the disclosure in the context of protesting against U.S. submarines, warships, and airplanes, some of which he claimed had violated Cuba's territorial waters. The State Department responded the following day that it was astonished by Castro's claim that "a Cuban patrol boat fired upon a United States submarine and chased it for thirty miles." The department spokesman said that the U.S. government had not raised the issue previously because it had not wanted to add to tensions in the Caribbean area, but that on May 6, the U.S.S. *Sea Poacher* had been on the high seas in a recognized and well-traveled sea lane between Guantánamo and Key West. It added that "neither the submarine commander nor this Government could take seriously what appeared to be a question of identification at sea and a failure of communication." On May 14, the State Department asked the Cuban chargé d'affaires in Washington to provide an explanation for this action. It received none, and on June 11, 1960, Fidel Castro said in a television interview that he would give none. A State Department memorandum titled "Provocative Actions of the Government of Cuba against the United States" protested the firing on the *Sea Poacher* to the Inter-American Peace Commission of the OAS as "an armed attack on a U.S. naval vessel on the high seas." Although Fidel had not implicated Guantánamo directly in his remarks, this incident reflected the growing overt hostility between the Castro government and the U.S. Navy.[65]

On July 12, 1960, Khrushchev vowed in a provocative international press conference to back Cuba in any effort to get rid of the U.S. naval base at Guantánamo. According to the report filed by the *New York Times* Moscow correspondent, Seymour Topping, Khrushchev said, "The Monroe Doctrine has died a natural death and should best be buried as every dead body is." He charged that it was "sheer iniquity that the United States should be maintaining its Cuban naval base . . . without a time limit." Khrushchev rejected the idea that the Soviet Union wanted a military base in Cuba as a "silly fabrication." He added that the Cubans themselves had replied, "The best base is the Soviet Union, whose rockets can hit any sector in any part of the globe."[66]

In August 1960, the *New York Times* military editor, Hanson Baldwin, who had visited Guantánamo many times, sought to define its importance within the context of the intensifying bilateral controversy. Baldwin admitted that in an all-out nuclear war, Guantánamo would be useless, but in a conventional conflict, it could perform a variety of important tactical and logistical functions. He emphasized, however, that "Gitmo's political and psychological importance transcends its military utility. . . . If we are bullied, bluffed, blackmailed, or persuaded to abandon Guantánamo . . . it would mark the ebb tide of American power."[67]

In early September 1960, Raúl Castro lashed out at Guantánamo as a haven for "war criminals . . . a fascist reserve . . . mobilized by Yankee gold," at which forces were being trained to invade Cuba. Raúl vowed that "if they don't die on the battlefield, they will . . . die on their knees, backs turned to the firing squad, which is the manner in which traitors are shot."[68]

Raúl's furious diatribe, apparently calculated to warn the U.S. government that Cuba was prepared to defeat any covert invasion, was a prelude to Fidel's denunciations of Guantánamo at the UN General Assembly on September 26. At that session, Fidel accused Washington of using the base to "justify an attack on Cuba." In his speech, Fidel referred to a statement made by Burke that the Soviet Union would not use rockets if the United States reacted militarily to a Cuban seizure of Guantánamo, because "the U.S.S.R. knows it would be destroyed." Fidel said, "Let us imagine that Admiral Burke is wrong. If he is wrong, he is playing with the most dangerous thing in the world." At that moment, Khrushchev, who was sitting in the audience, brandished his fist and reportedly shouted: "He [Burke] is mistaken!"[69]

Burke responded quickly and directly to Fidel. In an interview with *U.S. News & World Report* on October 3, 1960, he affirmed that the navy was concerned not just about Guantánamo, but the entire Cuban situation.

"Here is a country with a people normally very friendly to the United States. Yet here has come a man with a small, hard core of Communists determined to change all of that. Castro has taught hatred of the United States." A month later, Burke persuasively listed Guantánamo's attributes as a major training facility: "The weather is ideal and we are not interfering with a lot of airplanes. We can do gunnery exercises, bombing exercises, missile training . . . a lot of things we can't do anywhere else." Burke's defense of Guantánamo's utility echoed the comments made by Fenno, who had been quoted in the *San Diego Union* as saying that "Guantánamo is one of the most strategically located bases we have. . . . It is unrivaled in the Caribbean logistically and . . . it is of utmost importance in anti-submarine operations in the Caribbean and off the southern coast of the United States."[70]

At approximately the same time Burke was making his remarks, on October 30, the U.S.S. *Boxer* arrived at Guantánamo with a contingent of 1,450 marines on maneuvers. In response to Eisenhower's public approval for the marines to have shore leave, the official Cuban press portrayed the arrival of the *Boxer* as a deliberate act of provocation. For his part, Fidel did not mention the marines or Guantánamo, but instead challenged his enemies to invade Cuba and boasted that he had the means to destroy them.[71]

In this heightened state of tension, the U.S. Navy took effective countermeasures to enhance Guantánamo's base security. On November 2, the navy publicly disclosed that as a precautionary move against a possible assault by Cuban forces, it had put landmines along a twenty-four-mile dividing line between Guantánamo and the surrounding territory. The mines were placed inside a steel mesh and barbed wire fence with warning signs in Spanish and English. A navy spokesman admitted that such an attack seemed highly improbable, but if one should occur, it would be repelled. On November 6, the *Times* reported that U.S. marines, sailors, and Seebees (naval engineers) had just completed a twenty-four-hour exercise to test Guantánamo's ground defenses against any attack by Castro's forces, and that the exercise had persuaded the marine commander that Guantánamo's current strength would be sufficient to hold the base until it could be reinforced.[72]

On November 2, however, the commander of the Atlantic Fleet, Admiral Robert L. Dennison, learned for the first time that the CIA had an operative plan linked to the Bay of Pigs operation for an amphibious invasion of Cuba with the code-name "Bumpy Road." Dennison's briefer, CIA Deputy Director Richard Bissell, was unable to answer Dennison's question, Who would defend his undermanned outpost of Guantánamo in case of an immediate invasion? For the next three months, Dennison received almost no intelligence on Cuba even though he repeatedly asked Bissell for information on the capabilities of Castro's defense forces. As a consequence of being excluded from CIA planning for the Bay of Pigs operation, one of Dennison's warships almost sank a CIA vessel near the invasion site.

The exclusion of Dennison from any role in planning or preparing for the Bay of Pigs Operation is appalling and condemnatory evidence of the lack of oversight over covert operations in this era. Dennison was one of the navy's most experienced senior officers, having previously served as assistant chief of naval operations and President Truman's naval aide. Moreover, in his assignment as commander of the Atlantic Fleet, he was at the top of the chain of command for U.S. bases in the Atlantic and Caribbean area including Guantánamo.[73]

On November 1, 1960, Eisenhower made a forthright public declaration of the U.S. government position regarding Guantánamo. Repeating the language of the 1903 and 1934 bilateral treaties that the United States exercised complete jurisdiction and control over the designated area of the base, he asserted, "Our government has no intention of agreeing to the modification or abrogation of these agreements and will take whatever steps may be appropriate to defend the base." In the same message, Eisenhower sought to reassure Fidel and the Cuban people that the U.S. presence in Guantánamo posed "no threat whatever to the sovereignty of Cuba . . . or to the independence of any of the American countries." He then added that "in light of the intimate relations which now exist between the present Government of Cuba and the Sino-Soviet bloc, it is essential that our position in Guantánamo be clearly understood."[74]

On January 3, 1961, less than three weeks before leaving office, Eisenhower formally ended U.S. diplomatic relations with Cuba. The break came after Castro demanded that the U.S. Embassy in Havana reduce its staff to eleven diplomats, claiming that 80 percent of the 300 assigned officials were spies for the Federal Bureau of Investigation (FBI) and the Pentagon. Eisenhower publicly justified his action by simply saying, "There is a limit to what the United States in self-respect can endure. That limit has now been reached." On January 4, White House Press Secretary James Hagerty released the statement that the termination of diplomatic and consular relations with Cuba had no effect on the status of the naval station at Guantánamo.[75]

Privately, however, the president was worried about how breaking relations might affect the treaty guaranteeing the use of Guantánamo to the United States. Both he and his staff secretary, General Andrew Goodpaster, consulted Herter repeatedly on this issue. The State Department's legal adviser, Eric Hager, indicated that this was a gray area of international law. He found that there could be a potential problem involving the provision in the 1903 treaty for the return of fugitives at the base. The Cubans might charge that the U.S. government could not guarantee the return of fugitives in the absence of diplomatic relations. Hager believed that the United States and nations aligned with the Soviet Union could make good arguments on the fugitive issue, but he could not think of a forum in which the Castro government might initiate a challenge because it was a political, not a legal question. At one point, in evident exasperation, Eisenhower exclaimed, "If the Cubans attack Guantánamo, they will be kicked out with force."[76]

The events involving Guantánamo that transpired between June 27, 1958, and January 3, 1961, contributed significantly to the deterioration in bilateral relations between the United States and Cuba. Mary McCoy may be literally correct when she describes this interchange as largely a "war of words," but in the context of the Cold War, and especially involving a major U.S. naval base in a country increasingly under Soviet domination only ninety miles from the Florida coast, this war of words was a source of grave concern for all participants. As this account illustrates, frictions over Guantánamo could and did escalate to the highest levels of the governments in Washington, Havana, and even Moscow. Guantánamo was an ingredient in the genesis of planning for the ill-fated Bay of Pigs invasion and a subject of diplomatic anxiety when the United States broke relations with Cuba. Not only did the United States refuse to consider abrogating its lease of Guantánamo Bay, by the end of the Eisenhower administration, Washington's determination to keep this particular naval base was stronger than ever before.

7

The Cold War, Part 2
John F. Kennedy and Lyndon B. Johnson

BY THE TIME JOHN FITZGERALD KENNEDY (JFK) took office, Guantánamo had acquired a symbolic significance that greatly outweighed and bore little resemblance to its actual value as a naval and marine training center. To the U.S. military and particularly to the Joint Chiefs of Staff (JCS), Guantánamo was virtually sacrosanct, not to be preempted by actions they could not control or placed at risk by covert operations orchestrated by the Central Intelligence Agency (CIA) such as the invasion of the Playa de Girón (Bay of Pigs) or the follow-up Mongoose Operation. One of the first preventative measures undertaken by Defense Secretary Robert McNamara following the onset of the Cuban missile crisis was simultaneously to remove all dependents from Guantánamo and to reinforce its military preparedness with two marine battalions.

Ironically, throughout the JFK and Lyndon Baines Johnson (LBJ) administrations, Fidel Castro was also unwilling to place Guantánamo in real jeopardy. Despite his repeated criticisms and harassment tactics, the most provocative action undertaken by the Cuban regime was to remove a portion of the chain-link perimeter fence. Even after LBJ summarily began to fire Cuban workers at Guantánamo in response to a temporary cutoff of the base's potable water supply, Fidel sought a compromise by offering to turn on the water for one hour each day. Both Fidel and Raúl had vowed consistently that they would seek to obtain the base's return to Cuba through peaceful diplomacy. In many ways, the Castro regime's approach to Guantánamo mirrored the way it dealt with the U.S. embargo—largely exploiting it for anti-U.S. propaganda purposes.

President-Elect Kennedy, like his opponent, Richard Nixon, had ultimately taken a hard-line political stance toward Cuba in his campaign, but he was unwilling to endorse the White House's move to break relations.[1] Acting as JFK's spokesman, the designated secretary of state, Dean Rusk, said that "without complete information on all relevant factors, the new administration did not feel it could participate in the decision."[2] In his inaugural address, which was broadcast live in Cuba, JFK, however, alluded to the Monroe Doctrine by vowing "to oppose aggression and subversion anywhere in the Americas," and affirming that "this Hemisphere intends to remain the master of its own house."[3] On January 22, 1961, Rusk chaired a special meeting regarding Cuba that discussed among other topics the potential threat of the export of Cuban communism to other countries in the Western Hemisphere and the possibility that Castro might challenge the United States at Guantánamo. Army Chief of Staff General Lyman Lemnitzer identified the water supply as Guantánamo's key vulnerability, but saw no evidence of a buildup of Cuban forces around the base.[4] At his first press conference, on January 25, JFK said he had no plans to resume diplomatic relations with Cuba.

Fidel's approach to Guantánamo did not change in any fundamental way. He initially made a few conciliatory remarks such as "We are going to begin anew" and "Our attitude will not be one of resentment."[5] These statements did not lead to any alleviation of tensions over the base. On February 4, on Fidel's orders, Cuban forces took over the Yateras water plant, but did not shut off the water.

The idea of using Guantánamo to fake an attack on Cuba or to stage an incident there that would act as a pretext for a massive U.S. invasion of Cuba may have first surfaced in the meeting of the National Security Council (NSC) on January 3, 1961, when President Dwight D. Eisenhower decided to end diplomatic relations with Cuba. According to Trumbull Higgins, it was Secretary of State Christian Herter who first suggested "staging a fake attack on Guantánamo."[6] This proposal would resurface repeatedly during the JFK administration and would invariably be rejected by the JCS. It is not known whether reports that such a proposal existed or sheer paranoia caused Castro to believe that Guantánamo posed a direct threat to his regime, but this theme became prominent in Havana's propaganda.

Prior to the Bay of Pigs failed invasion—code named Operation Zapata—Rusk suggested that Guantánamo could serve as a staging area for the operation, but he met fierce opposition from the Pentagon's joint chiefs. According to Peter Wyden's account, the idea of placing the base in such an exposed and endangered position "had startled and appalled them." Rusk subsequently complained to the president's special assistant, Arthur Schlesinger Jr., "It is interesting to observe the Pentagon people. They are perfectly willing to put the President's head on the block, but they recoil from the idea of doing anything which might risk Guantánamo." In similar irritated tones, Rusk told the study group for Operation Zapata on May 4, 1961, "I do regret that consideration was not given to [my suggestion] that they land in the eastern portion of Cuba and then get a position with Guantánamo behind them. However, our military friends didn't want to spoil the virginity of Guantánamo."[7]

Aleksandr Fursenko and Timothy Naftali have found that on April 19, after the White House learned that the invasion had failed, Attorney General Robert F. Kennedy (RFK) urged his brother to initiate another covert operation involving a fake attack on Guantánamo to win hemispheric support for a massive U.S.-led military invasion of Cuba. In his letter to the president, the younger Kennedy was emphatic. He warned, "If we don't want Russia to set up missile bases in Cuba, we had better decide now what we are willing to do to stop it."[8]

At a retrospective conference in 1996 on the Bay of Pigs held at the Musgrove Plantation on St. Simons Island, Georgia, Philip Brenner asked CIA operative Jacob "Jake" Esterline why, prior to the invasion, Fidel had placed his brother Raúl in charge of defense forces in Oriente Province. "Did this mean that the Cubans believed the invasion was coming from the east?" Esterline answered, "That's possible." Brenner speculated, "Why might the Cubans have believed this? It raises questions for example about Guantánamo. There are indications that there was a unit preparing to land there as a diversion. But nothing has been said here about the use to which the U.S. naval base in Guantánamo would be put. What was to be its role in helping to ensure the success of the invasion?" Neither Esterline nor anyone else at the Musgrove conference addressed Brenner's query about Guantánamo. The best answer so far has been Peter Wyden's report that a boat captained by Cuban exile Nino Díaz had planned to land in Oriente Province not far from Guantánamo at approximately the same time as the main landing at Playa de Girón, but that for various reasons, including reports that landing on a rocky coastline in sight of Cuban forces there would be unnecessary as well as extremely dangerous, Díaz decided to abort the operation. According to the subsequent Memorandum No. 1, prepared by the Special Group—a high-level interagency committee that reviewed covert operations—Díaz's decision to abort the diversionary landing near Guantánamo "may have had a considerable effect on the main landing as the diversion was intended to draw Castro's forces to the east and confuse his command."[9]

After the acrimonious Vienna summit between JFK and Khrushchev in early June 1961 failed to reduce Cold War tensions over the hot spots Berlin and Cuba, new intelligence reports that the Soviets were sending armaments and military technicians to Cuba provoked a crisis atmosphere in Washington. In late July, after reading the National Intelligence Estimate Board report "The Military Buildup in Cuba," Admiral Arleigh Burke urged the White House to launch a preemptive military invasion before the Cubans were fully armed and trained. Responding to the query about what would happen if the United States attacked, Burke predicted that "all hell would break loose, but that someday we would have to do it."[10]

At approximately the same time, Cuban leaders, fearful that the United

States might attack their country again, sought to reduce bilateral tensions through discrete and indirect diplomatic approaches. At a lunch with *New York Times* correspondent Tad Szulc in mid-July, Cuban Ambassador to the OAS Carlos Lechuga voiced concern that U.S. policy was forcing Cuba to align with the Sino-Soviet bloc, and asked Szulc to act as an intermediary by seeking to reestablish diplomatic relations between Havana and Washington. On August 17 at an informal gathering in Punta del Este, Uruguay, just after the OAS conference had concluded, Ché Guevara initiated a friendly conversation with White House Aide Richard Goodwin by thanking him for solidifying Fidel's hold on Cuba by handing him the Bay of Pigs. Goodwin responded in kind, asking Ché to reciprocate by attacking Guantánamo. Guevara laughingly retorted that the Cubans were not that foolhardy. Then, in a more serious tone, he suggested that the United States propose diplomatic terms that could create "at least an interim modus vivendi." When Goodwin failed to answer, Guevara, obviously thinking out loud, hypothesized that Cuba might compensate the United States for expropriated commercial properties with trade concessions, agree not to make any alliances with the East (presumably China), hold free elections within the revolution's single party network, and possibly discuss Cuban revolutionary activities in other countries. Goodwin, who reported this conversation verbatim to JFK, also mentioned that an Argentine diplomat who was present called the next day to say that Guevara considered the discussion "profitable" and had found it "easier to talk with someone of the new generation."[11]

Neither of these informal Cuban approaches had any measurable impact in easing bilateral tensions. On the contrary, the White House continued to be obsessed with removing Castro and his cohort, and Guantánamo once again became a potential site in a major covert action scheme. According to information found in Russian archives by Fursenko and Naftali, an elaborate plot had been concocted to kill Fidel Castro on July 26—the anniversary of his attack on the Moncada barracks in 1953—and, at the same time, counterrevolutionaries in Oriente Province were to shell Guantánamo to create a pretext for a U.S. invasion. The Soviet KGB, however, reportedly managed to penetrate and foil this operation at an early stage. In any case the underground network, called Candela, never attracted a sufficient number of recruits to accomplish anything.[12]

Sometime in September 1961—the exact date has not been specified—U.S. marine Captain Arthur Jackson shot and killed Ruben López, a Cuban worker at Guantánamo, supposedly on Cuban soil, and then buried him secretly inside the base. The incident was potentially sensational news because Jackson, who had won the Congressional Medal of Honor for heroism at Peleliu in 1944, was denied a court-martial but forced to resign from the

Marine Corps eighteen months before he would have been eligible for a pension. When the Cuban government learned of López's violent death and demanded an explanation on October 24, 1961, the U.S. Defense Department promised a full investigation, but did not follow through. In June 1962, the U.S. State Department sent Cuba a note through the Swiss Embassy stating briefly that the cause of López's death was unexplained. The incident, however, resurfaced publicly in early May 1963, after JFK held a reception for all living Medal of Honor recipients, to which Jackson was invited but did not attend. Despite subsequent accounts of López's murder/manslaughter and the official coverup by *Newsweek, Time,* the *New York Times,* and the *Nation,* the Cuban response was remarkably restrained.[13]

Following the Bay of Pigs debacle, JFK and RFK turned to Brigadier General Edward Lansdale for advice on how to deal with Fidel. Lansdale, a former CIA operations officer who had run covert operations in the Philippines and Southeast Asia, had been highly critical of the Bay of Pigs operation, and, according to some accounts, the Kennedy brothers viewed him as a pragmatist. On December 14, 1961, at a meeting with top CIA officials at the White House, JFK authorized Lansdale to execute his proposal, which subsequently became known by its code name Operation Mongoose, to assist Cubans in overthrowing Fidel.[14] At that meeting, CIA Deputy Director for Intelligence Robert Amory proposed a review of the question, Should Guantánamo be used as a base of operations? Amory warned that "if the answer is in the affirmative and Castro attempts to throw the U.S. out, then the U.S. would be faced with formulating a new policy toward Cuba."[15]

During 1962, as tensions increased between the United States and Cuba, Guantánamo continued to be a focal point of mutual animosity. On February 8, Rusk sent a five-page memorandum to National Security Adviser McGeorge Bundy with a cover note stating that Rusk believed JFK would be interested in the interpretation of legal adviser Leonard Meeker of the rights and legal position of the United States with regard to Guantánamo in the event of a Cuban denunciation of the base arrangement. Meeker's interpretation was that, in Guantánamo, the United States had more than enough right to maintain a base on territory under the sovereignty of Cuba; that "by international agreement and treaty the United States [had] obtained the lease of a defined area and received from Cuba the right of 'complete jurisdiction and control' in that area." Meeker forcefully asserted that any declaration by Cuba that it denounced, repudiated, or abrogated its treaty concerning the Guantánamo base arrangements "would be legally ineffective." It is certain, given Bundy's assiduous attention to his duties and to serving the president's security needs, that he placed this document in the president's reading file. It can also be assumed that JFK read, absorbed, and fully agreed with its key points.[16]

In March 1962, Foreign Minister Raúl Roa formally complained through the Czechoslovakian Embassy to the U.S. State Department that U.S. troops at the naval base had repeatedly tried to provoke "military incidents" by throwing rocks and cans of burning gasoline at Cuban sentries. It may have been more than a coincidence that at the same time in Washington the joint chiefs had prepared a plan code named Operation Northwoods, under the direction of Lemnitzer, that consisted of a series of well-coordinated provocative incidents at Guantánamo intended to create the illusion of a credible Cuban attack on the base and thus provide justification for a massive U.S. military intervention. These proposed incidents included: (1) using a clandestine radio to start rumors the base would be attacked; (2) landing friendly Cubans in uniform "over the fence" to stage an attack on the base; (3) capturing friendly Cuban "saboteurs" inside the base; (4) starting riots (involving friendly Cubans) near the base's main gate; (5) blowing up ammunition inside the base that would start fires; (6) burning aircraft on the air base; (7) lobbing mortar shells into the base—this probably would cause some damage to installations; (8) capturing "assault or militia teams" approaching from the sea or from the vicinity of Guantánamo City; (9) sabotaging a ship in the harbor by using naphthalene to start large fires; (10) sinking a ship near the entrance to Guantánamo Harbor and conducting funerals for the mock victims.[17]

The joint chiefs justified this audacious proposal by intimating that time was running out before the Soviet Union would bind itself to the defense of Cuba, Cuba would join the Warsaw Pact, and the Soviets would establish military bases in Cuba. Lemnitzer and the other chiefs almost certainly viewed these deceptive operations as "drama" or mere trickery, none of which would put the base in serious jeopardy. But even well-conceived operations could go awry, and, given the international attention focused on Cuba in the aftermath of the Bay of Pigs invasion, if such deceptions had led to a shooting war, it could easily have been unmasked as a war that the generals had started but that U.S. citizens did not want.[18]

There are indications in the State Department's *Papers Relating to the Foreign Relations of the United States* that senior officials of the JFK administration gave some consideration to the JCS's proposal, but in a meeting with his top national security advisers on March 14, 1962, including Lemnitzer, JFK voiced skepticism that "circumstances will arise [to] justify and make desirable the use of American forces for overt military action" in Cuba.[19] Two days later, according to investigative journalist James Bamford, JFK bluntly told Lemnitzer he had no intention of using overt military force to oust Fidel. According to Bamford, Lemnitzer's continuing efforts to seek a pretext for invading Cuba eventually antagonized McNamara, who began treating Lemnitzer "like a schoolboy," denied him a second term as chair of the JCS, and then transferred him to Europe, making him head of NATO.[20]

The administration's decision not to initiate a second invasion of Cuba under any circumstances may have strengthened after JFK and his advisers read *National Intelligence Estimate (NIE) 85-62*, published on March 21, 1962, which described Cuba as "in effect, surrounded by an iron curtain." The estimate found that the forces available to Fidel "to suppress insurrection or repel invasion have been and are being greatly improved with substantial Bloc assistance." It judged these forces as essentially defensive in nature, and considered it unlikely that the bloc would "provide Cuba with strategic weapons systems."[21]

Operation Northwoods illustrated once again the importance of Guantánamo in the minds of both Cuban and U.S. leaders. Indeed, Lemnitzer's proposal may be viewed as a kind of U.S. counterpoint to earlier provocative moves by Raúl and Fidel, for example, holding U.S. naval personnel as hostages in June 1958. These were all threatening moves that, at the same time, were calculated to stop short of placing Guantánamo in harm's way. The fact that the JFK administration ultimately rejected the Northwoods proposal and then assigned Lemnitzer to a less influential position also reflects the reality that JFK had decided not to risk any elevation in bilateral hostilities at Guantánamo.

In early 1962, both Havana and Washington instituted new defensive measures on their respective sides of Guantánamo. Cuba began to construct six new access roads to the base, cleared a seventy-five-yard strip along the seventeen-mile fenceline, and planted the strip with a bayonet-grass "curtain." For its part, the U.S. Navy ordered 800 more marines to Guantánamo, bringing its total strength to 1,100 marines and 2,000 sailors. In May, Defense Minister Raúl Castro made new charges that U.S. soldiers were attempting to provoke their Cuban counterparts by stoning and shooting at them.[22] During June, Fidel established a six-mile militarized zone around the base and ordered that families be removed and farms vacated, and placed travel restrictions on all roads in the immediate vicinity. Both the United States and Cuba built perimeter fences and proceeded to install their respective minefields.[23]

In radio broadcasts, Fidel frequently accused the United States of using Guantánamo to conduct espionage against Cuba.[24] On July 26, at a commemorative rally, Fidel made one of his shrillest verbal attacks on Guantánamo, claiming that the United States was preparing a new armed invasion of Cuba. He charged that the U.S. Navy was holding the base "against our will," and that it provided "lodging for the drunken inhabitants and counterrevolutionaries."[25]

Operation Mongoose has incurred well-deserved derision both from former policymakers and from scholars for such escapades as exploding cigars, shampoo intended to make Fidel's beard turn green and fall out—ideas that were never implemented—but a few Cubans were killed by mortar shells, a shipment of sugar bound for Moscow was contaminated by concealed chemicals, and there were plans involving the Mafia to assassinate Fidel.

It is difficult to ascertain to what extent, if any, Guantánamo played a role in Operation Mongoose. Plans contained in an "Operation Mongoose Priority Operations Schedule" for the period May 21 to June 30, 1962, include "making the fullest possible use of the Cuban labor population on the base" to "intensify the psychological effort at Guantánamo." The operations schedule fails to define what is meant by "psychological effort," but it does mention sports and news broadcasts, U.S. Information Agency (USIA) publications in Spanish, and taped interviews with Cuban refugees—all of which could be used as propaganda instruments to influence Cuban employees at Guantánamo in the psychological war against communism and Fidel. The schedule also purports "to take the fullest possible advantage of this open U.S. listening post on Cuban soil for the purpose of intensifying the exploitation of the intelligence potential which exists on the base at Guantánamo." It is unclear from this brief description if Lansdale intended to use Guantánamo for intelligence-gathering or counterintelligence or for both objectives.[26]

Lansdale's proposed operations schedule was vetted at a meeting of the Special Group Augmented (SGA) on May 17, 1962.[27] According to a brief memorandum by CIA Director John McCone, the SGA accepted the schedule "for review, study, and decision at the meeting on Thursday, May 24." No record of the May 24 meeting has been found.[28]

On August 14, Lansdale distributed a memorandum titled "Alternate Course B" to the SGA that did not specifically mention but obviously intended to make use of Guantánamo. The aim of this ambitious plan was to isolate and discredit the Castro regime both in Cuba and in the Western Hemisphere. It contemplated the use of sabotage teams to infiltrate Cuba, the creation of protected arms caches, and the training of resistance cells. At the SGA's next meeting on August 16, Lemnitzer voiced strong opposition to the use of Guantánamo in any of these activities, and McCone said that he, too, was concerned about the use of Guantánamo, and recommended that planning for covert operations exclude Guantánamo.[29]

Researcher Gus Russo uncovered the most tantalizing, but also inconclusive, information linking Guantánamo to Operation Mongoose. Russo told the story of Lt. Commander John Gordon of the Office of Naval Intelligence (ONI), a Ph.D. in maritime history from Harvard and a "fast-tracker" in the navy, who was assigned as an intelligence officer to Guantánamo in spring 1961 following the Bay of Pigs invasion. Russo's account indicates that while there, Gordon found out the base was being used to plan the assassination of Fidel and Raúl Castro. According to his daughter, Gordon "worked around the clock, spoke fluent Spanish, and was always having Cubans over to their home. . . . The Cubans told Gordon's wife about plots to kill Castro." Gordon subsequently suffered a nervous breakdown, was sent to Bethesda Naval Hospital for eight months of observation during which he did not see his family, and was reassigned to duty only after he vowed to remain silent about the plots he had discovered at Guantánamo. During the Senate hearings conducted by Senator Frank Church (D-Idaho), committee staffers determined that Gordon's story about anti-Castro plots based at Guantánamo was accurate. According to Gordon, RFK had ordered these plots.[30] Gordon later hired noted attorney F. Lee Bailey to prosecute a medical malpractice case on behalf of Gordon's wife against the navy. According to Bailey, the parties reached an out-of-court settlement with the understanding that Gordon would remain mum on the subject of Guantánamo and drop the entire matter.[31]

Although there is no conclusive evidence that Guantánamo played a significant role in either the Bay of Pigs invasion or Operation Mongoose, there were recurrent efforts by members of the JFK administration to use the base's assets to oust the Castro regime. It is virtually certain that Fidel acquired some knowledge of these various plots, and therefore came to believe, rightly or wrongly, that Guantánamo might serve as the point of entry for a U.S. invasion of Cuba.[32]

In mid-August, when the JFK administration was focused on intensifying Operation Mongoose, it began to receive intelligence warnings of increased Soviet military assistance to Cuba, including military construction at several locations (whether by the Cubans or the Soviets was unknown). On August 17, General Maxwell Taylor sent a memorandum to JFK informing him that the SGA had tentatively approved a new course of action (for Mongoose) calculated to "increase added difficulties for the [Castro] regime and [to] increase the visibility of its failures."[33] It also predicted that "the noise level of Mongoose operations will probably rise."

On August 22, an intelligence memorandum presented by McCone to JFK warned that Soviet construction activity in the Matanzas area of Cuba could signify the creation of an air defense system—meaning offensive missiles—possibly aimed at Cape Canaveral and other U.S. installations. On the following day, JFK authorized Taylor to implement the new "line of activity for Operation Mongoose (known as Mongoose B Plus) . . . with all possible speed."[34] Also on August 23, JFK met with his senior national security advisers, including Rusk and McNamara, Taylor, McCone, Bundy, and Deputy Secretary of Defense Roswell Gilpatric, to discuss the situation in Cuba. According to the memorandum drafted by McCone, Rusk began by advocating the removal of restrictions on the use of Guantánamo by the Lansdale group. This recommendation was not approved because of strong opposition from the joint chiefs. After McCone stated that CIA photo interpreters could not currently differentiate between surface-to-air and ground-to-ground offensive missiles, JFK requested that the CIA National Intelligence Estimate Board work continuously on this problem.[35] JFK then issued National Security Action Memorandum No. 181, which directed the Department of Defense to study the possible military actions that would eliminate any installations in Cuba capable of launching a nuclear attack on the United States. This study would evaluate the pros and cons, for example, of a pinpoint attack, a general counterforce attack, and an outright invasion. The same action memorandum also directed the State and Defense Departments to make a joint study of the advantages and disadvantages of "liberating" Cuba by blockade, invasion, or other action beyond Mongoose B Plus in the context of an aggravated Berlin crisis.[36]

By the end of August 1962, bilateral antagonisms between the United States and Cuba, fueled by the Bay of Pigs invasion and Operation Mongoose, were probably at an all-time high, and Guantánamo was central to that particular equation.[37] McCone provided valuable insight into the thinking of senior members of the JFK administration regarding the merits of overt versus covert operations in Cuba in a memorandum for the record of a meeting in Rusk's office on August 21, 1962:

> McNamara expressed strong feelings that we should take every possible aggressive action in the fields of intelligence, sabotage, and guerrilla warfare, utilizing Cubans, and do such other things as might be indicated to divide the Castro regime. McCone pointed out that all of these things could be done. . . . Attorney General queried the meeting as to what other aggressive steps could be taken, questioning the feasibility of provoking an action against Guantánamo which would permit us to retaliate. . . . It was Bundy's opinion that all overt actions would involve serious consequences throughout the world and therefore our operations must be covert at this time.[38]

Correspondent Don Bohning's well-argued book *The Castro Obsession* has examined the recent scholarly literature on the Cuban missile crisis to find that the most revealing works by U.S., Soviet, and Cuban scholars all cite a common fear in Moscow and Havana that the United States was planning to launch another invasion of Cuba, and the activities and rumors surrounding Operation Mongoose enhanced that perception. Indeed, contingency plans had been updated to strike against Fidel by sending in Army Airborne and Marine Corps divisions, but JFK chose not to initiate any military action.[39] Nonetheless, as Bohning rightly claims, "Operation Mongoose, the program of covert action, and overt saber-rattling most certainly contributed to the Soviet decision to install the missiles."[40] Bohning does not mention Guantánamo, but throughout the missile crisis, this particular naval base was never far from the thoughts of U.S., Cuban, and Soviet policymakers.

It is instructive to read the "Cuban Developments" memoranda distributed by the CIA at the daily morning intelligence briefings at the White House. JFK, Bundy, and McCone were the principal participants at these briefings, the minutes of which were not recorded (standard procedure). On August 28, the CIA memorandum reported: "The U.S. Guantánamo base has been receiving a steady flow of reports that large numbers of [Soviet] Bloc personnel are engaged in some kind of unusual construction activity near Banes on the north coast of Oriente Province. These reports persistently link this activity with allegations that Soviet SAM missiles are arriving on the scene."

By September 1, the title of the CIA memoranda had been changed to "Cuban Highlights Prepared for the Special Group." The one for that day reported: "Information has reached the U.S. base at Guantánamo that Cubans in the nearby town of Caimanéra have been told to stay indoors today because of an invasion threat. The base also has reports that heavy military equipment is being moved through that area."

The most disturbing message was briefed on September 7: "The Cuban ambassador in Prague, son of Raúl Roa, told a clandestine source recently that the Soviets have provided Cuba with 'rockets of the same kind that shot down the U-2,' and that preparations have been made for the 'complete destruction' of the U.S. naval base at Guantánamo in the event of an attack on Cuba."

The same issue of "Cuban Highlights" also stated that "reports reaching Guantánamo, which seem to ring true, indicate that Soviet vessels have been unloading men and military gear near Banes in Oriente Province. We suspect these deliveries are related to the construction of what looks like another SA-2 site in the area."[41] Based on the give-and-take nature of the questions and answers—as well as the levying of new intelligence requirements—that often flowed from the briefing of such warning intelligence, it can be assumed that the participants at the morning meeting of September 7 discussed the possibility that Fidel Castro might fabricate a provocative incident at Guantánamo to justify a Soviet attack on the base.

JFK revealed just how seriously he took these warnings from the CIA at his news conference on September 13. In his preliminary statement, JFK said, "If the United States should find it necessary to take military action against communism in Cuba, all of Castro's communist-supplied weapons and technicians would not change the result." He then focused in on the most recent developments, threatening swift and effective retaliation "if at any time the communist buildup in Cuba were to endanger or interfere with our security in any way, including our base in Guantánamo, our passage to the Panama Canal, or if Cuba should ever attempt to export its aggressive purposes by force . . . or become an offensive military base of significant capacity for the Soviet Union." If any of these developments should occur, JFK vowed that "this country will do whatever must be done to protect its own security and that of its allies."[42]

On October 1, Taylor, on his first day as chair of the JCS, and McNamara received an intelligence briefing on Cuba in which they learned that new evidence obtained from recent U-2 flights over Cuba indicated that medium-range Soviet ballistic missiles were arriving in Cuba. On October 2, McNamara sent a memorandum to the JCS that listed six potential developments likely to trigger a U.S. military response: Soviet actions in Berlin, Soviet offensive weapons in Cuba, *an attack against the Guantánamo Naval Base,* an uprising in Cuba that called for U.S. assistance, Cuban armed subversion in the Western Hemisphere, and/or a presidential decision that "the situation in Cuba is inconsistent with U.S. national security." McNamara directed the joint chiefs to advise him as to the military preparation and force deployment necessary to respond effectively to each challenge.[43]

The Cuban missile crisis dates from the morning of October 14, 1962, when a U-2 aircraft piloted by Air Force Major Richard D. Heyser took 928 photographs during a six-minute reconnaissance mission over the western part of Cuba that verified the existence of Soviet offensive missile sites in Cuba. On the next day, two more U-2 flights found additional missile sites as well as medium-range ballistic missile transporters and erector launchers, plus crates for Soviet IL-28 medium-range bombers. After the CIA's National Photographic and Interpretation Center had interpreted the photographs from these missions, Deputy Director Marshall Carter reported the hard evidence to Bundy at 8:30 P.M. on October 15. Because JFK had been campaigning in New York, Bundy did not inform the president of these developments until the morning of October 16. On that same day, Algerian Premier Ahmed Ben Bella, who had just requested foreign aid from JFK, created additional tension at the White House by publicly embracing Fidel in Havana,

where Ben Bella attacked U.S. "imperialism" and joined the Cubans in calling for the United States to abandon Guantánamo.[44]

Early in the first meeting of the White House Executive Committee of the
NSC (ExComm) on October 16, Rusk advocated the declaration of a state
of national emergency and an announcement that "we intend to continue
our surveillance of Cuba and will enforce our right to do so, and that we
strengthen our forces in Guantánamo and in the southeastern part of the
United States."[45] Rusk's advice was persuasive with the other committee
members. At that time, the ExComm had no idea that Guantánamo itself
had been placed in jeopardy. It would not become known until after Soviet
archives were opened that the 106th Soviet Regiment—the only one without
a Luna rocket detachment—had moved into eastern Cuba specifically to
provide defense against a possible U.S. attack launched from Guantánamo.
According to General Anatoli Gribkov, the officer most responsible for the
deployment of Soviet troops and weapons to Cuba, a cruise missile unit occupied the hills above the U.S. base.[46] Former *Washington Post* correspondent and scholar Michael Dobbs has found that the Soviets had positioned
three FKR cruise missile launchers, "each with its own Hiroshima-sized
nuclear device" in the village of Vilorio, located about fifteen miles inland
from Guantánamo and aimed directly at the base. It obviously was because
of this discovery that Dobbs titled his book *One Minute to Midnight: Kennedy, Khrushchev, and Castro on the Brink of Nuclear War.* The work concludes with the persuasive observation that if the Soviets had obliterated
Guantánamo, "Kennedy would have been under enormous pressure to order
a nuclear response. It would have been difficult to confine a nuclear war to
Cuba."[47]

At an "Off the Record on Cuba" meeting of the ExComm held the evening
of October 16, RFK, probably brainstorming, made the startling suggestion
that the United States create an incident at Guantánamo that could justify
a U.S. invasion. According to the minutes of the meeting, he said, "One
other thing we should also think of [is] whether there is some other way we
can get involved in this through Guantánamo Bay . . . or whether there is
some ship that, you know, sink the *Maine* again or something." Taylor immediately moved to kill this idea from further consideration by countering,
"We think that, under any of the plans, we will probably get an attack on
Guantánamo, at least by fire. They have artillery and mortar easily within
range, and [with] any of the actions we take, we'll have to give air support
to Guantánamo and probably reinforce the garrison."[48]

RFK's subsequent memoir, *Thirteen Days,* makes no mention of this incident, which did not become public until 1983, but he does discuss the
controversial suggestion by UN Ambassador Adlai Stevenson at the meeting

of the NSC on October 20. Stevenson supported the idea of imposing a naval blockade, but to emphasize his aim of terminating the missile crisis without casualties and without escalation, he advocated that "we offer the Russians a settlement involving the withdrawal of our missiles from Turkey and our evacuation of Guantánamo." JFK immediately rejected the idea of surrendering Guantánamo, indicating that such an action would convey to the world that the White House had been frightened into abandoning its position. According to the minutes of the meeting, JFK was not opposed to discussing the withdrawal of U.S. missiles from Greece and Turkey, but was firm in saying that Washington should only make such a proposal in the future.[49]

According to Jeff Broadwater's biography of Stevenson, his behavior at the meeting appalled RFK. JFK's brother subsequently told him that Stevenson was "not strong enough or tough enough to be representing us at the UN at a time like this." JFK, however, took a broader view of Stevenson's capabilities. He later told his aide Theodore Sorensen, "You have to admire Adlai. He sticks to his position even when everyone is jumping on him." RFK also had second thoughts about Stevenson's proposal. In *Thirteen Days,* he wrote, "I think it should be emphasized that he [Stevenson] was presenting a point of view from a different perspective than the others. . . . Although I disagreed strongly with his recommendations, I thought he was courageous to make them."[50] For his part, Stevenson had confided to White House Special Assistant Kenneth O'Donnell after the NSC meeting, "Most of those fellows will probably consider me a coward for the rest of my life, but perhaps we need a coward in the room when we are talking about a nuclear war."[51] Stevenson's suggestions to his colleagues in private bore no comparison to his stern public demeanor and forceful defense of U.S. policy at the United Nations. On October 25, when Soviet Ambassador Valerian Zorin challenged Stevenson to present evidence of Soviet offensive missiles in Cuba, Stevenson retorted, "Do you, Ambassador Zorin, deny that the U.S.S.R. has placed and is placing medium- and intermediate-range missiles and sites in Cuba? Yes or no?" When the shaken Zorin promised an answer sometime later, Stevenson fired back that he would wait for an answer "until hell freezes over." Stevenson received high praise from JFK for his stirring public performance.[52]

While the president and his top advisers were debating how to resolve the missile crisis, the Defense Department was taking no chances that the Cubans or Soviets would do anything to threaten or endanger Guantánamo. At that time, approximately nine hundred U.S. families were living on the base, including about twenty-eight hundred women and children. When McNamara insisted that all dependents be evacuated, Navy Secretary Paul

Nitze countered with the proposal that marine combat troops replace the women and children. On October 22, McNamara ordered the evacuation of all dependents from Guantánamo, and, at the same time, endorsed Nitze's recommendation to make a show of strength by reinforcing the base with more than five thousand combat-ready marines (two battalions) plus four hundred Marine Corps aircraft. These aircraft would later play a significant role in monitoring the withdrawal of the Soviet missiles from Cuba.[53]

According to Michael Dobbs, Fidel first learned from Cuban spies who had infiltrated as workers at Guantánamo that the marine guard had been reinforced and women and children were being evacuated. He immediately reacted to this news by calling up Cuban militia reserves, thus tripling the size of his armed forces to 300,000 strong. Within seventy-two hours, Raúl had posted militiamen all over the island.[54]

Late the evening of October 26, Fidel, who had been largely on the sidelines during the missile crisis, sent a telegraph to Khrushchev that may have influenced the outcome of the crisis itself, and certainly conditioned subsequent Soviet thinking with regard to the status of Guantánamo. Earlier that day, apparently convinced that the United States was determined to invade Cuba on October 29 or 30, Fidel had dispersed fifty artillery batteries around the island and ordered that landmines be placed on all mountain passes between Guantánamo and all cities in Oriente Province. After consuming large amounts of sausage and beer with the senior KGB official at the Soviet Embassy in Havana, Fidel wrote ten drafts of a letter to Khrushchev that ultimately read: "If the imperialists invade Cuba with the goal of occupying it, the danger that that aggressive policy poses for humanity is so great that following that event the Soviet Union must never allow the circumstances in which the imperialists could launch the first nuclear strike against it."[55]

Meanwhile, at the Kremlin, Khrushchev had made his own decision on October 26 to withdraw the missiles from Cuba. According to Gribkov's account, when Fidel's letter arrived in Moscow on October 27, Kremlin policymakers were alarmed by his muddled appeal. "While they were working to resolve the crisis directly with Washington, they feared that Castro was seeking to escalate the conflict toward global nuclear war." This perception that Castro had become a sometimes irrational and dangerous ally would linger and influence subsequent decisions within the Soviet hierarchy pertaining to Soviet backing for Fidel's initiatives.[56]

On October 28, Fidel issued a set of five demands for normalizing relations between the United States and Cuba, including insisting that the United States evacuate its naval base at Guantánamo Bay. A few days later, Soviet Deputy Prime Minister Anastas Mikoyan, after having visited the United States, arrived in Havana, and, according to information obtained by the French Embassy, he reportedly advised Fidel to "either give up the government or take a long vacation." After a largely unproductive series of meetings with Fidel, Mikoyan returned to the United States, where he told senior U.S. officials that Moscow officially supported Fidel's position on Guantánamo, but would not press Washington further on this subject. According to JFK's senior adviser, John McCloy, on November 28, "Mikoyan mentioned Guantánamo, indicating he did not expect us to withdraw right away, but [he] thought it would be reasonable for us to set a time at which we would begin to negotiate about withdrawal."[57]

Given the high drama and complexity of the Cuban missile crisis, it is easy to overlook the scattered references to Guantánamo or to ignore its relevance to this dispute. Yet, as this discussion has shown, Guantánamo, if not central, was an important aspect of this tension-filled period. The outcome of the crisis was to reinforce U.S. determination to retain the base as Washington pressed forward on other fronts with new initiatives to persuade the Soviet Union to agree to arms reductions, creation of nuclear-free zones, and general retreat from the nuclear brinksmanship that had resulted in the missile crisis and frightened the entire world. Realizing that it had won a significant victory in both diplomatic and military terms over the Soviet Union and Cuba, the JFK administration was in no mood to make any concessions regarding the U.S. presence at Guantánamo.

LBJ: "I Sent One Little Admiral"

Within a few months after the assassination of JFK, LBJ faced almost simultaneous challenges to the U.S. presence in the Panama Canal Zone and Guantánamo Bay, Cuba. The faceoff between LBJ and Fidel over Guantánamo began with the low-key but illegal intrusion of four Cuban fishing vessels into the waters of the Florida Keys. In the early afternoon of Sunday, February 2, 1964, the Cuban boats arrived in the vicinity of East Key, Dry Tortugas, and, as they trolled amidst U.S. fishing boats, entered the territorial waters of the United States. After being alerted by radio to the situation, the U.S. Coast Guard Office in Miami directed the cutter *Cape Knox* to order the Cuban vessels to stop and anchor in their present locations. Subsequently, after boarding the vessels to question their captains and crew members, the coast guard determined that all four ships had violated both state and federal law by fishing 1.5 to 1.9 miles from the Florida coast and that at least two Cuban captains admitted they were intentionally fishing in U.S. waters.[58] When on the following day the ships were escorted to Key West, the crews were free to communicate by radio, and they notified Havana that they had been arrested and the ships would be impounded. On February

5, thirty-six of the original thirty-eight Cuban crewmen were placed in the custody of the assistant attorney general of Florida; the other two crewmen requested and received political asylum in the United States.[59]

Meanwhile, in Havana on February 3, Roa summoned Swiss Ambassador Emil Stadolhofer to protest the seizure of the fishing vessels through diplomatic channels. The following day, Roa publicly charged that the United States had committed an act of piracy in international waters against Cuba. He also made a formal protest to the U.S. government through the Czech Embassy, and instructed the Cuban delegation at the United Nations to inform the UN Security Council of this alleged "act of piracy." On February 6, shortly before noon, Roa presented a diplomatic note to Stadolhofer announcing that Cuba was shutting off the water supply to the Guantánamo Naval Base in retaliation for the seizure of the Cuban fishing boats and their crews. The note described the arrest of the fishermen as "insolent, arbitrary, and illegal" and stipulated that "the water will remain cut off until the fishermen are freed."[60]

One hour later, NSC Adviser Bundy telephoned LBJ, who was at the Waldorf-Astoria Hotel in New York preparing to have lunch with executives of the *New York Times* and to address the Weizmann Institute of Science. When Bundy told LBJ that the Castro regime had turned off the water to Guantánamo, the president responded, "We can't release the fishing boats, but I have to hold my fire. I have a meeting with the *New York Times*." Bundy advised, "Show them you're a man of peace." Beginning to grasp the seriousness of the situation confronting the naval base, a few minutes later LBJ called McNamara at the Pentagon. McNamara, who had already been apprised of the situation through military channels, told LBJ, "There is no problem militarily, but politically, its dynamite!" He explained, "We have 15 million gallons in storage—a ten- to twelve-day supply—and we can bring in tankers in five to six days. We can last indefinitely."[61] McNamara assured the president that the U.S. government was fully prepared for this contingency. "We have a precedent—October of last year when Hurricane Flora put out the water supply." McNamara suggested that if the crisis escalated, Guantánamo could fire its Cuban workers: "We have 3,000 [Cubans], 500 of whom live inside the base. The other 2,000 to 2,500 come in through the gate. We have told the State Department that we can get by without any Cuban workers. . . . We could send a tender down with U.S. workers to take over." When LBJ asked, "Should I cancel my speech at the Waldorf-Astoria and return to Washington?" McNamara shot back, "Absolutely not! Canceling the speech would dignify it with more importance than is due."[62]

Meanwhile, at Guantánamo, the new commander, Admiral John D. Bulkeley, was taking his own actions to free the base from its dependency on Cuba. As soon as he received the notice that the Castro government had shut off the water, Bulkeley placed the base on water condition "Alfa," which meant that limited water supplies would be provided to base houses three times daily and that laundry facilities and swimming pools would be closed for the duration of the crisis. Bulkeley also requested that ships in Guantánamo Bay be self-sufficient in their use of water.[63]

In Bulkeley, Fidel confronted one of the most determined adversaries he would ever face across Guantánamo's fenceline or "cactus curtain." Bulkeley, whose well-deserved nicknames were "Wild Man" and "Sea Wolf," had first won fame and his Congressional Medal of Honor for rescuing General MacArthur from Corregidor in World War II. He had also made a crucial reconnaissance of Utah Beach before the Normandy invasion. His mission in Cuba, as he saw it, was clear: to defend a major U.S. naval base and to counter Fidel Castro's intimidating moves and threats without igniting World War III.[64]

Having arrived at Guantánamo in early December 1963, Bulkeley had already dispelled one serious challenge from the Cuban military. Shortly after his arrival, Cuban Minister of State Security Major Ramiro Valdez had informed the base that 1,100 yards of the chain-link fence on the western side of the perimeter would be bulldozed, and that it would be imprudent for the United States to try to rebuild the fence. Bulkeley, having read the Permanent Treaty, viewed this provocative move as a calculated effort by the Castro regime to show that part of the base had been abandoned by U.S. forces, and therefore the treaty was no longer valid and the base should revert to Cuban ownership. Within an hour after Cuban soldiers bulldozed the fence, Bulkeley informed Valdez, "That fence is going back up at 10 A.M." At the appointed hour, Bulkeley was on the scene in full battle regalia, armed with a .357 Colt Magnum pistol and three hand grenades. Two thousand marines were dug in along the stretch of downed fence with loaded machine guns, rifles, and rocket launchers all aimed at Cuba. Circling overhead were Crusader jets, and just behind the fenceline were six helicopters armed with automatic weapons. Offshore in Guantánamo Bay, four destroyers were well positioned and ready for action. Amidst this impressive show of force, the navy's engineers, the Seebees, arrived with their truckloads of fencing, cranes, and other necessary equipment. By 4:00 P.M. they had erected a new chain-link fence along the line of demarcation, which had been double-checked for accuracy. No U.S. sentry had seen a single Cuban soldier until Valdez parked his jeep a mile away to watch the fence reconstruction through his high-power binoculars.[65] As one of Bulkeley's aides later recalled, "Castro's bluster and threats didn't phase Bulkeley one iota. He simply kept up his usual hectic pace, dashing all over the base, inspecting defenses and tightening security, often from before dawn until well after midnight."[66]

On January 9, 1964, another crisis had erupted in the Panama Canal

Zone when students from the United States attending Balboa High School precipitated violent and prolonged riots by illegally raising the U.S. flag over their school.[67] As angry mobs carrying Molotov cocktails and guns rampaged through the streets of Panama City shouting "*Viva Fidel!*" Bulkeley, who was closely monitoring the situation, wondered if Fidel might try to provoke similar riots at Guantánamo Naval Base. His suspicions mounted when, a few days later, Radio Havana made the unsubstantiated charge that "drunken marines had fired their machine guns indiscriminately at Cuban workers on the base."[68]

These were the experiences and thoughts that shaped Bulkeley's independent actions at Guantánamo on the afternoon of February 6 as he awaited guidance from Washington. At 1:00 P.M. Bulkeley and U.S. Navy Captain Zabisco "Zip" Trzyna, the base engineer, took a doctor's stethoscope and rushed to the point near the main gate where water from the Yateras River pipeline entered the base. For the next five hours they took turns listening to the water flowing through the intake valves of Guantánamo's pumping station. Just before 6:00 P.M. Trzyna took the stethoscope from his ears and said, "Admiral, the patient has died." At 7:35 P.M. Washington received the news that the flow of water from the Yateras pipeline had ceased.

An hour and a half later at the Waldorf-Astoria, LBJ deviated from his prepared remarks to members of the Weizmann Institute to announce that the Cuban government had shut off water to the Guantánamo Naval Base. Noting that the reason given by the Cubans for their action was the recent arrest by the U.S. government of Cuban fishermen, LBJ affirmed, "These fishermen were clearly inside the U.S. territorial waters." With greater oratorical emphasis, LBJ asserted, "The United States has known since Mr. Castro took over and allied himself with a foreign power that he would someday cut off the water to our Guantánamo base. We have made plans for such an eventuality. Our troops in Cuba and their families will have the water they need." The implication of LBJ's remarks was clear: the United States would never be driven out of Guantánamo for lack of water.[69]

That same evening, in Havana, Fidel held a lengthy press conference in which he described the arrest of the fishermen as "an act of cold war against Cuba, an aggression." He insisted that the area in which the Cuban boats were captured was in international waters, and that, to avoid any misunderstanding, the Cuban government had earlier advised Washington through the Swiss Embassy that those fishing boats, in pursuit of sawfish, would be fishing in that location. Fidel insisted that the U.S. seizure and arrests had come without warning in "a period of relative calm" in which "there was no incident of any kind." He also accused the United States of pressuring the fishermen to seek asylum, and said that "if they had all asked for asylum, they would not have been sent to jail." Finally, Fidel said that his government did not want to harm women and children at the U.S. base, and he therefore promised "to open the taps" for one hour each morning.[70] What Fidel did not know was that Yateras River water could no longer flow into Guantánamo because Bulkeley, worried that the Cuban leader might try to poison the water supply, had welded the intake valves shut at the pumping station just after Trzyna had pronounced the patient "dead."

On the morning of February 7, an editorial in the *Washington Post* with the catchy title "Base Motives" opened with the question: "Why has Fidel Castro suddenly made an issue out of Guantánamo Base?" The *Post*'s best guess was, "The most likely reason for the Cuban move lies in Panama. Castro may not have started the quarrel between the United States and Panama, but he has everything to gain by prolonging it. And injecting the Guantánamo issue into U.S. policies will make it harder for Washington to take a conciliatory line on Panama."[71]

At the White House, LBJ, who had returned to Washington after his talk, resumed his telephone consultations with his key advisers. Rusk mentioned that Cuba got $7 million in foreign exchange annually from having Cuban workers at Guantánamo and said, "We may want to stop that." In a brief chat with his longtime Texas friend A. W. Moursund,[72] LBJ mentioned that "Khrushchev has threatened us on Guantánamo. After they cut off our water, Khrushchev said, if we messed with them [the Cubans], they [the Soviets] would let us have it." Moursund shot back, "Tell him by God you're ready." LBJ mused, "I wish I was." LBJ then called McNamara, telling him to make sure that RFK attended the meeting of ExComm he was convening regarding Guantánamo. Searching for ideas on how to proceed, LBJ bluntly asked McNamara, "What should we do?" McNamara immediately responded, "Mr. President, we cannot do nothing. We can't let them turn off the water and just handle these crews through the courts and then send them back to Cuba. We can quarantine the subversive arms flows into Venezuela. There are lots of possible actions. . . . It's a political problem. We could restrict their access to some Latin American countries." LBJ then queried, "Do you think it [Castro's action] is closely tied in with the Panama action?" McNamara said, "Yes." LBJ replied, "I do, too."[73]

Later that morning, LBJ called his former political mentor, Senator Richard Russell (D-Ga.), who chaired the powerful Armed Services Committee. LBJ lamented that the committee had no ideas.

Bobby Kennedy said turn the seamen loose, but hold the boats. Give Castro 24 hours to turn the water on. I say to hell with that! The best thing I could suggest is that we had a contract with the water company that was nationalized by Castro. A contract that has been canceled. *We need to make our base inde-pendent of Cuba. We would staff it ourselves and supply our own water. We will cut Castro off of $7–8 million in foreign exchange.* . . . We need to get hold of Khrushchev and tell him this man is playing a dangerous game with his marbles. Tell Britain and France this is a serious matter with us. If they want to keep sickin' 'em on and egging 'em on, then we will have a difficult time with them![74]

Russell agreed: "We should make it clear to Khrushchev that this man is irrational. There will be a limit to our patience. If he [Castro] keeps on, we may have to take some very affirmative steps there. It would be tragic if he were to support a man who would be doing things that he [Khrushchev] would not tolerate himself. Remind him a little bit of Hungary."[75]

A few minutes later, LBJ spoke briefly with Senate Majority Leader Mike Mansfield, to whom he lamented, "We should treat the Cuban seamen bet-ter. The Coast Guard should have told them to get the hell out of there in-stead of turning them over to Florida. There are no bunks in their 8 ft. by 10 ft. cells." Mansfield responded, "They violated state law, not international law. The Cuban fishermen will receive justice. [There will be] no mixing of water and justice on our part. We will not be parched out of Guantánamo. Florida courts might release the seamen." LBJ opined, "It looks to me like their intrusion was deliberate." Mansfield agreed.[76]

On February 6, the Intelligence and Research Branch (INR) of the State Department prepared an intelligence note for the secretary of state titled "Possible Cuban Motivations for Fishing Boat Incident and Guantánamo Water Cutoff." This paper was forwarded to the NSC, which received it on February 7. The main points of this note may be summarized as follows: (1) The interrogations of the Cuban fishermen indicated that they were hand-picked crews explicitly instructed to violate U.S. territorial waters; (2) Fidel had decided to use the fishing incursion as the pretext to cut off the water at Guantánamo, and, thus, to shift the focus from territorial waters to the U.S. status and rights at Guantánamo because he wanted to link Guantánamo to the tail end of the Panama dispute, arguing that both the canal zone and the naval base were relics of a bygone imperialist age and had been forced upon new nations; (3) During Fidel's recent visit to Moscow, on January 17, Khrushchev had made a rare, explicit statement of support for Cuban de-mands for the return of Guantánamo; and (4) Fidel might think that Soviet military forces still in Cuba would inhibit any forceful U.S. response to the water cutoff.[77]

Just before his 4:30 P.M. meeting with the SGA, LBJ called Senator Russell to get his final input. LBJ began:

Nobody wants to do much. . . . Bobby Kennedy wants to turn everybody loose and let 'em go on home. McNamara feels that the sentiment in this country is that we have to do more than that. That we probably ought to do two things: (1) Declare the independence of that Base and furnish our own water—We don't want your damn water! (2) Tell the people that are on the Base that they can pledge allegiance to the United States and live there and tell the other 2,500 that we are going to quit financing Cuba, and we are going to operate the Base independently, so that our Base will be secure and we can operate independently. It's going to hurt you more than it hurts us, and we don't need you people. That's McNamara's feeling. He is the only one that feels that way. That's my feeling. I think they [the international press and foreign leaders] will say we're cruel and these people have been loyal for generations and have been working there. We're just firing them outright without any wrongdoing on their part.

Russell responded:

These nations aren't as silly as we seem to think they are. While they're envious of us, when they get down to where their self-interest is involved, they aren't as bad as everyone makes out. . . . None of the leaders want Castro to prosper. . . . Khrushchev will blow up and Mao Tse Tung will come in with a philippic. The world as a whole will say that it's a logical position to take. . . . If Khrushchev pulled them [the workers] all out at once, which he could do, and you had one hour's notice, you would need them; but now you're giving yourself an hour's notice and preparing against a probability that he [Castro] will do another asinine thing by declaring that no Cuban national can enter the base. You've got to be ready for that.

LBJ: "You think a lot of people are going to think that you're not headed anywhere when you fire a bunch of innocent people?" Senator Russell: "No, I don't think so. . . . I would make it perfectly clear that this situation is regrettable. Our association with these people has been pleasant and mutually profitable over a period of years, but they are within the power of Castro and not within our power. We had to make this base independent. In happier days our pleasant relationship with them could be renewed. I'd sure throw that in there."[78]

Two hours later at 6:30 P.M., after an inconclusive meeting, LBJ again conferred with Russell prior to the release of a White House statement on the Guantánamo dispute. The president began:

We may have a lot of U-2s shot down, and we may have a lot of people marching outside our gate. We've got a good deal of division in our government. It's about the line the three of us had—you, me, and McNamara versus Bundy, and Bobby, and McCone. Bobby and McCone were very much together. So we are putting out this statement: "When the Cuban government shut off the water supply to Guantánamo it deliberately broke an agreement made in 1938, reasserted in 1947, and personally supported by Fidel Castro in 1958. The United States is determined to guarantee the security of Guantánamo Naval Base, and does not intend to submit that security or the welfare of its servicemen to irresponsible activities by the Cuban government." Do you agree with that statement?

Russell: "Yes, I do." LBJ continued to read the statement:

"The President has instructed the Department of Defense to make Guantánamo Naval Base wholly self-sufficient. In response, the Secretary of Defense has issued instructions to: Assure the base's control over its own water supplies both by conversion of sea water to fresh water and by the transportation of water by ship. To reduce the employment of Cuban personnel who are subject to the control of the Cuban government, and whose wages contribute to its foreign exchange. The Castro government remains a constant threat to the peace of this hemisphere. The consequences of future provocations by Castro should be carefully weighed by all nations. These matters are being called to the attention of the members of the OAS for consideration in connection with charges now pending against Cuba. They will be discussed with members of NATO in order that they may take them into account in consideration of their own relations with Cuba and in connection with threats posed to the Western Hemisphere by the Castro regime."

Russell: "You're not going to say anything about Khrushchev?" LBJ:

We've already notified the Soviet ambassador this afternoon about what we've agreed upon. This is an irrational man! This is what they [Bundy, Kennedy, and McCone] wanted us to say: "That the President has instructed the Secretary of Defense to make Guantánamo wholly self-sufficient in fresh water, and to be prepared to take such other measures as may become necessary to insure against any future harassment by the Cuban government. . . . but to do nothing about it."

Russell: "I prefer the first statement."[79]

At 6:35 P.M. on February 7, 1964, White House Press Secretary Pierre Salinger issued the statement declaring the U.S. determination "to guarantee the security" of the base and announcing LBJ's instructions to the Department of Defense to make Guantánamo self-sufficient. One hour later,

McNamara instructed Nitze to send a U.S. Navy study group to Guantánamo to work out plans with Bulkeley to comply with the president's self-sufficiency directive, with special emphasis on implementing procedures to reduce the employment of Cubans on the base. This directive was incorporated into the message the JCS sent to the commander of the Atlantic Fleet at 11:13 P.M.[80]

With 1964 being a presidential election year, prominent politicians were quick to criticize LBJ's actions from various perspectives. On February 8, conservative Republican senator Barry Goldwater charged that Fidel's action was a slap in the face to the United States, and that the nation should send in the marines to seize the pumping station. New York governor Nelson Rockefeller, also a prospective presidential candidate, said that Fidel's action was one more sign of "the deterioration of U.S. leadership in world problems," but Rockefeller argued that deploying marines was not militarily feasible, given the continuing presence of Soviet troops and short-range missiles.

Meanwhile, RFK, who was in increasing disagreement with LBJ, wanted to downplay the whole incident by sending the Cuban fishermen back to Cuba and retaining the Cuban workers at Guantánamo.[81] It was largely because of RFK's opposition to the way the White House was handling this issue that Assistant Press Secretary Bill Moyers telephoned LBJ at his Texas ranch on Saturday, February 8. Moyers began:

Mr. President, I would suggest that you keep the pressure on Bundy, Rusk, McCone, and others to press forward on what we can do about Cuban subversion, espionage, and intelligence. We have got to do it! The Attorney General did not miss any opportunity yesterday to say that we are slapping at gnats. The big problems are subversion, the training of guerrillas for Africa, and nobody is giving any thought to that. Nobody seems to be concerned, nobody seems to be able to come up with a policy, and sooner or later we are going to get newspaper stories about how the President is more interested in gnats than the big problem.

LBJ calmly replied:

Tell Bundy that and tell Rusk that. I want him to appoint someone in State and see what we can do about this subversion—possibly Averil Harriman. I want the Attorney General and Bundy and someone from State—whoever Rusk wants—to see about this exportation of subversion from Cuba. You might ask Bundy to come down to the Ranch to talk about Cuba. Let Bobby study the exportation of subversion.[82]

At 4:30 P.M. LBJ spoke briefly with McNamara, who informed the president that he was having the study group divide the Cuban workers on the base into known subversives and suspected subversives. LBJ added, "We also need [to identify] possible subversives."

On February 10, another analytical paper produced by the INR, "Soviet Involvement in Cuban Fishing Boat–Guantánamo Water Escapade," arrived at the NSC. This study argued that Castro had probably planned to use the fishing boat incident to provoke the United States into a strong defense of its territorial rights, possibly to justify Soviet and Cuban use of similar arguments to protest U.S. overflights of Cuba. The paper also suggested that Moscow did not want to become enmeshed in a new international crisis in Cuba and that Soviet press coverage of the latest U.S.-Cuban developments had been restrained and largely factual.[83]

Shortly after noon, at Guantánamo, Bulkeley received his order from Nitze to terminate by February 12, 1964, the services of 300 Cuban commuters who were security risks or the poorest/most marginal performers. Nitze's cable also informed Bulkeley that negotiations were under way on an accelerated basis for the installation of a water desalinization plant that would provide an adequate and permanent on-base source of water.[84]

In a transparent move to avoid public outcry over the firings of Cuban commuters, on February 11, the Defense Department temporarily barred news reporters from traveling to Guantánamo for on-spot reporting of this latest U.S.-Cuban crisis. The Pentagon told the Associated Press that it would "continue to review the matter daily," but that "government-sponsored transport of newsmen to Guantánamo is not believed in the national interest at this particular time."[85]

In Havana, Fidel, seeing that his efforts to force the United States out of Guantánamo were collapsing, tried to embarrass Bulkeley by accusing him on Cuban radio and television of using suction pumps to siphon off 14,000 gallons per hour from the Yateras water plant. When these charges were repeated verbatim by major U.S. newspapers, and Nitze called Bulkeley to account on the issue of "taking water from Fidel Castro," the admiral, whose integrity had never been questioned, exploded: "Sir, that's it. I'm going to cut the pipe and prove to the world that it's dry."[86] He then ordered Cuban laborers to dig a hole at the water-intake station on the base to expose the pipe. With fourteen reporters watching, Trzyna used his acetylene torch to cut a thirty-inch section of the pipe. As newspapers across the United States reported Bulkeley's action, Trzyna enshrined the hole with a hand-lettered sign "U.S. Answer to Castro . . . GITMO Water Liberated from Cuba at This Point." This site would quickly become Guantánamo's symbolic version of the Liberty Bell. As Bulkeley's biographer William Breuer wrote: "In the months and years ahead, no senator, Congressman, movie star, navy secretary . . . or other VIP would visit Gitmo without having his picture taken next to the sign at the pipe-surgery excavation."[87]

With regard to the water desalinization plant, events moved swiftly. On February 13, the navy announced it had selected Westinghouse International as the primary contractor, and two weeks later, it estimated that the final design and engineering work on the desalinization and power-generating plant would be completed in March. Construction of the facility began on April 1, and on July 26 the first of three units of the plant began operating. Bulkeley officially opened the facility in a low-key ceremony on July 30, when water use returned to normal and the swimming pools on base were filled again. Two additional desalinization facilities were completed by the end of 1964. As the *Science News Letter* accurately predicted on February 29, Guantánamo would soon join other major desalinization facilities in the Persian Gulf, Israel, Italy, and the Virgin Islands.[88]

For several months following LBJ's initial instructions to McNamara to fire the Cuban commuters, the president continued to monitor this issue. On April 2, for example, LBJ called McNamara to inquire, "How many more have you fired in Cuba?" McNamara replied, "We haven't fired any more. We're holding at 1,000. We can fire a few more if necessary." "I would," LBJ shot back. "I want to be as tough on Cuba as I can. . . . I'd just tighten it down and operate as frugally and as tight as 'Dick's hatband,' and let them know that they have got some things to lose if they get too tough with us."[89] By early August, however, Bundy told his assistant Gordon Chase he doubted "if the President wants to press the commuters to zero right now. He [LBJ] is on pretty good ground right now." On August 28, 1964, McNamara wrote his official memorandum to LBJ that summarized his efforts to make Guantánamo self-sufficient and to reduce the gold flow into the Cuban economy. McNamara reported that the number of Cuban commuters had been reduced by 1,504 (or 67 percent), but to maintain the base at its required operational level, 415 additional enlisted personnel had been assigned to Guantánamo from Atlantic Fleet resources, and there had been an increase of 236 in the resident Cuban population at the base and recruitment of 425 Jamaican workers. McNamara also recorded that the annual gold flow into Cuba had been reduced by approximately $3 million.[90]

LBJ was obviously proud of the way he had resolved the water crisis at Guantánamo, and he used it to his political advantage in speeches over the next several months.[91] On February 21, at the University of California–Los Angeles, he said, "We have dealt with the latest challenge and provocation from Havana without sending the marines to turn on a water faucet. We believed it far wiser to send an admiral to cut the water off than to send a

battalion of marines to turn it back on."[92] On March 15, in an interview
with major radio and television broadcasters, LBJ said, "Sometimes our
people become very impatient. They cut the water off on us in Cuba and I
got recommendations from all over the country. . . . Some of them wanted
me to run in the marines." As if he were observing his own self-restraint,
LBJ counseled, "Upon reflection, evaluation, and study, you can chart a
course that will preserve your dignity and self-respect." A week later, LBJ
told American Federation of Labor–Congress of Industrial Organization
(AFL-CIO) leaders, "The water problem that disturbed us at Guantánamo
was solved not by a battalion of marines bayoneting their way in to turn on
the water, but we sent a single admiral over to cut it off. I can say to you that
our base is self-sufficient—in lean readiness. And a source of danger and disagreement has been removed." When he spoke one month later to the U.S.
Chamber of Commerce, LBJ adopted a folksy manner to recall, "I talked to
Lady Bird about it, and I decided we don't have to shoot from our hip, and
let's not just go berserk because Castro talked in a strong voice. Wouldn't it
be better to send one little admiral in there to cut that water off than to send
all of these marines to turn it on?"[93]

The water dispute between LBJ and Fidel had ended quickly without
bloodshed and not even saber-rattling.[94] It could have been dismissed as a
minicrisis or possibly even a historical footnote had LBJ not chosen to turn it
into a major bilateral issue. Within the context of the Cold War, LBJ, Rusk,
McNamara, Russell, and Bulkeley, acting together, had made the U.S. naval
base truly autonomous of Cuba in such a way that neither Havana nor Moscow had any recourse but to accept its self-sufficient status as a new reality.
Rusk had given LBJ the idea of making the base autonomous, McNamara
had helped to develop a plan to achieve it, Russell had approved the decisions involved, and Bulkeley had executed the orders.

Even LBJ and his advisers did not fully recognize the longer-term consequences of their actions. At the outset of a new administration complicated
by an upcoming presidential election, LBJ and his aides were largely reacting
to Fidel's provocations and to Republican hopefuls Goldwater's and Rockefeller's efforts to exploit international disputes for their own political advantage. What LBJ and Bulkeley had done, however, was of lasting significance.
They had moved Guantánamo Naval Base from the center to the periphery
of U.S.-Cuban relations. Never again would Fidel Castro or Soviet leaders
threaten the U.S. presence at Guantánamo. It was as if a knight or more
aptly a castle simply and quietly had been removed from the chessboard.

8

Guantánamo Endures

IT IS A HISTORICAL IRONY THAT at the same time Guantánamo Naval Base achieved its autonomous status vis-à-vis Cuba, its operational value to the U.S. military was declining.[1] Two of its major justifications, in historical terms, had suddenly become less important in the Cold War era, namely protecting the Caribbean and guarding the approaches to the Panama Canal.[2] The two-ocean navy of the first half of the twentieth century had been transformed into a four fleet, multiocean navy that in the Cold War would rely increasingly on nuclear-powered submarines and Nimitz-class aircraft carriers—too wide to pass through the Panama Canal—than on forward land bases. According to the research of Lars Schoultz, by the 1970s, in a typical noncrisis year, approximately twenty-five U.S. naval vessels, mostly destroyers, frigates, and submarines, would pass through the canal.[3]

In 1977, David Binder of the *New York Times* reported that senior State Department officials and navy commanders viewed Guantánamo as having "negligible" strategic importance, but that because of ongoing antagonism with the Castro government, no one anticipated any changes in the status of this military outpost.[4] Binder suggested that Guantánamo might serve as "a political bargaining chip" to normalize bilateral relations. He observed that Fidel had toned down his anti-Guantánamo rhetoric from describing it as "a dagger pointed at the heart of the Cuban revolution" to treating it as "a relatively insignificant wart on the body of his nation."[5] In this context, Binder's analysis made reference to the diplomatic initiative of President Jimmy Carter's administration to relinquish the Panama Canal by the year 2000. Binder further noted that the new Panama treaty "puts Guantánamo Bay more sharply in focus as anachronistic in an age of national independence and sovereignty."[6]

The thrust of Binder's piece was clearly in line with the Carter administration's initial moves to reduce bilateral tensions with Cuba. Shortly after taking office on January 20, 1977, the president quietly canceled the U-2 reconnaissance flights over Cuba that had been a routine intelligence activity since the missile crisis of 1962. He also lifted restrictions on the travel of U.S. citizens to Cuba.[7] Additionally, during his confirmation hearings before the Senate Foreign Relations Committee, designated secretary of state Cyrus Vance stated that "if Cuba is willing to live within the international system, then we ought to seek ways . . . to eliminate the impediments which exist between us."[8]

Fidel promptly responded. In February, he suggested bilateral talks to ease restrictions on Cuban fishing within the 200-mile maritime zone the U.S. government had established. In early April first Raúl and then Fidel publicly insisted that the United States leave Guantánamo before full diplomatic relations between the United States and Cuba could be restored.[9]

There is no available evidence that Carter's senior Latin American advisers gave serious consideration to this latter request. According to one former assistant secretary for Latin America, Ambassador Viron Vaky, "The issue [of abandoning Guantánamo] was never put on the table at the State Department." National Security Adviser for Latin America Robert Pastor, who participated in secret talks in 1977 with Cuba's top leaders, said some initial thought may have been given to "a large bargain, involving Guantánamo, that would also have required Castro to break military relations with the Soviets," but he also said, "There was no chance [and] nothing like that was ever put forward." Fidel and Deputy Prime Minister Carlos Rafael Rodriguez, however, both raised the subject of Guantánamo in the secret talks when they asserted that the United States "had no right to be there." Pastor reminded them that it was Batista who, as the real authority in Cuba's government, had approved the 1934 treaty that abrogated the Platt Amendment but approved the retention of Guantánamo, and that had not inhibited Rodríguez from becoming one of Batista's cabinet ministers several years later.[10]

The inconclusive discussion regarding Guantánamo's future did not derail the secret talks. On June 3, 1977, Cuba announced that "interest sections" would be established in neutral embassies in Havana and Washington to facilitate future diplomatic exchanges—an important step toward normalizing bilateral relations. This warming trend ended abruptly on November 17, 1977, when the White House announced it had evidence of a recent, dramatic increase in Cuban military forces in Angola as well as a Cuban military presence in eleven other African countries. Carter denounced what he called Castro's "military intrusion policy" as a "threat to the permanent peace in Africa," and he also stated publicly that "there is no possibility that we would see any substantial improvement in our relationship with Cuba."[11]

In July 1978, Fidel accused the Carter administration of hypocrisy in its emphasis on human rights and its demands that Cuba pull its troops out of Africa. In a speech to an international communist youth conference, Fidel called attention to serious socioeconomic inequities and discrimination based on race and ethnicity in the United States and defended Cuba's military deployments in Africa as being requested by sovereign governments, "but the United States has thousands of marines in Cuban territory [at Guantánamo] against the will of our nation."[12]

By mid-November 1978, U.S. spy planes were once again conducting reconnaissance missions over Cuba. Now it was SR-71s—flying at higher altitudes and with more sophisticated sensors than the U-2—that uncovered the presence of a squadron of Soviet MIG-23s in Cuba. The immediate response of the Carter administration was to invite its British allies to conduct a joint air and naval exercise, named Gulf EX79, that would range over 2,500 square miles of the Caribbean Sea. The Soviet Fleet, possibly in response to this heightened surveillance, had further aroused Washington's concern by entering Cuban waters twice in 1978 instead of the usual once-a-year visit.[13] As the *Washington Post* editorialized on November 18, 1978, "It was the military edge to the Carter administration's effort to impress both Havana and Moscow that the United States stands ready to combat any offensive threat in its back yard." In many ways, the scene was reminiscent of earlier confrontations during the Cold War.[14] It is virtually certain that Guantánamo and other U.S. naval assets, including Roosevelt Roads in Puerto Rico, were keeping a close watch on Soviet movements in the Caribbean.

In mid-July 1979, the National Security Agency (NSA) reported to senior U.S. policymakers that there was a Soviet "combat" brigade in Cuba. Until then the only known Soviet military personnel were members of an advisory group who had been there since the early 1960s. Subsequent investigation revealed that indeed this was the same Soviet unit that had been stationed in Cuba since 1963 and that it was primarily a training mission. Additionally, the NSA's use of the term *combat* was not based on hard evidence, and the interpretation of satellite photography of a brigade on maneuvers proved alarmist.

This intelligence failure proved highly embarrassing to the Carter administration and had significant policy repercussions. By the time the White House fully realized the mistakes involved in the "combat brigade" misinterpretation, 1,800 marines in battle gear had landed at Guantánamo to make a show of force, and the U.S. Senate decided to postpone indefinitely ratification of the second Strategic Arms Limitation Treaty (SALT II) that Carter and Soviet leader Leonid Brezhnev had signed six months earlier. Carter would later say that his failure to secure ratification of the SALT II agreement was "the most profound disappointment of [his] presidency." Pastor has suggested a link between the incipient clash over the Soviet brigade and the 1962 missile crisis by observing that, as in previous strategic confrontations in Cuba, the Soviet brigade issue had less to do with Cuba than with the perceived balance of power between the Soviet Union and the

United States. He overlooked, however, the involvement of Guantánamo in both cases.[15]

Throughout the 1980s and early 1990s Guantánamo continued to function as an important Caribbean site for the U.S. Fleet. Guantánamo also figured in the occasional displays of U.S. naval force in the Caribbean under President Ronald Reagan. From April 20 to May 6, 1983, a few warships deployed from Guantánamo to participate in a massive military exercise called Ocean Venture 1, which involved 350 warships and 30,000 service-members. The official purpose was "to protect our national interests by projecting military power." Shortly after the U.S.-led invasion of Grenada in October 1983 known as Operation Urgent Fury, the Cuban government planted its own minefields in the no-man's land between Cuban territory and Guantánamo Naval Base.[16] As late as 1985, eighty-three ships, large numbers of aircraft, and approximately twenty thousand sailors and marines used the base for various training purposes and military exercises.[17] Nevertheless, in a time of mounting inflation and public criticism of unnecessary government expenditures, in April 1990, a Pentagon naval committee included Guantánamo in a target list of ninety-four bases and facilities for "possible closing or realignment."[18]

It was in this climate of uncertainty that Guantánamo began to play a new and even more controversial role as a center for Haitian and Cuban refugees seeking political asylum in the United States. On September 29, 1991, Haitian military forces led by Brigadier General Raoul Cedras ousted the democratically elected government of President Jean-Bertrand Aristide, and in the following weeks unrecorded numbers—probably thousands—of Aristide's followers were beaten, shot, hacked with machetes, jailed, or terrorized into hiding. One month later, Haitians began fleeing their country in any rickety boat they could quickly build or find. Around Halloween, the U.S. Coast Guard began intercepting these refugees, taking everyone onboard and destroying their vessels as "hazards to navigation." By mid-November, the *Miami Herald* reported that more than one thousand Haitians were crammed onto the coast guard cutter decks and then suddenly there were two thousand.[19] Even with the coast guard deploying fifteen cutters, there were reports of boats being lost at sea and of hundreds of Haitians missing and presumed drowned. Despite urgent pleas to President George H. W. Bush to grant the Haitians "temporary protected status" in the United States until they could be processed by the Immigration and Naturalization Service (INS), the White House refused to bring them to Miami, and, as a temporary measure, sent approximately five hundred to Guantánamo.[20]

On November 18, 1991, the State Department announced that the U.S. Coast Guard would begin to return Haitian refugees to Port-au-Prince. It justified this decision with the argument that allowing large numbers of Haitians to enter the United States without legitimate claim to asylum would provoke more massive outflows, possibly resulting in large numbers of deaths on the high seas. It was at that point that attorney Ira Kurzban and other immigration lawyers in Miami moved to halt the forced repatriations by filing a lawsuit against the Bush administration, *Haitian Refugee Center v. Baker.*

After Federal District Judge C. Clyde Atkins issued an order halting the repatriations, on November 25 the first Bush administration dispatched a military task force to Guantánamo to erect emergency refugee camps, or tent cities, to accommodate the waves of Haitian boat people. Hundreds of U.S. soldiers from all service branches arrived at Guantánamo to carry out Operation Safe Harbor, which involved the installation of thousands of tents, showers, and portable latrines at an unused training site and the inactive McCalla Airfield. Razor wire would surround each of these refugee camps along with the more isolated Camp Bulkeley that would later be built to accommodate Haitians diagnosed with the HIV/AIDS virus. By December 24, more than six thousand Haitians were being "warehoused" at Guantánamo, guarded by almost two thousand soldiers.

Senior officials at the State and Justice Departments offered several explanations for the choice of Guantánamo including that it would be easier for the INS to screen the refugees on land. The base was only 125 miles from Haiti, but well outside U.S. borders. Because it was a military facility, it could provide a protective environment for the refugees, and, at the same time, restrict the access of the press and other groups that might seek to contact the refugees. The most important reason, however, was the belief by Justice Department officials that the rights and privileges granted to U.S. citizens by the Constitution, namely due process, did not apply to foreigners on overseas military bases. That meant that INS officials processing Haitian requests for political asylum did not have to follow the requirements of domestic immigration law. Moreover, Guantánamo had its unique or anomalous legal features. Because of the leasing arrangement with the Cuban government, it could be treated as a foreign territory.[21]

In early February 1992, the Eleventh Circuit Court of Appeals in Atlanta threw out Atkins's decision. Its ruling was based on the principle that since the Haitians were outside the United States, they were not entitled to the protection of U.S. laws. In fact, the court's ruling implied that the Haitians had no rights at all. Kurzban and his colleagues appealed the Eleventh Circuit Court decision to the U.S. Supreme Court. In the meantime, the Coast Guard began returning the Haitians that they rescued to Port-au-Prince. Then the Supreme Court refused to review the *Baker* case, with only Justice

Harry Blackmun voting to hear it. Blackmun's dissent, however, would serve to inspire subsequent litigation on behalf of the Haitian refugees. He wrote, "If indeed the Haitians are to be returned to an uncertain future in their strife-torn homeland, that ruling should come from this Court, after full and careful consideration of the merits of their claims."[22]

According to Brandt Goldstein's well-researched legal history, *Storming the Court,* these words inspired distinguished Yale Law School professor Harold Hongju Koh, together with his students and human rights advocate Michael Ratner, to file a new lawsuit on behalf of the Haitian refugees being detained at Guantánamo and their right to legal counsel before being forcibly repatriated to Haiti.[23] The new case, known as *Sale v. Haitian Centers Council,* was initiated in the Eastern District Court of New York (Brooklyn), and in their first appearance before Judge Sterling Johnson Jr., Koh and his Yale Law School litigation team won a temporary restraining order. As an appeal on that case was pending, however, President Bush Senior issued an executive order authorizing the coast guard to return all fleeing Haitians directly to Haiti without any process at all. This would be only the first of several challenges from the White House and the U.S. attorney general's office that Koh and his legal team would confront. President-Elect Bill Clinton would praise Judge Johnson for making the "right decision in overturning the Bush administration's cruel policy of returning Haitian refugees to a brutal dictatorship without an asylum hearing." Just before his inauguration, however, Clinton shifted course and announced that he would continue the Bush administration policies of summarily returning Haitians without giving them the chance for asylum, and keeping those interned at Guantánamo indefinitely.[24]

Eventually the attorney general's office allowed Koh, Ratner, and their legal team to visit their Haitian clients at Guantánamo. There they discovered that those Haitians who had been assigned to Camp Bulkeley were enduring sweltering heat in cramped quarters—often twelve assigned to a hut measuring twenty feet by forty feet—with some sleeping on cots and others on flattened cardboard boxes.[25] The Haitians interviewed would reveal that if they protested their living conditions and indeterminate detention, they would be handcuffed, blasted with fire hoses, and imprisoned in small razor-wire pens. As Koh would later write of his clients, "All had credible claims of political persecution, and many had already established full-fledged claims of political asylum. Nevertheless, they were barred from entering the United States because most had the HIV virus."

When it returned to the Eastern District Court, the Yale team amended its complaint to challenge directly the legality of its clients' confinement in what the lawyers described as the first U.S. HIV concentration camp. After a two-week trial, Judge Johnson ordered the immediate release of the Guantánamo detainees, basing his decision on the conclusion that the Due Process Clause of the Constitution applied to Guantánamo. He reasoned that the U.S. government had seized the refugees on the ocean and taken them to territory exclusively controlled by the United States. Once there, however, the military authorities had been deliberately indifferent to the refugees' medical needs and had incarcerated them indefinitely for no legitimate reason. Johnson declared it "totally unacceptable." The Clinton administration chose not to fight Johnson's ruling, and shortly thereafter acting Attorney General Webster Hubbell settled the case. On June 21, 1993, almost two years after Aristide had been overthrown, the last of the Guantánamo Haitians were permitted to enter the United States.[26]

From Detention to Imprisonment

The use of Guantánamo as a detention center for undocumented aliens, and particularly for Haitian refugees that both the former Bush and Clinton administrations determined were ineligible to enter the United States, was a historical prelude to Guantánamo's status as a maximum security prison for suspected terrorists. In particular, the arguments used by both the federal government and by the advocates for the Haitian detainees in *Baker* and in *Sale* would be cited and raised again in cases concerning the rights of terrorist suspects to decent treatment and fair trials.

Following the devastating terrorist attacks of September 11, 2001, on the World Trade Center and the Pentagon, President George W. Bush signed an executive order dated November 13, 2001, that authorized the secretary of defense to hold non-U.S. citizens in indefinite detention. On December 27, 2001, Defense Secretary Donald Rumsfeld confirmed that the Pentagon would transfer alleged terrorist detainees from Afghanistan to the U.S. naval base at Guantánamo, Cuba. In his press conference, Rumsfeld admitted, "We have made no plans to hold any kind of tribunal there," and he described Guantánamo as "the least worst place we could have selected." What Rumsfeld meant by this cryptic remark may have been that the Defense Department had examined other offshore U.S. possessions and made the determination that only Guantánamo contained the sufficient infrastructure necessary to accommodate large numbers of incarcerated "enemy combatants."[27] Karen Greenberg's well-documented study *The Least Worst Place: Guantanamo's First 100 Days* presents information that challenges this perspective: specifically, the existing detention facility, Camp X-Ray, built in the mid-1990s to incarcerate unruly migrants who had been reclassified as criminals, was a ramshackle collection of approximately forty open-air cages with cement floors, lacking running water and now overgrown with weeds; additionally, the base hospital was essentially an out-patient facility with fewer than ten beds and weak emergency capabilities—hardly adequate to address the medical needs of hundreds of detainees who may have been wounded when taken prisoner or suffering from serious illnesses.[28]

The detainees began arriving in military transports in January 2002. According to Greenberg's research, the first head of Joint Task Force (JTF) 160, Marine Brigadier General Michael Lehnert, was morally committed to treating these prisoners in a manner consistent with the Geneva Conventions, which mandate basic standards of humane treatment. Lehnert and his subordinates issued each detainee a copy of the Koran, a skullcap, and prayer beads if requested. When the detainees initiated a hunger strike to protest their detention, Lehnert responded by sitting bare-headed on the ground outside the wire-mesh cells trying to persuade the prisoners to resume eating. On one occasion, frustrated by a detainee's refusal to cooperate, this tough marine began to cry, "the unmistakable flow of tears cascading down his face." This respect for prisoners' basic rights, however, began to diminish after Rumsfeld appointed the ambitious army reservist and former interrogator Major General Michael Dunlavey to head a second command, JTF 170, to be concerned solely with interrogation. As Greenberg concludes, "The fabric of prisoners' rights that Lehnert had woven [began] to unravel. . . . Interrogations, not trials, had become the future of Guantánamo."[29]

By mid-2002, the United States was holding more than six hundred suspected terrorists, who had been arrested in more than forty countries, in a modern maximum-security facility named Camp Delta at Guantánamo. Greenberg writes that "in these cells the prisoners couldn't communicate with anyone. . . . They were here to stay—without charge, without lawyers, without process, without a trial. Encased in concrete, they had been buried alive."[30] Meanwhile, the members of the JTF assigned to guard them were quartered in new, air-conditioned barracks at Camp Bulkeley, the former quarantine center for HIV-infected Haitians.

On February 19, 2002, a team of lawyers representing the Center for Constitutional Rights that included Ratner filed a habeas corpus petition in federal court in Washington, D.C., on behalf of the Guantánamo detainees. The case, *Rasul v. Bush,* asserted that holding the suspected terrorists indefinitely at Guantánamo violated the Due Process Clause and other laws. In support of their arguments, the lawyers relied in part on Judge Johnson's ruling in *Haitian Centers Council v. Sale.* In response, lawyers representing the Bush administration asked the court to dismiss *Rasul v. Bush* on the grounds that Guantánamo was not within U.S. jurisdiction, that no U.S. law applied there, that the detainees had no enforceable rights, and that the court itself had no authority—or legal jurisdiction—to hear the case.[31]

On November 10, 2003, the U.S. Supreme Court agreed to hear *Rasul v. Bush.* By then, Guantánamo had become the target of intense criticism, both domestic and international, and many foreign governments had called on the United States to release their citizens. Dozens of amicus briefs had been filed in support of the constitutional rights of the detainees, including one submitted by Koh. Much of the international outcry was in response to the use of torture tactics at Abu Ghraib, but there was also widespread knowledge that Rumsfeld had authorized and then subsequently rescinded an order for harsh interrogation tactics at Guantánamo, including forcing prisoners into "stress positions," interrogating them for twenty hours at a time, removing their clothing, and intimidating them with dogs. In a letter to the *New York Times,* Ratner charged that two detainees he represented had been in solitary confinement for three months and that they had been interrogated for twelve hours at a time while shackled to the floor. These individuals were subsequently released without charges filed against them.[32]

The question must be asked, Have these interrogations produced useful intelligence that would facilitate the apprehension of other dangerous terrorists or prevent acts of international terrorism? A disturbing answer has been provided by one senior military intelligence officer, Lieutenant Commander James R. Van de Velde, who visited the detention facility at Guantánamo twice in 2003. He described chaotic conditions in which "those in charge have a poor idea of what they are doing, . . . crucial information is not being learned, . . . and some [interrogators] possess very sensitive clearances and see the big picture; [whereas] others have low-level clearances and understand little."[33]

On June 28, 2004, the Supreme Court decided *Rasul v. Bush.* Using broad language, the Court ruled that Guantánamo detainees had the right to challenge their captivity in U.S. federal courts. Speaking for the 6–3 majority, Justice John Paul Stevens wrote that if, as many of the detainees claimed, they had not been engaged in terrorist acts, then holding them for up to two years at Guantánamo "unquestionably" violated the Constitution as well as other laws and treaties of the United States. Justice Anthony Kennedy wrote a separate concurring opinion in which he asserted, "What matters is the unchallenged and indefinite control that the United States has long exercised over Guantánamo Bay. From a practical perspective, the indefinite lease of Guantánamo Bay has produced a place that belongs to the United States, extending the 'implied protection' of the United States to it."

Justice Antonin Scalia, joined by Chief Justice William Rehnquist and

Justice Clarence Thomas, dissented. In an angry, lengthy opinion, Justice Scalia wrote, "Today the Court springs a trap on the Executive, subjecting Guantánamo Bay to the oversight of the federal courts even though it has never before been thought to be within their jurisdiction. . . . For this Court to create such a monstrous scheme in time of war . . . is judicial adventurism of the worst sort."[34]

This decision, landmark though it may be, did not resolve the issue of indeterminate detention at Guantánamo or the most important legal question, Does the U.S. Supreme Court have the legal authority to review the decisions of military tribunals at Guantánamo? Although the Supreme Court ruled in *Rasul v. Bush* that U.S. courts did have jurisdiction over suspected terrorists incarcerated at Guantánamo, it did not discuss the merits of the petitioner's habeas corpus claims, nor did it provide the lower courts clear guidance on how to handle such claims.[35] On October 17, 2006, President George W. Bush signed into law the Military Commissions Act. This new law's stated purpose was to "facilitate bringing to justice terrorists and other unlawful enemy combatants through full and fair trials by military commissions." Its provisions specified that "no court, *justice*, or judge, shall have jurisdiction to hear or consider an application for a writ of habeas corpus filed by or on behalf of an alien detained by the United States who has been determined by the United States to have been properly detained as an enemy combatant or is awaiting such determination."[36]

Clearly, from Bush's perspective, neither the U.S. Constitution nor the Supreme Court exercised jurisdiction over Guantánamo Bay, Cuba. The position of this offshore U.S. naval base was both autonomous and anomalous.

Since 2002 the official Cuban position vis-à-vis the detention center has changed radically. Initially, Raúl Castro stated publicly that "if anyone is lucky to escape [from Guantánamo], I doubt he would get through the minefields. . . . But if anyone gets out alive, we would send him back to the Americans."[37] Following, however, the shocking revelations of the abusive treatment of prisoners at Abu Ghraib and the use of harsh interrogation procedures at Guantánamo and other detention centers—including the Bagram Theater Internment Facility at Bagram Air Base in Afghanistan—both Fidel and Raúl have castigated the detention center and renewed their demands for the unconditional return of Guantánamo Bay to Cuba. According to a focused study of the history of leasing arrangements for Guantánamo, international relations scholar Michael Strauss has found that Cuba's revolutionary government both under Fidel and Raúl Castro has not mounted any formal initiative to utilize international legal procedures to terminate the U.S. leasing of Guantánamo. As Strauss finds: "It appears that Cuba has never sought arbitration on the matter, and has never accepted the compulsory jurisdiction of the International Court of Justice, the logical tribunal for adjudicating such issues."[38]

It has not been the purpose here to argue or even to suggest that there are easy answers to the question of how the U.S. government should treat or prosecute dangerous, ideologically committed terrorists who constitute a security threat to the United States. As a historical study, however, this work does suggest that the torrent of international and domestic criticism provoked by the base's use as an interrogation and detention center outside of the confines of constitutional procedures and due process threatened to tarnish permanently the proud history of Guantánamo for both the U.S. Navy and Marine Corps. Bush's stubborn insistence on controlling the fate of all suspected international terrorists at Guantánamo also elevated this particular facility into a high-profile topic for Barack Obama as a presidential campaign issue of 2008. On January 22, 2009, the third day of his administration, President Obama signed an executive order aimed at closing the Guantánamo detention center within one year. The key issue the executive order did not address is where the U.S. government will incarcerate, interrogate, and prosecute or release current and future alleged enemy combatants. One answer is clear: it will not be Guantánamo.

The Necessity for Diplomacy at Guantánamo

During the 106 years the United States has occupied Guantánamo Bay, perhaps the most remarkable role the naval base has played has been to facilitate "fenceline talks" between Cuban and U.S. officials, which began in 1994 and continue to the present. These discussions began at a time when thousands of Haitian and Cuban rafters were at Guantánamo.[39] There was an escalation in accidents in minefields as migrants tried to escape from Guantánamo and the Cubans persisted in efforts to migrate to the United States through Guantánamo. As the Cuban Foreign Ministry dispassionately outlined the situation, "Accidents occurred, and often our soldiers had to take major risks to rescue people from mined fields. Such actions also required information and cooperation from people stationed at the base. Additionally, there were the heavy rains and swollen rivers in the area that swept away mines and blurred their markings, which gave rise to similarly hazardous situations for all."[40]

In May 1995, the United States agreed to return most Cubans who intruded into the naval base or were interdicted at sea by the coast guard. Both sides agreed not to take any action against the returned migrants as a consequence of their attempts to immigrate illegally.[41] To work out the modalities of repatriation at Guantánamo, the senior local U.S. and Cuban military commanders were authorized to meet at the single gate in the fenceline demarcating the naval base. These exchanges of information soon became regularized as monthly meetings and led to an improvement in relations in which other local operational issues that had the potential to escalate into more serious problems were quickly resolved. These included minor, but potentially explosive incidents such as U.S. marines and Cuban soldiers (or sentries) making offensive remarks and/or gestures. Surprisingly, the Cuban government was receptive to a request to permit U.S. military aircraft to use a portion of adjacent Cuban airspace for takeoffs and landings at Guantánamo. Until the granting of this concession, the beeline approach between the base and international waters was difficult and potentially dangerous for larger aircraft, but the Cubans justified their decision by explaining that it was not in their national interests to have U.S. aircraft crash on Cuban soil.[42] These fenceline talks have also addressed the issue of how to medically treat potential burn victims, Cuban and American, should serious brushfires break out along the fenceline. Should this happen, both Cuban and U.S. soldiers would be treated at the burn unit in the Guantánamo City hospital or possibly airlifted to Havana. The most recent example of fenceline cooperation occurred in mid-July 2009, when a Cuban army helicopter overflew the naval base to extinguish burning plywood by dropping 500 gallons of saltwater during this simulation of a wildfire. American sailors joined members of the Cuban Frontier Brigade outside the fenceline to create a mock triage medical center that both forces would staff and operate should such a catastrophe occur.[43]

The Cuban government has provided additional insights regarding its perspective on the fenceline initiative. In 1999, during the war in Kosovo, the U.S. government gave serious consideration to using Guantánamo to shelter Kosovar refugees. Although, according to the Cubans, they were almost never consulted on such matters, on this occasion, they were informed. Even though Havana opposed the war, it had no reason to refuse the assistance the Kosovars might need, and it offered medical care or any other services that might be required. Ultimately, the decision was made not to send those refugees to Guantánamo.

According to the Cuban government's stated view, "that military enclave [Guantánamo] is the exact place where American and Cuban soldiers stand face to face, [and] thus the place where serenity and a sense of responsibility are most required. . . . Consequently, what prevails there today is not what could be described as an atmosphere of hostility or war." Even if this is interpreted as propaganda, it is documented by recent history.[44]

Guantánamo and the Embargo

It is appropriate to note parenthetically that, during the four and a half decades of the Castro era, Guantánamo's role has undergone changes as dramatic as those undergone by the U.S. embargo, which began on October 19, 1960, in the final days of President Dwight D. Eisenhower's administration as a partial economic embargo that excluded the export of medicine and food to Cuba. It was broadened under President John F. Kennedy to prohibit travel as well as all commercial and financial exchanges between the United States and Cuba. The travel ban was relaxed in 1977 by Carter, who also allowed U.S. residents to send money to Cuban relatives. Reagan tightened the embargo, President Clinton relaxed it somewhat, and George W. Bush imposed new restrictions. Overall, the strategy behind the embargo has evolved from an effort to isolate Cuba as the communist pariah within the Western Hemisphere to a more concerted effort to bring an end to the Castro brothers' domination of Cuba. Today Fidel is close to the end of his domination of Cuba, but the Castro regime is likely to persist, probably in an amended form, into the indeterminate future. As a probable consequence, Guantánamo will endure under full U.S. control, and the embargo is also likely to persist until and unless democratic norms are restored in Cuba.[45]

Obama has said that he wants to improve bilateral relations and, as a first step, he has lifted restrictions on travel to Cuba. Whether this initiative will lead to removing the trade embargo or other major U.S. concessions, however, is uncertain. As long as the Castro brothers retain power, they almost certainly will insist on trying to manage all aspects of their country's future. Cuban resistance to economic and political liberalization could easily derail subsequent moves by the Obama administration to place U.S.-Cuban relations on a better footing. As George Friedman, editor of the on-line analytical news service Stratfor, recently commented: "The Cubans must be thoroughly convinced of the benefits of increased engagement with the United States. . . . If Cuba opens too much to the United States, the Cuban regime might fall."[46]

Retrospective

In concluding the history of this military outpost that has provided a unique setting for conflict and compromise, it seems fitting to recall the origins of Guantánamo's importance to the United States. In popular literature, Elmore Leonard painted a picture of the first and only time that Guantánamo was a battleground.

Once it was decided Guantánamo Bay would make a dandy coaling station, Huntington's marines were sent in to secure the area. . . . What they needed was a coaling station in a sheltered area not far from Santiago, where they had the Spanish Fleet blockaded, and even closer to where the American troops would come ashore to engage the enemy, and Guantánamo Bay filled the bill. There were six thousand Spanish troops fifteen miles away in the city of Guantánamo, but insurgents were up there keeping them busy. They also had a fort up the bay at Caimanéra; but the *Marblehead* and the *Texas* would cruise up there and pound it to hell. So once the high ground around here was secured they'd have a coaling station: the reason for starting the war here.[47]

It is not surprising, given its rancorous history and controversial present, that fiction writers usually treat Guantánamo as a setting for conflict, espionage, and even murder. Dan Fesperman's novel *The Prisoner of Guantánamo* is a virtual reality tour of interrogations accompanied by chains, blinding lights, and deafening music as well as deception and subterfuge. And yet the historian, unlike the novelist, must also recognize the significance of Raúl Castro's astonishing promise made in January 2002 that Cuba would return any prisoner who made it through the minefields to Guantánamo. The implication was clear: Cuba's leaders would not provide sanctuary to suspected terrorists. It also seemed that Raúl had finally come to terms with Guantánamo's enduring presence. He concluded his promise by stating that Cuba had no intention of reinforcing its side of the border at Guantánamo Bay. "We don't have to add more troops because it's not necessary. There is a situation of calm."[48]

Since 1898, Guantánamo has provided a unique focus for U.S. and Cuban interests. The occupation of Guantánamo Bay by U.S. marines with the essential aid and participation of Cuban auxiliaries was the beginning of U.S. participation in Cuba's war for independence, and it also facilitated a rapid end to that conflict. Since then, Guantánamo has often been a flashpoint for controversy and heightened nationalistic tensions for both nations, but even in its tensest moments it also has functioned as a center for dialogue and diplomatic accommodation. In 1903, when President Theodore Roosevelt was determined to take control of at least one and possibly four naval stations in Cuba, President Tomás Estrada Palma negotiated the ceding of only one station—Guantánamo—and under the terms of a lease, not a purchase. In 1934, when President Franklin Delano Roosevelt abrogated the Platt Amendment, even though his administration ignored nationalist opposition to its retention of Guantánamo, it managed to establish positive relations with Cuba and to strengthen hemispheric cooperation under the rubric of the "good neighbor" policy.

The most dramatic clashes and accommodations involving Guantánamo, of course, have occurred during the Castro era. Yet, despite Fidel and Raúl's harsh condemnations of the base as a vestige of U.S. imperialism, the closest they ever came to endangering the base's security was shutting off the potable water supply in February 1964, and they were willing to rescind that action when confronted with President Lyndon B. Johnson's unflinching retaliatory moves to fire the Cuban commuters and to construct the desalination plant.

For ideological reasons, the Castro government continues to argue that Guantánamo "has been put to multiple uses, none of them contemplated in the agreement that justified its presence," and, moreover, that the naval base is on a "portion of national territory occupied against the will of our people." This is clearly the unwavering position of the Castro government. In 1979, the Cuban Ministry of Foreign Relations published its version of the history of Guantánamo, in which it stated that "in the history of all the [naval] bases in the world today, the most tragic case is Cuba: a base [located] unmistakably in Cuba—which is a good distance from the United States—against Cuba and against its people, imposed by force and [thus constituting] a threat and a preoccupation for our people."[49] These repeated official assertions of irredentism probably evoke a sense of unrequited nationalism more widely shared among the Cuban people. Yet, at the same time, the Castro brothers have come to accept the reality of the indeterminate nature of the U.S. occupation of Guantánamo Bay and to work toward the solution of bilateral problems that might arise from the enduring U.S. presence there calmly and quietly.[50]

The final words should be those of modern Cuban historians José Sánchez Guerra and Wilfredo Campos Cremé. They concluded their study *La Batalla de Guantánamo 1898* by recalling a prediction made by Manuel Sanguilí in June 1898. Upon reading in a New York newspaper that the U.S. Fleet had taken the bay, Sanguilí told his friend Enrique Trujillo, "Now that they have seen Guantánamo, they will never renounce its possession."[51]

Appendix A
Imperial Germany and the Caribbean, 1890s–1917

In his research in the military archives in Freiburg, Germany, historian Holger Herwig found that beginning in the late 1890s, the German government had prepared operational war plans to seize poorly defended U.S. Caribbean bases with the intention of using them to attack U.S. trade centers.[1] There had been strong frictions between Germany, Great Britain, and the United States over Samoa in the mid-1880s, when the United States wanted to annex the deepwater port at Pago Pago, and war was narrowly averted by the establishment of a tripartite protectorate. German and U.S. overseas ambitions also clashed in the Philippines, China, and even in the Congo as various interest groups in both nations competed for access to foreign markets, political influence, and the right to establish coaling and naval stations.[2]

On March 10, 1898, the German military attaché in Washington, Count Gustav Adolf von Göetzen, sent a memorandum to Berlin titled "The Strategic Importance of a Shipping Canal through Central America for the United States, England, and Germany." Citing writings by Captain Alfred Thayer Mahan that advocated U.S. control of Cuba and other Caribbean islands to protect Atlantic approaches to the future isthmian canal, von Göetzen argued that Germany's international prestige as well as its strategic and commercial objectives dictated that it establish a naval station at a port in the Caribbean Sea even if it had to challenge the Monroe Doctrine.[3]

In summer 1898, during the U.S. naval blockade of Santiago de Cuba, the German cruiser *Geier* was stationed in the West Indies and permitted to pass in and out of Cuba's blockaded ports. Its chief officer, Commander Jacobsen, who wrote under the pseudonym Commander J . . . . , subsequently published a series of "Sketches from the Spanish-American War" in Berlin's *Marine-Rundschau,* which the U.S. Office of Naval Intelligence (ONI) translated in their entirety. Jacobsen began by emphasizing Alfred Mahan's early and accurate perception of the importance of Cuba to future strategic and commercial U.S. interests. Observing that "almost nine-tenths of all the sugar from Cuba is already going to the American market," he predicted, "If America succeeds in getting Cuba into her hands . . . it will insure an immense advantage to the American market and drive all other kinds of sugar entirely out of America." Obviously believing that imperial Germany had missed a great opportunity in Cuba by not being the first great power to declare war on a weakened Spain, he lamented, "The United States of America has done what other nations in its place might have accomplished long ago. According to the old adage that a war arises out of the needs of nations, the Union has taken advantage of the opportunity to secure for herself the first place in the West Indies."[4]

During the Venezuelan crisis of 1902, in which Germany joined in a naval blockade with England and Italy to force Caracas to pay its foreign obligations, some U.S. naval officers acted as if a war with Germany were imminent. The chief of the ONI, Captain Charles Sigsbee, warned the secretary of the navy that in the event of war the German Fleet would almost certainly defeat the U.S. Fleet, and could conceivably steam through the Chesapeake Bay to Annapolis, and from there launch an attack on Washington.[5]

In 1903 the German high command devised a formal war plan, designated Operation Plan III, to attack and invade the United States by sending the German Fleet into the Caribbean to seize a naval base in or near Puerto Rico, and from there to attack various targets along the eastern seaboard of the United States. Although these plans were reviewed and updated periodically, historian Nancy Mitchell has found that sometime between 1903 and 1905, German war planning efforts shifted from the Caribbean–Latin American region to Europe, Africa, and Asia.

As for U.S. war plans against Germany, naval historian Steven T. Ross has found that in 1905, the Joint Army-Navy Board reviewed a plan prepared by the Naval War College that proposed, in the event of a global conflict, that U.S. forces occupy the island of Hispaniola (Haiti and the Dominican Republic) and concentrate the U.S. Fleet at Guantánamo Bay to protect the Caribbean and provide a shield for the United States.[6]

Mitchell makes a well-documented revisionist argument that Berlin's seemingly belligerent actions in the Caribbean region in the early 1900s—to include Germany's joining Great Britain and Italy in the naval blockade of Venezuela's ports—were an exaggerated form of gunboat diplomacy. Mitchell sees Germany's moves as more of a probing and testing of U.S. naval might and political determination to protect its interests than a realistic threat. She writes, "In 1823 the Monroe Doctrine had been blithely arrogant rhetoric, but by 1902 the United States had staked out Cuba and Puerto Rico, and its navy was substantial and growing. . . . What did Germany actually do to establish hegemony in the region? The simple answer is nothing. Why then did the United States persist in seeing Germany as the threat to the region?"[7]

In part, Mitchell may be accused of pushing her analytical perspective too far when she suggests that the United States exploited the German threat merely for opportunistic goals—"to build the naval strength and develop the trade and diplomatic ties to claim [the hemisphere as] its sphere." It may well be argued and documented from hindsight that this was the eventual outcome, but it seems overly cynical to dismiss the expressed concerns of senior policymakers such as Elihu Root and Theodore Roosevelt regarding the potential German threat to the Caribbean and Western Hemisphere in 1901 and 1902 as sheer paranoia, or worse, as hypocrisy. This is really what Mitchell is saying in her sweeping condemnation: "It was simple imperialism: we presumed it was ours, we had the power to take it, and the cost was extraordinarily low."[8]

A more penetrating interpretation has been provided by Paul Schroeder, who argues that Germany's foreign policy after Bismarck oscillated between its overriding need to protect its vital interests on the European Continent by avoiding conflict and Kaiser William II's dreams of foreign aggrandizement. Schroeder writes:

> It is commonly said that after 1890 Germany played the game of international politics like a plunger on the stock market, always looking for quick short-term gains. The truth is worse than this. Germany played it like a plunger looking for quick gains without making any investment, a gambler trying to win without betting. The Germans were always expecting to be feared and respected because of the power they possessed but dared not exert.[9]

William's apparently uncontrollable desire to be a player in *Weltpolitik* frequently led the Second Reich into imperialistic adventures and aggressive moves—in such places as the Caribbean and South Pacific—from which Germany would frequently be forced to withdraw in order to protect her greater interests on the European Continent. Nonetheless, Germany's antagonistic maneuvers created fear, suspicion, and ill will that would linger in nations such as the United States until World War I. Diplomatic historian Frederick Marks finds that even before the U.S. entry into the war in 1917, President Woodrow Wilson's intrusive Caribbean policies were largely shaped by his fear of potential German aggression. This is why he authorized a preemptive invasion of Haiti and threatened to seize the Virgin Islands when Denmark seemed reluctant to sell them.[10]

Appendix B
Transcriptions of Letters
from Elihu Root, 1901

Letter from Elihu Root to Major General Leonard Wood,
January 9, 1901

War Department,
Washington.
January 9, 1901.
My dear General:

Your letter with the petition relative to the tariff has been received and the petition has been formally transmitted to the President. He has been too ill to see any one since Saturday, and Rixay and Sternberg say that he has a well defined case of grip. He certainly will not be able to attend to business before next week. The Diplomatic Reception which was to have been tonight has been called off, and Mrs. Root is about withdrawing her invitations for a Cabinet dinner which we would have given Saturday night. It makes no difference, however, so far as this petition goes for you might as well ask a foot-ball team in full play for their autographs as expect to get legislation on any important new subject from Congress at present; nor do I think that at the present stage of Cuban affairs it is desirable. In the fall of 1899 I was in favor of legislation giving special advantages to Cuba during our occupation, but matters have gone so far now that I think any action on that subject must necessarily wait until after the presentation to Congress of the whole subject of the relations between the two countries, which will come up on the transmittal of the proposed constitution and of such expression as the convention may make on the subject of relations, or upon their refusal to make any expression. When that time comes I think we are in great danger of finding ourselves in a very awkward and untenable position. It seems clear enough to me that we can not justify the demand that Cuba shall treat us as a kind of foster-mother, on whose benevolent protection she is to rely and to whom she is to give special privileges in the way of naval stations and rights of supervision and intervention while we treat her commercially at arms length just as we do our most unfriendly competitors, and grant her absolutely no privileges or advantages in her intercourse with us. It is, however, exceedingly doubtful whether Congress can be induced to make any abatement whatever in the United States tariff on Cuban sugar and tobacco. The Senate has not ratified any of the reciprocity treaties providing for the reduction of duties upon the products of other West Indian islands, and the present indications are that they will not be ratified. The proposition to reduce the duties on Cuban sugar and tobacco would be met with a great outcry and a strong pressure on the part of the cane sugar, beet sugar and tobacco people, and it is doubtful whether in view of the democratic tendency to unite with any republican minority for the purpose of embarrassing the republican administration any such measure could be carried. It certainly could not be except after a long protracted and heated discussion. I hope that the convention will not take it into their heads to present any such proposition as a part of a scheme under which they will consent to such rights and powers as we think we ought to have in Cuba. I hope that the whole subject of commercial relations may be postponed for future consideration.

Under all the circumstances I have come to the conclusion that the sooner the convention finishes its labors and sends its conclusion to the President the better. I think they should be promptly confronted with the proposition that we desire as soon as possible to be relieved from the burden and annoyance of their government, and the expense of maintaining troops there which must be about half a million dollars a month. They have been talking about getting their constitution here by the first of February. I think they should be urged to do so, and we will get it before Congress as soon as possible. I am led to this view by several considerations. First, as to the situation in Cuba. It is utterly hopeless to expect any relief from Congress in regard to the Foraker resolution. Nothing could be more reasonable than your letter to Foraker, but it will be wholly ineffective. I have been trying to accomplish something on the same line and everybody is afraid to touch it. I do not think that this is fair towards Cuba, or that we ought to prolong our government there and at the same time prohibit Cuba from developing her own resources. We ought not to say that Cuba shall not, and that we will not, offer the necessary opportunities for the introduction of capital and the inauguration of such great private enterprises as have built up this country.

It seems to me, moreover, that the people of Cuba will never come to a realizing sense of what is before them, or of what the relations of this country mean, until they are brought face to face with the prospect of being abandoned to their own devices, and I think the sooner we have the round up the better.

Second, as to the situation here. I am getting pretty tired of having

Congress on the one hand put us under independence of Cuban resolutions, and Foraker franchise resolutions and resolutions of hostile inquiry and criticism, and on the other hand shirk all responsibility; and I do not relish the prospect of having the Cuban constitution and proposals as to our relations just too late for Congress to act, compelling us to go on and govern for another year with the Cubans howling at us to do something and the democratic press abusing us because we do not do something, and with the certainty that we will be met by a denial of our lawful authority if we undertake to do anything, and with a possibility of a change for the worse in Cuban conditions. I have talked it over with the President and he agrees with the view that we should get the conclusions of the convention before Congress as speedily as possible, and he is prepared, when the subject is once fairly before Congress, to urge prompt action, which he thinks can be secured. At all events, if it should not be, the responsibility will be upon Congress and it will be plain to everyone that, failing Congressional action, the administration will be dealing with a situation for which it is not responsible.

I do not think that the plan of having a Cuban Legislature while the Military Governor continues and exercises the veto power over their acts, is safe. I think matters should be shaped so that we can make a clean cut between the military government and the new Cuban government, turn over the administration and get out, except in so far as we may keep some troops in place until the stability of the government is assured: and this should be clearly understood to be not a favor to us but a favor to them.

Of course, you are taking special care not to permit anyone with whom you talk to have the opportunity to say that you are making demands, or even official suggestions. It seems to me important that the convention shall be required either to take the initiative in stating what they want the relations to be, or to distinctly refuse it. It might be wise for you, in talking with such members of the convention as come to you, to disabuse their minds of the idea that they are certain of being protected by the United States no matter what they do or refuse to do. If Cuba declines to accord to this government the authority and facilities for her protection, she will have to look out for herself in case of trouble with any other nation, and we will deal with that other nation. And we should probably deal with the other nation not on account of Cuba, but on our own account. If the American people get the impression that Cuba is ungrateful and unreasonable they will not be quite so altruistic and sentimental the next time they have to deal with Cuban affairs as they were in April, 1898.

Another fact which the Cubans should consider is that in international affairs the existence of a right recognized by international law is of the utmost importance. We have now by virtue of our occupation of Cuba and the terms under which sovereignty was yielded by Spain, a right to protect her which all foreign nations recognize. It is of great importance to Cuba that that right, resting upon the treaty of Paris and derived through that treaty from the sovereignty of Spain, should never be terminated but should be continued by a reservation, with the consent of the Cuban people, at the time when the authority which we now exercise is placed in their hands. If we should simply turn the government over to the Cuban administration, retire from the island, and then turn round to make a treaty with the new government, just as we would make treaties with Venezuela, and Brazil, and England, and France, no foreign State would recognize any longer a right on our part to interfere in any quarrel which she might have with Cuba, unless that interference were based upon an assertion of the Monroe Doctrine. But the Monroe Doctrine is not part of international law and has never been recognized by European nations. How soon some one of these nations may feel inclined to test the willingness of the United States to make war in support of her assertion of that doctrine, no one can tell. It would be quite unfortunate for Cuba if it should be tested there.

Whenever you consider that matters have reached such a point that a conference would be useful, cable for an order and come up.

With kind regard to Mrs. Wood,

Faithfully yours,

ELIHU ROOT

Major-General Leonard Wood,
Military Governor of Cuba
Havana, Cuba

Letter from Elihu Root to John Hay, *January 11, 1901*

War Department,
Washington.

CONFIDENTIAL. January 11
1901.

My dear Mr. Hay:

I wish to bring the question of the ultimate relations of this country to Cuba to a point as soon as possible, and, that being determined, to organize the permanent Cuban government to take the control of the island out of the hands of the present military authorities without any avoidable delay. I have directed General Wood to urge the Constitutional Convention, now in session in Havana, to bring its labors to a conclusion in time to lay them before Congress at the present session. When that is done, it is of course desirable that the policy which in a general way we have agreed upon should be made as definite as possible. Will you turn over in your mind, until our next meeting, the advisability of requiring the incorporation into the fundamental law of Cuba of provisions to the following effect: 1. That in transferring the control of Cuba to the Government established under the new constitution, the United States reserves and retains the right of intervention for the preservation of Cuban independence and the maintenance of a stable Government, adequately protecting life, property and individual liberty. 2. That no government organized under the constitution shall be deemed to have authority to enter into any treaty or engagement with any foreign power which may tend to impair or interfere with the independence of Cuba, or to confer upon such foreign power any special right or privilege without the consent of the United States, and that the United States shall be entitled to be a party, in the first instance, to any negotiation having in view any such provision. 3. That to facilitate the United States in the performance of such duties as may devolve upon her under the foregoing provisions and for her own defense, the United States may acquire and hold the title to land, and maintain naval stations at certain specified points. 4. That all the acts of the Military Governor, and all rights acquired thereunder, shall be valid and be maintained and protected.

I recall that there was at one time a great deal of discussion over the effect which the vesting in England of a right of intervention in Egypt would have, and my impression is that some good authorities were of the opinion that it would enable England to retire and still maintain her moral control, and prevent the backsliding of the Egyptian Government. Perhaps some of your people in the State Department have that subject at their fingers' ends. It is important now to consider and reach sound conclusions upon the scope and effect which the reservation of a right of intervention in Cuba would have.

I send you a copy of a confidential letter which I have recently sent to General Wood, which further explains what I consider to be the present situation.

Faithfully yours,
ELIHU ROOT, Secretary of War

Hon. John Hay, Secretary of State
Washington, D. C.

Letter from Elihu Root to Major General Leonard Wood, February 9. 1901

War Department
Office of the Secretary,
Washington.
February 9, 1901.
Sir:

As the time approaches for the Cuban Constitutional Convention to consider and act upon Cuba's relations with the United States, it seems desirable that you should be informed of the views of the Executive Department of our government upon that subject in a more official form that that in which they have been communicated to you hitherto. The limitations upon the power of the Executive by the Resolution of Congress of April 20th, 1898, are such that the final determination upon the whole subject may ultimately rest in Congress and it is impracticable now to forecast what the action of Congress will be. In the meantime, until Congress shall have acted, the military branch of the government is bound to refrain from any committal, or apparent committal, of the United States to any policy which should properly be determined upon by Congress, and, at the same time, as far as it is called upon to act or to make suggestions bearing upon the course of events, it must determine its own conduct by reference to the action already taken by Congress, the established policy of the United States, the objects of our present occupation, and the manifest interests of the two countries.

The Joint Resolution of Congress of April 20, 1898, which authorized the President to expel the Spanish forces from Cuba, declared

"that the United States hereby disclaim any disposition or intention to exercise sovereignty, jurisdiction or control over said Island except for the pacification thereof and asserts its determination, when that is accomplished, to leave the government and the control of the Island to the people."

The Treaty of Peace concluded at Paris on the tenth of December, 1898, and ratified by the Senate on the 6th of February, 1899, provides in the First Article that,

"as the island is, upon its evacuation by Spain, to be occupied by the United States, the United States will, so long as such occupation shall last, assume and discharge the obligations that may under international law result from the fact of its occupation, for the protection of life and property."

It contains numerous obligations on the part of the United States in respect of the treatment of the inhabitants of the territory relinquished by Spain such as the provision of the Tenth Article, that the inhabitants shall be secured in the free exercise of their religion; of the Eleventh Article that they shall be subject to the jurisdiction of the courts, pursuant to the ordinary laws governing the same, and of the Ninth Article, that they shall retain all the rights of property, including the right to sell or to dispose thereof, and the right to carry on their industry, commerce and professions. The Sixteenth Article of the Treaty provides that the obligations assumed in the treaty by the United States with respect to Cuba limited to the time of its occupancy thereof, but that it shall, upon the termination of such occupancy, advise any government established in the Island to assume the same obligations.

Our occupancy of Cuba has been under the binding force both of the Resolution and of the Treaty, and the pacification mentioned in the Resolution has necessarily been construed as co-extensive with the occupation provided for by the Treaty, during which we were to discharge international obligations, protect the rights of the former subjects of Spain and cause or permit the establishment of a government to which we could, in good faith, commit the protection of the lives and property and personal rights of those inhabitants, from whom we had compelled their former sovereign to withdraw its protection. It is plain that the government to which we were thus to transfer our temporary obligations should be a government based upon the peaceful suffrages of the people of Cuba, representing the entire people and holding their power from the people, and subject to the limitations and safeguards which the experience of constitutional government has shown to be necessary to the preservation of individual rights. This is plain as a duty to the people of Cuba under the resolution of April 20, 1898; and it is plain as an obligation of good faith under the Treaty of Paris. Such a government we have been persistently, and with all practicable speed, building up in Cuba, and we hope to see it established and assume control under the provisions which shall be adopted by the present Convention. It seems to me that no one familiar with the traditional and established policy of this country in respect to Cuba can find cause for doubt as to our remaining duty. It would be hard to find any single statement of public policy, which has been as often officially declared by so great an array of distinguished Americans authorized to speak for the Government of the United States, as the proposition stated, in varying but always uncompromising and unmistakable terms, that the United States would not under any circumstances permit any foreign power other than Spain to acquire possession of the Island of Cuba. Jefferson and Monroe and John Quincy Adams and Jackson and Van Buren and Grant and Clay and Webster and Buchanan and Everett have all agreed in regarding this as essential to the interests and protection of the United States. The United States has, and will always have, the most vital interest in the preservation of the independence which she has secured for Cuba, and in preserving the people of that Island from the domination and control of any foreign power whatever. The preservation of that independence by a country so small as Cuba, so incapable, as she must always be, to contend by force against the great powers of the world, must depend upon her strict performance of international obligations, upon her giving due protection to the lives and property of the citizens of all other countries within her borders, and upon her never contracting any public debt which in the hands of citizens of foreign powers shall constitute an obligation she is unable to meet. The United States has, therefore, not merely a moral obligation arising from her destruction of Spanish sovereignty in Cuba, and the obligations of the Treaty of Paris, for the establishment of a stable and adequate government in Cuba, but it has a substantial interest in the maintenance of such a government. We are placed in a position where for our own protection we have, by reason of expelling Spain from Cuba, become the guarantors of Cuban independence and the guarantors of a stable and orderly government protecting life and property in that Island. Fortunately, the condition which we deem essential for our own interests is the condition for which Cuba has been struggling, and which the duty we have assumed towards Cuba on Cuban grounds and for Cuban interests requires. It would be a most lame and impotent conclusion if, after all the expenditure of blood and treasure by the people of Cuba for the same object, we should, through the constitution of the new government, by inadvertence or otherwise, be placed in a worse condition in regard to our own vital interests than we were while Spain was in possession, and the people of Cuba should be deprived of the protection and aid from the United States which is necessary to the maintenance of their independence. It was, undoubtedly, in consideration of these special relations between the United States and Cuba that the President said in his message to Congress on the 11th of April, 1898:

> "The only hope of relief and repose from a condition which can no longer be endured is the enforced pacification of Cuba. In the name of humanity, in the name of civilization, in behalf of endangered American interests which give us the right and duty to speak and to act, the war in Cuba must stop. . . . In view of these facts and of these considerations I ask the Congress to authorize and empower the President to make measures to secure a full and final termination of hostilities between the Government of Spain and the people of Cuba, and to secure in the Island the establishment of a stable government, capable of maintaining order, observing its international obligations, insuring peace and

tranquility and the security of its citizens as well as our own, and to use the military and naval forces of the United States as may be necessary for these purposes."

And in his message of December 5, 1899:

"This nation has assumed before the world a grave responsibility for the future good government of Cuba. We have accepted a trust the fulfillment of which calls for the sternest integrity of purpose and the exercise of the highest wisdom. The new Cuba yet to arise from the ashes of the past must needs be bound to us by ties of singular intimacy and strength if its enduring welfare is to be assured. Whether those ties shall be organic or conventional, the destinies of Cuba are in some rightful form and manner irrevocably linked with our own, by how and how far is for the future to determine in ripeness of events. Whatever be the outcome, we must see to it that free Cuba be a reality, not a name, a perfect entity, not a hasty experiment bearing within itself the elements of failure. Our mission to accomplish for which we took up the wage of battle, is not to be fulfilled by turning adrift any loosely framed commonwealth to face the vicissitudes which too often attend weaker states whose natural wealth and abundant resources are offset by the incongruities of the political organization and the recurring occasions for internal rivalries to sap their strength and dissipate their energies."

And it was with a view to the proper settlement and disposition of these necessary relations that the order for the election of delegates to the present Constitutional Convention provided that they should frame and adopt a constitution for the people of Cuba, and as a part thereof provide for and agree with the Government of the United States upon the relations to exist between that government and the government of Cuba.

The people of Cuba should desire to have incorporated in her fundamental law, provisions in substance as follows:

1. That no Government organized under the constitution shall be deemed to have authority to enter into any treaty or engagement with any foreign power which may tend to impair or interfere with the independence of Cuba, or to confer upon such foreign power any special right or privilege without the consent of the United States.

2. That no Government organized under the constitution shall have authority to assume or contract any public debt in excess of the capacity of the ordinary revenues of the island after defraying the current expenses of Government to pay the interest.

3. That upon the transfer of the control of Cuba to the Government established under the new constitution Cuba consents that the United States reserve and retain the right of intervention for the preservation of Cuban independence and the maintenance of a stable Government, adequately protecting life, property and individual liberty, and discharging the obligations with respect to Cuba imposed by the Treaty of Paris on the United States and now assumed and undertaken by the Government of Cuba.

4. That all the acts of the Military Government, and all rights acquired thereunder, shall be valid and shall be maintained and protected.

5. That to facilitate the United States in the performance of such duties as may devolve upon her under the foregoing provisions and for her own defense, the United States may acquire and hold the title to land for naval stations, and maintain the same at certain specified points.

These provisions may not, it is true, prove to be in accord with the conclusions which Congress may ultimately reach when that body comes to consider the subject, but as, until Congress has acted, the Executive must necessarily within its own sphere of action be controlled by its own judgment, you should now be guided by the views above expressed.

It is not our purpose at this time to discuss the cost of our intervention and occupation, or advancement of money for disarmament, or our assumption under the Treaty of Paris of the claims of our citizens against Spain for losses which they had incurred in Cuba. These can well be the subject of later consideration.

Very respectfully,
ELIHU ROOT
Secretary of War.

Major-General Leonard Wood
Military Governor of Cuba,
Havana, Cuba.

Appendix C
Theodore Roosevelt's Message to Congress for Representation in Cuba, 1902

MESSAGE FROM THE PRESIDENT OF THE UNITED STATES COMMENDING TIMELY CONSIDERATION OF MEASURES FOR MAINTAINING DIPLOMATIC AND CONSULAR REPRESENTATIVES IN CUBA AND FOR CARRYING OUT THE PROVISIONS OF THE ACT MAKING APPROPRIATION FOR THE SUPPORT OF THE ARMY FOR THE FISCAL YEAR ENDING JUNE 30, 1902.

To the Congress of the United States:

I commend to the Congress timely consideration of measures for maintaining diplomatic and consular representatives in Cuba and for carrying out the provisions of the act making appropriation for the support of the Army for the fiscal year ending June 30, 1902, approved March 2, 1901, reading as follows:

Provided further, That in fulfillment of the declaration contained in the joint resolution approved April 20, 1898, entitled "For the recognition of the independence of the people of Cuba, demanding that the Government of Spain relinquish its authority and government in the island of Cuba, and to withdraw its land and naval forces from Cuba and Cuban waters, and directing the President of the United States to use the land and naval forces of the United States to carry these resolutions into effect," the President is hereby authorized to "leave the government and control of the island of Cuba to its people" so soon as a government shall have been established in said island under a constitution which, either as a part thereof or in an ordinance appended thereto, shall define the future relations of the United States with Cuba substantially as follows:

I.

That the government of Cuba shall never enter into any treaty or other compact with any foreign power or powers which will impair or tend to impair the independence of Cuba, nor in any manner authorize or permit any foreign power or powers to obtain by colonization or for military or naval purposes or otherwise, lodgment in or control over any portion of said island.

II.

That said government shall not assume or contract any public debt to pay the interest upon which, and to make reasonable sinking fund provision for the ultimate discharge of which, the ordinary revenues of the Island, after defraying the current expenses of government, shall be inadequate.

III.

That the Government of Cuba consents that the United States may exercise the right to intervene for the protection of Cuban independence, the maintenance of a government adequate for the protection of life, property, and individual liberty, and for discharging the obligations with respect to Cuba imposed by the treaty of Paris on the United States, now to be assumed and undertaken by the Government of Cuba.

IV.

That all acts of the United States in Cuba during its military occupation thereof are ratified and validated, and all lawful rights acquired thereunder shall be maintained and protected.

V.

That the government of Cuba will execute, and as far as necessary extend, the plans already devised, or other plans to be mutually agreed upon, for the sanitation of the cities of the island, to the end that a recurrence of epidemic and infectious diseases may be prevented, thereby assuring protection to the people and commerce of Cuba, as well as to the commerce of the southern ports of the United States and the people residing therein.

VI.

That the Isle of Pines shall be omitted from the proposed constitutional boundaries of Cuba, the title thereto being left to future adjustment by treaty.

VII.

That to enable the United States to maintain the independence of Cuba, and to protect the people thereof, as well as for its own defense, the Government of Cuba will sell or lease to the United States lands necessary for coaling or naval stations at certain specified points, to be agreed upon with the President of the United States.

VIII.

That by way of further assurance the Government of Cuba will embody the foregoing provisions in a permanent treaty with the United States.

The people of Cuba having framed a constitution embracing the foregoing requirements, and having elected a President who is soon to take office, the time is near for the fulfillment of the pledge of the United States to leave the government and control of the island to the people. I am advised by the Secretary of War that it is now expected that the installation of the Government and the termination of the military occupation of that island by the United States will take place on the 20th of May next [1902].

It is necessary and appropriate that the establishment of international relations with the Government of Cuba should coincide with its inauguration, as well to provide a channel for the conduct of diplomatic relations with the new State as to open the path for the immediate negotiation of conventional agreements to carry out the provisions of the act above quoted. . . .

THEODORE ROOSEVELT
White House
Washington, March 27, 1902.

Appendix D
Leasing Agreement between the United States and Cuba, 1903

LEASE OF COALING OR NAVAL STATIONS TO THE UNITED STATES.
Agreement between the United States of America and the Republic of Cuba for the lease (subject to terms to be agreed upon by the two Governments) to the United States of lands for coaling and naval stations.

Signed by the President of Cuba, February 16, 1903.

Signed by the President of the United States, February 23, 1903.

The United States of America and the Republic of Cuba, being desirous to execute fully the provisions of Article VII of the Act of Congress approved March second, 1901, and of Article VII of the Appendix to the Constitution of the Republic of Cuba promulgated on the 20th of May, 1902, which provide:

"Article VII. To enable the United States to maintain the independence of Cuba, and to protect the people thereof, as well as for its own defense, the Cuban Government will sell or lease to the United States the lands necessary for coaling or naval stations, at certain specified points, to be agreed upon with the President of the United States," have reached an agreement to that end, as follows:

Article I

The Republic of Cuba hereby leases to the United States, for the time required for the purposes of coaling and naval stations, the following described areas of land and water situated in the Island of Cuba.

1st. In Guantánamo (see Hydrographic Office Chart 1857): From a point on the south coast, 4.37 nautical miles to the eastward of Windward Point Light House, a line running north (true) a distance of 4.25 nautical miles; From the northern extremity of this line, a line running west (true) a distance of 5.87 nautical miles;

From the western extremity of this last line, a line running south-west (true), 3.31 nautical miles;

From the southwestern extremity of this last line, a line running south (true), to the seacoast.

This lease shall be subject to all the conditions named in Article II of this agreement.

2nd. In Northwestern Cuba (see Hydrograpic Office Chart 2036). In Bahía Honda (see Hydrographic Office Chart 520b).

All that land included in the peninsula containing Cerro del Morillo and Punta del Carenero situated to the westward of a line running south (true) from the north coast at a distance of thirteen hundred yards east (true) from the crest of Cerro del Morillo, and all the adjacent waters touching upon the coast line of the above described peninsula and including the estuary south of Punta del Carenero with the control of the headwaters as necessary for sanitary and other purposes. And in addition all that piece of land and its adjacent waters on the western side of the entrance to Bahía Honda included between the shore line and a line running north and south (true) distant one nautical mile form Pt. del Cayman.

Article II

The grant of the foregoing Article shall include the right to use and occupy the waters adjacent to said areas of land and water, and to improve and depend the entrances thereto and the anchorages therein, and generally to do any and all things necessary to fit the premises for use as coaling or naval stations only, and for no other purpose. Vessels engaged in the Cuban trade shall have free passage through the waters included within this grant.

Article III

While on the one hand the United States recognizes the continuance of the ultimate sovereignty of the Republic of Cuba over the above described areas of land and water, on the other hand the Republic of Cuba consents that during the period of the occupation by the United States of said areas under the terms of this agreement the United States shall exercise complete jurisdiction and control over and within said areas with the right to acquire (under conditions to be hereafter agreed upon by the two Governments) for the public purposes of the United States any land or other property therein by purchase or by exercise of eminent domain with full compensation to the owners thereof.

Done in duplicate at Habana, and signed by the President of the Republic of Cuba this sixteenth day of February, 1903.

T. ESTRADA PALMA

Signed by the President of the United States the twenty-third of February, 1903.

THEODORE ROOSEVELT

Lease to the United States by the Government of Cuba of certain areas of land and water for naval or coaling stations in Guantánamo and Bahía Honda.

Signed at Habana, July 2, 1903.
Approved by the President October 2, 1903.
Ratified by the President of Cuba August 17, 1902.
Ratifications exchanged at Washington October 6, 1903.

The United States of America and the Republic of Cuba, being desirous to conclude the conditions of the lease of areas of land and water for the establishment of naval or coaling stations in Guantánamo and Bahía Honda the Republic of Cuba made to the United States by the Agreement of February 16/23, 1903, in fulfillment of the provisions of Article Seven of the Constitutional Appendix of the Republic of Cuba, have appointed their Plenipotentiaries to that end.—The President of the United States of America, Herbert G. Squires, Envoy Extraordinary and Minister Plenipotentiary in Havana. And the President of the Republic of Cuba. José M. Garcia Montes, Secretary of Finance, and acting Secretary of State and Justice, who, after communicating to each other their respective full powers, found to be in due form, have agreed upon the following Articles;—

Article I

The United States of America agrees and covenants to pay to the Republic of Cuba the annual sum of two thousand dollars, in gold coin of the United States, as long as the former shall occupy and use said areas of land by virtue of said Agreement.

All private lands and other real property within said area shall be acquired forthwith by the Republic of Cuba.

The United States of America agrees to furnish to the Republic of Cuba the sums necessary for the purchase of said private lands and properties and such sums shall be accepted by the Republic of Cuba as advance payment on account of rental due by virtue of said Agreement.

Article II

The said areas shall be surveyed and their boundaries distinctly marked by permanent fences or inclosures.

The expenses of construction and maintenance of such fences or inclosures shall be borne by the United States.

Article III

The United States of America agrees that no person, partnership, or corporation shall be permitted to establish or maintain a commercial, industrial or other enterprise within said areas.

Article IV

Fugitives from justice charged with crimes or misdemeanors amenable to Cuban law, taking refuge within said areas, shall be delivered up by the United States authorities on demand by duly authorized Cuban authorities.

On the other hand, the Republic of Cuba agrees that fugitives from justice charged with crimes or misdemeanors amenable to United States law, committed within said areas, taking refuge in Cuban territory, shall on demand, be delivered up to duly authorized United States authorities.

Article V

Materials of all kinds, merchandise, stores and munitions of war imported into said areas for exclusive use and consumption therein, shall not be subject to payment of customs duties nor any other fees or charges and the vessels which may carry same shall not be subject to payment of port, tonnage, anchorage or other fees, except in case said vessels shall be discharged without the limits of said areas; and said vessels shall not be discharged without the limits of said areas otherwise than through a regular port of entry of the Republic of Cuba when both cargo and vessel shall be subject to all Cuban Customs laws and regulations and payment of corresponding duties and fees.

It is further agreed that such materials, merchandise, stores and munitions of war shall not be transported from said areas into Cuban territory.

Article VI

Except as provided in the preceding Article, vessels entering into or departing from the Bays of Guantánamo and Bahía Honda within the limits of

Cuban territory shall be subject exclusively to Cuban laws and authorities and orders emanating from the latter in all that respects port police, Customs and Health, and authorities of the United States shall place no obstacle in the way of entrance and departure of said vessels except in case of a state of war.

Article VII

This lease shall be ratified and the ratifications shall be exchanged in the City of Washington within seven months from this date.

In witness whereof, We, the respective Plenipotentiaries, have signed this lease and hereunto affixed our Seals.

Done at Havana, in duplicate in English and Spanish this second day of July nineteen hundred and three.

[seal] H. G. Squires.

[seal] José M. García Montes

I, Theodore Roosevelt, President of the United States of America, having seen and considered the foregoing lease, do hereby approve the same, by virtue of the authority conferred by the seventh of the provisions defining the relations which are to exist between the United States and Cuba, contained in the Act of Congress approved March 2, 1901, entitled "An Act making appropriation for the support of the Army for the fiscal year ending June 30, 1902."

Washington, October 2, 1903.

THEODORE ROOSEVELT

Appendix E
Treaty Agreement between the United States and Cuba, 1934

TREATY OF RELATIONS BETWEEN THE UNITED STATES AND CUBA
SIGNED MAY 29, 1934

The United States of America and the Republic of Cuba, being animated by the desire to fortify the relations of friendship between the two countries and to modify, with this purpose, the relations established between them by the Treaty of Relations signed at Habana, May 22, 1903, have appointed with this intention as their Plenipotentiaries:

The President of the United States of America; Mr. Cordell Hull, Secretary of State of the United States of America, and Mr. Sumner Welles, Assistant Secretary of State of the United States of America; and The Provisional President of the Republic of Cuba, Señor Dr. Manuel Márquez Sterling, Ambassador Extraordinary and Plenipotentiary of the Republic of Cuba to the United States of America; Who after having communicated to each other their full powers which were found to be in good and due form, have agreed upon the following articles:

Article I

The Treaty of Relations which was concluded between the two contracting parties on May 22, 1903, shall cease to be in force, and is abrogated, from the date on which the present Treaty goes into effect.

Article II

All the acts effected in Cuba by the United States, during its military occupation of the island, up to May 20, 1902, the date on which the Republic of Cuba was established, have been ratified and held as valid; and all the rights legally acquired by virtue of those acts shall be maintained and protected.

Article III

Until the two contracting parties agree to the modification or abrogation of the stipulations of the agreement in regard to the lease to the United States of America of lands in Cuba for coaling and naval stations signed by the President of the Republic of Cuba on February 16, 1903, and by the President of the United States of America on the 23rd day of the same month and year, the stipulations of that agreement with regard to the naval station of Guantánamo shall continue in effect. The supplementary agreement in regard to naval or coaling stations signed between the two Governments on July 2, 1903, also shall continue in effect in the same form and on the same conditions with respect to the naval station of Guantánamo. So long as the United States of America shall not abandon the said naval station of Guantánamo or the two Governments shall not agree to a modification of its present limits, the station shall continue to have the territorial area that it now has, with the limits that it has on the date of the signatures of the present Treaty.

Article IV

If at any time in the future a situation should arise that appears to point to an outbreak of contagious disease in the territory of either of the contracting parties, either of the two Governments shall, for its own protection, and without its act being considered unfriendly, exercise freely and at its discretion the right to suspend communications between those of its ports that it may designate and all on part of the territory of the other party, and for the period that it may consider to be advisable.

Article V

The present treaty shall be ratified by the contracting parties in accordance with their respective constitutional methods; and shall go into effect on the date of the exchange of their ratifications, which shall take place in the city of Washington as soon as possible.

IN FAITH WHEREOF, the respective Plenipotentiaries have signed the present Treaty and have affixed their seals hereto.

Done in duplicate, in the English and Spanish languages, at Washington on the twenty-ninth day of May, one thousand nine hundred and thirty-four.

[seal] CORDELL HULL

[seal] SUMNER WELLES

[seal] M. MÁRQUEZ STERLING

Note.—Ratification was advised by the Senate, May 31, 1934; ratified by the President, June 5, 1934; ratified by Cuba, June 4, 1934. Ratifications were exchanged at Washington, June 9, 1934; proclaimed by the President of the United States, June 9, 1934.

Appendix F
Statement by the
Government of Cuba, 2002

STATEMENT BY THE GOVERNMENT OF CUBA TO THE NATIONAL AND INTERNATIONAL PUBLIC OPINION—RELEASED BY THE FOREIGN MINISTRY OF CUBA (Received by U.S. government on January 11, 2002)

The American Naval Base at Guantánamo is a facility located in an area of 117.6 square kilometers of the national territory of Cuba occupied since 1903 due to an Agreement on Coaling and Naval Stations signed by the Government of the United States and the Government of Cuba under President Tomás Estrada Palma. At that time, our country was not really independent since an amendment—known as Platt Amendment—had been passed by the U.S. Congress and signed by President McKinley on [in] March 1901 while our country was under occupation by the U.S. army after its intervention in the independence war waged by the Cuban people against the Spanish metropolis.

The Platt Amendment, which granted the United States the right to intervene in Cuba, was imposed to the text of our 1901 Constitution as a prerequisite for the withdrawal of the American troops from the Cuban territory. Following that clause, the aforementioned Agreement on Coaling and Naval Stations was signed on [in] February 1903 in Havana and Washington, respectively. It actually included two areas of our national territory: Bahía Honda and Guantánamo, although a naval base was never established in the former.

In Article II of that Agreement, the right was literally granted to the United States to do "all that is necessary to outfit those places so they can be used exclusively as coaling or naval stations, and for no other purpose."

In addition to that treaty of February 1903, on May 22 that same year a Permanent Treaty of Relations was signed by Cuba and the United States of America using the exact text of the 8 clauses contained in the Platt Amendment which were thus turned into articles of said treaty.

Twenty-one years later, on May 29, 1934, in the spirit of the American "Good Neighbor" policy under President Franklin Delano Roosevelt, a new Treaty of Relations was subscribed between the Republic of Cuba and the United States of America that abrogated the previous 1903 Treaty, thereby abrogating the Platt Amendment. The new Treaty definitely excluded Bahía

Honda as a possible base, but it sustained the presence of Guantánamo Naval Base and kept in effect the rules of establishment. As for such rules that remained in force, the Article III of the new Treaty literally stated:

"Until the two contracting parties agree to the modification of the agreement in regard to the lease to the United States of America of lands in Cuba for coaling and naval stations signed by the President of the Republic of Cuba on February 16, 1903, and by the President of the United States of America on the 23rd day of the same month and year, the stipulations of that agreement with regard to the naval station of Guantánamo shall continue in effect. The supplementary agreement in regard to coaling and naval stations signed between the two Governments on July 2, 1903 also shall continue in effect in the same form and on the same conditions with respect to the naval station at Guantánamo. So long as the United States of America shall not abandon the said naval station of Guantánamo or the two Governments shall not agree to a modification of the present limits, the station shall continue to have the territorial area that it now has, with the limits that it has on the date of the signature of the present Treaty."

As evidence of the abusive conditions imposed by that Treaty, the above-mentioned supplementary agreement established that the United States would compensate the Republic of Cuba for the leasing of 117.6 square kilometers—that is, 11,760 hectares comprising a large portion of one of the best bays in the country—with the sum of $2,000 U.S. dollars annually— that is, 34.7 cents per hectare—to be paid to Cuba in yearly checks. An elemental sense of dignity and absolute disagreement with what happens in that portion of our national territory has prevented Cuba from cashing those checks which are issued to the Treasurer General of the Republic of Cuba, a portion and an institution that ceased to exist a long time ago.

After the victory of the Revolution in Cuba, that base was the source of numerous frictions between Cuba and the United States. The overwhelming majority of the over three thousand Cubans who worked there were fired from their jobs and replaced by people from other countries. At present, only 10 Cubans work there.

In the past, shots were often made from that facility against our territory, and several Cuban soldiers died as a result. Counterrevolutionaries found haven and support over there. Following unilateral decisions by leaders of the U.S. government throughout the revolutionary period in Cuba, tens of thousands of immigrants—Haitians and Cubans who tried to make it to the United States by their own means—were taken to that military base. Throughout more than four decades, that base has been put to multiple uses, none of them contemplated in the agreement that justified its presence in our territory.

But, Cuba could do absolutely nothing to prevent it.

On the other hand, for almost half a century propitious conditions have never existed for a calmed, legal and diplomatic analysis aimed at the only logical and fair solution to this prolonged, chronic and abnormal situation, that is, the return to our country of that portion of our national territory occupied against the will of our people.

However, a basic principle of Cuba's policy toward this bizarre and potentially dangerous problem between Cuba and the United States, which is decades long, has been to avoid that our claim would become a major issue, not even a specially important issue, among the multiple and grave differences existing between the two nations, in the Pledge of Baraguá presented on February 19, 2000, the issue of the Guantánamo base is dealt with in the last point and formulated in the following way: "In due course, since it is not our main objective at this time, although it is our people's right and one that we shall never renounce, the illegally occupied territory of Guantánamo should be returned to Cuba!"

That military enclave is the exact place where American and Cuban soldiers stand face to face, thus the place where serenity and a sense of responsibility are most required. Although we have always been willing to fight and die in defense of our sovereignty and our rights, the most sacred duty of our people and their leaders has been to preserve the nation from avoidable, unnecessary and bloody wars.

At the same time, that is also the place where it would be easier for people interested in bringing about conflicts between the two countries to undertake plans aimed at attracting aggressive actions against our people in their heroic political, economic, and ideological resistance vis-à-vis the enormous power of the United States.

Our country has been particularly thoughtful about applying there a specially cautious and equable policy.

It should be pointed out, however, that even if for decades there was quite a lot of tension in the area of the Guantánamo naval base, there have been changes there in the past few years and now an atmosphere of mutual respect prevails.

In 1994, when a large number of rafters sent by the U.S. authorities concentrated there, the situation created determined the need to solve the numerous problems that had been accumulating, which endangered the lives of many. Some people interested in migrating to the United States from our own territory attempted to do so through the base, while not a few tried to leave the American military base and return to our country crossing mined fields. Accidents occurred and often our soldiers had to take major risks to rescue people from the mined fields. Such actions also required information and cooperation from the personnel stationed at the base. Additionally, there were the heavy rains and swollen rivers in the area that swept away mines and blurred their markings which gave rise to similarly hazardous situations for all.

Such circumstances contributed to an improvement of the atmosphere there and to authorized, albeit minimal, contacts that were indispensable to those in positions of responsibility on both sides of the base area. Consequently, what prevails there today is not what could be described as an atmosphere of hostility or war.

Two new international developments have had a bearing on the situation in that base: the war in Kosovo in 1999 and the war in Afghanistan after the terrorist acts of September 11. In both cases, the United States has played a protagonist role.

In the former case there was a large number of Kosovars refugees. The Government of the United States of America, in accordance with previous commitments, made the decision to use the military base to shelter a number of them. Such decisions are always made unilaterally; over views are never previously asked; and, we were never even informed. However, on that occasion, for the first time, we were informed of the decision and the rationale behind it. We then gave a constructive response.

Although we were opposed to that war, there was no reason for us to oppose the assistance that the Kosovars refugees might need. We even offered our country's cooperation, if necessary, to provide medical care or any other services that might be required. Ultimately, the refugees were not sent to Guantánamo naval base.

This time the decision has been adopted to bring prisoners of the war in Afghanistan to that military base. The same as in the past, we were not consulted but there was a gesture in previously providing ample and detailed information on the steps that would be taken to accommodate the prisoners there and ensure that the security of our people is not in anyway jeopardized. The latest details were given to the Cuban authorities last Monday, January 7, 2002.

The information supplied indicates that there will be a strong reinforcement of the military personnel at the base in charge of taking the necessary measures for the accomplishment of their objectives.

Despite the fact that we hold different positions as to the most efficient way to eradicate terrorism, the difference between Cuba and the United States lies in the method and not in the need to put an end to that scourge,— so familiar to our people who have been its victim for more than 40 years— the same that last September 11 dealt a repulsive and brutal blow to the American people.

Although the transfer of foreign war prisoners by the United States government to one of its military facilities—located in a portion of our land over which we have no jurisdiction, as we have been deprived of it—does not abide by the provisions that regulated its inception, we shall not set any obstacles to the development of the operation.

Having been apprised of the operation and aware of the fact that it demands a considerable movement of personnel and means of air transportation, the Cuban authorities will keep in contact with the personnel at the American naval base to adopt such measures as may be deemed convenient to avoid the risk of accidents that might put in jeopardy the lives of the personnel thus transported.

Despite the major increase of military personnel that such an operation will require, we feel that it does not pose any threat to the national security of our country. Therefore, we will not increase the Cuban personnel or the military means stationed in the area of that facility. Our highly disciplined and qualified personnel suffice to ensure the safety of the population in the region in case of any danger that might originate with the transfer of the foreign prisoners to that base.

Cuba will make every effort to preserve the atmosphere of détente and mutual respect that has prevailed in that area in the past few years.

The government of Cuba appreciates the previous information supplied and has taken note with satisfaction of the public statements made by the U.S. authorities in the sense that the prisoners will be accorded an adequate and humane treatment that may be monitored by the International Red Cross.

Although the exact number of prisoners that will be concentrated there is not yet known, just like on the occasion of the project to transfer to that place thousands of Kosovars refugees, we are willing to cooperate with the medical services required as well as with sanitation programs in the surrounding areas under our control to keep them clean of vectors and pests. Likewise, we are willing to cooperate in any other useful, constructive and humane way that may arise.

This is the position of Cuba!

Government of the Republic of Cuba
January 2002

NOTES

Introduction: The Significance of Guantánamo

1. K. C. McIntosh, "Guantánamo Bay," *American Mercury* 10 (January 1927): 106–112. McIntosh had a lengthy career in the U.S. Navy. He was first assigned to Guantánamo in 1906 and again in 1926. During World War II, Captain McIntosh served as the naval commandant at Harvard, where he participated in the swearing-in ceremony of Ensign John Roosevelt, son of President Franklin D. Roosevelt. *Washington Post*, September 13, 1941, 6.

2. Shortly after coming to power, Castro's officials reportedly cashed the first check issued in July 1959. For more information, see Chapter 6, Note 43.

3. Jana K. Lipman, *Guantánamo: A Working-Class History between Empire and Revolution* (Berkeley: University of California Press, 2009). Surprisingly Guantánamo has long been known worldwide through the song "Guantanamera," which, according to folk singer Pete Seeger, was originally conceived to satirize the Cuban women who went out with U.S. sailors. It was first popularized in Havana in 1949 by radio personality José "Joseito" Fernandez Dias, who would open the daily newspaper and improvise verses based on the latest scandal. Its most frequently sung stanzas are those adapted from the poems *Versos Sencillos* (Simple Verses) by Cuban hero and writer José Marti. However, Seeger, whose recordings helped make the song famous, observes that Cuban singers continue to improvise new verses to "Guantanamera," and he gives the example, "Fidel's beard is a broom to sweep the Yankees out of Latin America." Pete Seeger, *Where Have All the Flowers Gone: A Singer's Stories, Songs, Seeds, Robberies,* ed. Peter Blood (Bethlehem, N.H.: Sing Out Corporation, 1993), 128–130.

4. As I indicated, Guantánamo has functioned as an offshore naval base and as a coaling station. In primary sources, it is also called a naval station. At different times in its history, it has served as an emergency repair facility, an advanced base, the winter headquarters for the U.S. Navy Atlantic Fleet, and as a naval, marine, and coast guard training center. As soon as it became a U.S. naval facility in December 1903, for the bureaucratic purposes of the Navy Department, it came under the authority of the Bureau of Yards and Docks.

5. Lipman, *Guantánamo*, 18.

6. The Fifth Amendment of the U.S. Constitution specifies that "no person shall be deprived of life, liberty, or property without due process of law." With regard to legal procedures, the term *due process* includes, at a minimum, an individual's right to be notified of charges or proceedings confronting him or her as well as the opportunity to be heard at these proceedings. The term also implies legal fairness as well as the right to a fair and speedy trial.

7. Bradley M. Reynolds, "Guantánamo Bay, Cuba: The History of an American Naval Base and Its Relationship to the Formulation of United States Foreign Policy and Military Strategy toward the Caribbean, 1895–1910" (Ph.D. diss., University of Southern California, 1982), 6–7.

8. According to historian John Maurer's research, Navy Secretary Long had established the General Board not to make recommendations concerning the "construction, manning, arming, and equipping of ships" but rather to make "recommendations as to the proper distribution of the Fleet." The board's views carried special weight when its chair, Admiral George Dewey, argued its strategic recommendations. John H. Maurer, "American Naval Concentration and the German Battle Fleet, 1900–1918," *Journal of Strategic Studies* 6 (June 1983): 147–148.

9. Thomas B. Buell, *Master of Sea Power: A Biography of Fleet Admiral Ernest J. King* (Annapolis, Md.: Naval Institute Press, 1995), 123.

10. Mary Ellene Chenevey McCoy, "Guantánamo Bay: The United States Naval Base and Its Relationship with Cuba" (Ph.D. diss., University of Akron, 1995), 107.

11. Ibid., iv.

12. For the historical background to the 1903 treaty, which permitted the United States to lease Guantánamo for an unspecified period, see Chapters 1–3 of this volume.

13. *Vienna Convention on the Law of Treaties, 1969,* United Nations Treaty Series, vol. 1155, 2005. See also Joseph Lazar, "International Legal Status of Guantánamo Bay," *American Journal of International Law* 62, no. 3 (July 1968): 730–740; Lazar, "Cession in Lease of the Guantánamo Bay Naval Station and Cuba's Ultimate Sovereignty," *American Journal of International Law* 63, no. 1 (January 1969): 116–118.

14. Bradley Reynolds, "Guantánamo Bay, Cuba," in *United States Navy and Marine Corps Bases Overseas,* ed. Paolo E. Coletta (Westport, Conn.: Greenwood, 1985), 146–157.

15. How can these dissertations document almost diametrically opposed theses, given the paucity of published information and the scattered nature of primary sources? The answer is in the assiduous efforts of both Reynolds and McCoy to obtain information about this unique base, which, from its acquisition by President Theodore Roosevelt until it ceased to be dependent on Fidel Castro's government for its water supply under President Lyndon Johnson, played a central role in U.S.-Cuban relations. They have uncovered sources that have informed and guided my own research, and I have also felt frustrations akin to those voiced by Bradley Reynolds when he thanked his wife for enduring his "constant groaning and griping about the dissertation."

16. For an excellent, balanced discussion of Guantánamo's recent legal history, see Jay Bauer, "Detainees under Review: Striking the Right Constitutional Balance between the Executive's War Powers and Judiciary Review," *Alabama Law Review* 57, no. 4 (Summer 2006): 1081–1104.

17. A Navy Department memorandum written in response to a request by a flag-ranking officer for a history of Guantánamo Naval Base illustrates the fragmentary nature of primary source materials on this subject. The author reports, "I have been glad to have a search made of the records and regret that very little manuscript material was uncovered." The memorandum then cites a few key sentences and paragraphs culled from various letters and official documents that sketch the history of Guantánamo from 1902 to 1916. Alma R. Lawrence, Memorandum for Rear Admiral E. E. Duvall, U.S.N., December 10, 1952, OP-296/fes, Operational Archives Branch, Naval Historical Center.

18. There is no explicit definition for the term *forward base*. Various naval

strategists and military historians, however, have used the term to describe an off-shore base of which the primary function is to project military force.

19. Harold Sprout and Margaret Sprout, *The Rise of American Naval Power, 1776–1918* (Princeton, N.J.: Princeton University Press, 1939), 293–294.

20. Hugh Thomas, "The U.S. and Castro," *American Heritage Magazine* 29, no. 6 (October–November 1978): 26–35. See also Georgie Anne Geyer, *Guerrilla Prince: The Untold Story of Fidel Castro* (Boston: Little, Brown, 1991), 29.

21. Willis Fletcher Johnson, *The History of Cuba,* vol. 2 (New York: B. F. Buck, 1920), 261–262. It is likely that a State Department clerk would have copied such an important communiqué and filed it as "Important Background Information" on Cuba and the Caribbean. For historical information on clerks in the Department of State in the early nineteenth century, see Elmer Plischke, *U.S. Department of State: A Reference History* (Westport, Conn.: Greenwood, 1999), 70–73. Diplomatic historian Samuel Flagg Bemis discusses Adams's belief that Cuba and Puerto Rico formed outlying natural defenses for Florida and Louisiana. According to Bemis, during the political turmoil that gripped Spain under the autocratic but weak King Ferdinand VII from 1820 to 1823, Adams feared that France or England might occupy Cuba. After the cabinet meeting of September 30, 1822, Adams confided to his diary that the "Cuban question was of deeper importance and greater magnitude than had occurred since the establishment of our Independence." In April 1823 Ferdinand managed to persuade his cousin King Louis XVIII of France to invade Spain for the purpose of abolishing the constitutional liberties Liberals had forced Ferdinand to concede in 1820. According to Hugh Thomas's account, forty thousand Spanish troops were dispatched to Cuba "to crush Cuban liberalism." These events played a significant role in spurring Adams to articulate the Monroe Doctrine. Samuel Flagg Bemis, *John Quincy Adams and the Foundations of American Foreign Policy* (New York: Norton Library, 1973), 372–373. See also Hugh Thomas, *Cuba: The Pursuit of Freedom* (New York: Harper & Row, 1971), 102–103.

22. At the presidential level, Franklin Pierce was interested in purchasing Cuba. According to former president of Guatemala Juan José Arevalo, in 1848 the United States offered the Spanish government $100 million "for that one island." Juan José Arevalo, *The Shark and the Sardines* (New York: Lyle Stuart, 1961), 76.

23. Seward apparently foresaw the Virgin Islands' potential as offshore naval stations. St. Thomas, in particular, has an excellent harbor and borders on the Anegada Passage—a key shipping lane between the Caribbean and the Atlantic. The U.S. interest in obtaining the Virgin Islands persisted. In 1896, the Republican platform listed its acquisition in one of its planks. Bartholomew H. Sparrow, *The Insular Cases and the Emergence of American Empire* (Lawrence: University Press of Kansas, 2006), 232.

24. Culebra Island is approximately seventeen miles east of Puerto Rico, twelve miles west of St. Thomas, and nine miles north of Vieques. It now belongs to Puerto Rico, but it is sometimes called the last of the Spanish Virgin Islands. Its principal harbor, Ensenada Hondo, is considered one of the most secure from hurricanes in the Caribbean.

25. Frederick Bancroft, "Seward's Ideas of Territorial Expansion," *North American Review* 167 (July 1898): 79–90. The publication of this article was timely. As subscribers and frequent contributors to the *North American Review,* Roosevelt and Mahan almost certainly read it.

26. Walter LaFeber, *The New Empire: An Interpretation of American Expansion, 1860–1898,* 2nd ed. (Ithaca, N.Y.: Cornell University Press, 1963), 24–32.

27. Henry Adams, "The Session," *North American Review* 111 (July 1870): 29–62.

28. Donald Yerxa, *Admirals and Empire: The United States Navy and the Caribbean, 1898–1945* (Columbia: University of South Carolina Press, 1991), 2. The controversy over whether the United States became an imperialist power in the Spanish-American War, or even earlier when we invaded Mexico in 1846, probably will never be answered definitively. In an eye-catching article with the ironic title "American Imperialism: The Worst Chapter in Almost Any Book" published in the *American Historical Review,* James Field concluded, "The New Navy was a defensive answer to European developments; its deployment reflected a shrunken rather than an enlarged strategic perspective. The search for bases was a response to the strategic problems of isthmus, Caribbean, and eastern Pacific. . . . In the circumstances of the time, such a defensive policy seems quite reasonable." James A. Field, "AHR Forum—American Imperialism: The Worst Chapter in Almost Any Book," *American Historical Review* 83, no. 3 (June 1978): 644–668. Walter McDougall presents a different but equally well-argued perspective in *Promised Land, Crusader State,* where he asserts that the United States "went off the rails in terms of its honored traditions" when it declared war on Spain. Walter A. McDougall, *Promised Land, Crusader State: The American Encounter with the World since 1776* (Boston: Houghton Mifflin, 1997), 118. Still worthy of consideration is William L. Langer's eloquent essay "Farewell to Empire," which attempts to strike a philosophical balance by acknowledging that "imperialism's one great achievement was to open up all parts of the world and to set all humanity on the high road to eventual association and collaboration," and at the same time voices the hope that "the world has outgrown the mentality of imperialism." William L. Langer, "Farewell to Empire," *Foreign Affairs* 41, no. 1 (October 1962): 115–130.

29. Yerxa, *Admirals and Empires,* 5–9. See also Bradford Perkins, *The Great Rapprochement: England and the United States, 1895–1914* (New York: Atheneum, 1968), 125, 183.

30. "Foreword," *Naval Strategy,* Fleet Marine Force Reference Publication (FM-FRP) 12–32 (Washington, D.C.: Department of the Navy, 1991); Thomas H. Etzold, "Is Mahan Still Valid?" *Proceedings of the U.S. Naval Institute* 106 (August 1980): 38–43.

31. My book does not investigate or barely mentions those U.S. presidential administrations that ignored or paid scant attention to Guantánamo. For example, President Calvin Coolidge, who is the only chief executive to pay a state visit to Cuba, is only briefly mentioned in Chapter 4, in the context of his views on the Platt Amendment and Guantánamo. President Harry Truman briefly visited Guantánamo in 1948 during a "goodwill" trip to the Caribbean that also included Puerto Rico and the Virgin Islands, but it was not a state visit, as he did not meet with Cuban leaders. Moreover, Guantánamo received comparatively little top-level attention during Truman's administration, even though ships activated for service in the Korean War frequently conducted shakedown preparations at Guantánamo before departing for the Orient.

32. To borrow from the thought of cultural geographer D. W. Meinig, Guantánamo has often been a site for "sudden and harsh" encounters between different cultures that transformed them even if it failed to unite them. Cited in Bernard Bailyn, *Atlantic History: Concept and Contours* (Cambridge, Mass.: Harvard University Press, 2005), 55–56.

33. Tom Miller, *Trading with the Enemy: A Yankee Travels through Castro's Cuba* (New York: Atheneum, 1992), 196–205. See also Louis A. Perez Jr., *On Becoming Cuban: Identity, Nationality, and Culture* (Chapel Hill: University of North Carolina Press, 1999), 238–239.

Chapter One. The Rise of the U.S. Navy and Theodore Roosevelt

1. Clark G. Reynolds, *Command of the Sea: The History and Strategy of Maritime Empires* (New York: Morrow, 1974), 418.
2. Walter LaFeber, *The New Empire: An Interpretation of American Expansion, 1860–1898,* 2nd ed. (Ithaca, N.Y.: Cornell University Press, 1963), 93.
3. Theodore Roosevelt, *The Naval War of 1812* (New York: Da Capo, 1999 [1882]), 2.
4. Harold Sprout and Margaret Sprout, *The Rise of American Naval Power, 1776–1918* (Princeton, N.J.: Princeton University Press, 1939), 180.
5. Kurt Hackemer, *The U.S. Navy and the Origins of the Military-Industrial Complex, 1847–1883* (Annapolis, Md.: Naval Institute Press, 2001), 119–125.
6. Robert G. Albion, "Richard W. Thompson," in *American Secretaries of the Navy,* vol. 1, ed. Paolo E. Coletta (Annapolis, Md.: Naval Institute Press, 1980), 381–383.
7. Sprout and Sprout, *Rise of American Naval Power,* 181.
8. Albion, "Thompson," 383. President Hayes was so shocked and outraged by the news that Ferdinand de Lesseps was selling stock subscriptions in the United States that he immediately warned the French government that the United States would insist on a U.S.-controlled canal. David M. Pletcher, *The Diplomacy of Trade and Investment: American Economic Expansion in the Hemisphere, 1865–1900* (Columbia: University of Missouri Press, 1998), 376.
9. Thompson's departure came so late in Hayes's administration that his stop-gap replacement, Nathan Goff Jr., served less than two months as Secretary of the Navy (January 7, 1881, to March 6, 1881) prior to the inauguration of President James A. Garfield.
10. Between 1865 and 1898 U.S. exports increased from $281 million to $1,231 million. After the Civil War, U.S. cotton production had largely revived by 1871, and wheat and flour emerged along with pork as major agricultural exports. Shipments of kerosene and other petroleum products began in the 1860s, and soon Standard Oil dominated this industry. Iron and steel products, including tools and machinery, became major export items—by 1902, the United States was producing more iron and steel than Germany and Great Britain combined. Pletcher, *Diplomacy of Trade,* 15–17.
11. Department of the Navy, *Annual Reports of the Navy Department for the Year 1881: Report of the Secretary of the Navy,* vol. 1 (Washington, D.C.: Government Printing Office, 1898), 3.
12. Jeffery M. Dorwart, *The Office of Naval Intelligence: The Birth of America's First Intelligence Agency* (Annapolis, Md.: Naval Institute Press, 1979), ix, 12.
13. Thomas Hunt, *The Life of William H. Hunt* (Brattleboro, Vt.: E. L. Hildreth, 1922), 251; *Puck,* September 14, 1881, 23; George T. Davis, *A Navy Second to None: The Development of Modern Naval Policy* (New York: Harcourt, Brace, 1940), 19; Walter R. Herrick Jr., "William H. Hunt," in *American Secretaries of the Navy,* vol. 1, ed. Paolo Coletta (Annapolis, Md.: Naval Institute Press, 1980), 389–394.

14. According to the biography written by his son, President Arthur never informed Hunt of the reasons for his transfer to diplomatic service, which Hunt regarded as an unjust dismissal from the Navy Department. Hunt died in St. Petersburg on February 27, 1884. Hunt, *Life of William Hunt,* 253–255, 356–358.

15. Department of the Navy, *Annual Reports of the Navy Department for the Year 1884,* vol. 1, 3–8. Hackemer has come to Chandler and Roach's defense, arguing that Roach's firm had the requisite experience in shipbuilding and submitted the lowest of twelve bids. For its part, the Navy Department, in awarding and supervising the contract, had required Roach to carry appropriate insurance and adhere to various quality controls. According to Hackemer's analysis, partisan attacks by the incoming Cleveland administration prevented payments for the *Dolphin* and drove Roach into bankruptcy, with subsequent work on the three cruisers completed by the U.S. Navy in Roach's shipyard. Hackemer, *U.S. Navy and Origins of the Military-Industrial Complex,* 126–131. See Note 23 for historian Allan Nevins's contrasting treatment of this issue.

16. Department of the Navy, *Annual Reports (1884),* vol. 1, 41.

17. Pletcher, *Diplomacy of Trade,* 148–150.

18. Ibid., 49.

19. Walter R. Herrick Jr., "William E. Chandler," in *American Secretaries of the Navy,* vol. 1, ed. Paolo E. Coletta (Annapolis, Md.: Naval Institute Press, 1980), 397–403; *The Letters of Theodore Roosevelt,* vol. 1, ed. Elting E. Morison (Cambridge, Mass.: Harvard University Press, 1951), 691–692.

20. Paolo Coletta considers John Roach "probably America's greatest shipbuilder" of the era, who was simply undone by the underdevelopment of the U.S. steel industry. The British, by comparison, "were far ahead, be it in power supply, forced air furnaces, or guns." Paolo Coletta, *French Ensor Chadwick: Scholarly Warrior* (Lanham, Md.: University Press of America, 1980), 25–26.

21. John F. Beeler, *British Naval Policy in the Gladstone-Disraeli Era, 1866–1880* (Palo Alto, Calif.: Stanford University Press, 1997), 2.

22. Theodore Roosevelt, Letter of the Assistant Secretary of the Navy to the Department, Transmitting the Proposed Personnel Bill, Senate Document no. 97, December 9, 1897.

23. Walter R. Herrick Jr., "William C. Whitney," in *American Secretaries of the Navy,* vol. 1, ed. Paolo E. Coletta (Annapolis, Md.: Naval Institute Press, 1980), 405–411. Noted historian Allan Nevins in his biography of Grover Cleveland not only names Whitney the true father of the U.S. Navy but derides Chandler as a "hack politician," paints Roach as an illiterate, doddering has-been, and fails to mention the contributions of William Hunt. Allan Nevins, *Grover Cleveland: A Study in Courage* (New York: Dodd, Mead, 1966), 217–223. For a diametrically opposed historical appraisal of Chandler's handling of the ABCD contract, see note 15.

24. In recognition of Tracy's bravery at the battle of Spotsylvania in 1864, the War Department had brevetted him brigadier general and nominated him for the Congressional Medal of Honor, an award he finally received in 1895. Walter R. Herrick Jr., "General Benjamin F. Tracy," in *American Secretaries of the Navy,* vol. 1, ed. Paolo E. Coletta (Annapolis, Md.: Naval Institute Press, 1980), 415–422.

25. Walter Russell Herrick Jr., "General Tracy's Navy: A Study of the Development of American Sea Power, 1889–1893" (Ph.D. diss., University of Virginia, 1962), 121.

26. Ibid., 92–93.

27. Sprout and Sprout, *Rise of American Naval Power,* 207.

28. Department of the Navy, *Annual Reports of the Navy Department for the Year 1889,* vol. 1, 3–4.

29. Ibid., 10–11.

30. Senate Executive Document no. 43, 51st Cong., 1st sess.; *New York Herald,* January 31, 1890, 6.

31. Congress approved the construction of these three battleships, which Tracy named the *Indiana,* the *Massachusetts,* and the *Oregon.* Together they cost an unprecedented $18 million.

32. The italics are mine. *Congressional Record,* 51st Cong., 1st sess., no. 21 (1890), 3163.

33. Herrick, "General Tracy's Navy," 154–157.

34. The long-term impact of Blaine's letter to the president is unknown. It is virtually certain that Harrison carefully filed this letter in an important background folder in the White House. We do not know, however, if Harrison shared its contents with other cabinet officials including the secretary of the navy. For his part, Blaine rarely made copies of his own letters and was careless about preserving his correspondence. *The Correspondence between Benjamin Harrison and James G. Blaine, 1882–1893,* ed. Albert T. Volwiler (Philadelphia, Penn.: American Philosophical Society, 1940), ix–x, 1–2, 173–174; Herrick, "General Tracy's Navy," 161.

35. Herrick, "General Benjamin F. Tracy," 421.

36. Department of the Navy, *Annual Reports of the Navy Department for the Year 1892,* 3–6; Walter R. Herrick Jr., *The American Naval Revolution* (Baton Rouge: Louisiana State University Press, 1966), 151–152.

37. Alfred T. Mahan, "The Isthmus and Sea Power," *Atlantic Monthly* 72 (October 1893): 459–472.

38. Benjamin Franklin Cooling, *Gray Steel and Blue Water Navy: The Formative Years of America's Military-Industrial Complex* (Hamden, Conn.: Archon, 1979), 113–137.

39. Department of the Navy, *Annual Reports (1894),* 28–29.

40. At the beginning of his report, Herbert cited seventeen nations ahead of the United States in the construction of torpedo boats, noting that the smallest number possessed by any of them was twenty-two, whereas the United States, with more seacoast and more ports to defend than any of them, had only six, including three under construction. He criticized the navy's reliance on monitors and unarmored cruisers, observing that "unarmored cruisers are not fighting vessels." Ibid., 4, 37.

41. Ibid., 40.

42. Department of the Navy, *Annual Reports of the Navy Department for the Year 1896,* 5, 9, 56–57.

43. Mark Russell Shulman, *Navalism and the Emergence of American Sea Power, 1882–1893* (Annapolis, Md.: Naval Institute Press, 1995), 95, 117.

44. Hilary A. Herbert, "The Lessons of the Naval Review," *North American Review* 156 (June 1893): 641–647.

45. Richard Turk, in an in-depth study of the two, identifies three stages in the relationship between Mahan and Roosevelt: close collaboration and friendship from 1888 to 1898, distance and disagreement from 1899 through 1907, and some rapprochement from 1908 through 1914, although this period lacked the warmth and intensity of the initial period. Richard W. Turk, *The Ambiguous Relationship: Theodore Roosevelt and Alfred Thayer Mahan* (Westport, Conn.: Greenwood, 1987), 101.

46. Ibid., 400–401.

47. H. W. Brands, "Introduction," in *Naval War of 1812*, by Theodore Roosevelt (New York: Da Capo, 1999 [1882]), xx.

48. At some point, Roosevelt had probably read Mahan's first book, *The Gulf and Inland Waters*, published in 1883. This work did not contain any hint of Mahan's subsequent "sea power hypothesis," which Roosevelt and others found so attractive, but it did qualify him as a naval historian and led to Luce's hiring him at the Naval War College. Turk, *Ambiguous Relationship*, 10, 15.

49. Alfred Thayer Mahan, *The Influence of Sea Power upon History, 1660–1783* (Boston: Little, Brown, 1890), 33. Mahan was one of the first major geopolitical thinkers. Another was H. J. Mackinder, a reader in geography at Oxford University, who in 1904 observed that there was "scarcely a region left [in the world] for the pegging out of a claim of ownership, unless as the result of a war between civilized or half-civilized powers." H. J. Mackinder, "The Geographical Pivot of History," *Geographical Journal* 23, no. 4 (April 1904): 421–444.

50. In 1890, Congressman Lodge was the second-ranking member of the House Naval Affairs Committee and already an outspoken advocate of building a modern navy.

51. *The Letters of Theodore Roosevelt*, vol. 1, 221–222.

52. The *Atlantic Monthly* did not include the names of authors of its book reviews (a peculiar practice), but Roosevelt's accompanying letter to Scudder may be found in *The Letters of Theodore Roosevelt*, vol. 1, 229.

53. The tactic of "commerce-destroying" could apply to sinking an enemy's merchant vessels in open seas or attacking an enemy's port.

54. Theodore Roosevelt, "The Influence of Sea Power upon History," *Atlantic Monthly* 66, no. 396 (October 1890): 563–567.

55. Turk, *Ambiguous Relationship*, 16.

56. Theodore Roosevelt, "The Influence of Sea Power upon the French Revolution and Empire, 1793–1812," *Atlantic Monthly* 71 (April 1893): 556–559.

57. Mahan, "The Isthmus and Sea Power," 467–472.

58. Ibid.

59. *Letters of Theodore Roosevelt*, vol. 2, 379, 409.

60. On May 1, 1893, Roosevelt lamented to Mahan, "I fear all hope for the War College (which is nothing without you) is gone; our prize idiots here have thrown away the chance to give us an absolutely unique position in Naval affairs." Ibid., 315.

61. Turk, *Ambiguous Relationship*, 17–20.

62. "Extracts from Memorandum by Theodore Roosevelt," February 10, 1908, in *Selections from the Correspondence of Theodore Roosevelt and Henry Cabot Lodge, 1884–1918*, vol. 1, ed. Henry Cabot Lodge (New York: Scribner's, 1925), 25.

63. Lodge's use of the term *empire* in his first major public speech indicates the expansive nature of his nationalistic pride. William C. Widenor, *Henry Cabot Lodge and the Search for an American Foreign Policy* (Berkeley: University of California Press, 1980), 69–70.

64. *Letters and Papers of Alfred Thayer Mahan*, ed. Robert Seager II and Doris D. McGuire, vol. 1 (Annapolis, Md.: Naval Institute Press, 1975), 544; Robert Seager II, *Alfred Thayer Mahan: The Man and His Letters* (Annapolis, Md.: Naval Institute Press, 1977), 138–139; Warren Zimmermann, *First Great Triumph: How*

Five Americans Made Their Country a World Power (New York: Farrar, Straus & Giroux, 2002), 87.

65. Seager, *Alfred Thayer Mahan*, 139.

66. *Correspondence of Roosevelt and Lodge*, vol. 1, 63.

67. Letters of Theodore Roosevelt to William Sheffield Cowles, BMS AM 1834 (788–820), Theodore Roosevelt Collection, Houghton Library, Harvard University.

68. Ibid., December 22, 1895. In these letters to members of his family—which included his brothers-in-law, Cowles and Douglas Robinson—Roosevelt would frequently express private thoughts and emotions he did not convey to anyone else, including Henry Cabot Lodge.

69. Quick-firer guns was a British term for naval artillery that could fire several times per minute.

70. *Letters of Theodore Roosevelt*, vol. 1, 527.

71. Ibid., 522.

72. The italics are mine. Henry Cabot Lodge, "Our Blundering Foreign Policy," *Forum* (March 1895): 8–17.

73. *Correspondence of Lodge and Roosevelt*, vol. 1, 211–214. Lodge amplified his remarks in his subsequent article "Our Duty to Cuba," in which he castigated Spain as "an anachronism in the Western Hemisphere" and asserted, "It is impossible that she should long retain even this last foothold." Suggesting that Spain could only be defeated by an equal or greater sea power, Lodge wrote, "It has been urged against the insurgents that they have no port. This is due to the fact that they have no ships. . . . Although they have taken several of the seaport towns, they have been unable to hold them, because they did not have command of the sea and were without heavy ordnance." Lodge then warned the Cleveland administration that if it failed to intervene, "There will be put in power another Administration which will neither neglect nor shun its duty . . . to the cause of freedom and humanity." Henry Cabot Lodge, "Our Duty to Cuba," *Forum* (May 1896): 278–288.

74. Letters of Roosevelt to Cowles, BMS AM 1834 (788–820), Theodore Roosevelt Collection, Houghton Library, Harvard University. One of the reasons Roosevelt's correspondence was so extensive is that he generally wrote one to two paragraphs, often on a postcard or a single piece of stationery. One of his curious traits is that even when writing to his beloved sisters "Bye" and Corrine, he frequently would end "Ever yours, Theodore Roosevelt."

75. *Correspondence of Roosevelt and Lodge*, vol. 1, 240–241. Roosevelt responded to Lodge's account of the meeting with McKinley with enthusiasm: "I am delighted at what you say about McKinley. I do hope he will take a strong stand about Hawaii and Cuba. I do not think a war with Spain would be serious enough to cause much strain on the country, or much interruption to the revival of prosperity, but I certainly wish the matter could be settled this winter." Ibid., 243.

76. John A. Garraty, *Henry Cabot Lodge: A Biography* (New York: Knopf, 1953), 104.

77. Theodore Roosevelt, *Letters from Theodore Roosevelt to Anna Roosevelt Cowles, 1870–1918* (New York: Scribner's, 1924), 182–183.

78. Zimmermann, *First Great Triumph*, 228.

79. *Letters of Theodore Roosevelt*, vol. 1, 709.

80. Turk, *Ambiguous Relationship*, 114–117.

81. Ibid., 29–31; Dorwart, *Office of Naval Intelligence*, 57. The president of the Naval War College, Captain Henry Taylor, who was also serving on the special

advisory board, disagreed with Kimball. Taylor argued that, in the event of war, all U.S. naval forces should be concentrated on Cuba. Ronald Spector, *Admiral of the New Empire: The Life and Career of George Dewey* (Baton Rouge: Louisiana State University Press, 1974), 35.

82. Assistant Secretary of the Navy Roosevelt was largely responsible for personnel matters. According to Spector's biography, Roosevelt picked Dewey to command the Asiatic Squadron. As Roosevelt would justify his decision in his autobiography, "Here was a man who could be relied upon to prepare in advance and to act fearlessly and on his own responsibility when the emergency arose." Spector, *Admiral of the New Empire*, 36.

83. Papers of Theodore Roosevelt, series 1, subseries A (Microfilm Reel 308), Manuscript Division, Library of Congress.

84. *The Journal of John D. Long*, ed. Margaret Long (Rindge, N.H.: Richard R. Smith, 1956), 217.

85. Paolo E. Coletta, "The Peace Negotiations and the Treaty of Paris," in *Threshold to American Internationalism*, ed. Paolo E. Coletta (Jericho, N.Y.: Exposition, 1970), 144; *Letters of Theodore Roosevelt*, vol. 1, 685.

86. *Letters of Theodore Roosevelt*, vol. 1, 685.

87. Roosevelt first met Wood at a dinner party in Washington, D.C., in June 1897, where he was enthralled by Wood's tales of fighting Apaches. Jack McCallum, *Leonard Wood: Rough Rider, Surgeon, Architect of American Imperialism* (New York: New York University Press, 2006), 52–53. The two men quickly discovered that they shared a love of physical fitness, and soon they were hiking, swimming, and playing football together. As Roosevelt joyfully told Lodge, "I finally developed a playmate who walked me off my legs; a Massachusetts man moreover, an army surgeon named Wood." *Correspondence of Roosevelt and Lodge*, vol. 1, 285.

88. On July 27, 1898, following his celebrated charge up San Juan Hill, Roosevelt wrote Robinson: "The charge was great fun. Frankly, it did not enter my head that I could get through without being hit, but I judged that even if hit the chances would be about three to one against my being killed. . . . It makes me feel as though I could now leave something to my children which will serve as an apology for my having existed." Letters of Theodore Roosevelt to Corinne Roosevelt and Douglas Robinson, BMS AM 1540 (63–127), Theodore Roosevelt Collection, Houghton Library, Harvard University.

89. Letters of Theodore Roosevelt to Anna Roosevelt Cowles, February 25, 1898, BMS AM 1834 (111–787), Theodore Roosevelt Collection, Houghton Library, Harvard University.

90. White, who moved with equal facility in influential circles in London and Washington, served for many years as an aide to the U.S. ambassador to Great Britain, where he played a key role in the negotiations leading to the Hay-Pauncefote Treaty. Theodore Roosevelt subsequently appointed White as U.S. ambassador to Italy and then to France. Roosevelt also proclaimed White "the most useful man in the entire diplomatic service during my Presidency and for many years before." *Letters of Theodore Roosevelt*, vol. 1, 790.

91. Jonathan M. Hansen, in *The Lost Promise of Patriotism*, makes the argument that Theodore Roosevelt embraced U.S. imperialism as a means to revive the country's vitality, which had been jeopardized by the closing of the frontier and material decadence. According to Hansen, for Roosevelt U.S. imperialism "was ordained, not fortuitous—the natural course for an evolving nation-state." Hansen bases his

argument largely on Roosevelt's famous postwar speech "The Strenuous Life," delivered to Chicago's Hamilton Club on April 10, 1899. In that address, Roosevelt certainly emphasized the value of a vigorous approach to life, but with regard to the new U.S. responsibilities in Hawaii, Cuba, Puerto Rico, and the Philippines, he warned, "We cannot avoid the responsibilities that confront us. . . . All we can decide is whether we shall meet them in a way that will redound to the national credit, or whether we shall make of our dealings with these new problems a dark and shameful page in our national history." Hansen does not take full account of Roosevelt's warning of the dangers of imperialism. Jonathan M. Hansen, *The Lost Promise of Patriotism: Debating American Identity, 1890–1920* (Chicago, Ill.: University of Chicago Press, 2003), 4, 21–24.

92. *Correspondence of Roosevelt and Lodge*, vol. 1, 299, 309.

93. Cosme de la Torriente, "Teodoro Roosevelt," in *Cuarenta Años de mi Vida* (Havana, Cuba: El Siglo 20, 1939), 441–447.

94. Ibid. My translation of the phrase "que abrogó para siempre el Tratado Permanente y con él la Enmienda Platt y convirtió en material convencional entre las dos naciones, en vez de la imposición que había implicado antes, el problema de la estación naval en Guantánamo," 445.

95. In the same address, in his discussion of the Spanish-American War, Portell Vilá failed to mention Guantánamo, but he recognized the significance of the "naval victory of Santiago de Cuba," which, as he indicated, led to the "surrender of the city under siege" and meant that "the adventure had ended for Theodore Roosevelt." The Spanish text of my translation is: "No hay duda de que Theodore Roosevelt era imperialista; pero el plan imperialista de Wood no le entusiasmó en lo más mínimo. . . . La inauguración de la República de Cuba constituyó para él, como siempre debe ser para todo hombre de honor y de convicción liberal la libertad de un pueblo, un motivo de grande y legítima satisfacción. . . . En cuanto a Cuba fueron más sus aciertos que sus errores. . . . Cuando murió Theodore Roosevelt, el pueblo cubano expresaba su sincero dolor por la pérdida del major amigo que tenía entre los norteamericanos." Herminio Portell Vilá, *Theodore Roosevelt en la Historia de Cuba* (Havana, Cuba: La Habanera, 1950), 3–28.

Chapter Two. The Battle for Guantánamo in 1898

1. *The War Dispatches of Stephen Crane*, ed. R. W. Stallman and E. R. Hagemann (New York: New York University Press, 1964), 145.

2. M. E. Murphy, *The History of Guantánamo Bay, 1494–1964*, vol. 1 (Guantánamo, Cuba: U.S. Naval Base), http://www.nsgtmo.navy.mil/history/gtmohistory murphyvol1ch1.htm. Murphy quotes Frederick Hervey's *Naval History of Great Britain*, published in 1779, which described Guantánamo as "a large and secure haven."

3. Charles E. Nowell, "The Defense of Cartagena," *Hispanic American Historical Review* 42, no. 4 (November 1962): 477–501.

4. G. J. A. O'Toole, *The Spanish War: An American Epic—1898* (New York: Norton, 1984), 256. Forrest Sherman, "The British Occupation of Guantánamo Bay," in *Proceedings of the U.S. Naval Institute* 57 (April 1931): 509–512.

5. Edwin North McClellan, "The American Marines of 1740–1742," *Marine Corps Gazette* 14 (December 1929): 286–297.

6. Richard Gott, *Cuba: A New History* (New Haven, Conn.: Yale University

Press, 2004), 39–42; Tobias Smollett, *The Adventures of Roderick Random* (New York: New American Library, 1964), 202–215; Frank Burt Freidel, *The Splendid Little War* (Boston: Little, Brown, 1958), 56, 77.

7. Not surprisingly, different historians choose different factors to emphasize in interpreting the reasons for McKinley's decision to intervene in Cuba. Louis Pérez Jr. states that "in 1898 Cuba was lost to Spain, and if Washington did not act, it would also be lost to the United States." Louis A. Pérez Jr., *The War of 1898: The United States and Cuba in History and Historiography* (Chapel Hill: University of North Carolina Press, 1998), 12. The Cuban revolutionary and diplomat Cosme de la Torriente would qualify Perez's assertion that Cuba was already lost to Spain. In his essay "Dios Nos Hizo Vecinos," he argues that because Cuba lacked a battle fleet that could destroy the Spanish Armada, its future independence required the decisive intervention of the U.S. Navy. Cosme de la Torriente, "¡Dios Nos Hizo Vecinos, Que La Justicia Nos Conserve Amigos!" in *Cuba y Los Estados Unidos* (Havana, Cuba: Imp. y Papeleria de Rambla, Bouza, 1929), 291–317. John Offner sees domestic partisan politics as the key ingredient when he asserts that "Republican legislators made war on Spain not to obtain control of Cuba but to retain control of Washington [in the 1898 elections]." John L. Offner, *An Unwanted War: The Diplomacy of the United States and Spain over Cuba, 1895–1898* (Chapel Hill: University of North Carolina Press, 1992), 234. Yet another view is presented by Douglas Porch, who argues that the motives for U.S. intervention were complex and idealistic, but that the explosion of the U.S.S. *Maine* provided the catalyst to unite very diverse interests. Douglas Porch, *Wars of Empire* (London: Cassell, 2000), 147–148. Virginia Bouvier sees McKinley's decision to intervene in Cuba and in the Philippines as laying the basis for a diplomatic and military approach to U.S.–Latin American relations that would persist. Her major criticism of that approach is that, in each of its military interventions, the United States has claimed to be promoting democracy abroad, but it also has insisted on controlling the political outcome of its intervention. Virginia M. Bouvier, *Whose America? The War of 1898 and the Battles to Define the Nation* (Westport, Conn.: Praeger, 2001), 1–7.

8. Lewis L. Gould, *The Spanish-American War and President McKinley* (Lawrence: University Press of Kansas, 1982), 25.

9. Bartholomew H. Sparrow, *The* Insular Cases *and the Emergence of American Empire* (Lawrence: University Press of Kansas, 2006), 33, 64.

10. The *Maine* was a 6,682-ton armored cruiser, also known as a second-class battleship, built at the New York Navy Yard and commissioned in 1895. Prior to being assigned to Havana Harbor, it had operated along the U.S. East Coast and in Caribbean waters.

11. On the day before his appeal to Congress, McKinley received word that the Spanish government was ready to suspend hostilities and grant autonomy to Cuba. McKinley mentioned this development in an offhand way at the end of his message, thereby suggesting that he really was not interested in further negotiations.

12. Lewis L. Gould, *The Presidency of William McKinley* (Lawrence: University Press of Kansas, 1980), 85.

13. H. H. Kohlsaat, *From McKinley to Harding* (New York: Scribner's, 1923), 67.

14. Winston Churchill, *My Early Life: A Roving Commission* (London: Cooper, 1989), 96–97.

15. In 1890 Captain Mahan predicted that the Marine Corps "will constitute a

most important reinforcement, nay the backbone to any force landing on the enemy's coast," and he recommended that in the event of war the U.S. Navy train and assign the entire Marine Corps as an expeditionary force. Graham A. Cosmos and Jack Shulimson, "Continuity and Consensus: The Evolution of the Marine Advanced Base Force, 1900–1922," *Proceedings of the Citadel Conference on War and Diplomacy* (1977): 31–36.

16. Frank O. Hough, Verle E. Ludwig, and Henry I. Shaw Jr., *Pearl Harbor to Guadalcanal: History of U.S. Marine Corps Operations in World War II*, vol. 1 (Washington, D.C.: Historical Branch, G-3 Division, U.S. Marine Corps, 1958), 4–5.

17. Richard W. Turk, *The Ambiguous Relationship: Theodore Roosevelt and Alfred Thayer Mahan* (Westport, Conn.: Greenwood, 1987), 29–31; Hough et al., *Pearl Harbor to Guadalcanal*, 5.

18. Bradley M. Reynolds, "Guantánamo Bay: The History of an American Naval Base and Its Relationship to the Formulation of United States Foreign Policy and Military Strategy toward the Caribbean, 1895–1910" (Ph.D. diss., University of Southern California, 1982), 96; Robert D. Heinl Jr., "How We Got Guantánamo," *American Heritage* 13, no. 2 (February 1962): 19–21, 94–97.

19. Herbert H. Sargent, *Campaign of Santiago de Cuba*, vol. 3 (Chicago, Ill.: McClurg, 1907), app. N, 199.

20. According to Marine Corps historian Colonel Robert Heinl, Commander Reiter, acting on a whim "to put the marines on their mettle," had dumped the battalion in "a pestiferous swamp." Robert D. Heinl Jr., *Soldiers of the Sea: The United States Marine Corps, 1775–1962* (Annapolis, Md.: U.S. Naval Institute, 1962), 115.

21. Trevor K. Plante, "New Glory to Its Already Gallant Record: The First Marine Battalion in the Spanish-American War," *Prologue* 30, no. 1 (Spring 1998): 23.

22. Reynolds, "Guantánamo Bay," 99.

23. Ibid., 100–105.

24. The U.S. Navy had first spotted some of Cervera's ships near Martinique on May 13, but then lost sight of him until May 19, when a U.S. secret agent in Havana telegraphed Washington that the Spanish fleet had slipped into the well-fortified harbor of Santiago on Cuba's southern coast. Graham A. Cosmas, *An Army for Empire* (College Station: Texas A&M University Press, 1994), 173.

25. Schley's squadron was so named because it was a squadron of observation capable of moving quickly from place to place.

26. Department of the Navy, *Annual Reports of the Navy Department for the Year 1898*, 397.

27. Ibid., 397–399. As Salvatore Mercogliano has noted, the blockading of Admiral Cervera's ships inside Santiago Harbor should have allowed U.S. transports to carry troops and cargo to Havana without fear of interception, but Sampson's overriding preoccupation with the enemy fleet inhibited such logistical support. Salvatore Robert Mercogliano, "Sealift: The Evolution of American Military Sea Transportation" (Ph.D. diss., University of Alabama, 2004), 35–36.

28. Ibid., 400, 478.

29. Ibid., 478.

30. Ralph D. Paine, *Roads of Adventure* (Boston: Houghton Mifflin, 1925), 220.

31. Ibid., 414.

32. Walter Millis, *The Martial Spirit* (Cambridge, Mass.: Riverside, 1931), 259.

33. Department of the Navy, *Annual Reports (1898)*, 480.

34. The author, G. J. A. O'Toole, notes that this "inferential version" of the El Aserradero conference is based on the accounts of García, Shafter, and Shafter's aide, Lieutenant John Miley. O'Toole, *The Spanish War*, 255–265. In regard to the assault on Daiquirí, historian Philip S. Foner documents the invaluable assistance of the Cuban auxiliaries. "The United States forces went ashore in a heavy surf on beaches covered by fifteen hundred Cuban soldiers while other Cuban units attacked Spanish troops in the interior. . . . Thus protected, the expedition disembarked without having to fight a single Spaniard." Philip S. Foner, *The Spanish-Cuban-American War and the Birth of Imperialism*, vol. 2, *1898–1902* (New York: Monthly Review Press, 1972), 354–355.

35. In his report on the isthmus expedition, McCalla had suggested that marine officers needed advanced training in the use of machine guns and artillery, that they participate in summer maneuvers in conjunction with the fleet and the U.S. Army, and that the Navy Department purchase its own transports to carry future brigades. Although Marine Corps Commandant Colonel Charles McCawley bristled at what he viewed as McCalla's criticisms, the Navy Department published McCalla's report as written. According to Jack Shulimson, McCalla's recommendation had little immediate effect, but he was clearly recommending the creation of an expeditionary force. Jack Shulimson, *The Marine Corps' Search for a Mission, 1880–1898* (Lawrence: University Press of Kansas, 1993), 61–62.

36. Jeffery M. Dorwart, *The Office of Naval Intelligence: The Birth of America's First Intelligence Agency* (Annapolis, Md.: Naval Institute Press, 1979), 28; Paolo E. Coletta, *Bowman Hendry McCalla: A Fighting Sailor* (Lanham, Md.: University Press of America, 1979), 33.

37. Reynolds, "Guantánamo Bay," 118–119. By this time, Sampson was totally exasperated with Shafter's delay. On the morning of June 7, he wired Secretary Long, "If 10,000 men were here, city and [enemy] fleet would be ours within forty-eight hours. Every consideration demands army movement." French Ensor Chadwick, *Relations of the United States and Spain: The Spanish-American War*, vol. 1 (New York: Scribner's, 1911), 451–452.

38. William T. Sampson, "The Atlantic Fleet in the Spanish War," *Century Illustrated Magazine* 57, no. 6 (April 1899): 903. See also Sargent, *Campaign of Santiago*, vol. 1, 228–231, for a detailed description of the Battle of Guantánamo.

39. Oriente, the former province in which Guantánamo was located, was the birthplace of Cuban independence. Bartolomé Masó from Manzanillo and Guillermón Moncada, the "ebony giant" of Santiago, played leading roles as insurgent commanders in Oriente in both of Cuba's struggles for liberation from colonial rule in the nineteenth century and gained national fame as patriots. So did Antonio Maceo, the "titan of bronze," who was born in Santiago, fought in the Ten Years War, and was killed in action in 1896. Fidel and Raúl Castro were born on a sugar plantation near Biran in Oriente Province. According to the *Encyclopedia de Cuba*, in 1976, the traditional six Cuban provinces were reorganized. Consequently, Oriente Province no longer exists; there is now a Guantánamo Province.

40. See map of the port of Guantánamo.

41. Letter seized by the Cubans en route to Santiago, *Annual Reports of the Navy Department for the Year 1898: Report of the Chief of the Bureau of Navigation*, 451–452; Heinl, "How We Got Guantánamo."

42. Department of the Navy, *Annual Reports (1898)*, 488.

43. Herbert P. McNeal, "How the Navy Won Guantánamo Bay," *Proceedings of the U.S. Naval Institute* 79 (June 1953): 616–619.

44. Paine, *Roads of Adventure*, 241–242.

45. Cuban revolutionaries, of course, employed guerrilla tactics beginning with the first prolonged insurgency, known as the Ten Years War (1868–1878). The Spanish, who had mastered guerrilla tactics a century earlier in the Peninsular Campaign against the forces of Napoleon, responded in kind. Correspondents Paine and Crane both applied the term "guerrilla" to the Spanish fighters who fired on their encampment and who fought at Cuzco. Paine wrote, "The woods are full of Spanish gorillas [*sic*] the *Escuadra* de Guantánamo." Crane also described the *Escuadra* as using guerrilla tactics: "The regiment was composed solely of *practicos*, or guides, who knew every shrub and tree on the ground over which they moved." Ibid., 242–243; Crane, "Marines Signaling under Fire at Guantánamo," in *The War Dispatches of Stephen Crane*, ed. R. W. Stallman and E. R. Hagemann (New York: New York University Press, 1964), 149; Reynolds, "Guantánamo Bay," 120.

46. Heinl, "How We Got Guantánamo," 21; Murphy, *History of Guantánamo Bay*.

47. Crane, "Marines Signaling under Fire at Guantánamo," 150.

48. Ibid., 146, 268; see also Charles H. Brown, *The Correspondents' War: Journalists in the Spanish-American War* (New York: Scribner's, 1967), 281–282. Gibbs was a cousin—by marriage—of Theodore Roosevelt, who encouraged him to enlist. Gibbs joined the U.S. Navy's Medical Corps and was assigned to the First Marine Battalion. Brown writes that Gibbs's death was "an intensely felt personal experience for Crane" and that other correspondents also mentioned his death in their accounts of the fighting.

49. Department of the Navy, *Annual Reports (1898)*, 824.

50. Reynolds, "Guantánamo Bay," 121.

51. Murphy, *History of Guantánamo Bay*.

52. George Kennan, *Campaigning in Cuba* (New York: Century, 1899), 72.

53. Department of the Navy, *Annual Reports (1898):* "Appendix to the Report of the Chief of Bureau of Navigation," 94–95.

54. Elliott to Huntington, June 15, 1898, Department of the Navy, *Annual Reports (1898)*, 845. Crane's account of the battle at Cuzco Well has been corroborated by recent field research conducted under the auspices of the Guantánamo Naval Station.

55. Stephen Crane, "The Red Badge of Courage Was His Wig-Wag Flag," in *The War Dispatches of Stephen Crane*, ed. R. W. Stallman and E. R. Hagemann (New York: New York University Press, 1964), 141–142.

56. Crane, "Marines Signaling under Fire at Guantánamo," 153.

57. Department of the Navy, *Annual Reports (1898)*, 838.

58. Department of the Navy, *Annual Reports (1898):* "Appendix to Report of Chief of Bureau of Navigation," 492.

59. Ibid., 494; McNeal, "How the Navy Won Guantánamo Bay," 618.

60. Ibid., 49; Plante, "New Glory to Its Already Gallant Record," 26–27; Brown, *Correspondents' War*, 288–289.

61. Kennan, *Campaigning in Cuba*, 75.

62. Department of the Navy, *Annual Reports (1898):* "Appendix to Report of Chief of Bureau of Navigation," 499–502; José Müller y Tejeiro, "Battles and Capitulation

of Santiago de Cuba," in *Notes on the Spanish War: War Notes,* vol. 1 (Washington, D.C.: Department of the Navy, Office of Naval Intelligence, 1899), 49.

63. Ibid., 497; David F. Trask, *The War with Spain in 1898* (New York: Macmillan, 1981), 228; Reynolds, "Guantánamo Bay," 121–122.

64. On July 1, 1898, Theodore Roosevelt led his famous Rough Riders up San Juan Hill overlooking Santiago.

65. To give the appearance of objectivity, Secretary Alger dedicated his work to "the American soldier and sailor." He also wrote in the text that "the record of our navy during the war with Spain is of such a character that every American citizen can refer to it with unqualified pride and satisfaction." That said, Alger devoted remarkably little attention to the importance of the naval blockade and said nothing about the marines at Guantánamo. His silence on these subjects can only be attributed to his intention to discredit Sampson. R. A. Alger, *The Spanish-American War* (New York: Harper, 1901), 86–88, 189–192, 221–254. See also Graham A. Cosmas, *Army for Empire,* 205–230; Graham A. Cosmas, "Joint Operations in the Spanish-American War," in *Crucible of Empire: The Spanish American War and Its Aftermath,* ed. James C. Bradford (Annapolis, Md.: Naval Institute Press, 1993), 110. For more on Shafter's insult to the Cubans, see footnote 149 of *Crucible of Empire.*

66. Distinguished historian Allan Millett, for example, has dismissed the military action at Guantánamo as "a minor skirmish of no consequence to the course of the war." To be fair to Millett, he is comparing the battle at Cuzco Hill with the campaign against Santiago, and in this restricted context, his comment may be justified, but as I argue in this book, Guantánamo needs to be viewed in the broader context of naval strategy, which is how Admiral Sampson, Captain McCalla, and Secretary Long saw it. Allan Millett, *Semper Fideles: The History of the United States Marine Corps* (New York: Macmillan, 1980), 133.

67. Brown, *Correspondents' War,* 289.

68. Foner, *Spanish-Cuban-American War,* vol. 2, 349.

69. Department of the Navy, *Annual Reports* (1898), 846.

70. Ibid., 847.

71. Crane, *War Dispatches,* 147; Brown, *Correspondents' War,* 288.

72. Howbert Billman, "Marines at Cusco [*sic*] Hill," *Chicago Record's War Stories by Staff Correspondents in the Field* (Chicago, Ill.: *Chicago Record,* 1898), 46–50. Billman's account of the battle at Cuzco Hill is a particularly well-written and perceptive account, but it also reveals that Billman did not comprehend why the marines had landed at Guantánamo, for he writes, "The brave, hardy fellows of the marine corps were well nigh exhausted by continuous fighting . . . to defend a position of no natural strategic strength, into which they had been thrust by an impulsive naval officer." It can be deduced that at this time, the U.S. military did not have any established procedures for briefing newspaper correspondents on the nature and purpose of specific missions.

73. The U.S. correspondents who covered the Spanish-American War were a distinguished group of journalists and writers. Stephen Bonsal, who wrote for the *New York Herald,* subsequently advocated making Guantánamo the key U.S. naval base in the Caribbean. He was the father of diplomat Philip Bonsal, who served as U.S. ambassador to Cuba until the termination of relations in 1961.

74. In April 1899, the funeral ship *Crook* transported several of the bodies of marines killed at Guantánamo back to the United States to be buried in the Brooklyn Navy Yard and in Arlington National Cemetery. John Gibbs was honored in

memorial services at Trinity Church in New York and at Rutgers College. His body
was later buried in Portsmouth, New Hampshire. *New York Times*, April 26, 1899,
5; *New York Times*, April 30, 1899, 6; *New York Times*, November 11, 1898, 3.

75. Department of the Navy, *Annual Reports (1898)*: "Appendix to Report of the
Chief of Bureau of Navigation," 441–442; Plante, "New Glory to Its Already Gallant
Record," 30.

76. Historian Louis Pérez Jr. has noted that "Cubans not only seem to have van-
ished from the war, they were excluded from the peace." He is referring to the refusal of U.S. military leaders to allow Cuban soldiers and their commander, General
Calixto García, to enter the city of Santiago after the Spanish surrendered. Shafter
reportedly told General García, "This war is between the United States and the King-
dom of Spain and . . . the surrender . . . was made solely to the American Army."
Pérez, *War of 1898*, 97.

77. Mercogliano, "Sealift: The Evolution of American Military Sea Transportation," 28–29.

78. According to information that the Spanish Ministry of War provided to the
U.S. Legation in Madrid in June 1903, there had been 17 general and field officers,
175 company officers, and 5,800 enlisted men assigned to Guantánamo in 1898.
Sargent, *Campaign of Guantánamo*, vol. 3, app. A, 159.

79. Bowman McCalla, *Memoirs*, reel 2, ch. 23, 34B and 34E; Müller y Tejeiro,
Notes on the Spanish War, 163.

80. The Cuban insurgents also needed food. According to correspondent George
Kennan's account in *Campaigning in Cuba*, Captain McCalla was in regular communication with General Pérez, an insurgent leader who was besieging Guantánamo
City, and it was through Pérez that McCalla was sending food to Cubans who had
taken refuge in the woods north of the bay. McCalla had already sent all the food he
could spare, but it was not nearly enough. Then, according to Kennan, Clara Barton
arrived in Guantánamo Bay with about fourteen hundred tons of food intended for
the Cuban "reconcentrados." McCalla instructed General Pérez to send pack animals
and an escort for five thousand rations, which could be landed on the western side
of the lower bay. Kennan, *Campaigning in Cuba*, 68–69; McNeal, "How the Navy
Won Guantánamo Bay," 619.

81. "Spain's View of the War: Her Council Says Naval Blockade Led to Surrender
of Santiago," *New York Times*, October 30, 1899, 7.

82. Müller y Tejeiro, *Notes on the Spanish War*, 111.

83. Department of the Navy, *Annual Reports (1898)*, 849. Allan Millett notes
that the remarkable health record of Huntington's battalion "made it a national
sensation." Millett, *Semper Fideles*, 134.

84. Department of the Navy, *Annual Reports (1898)*, 884–887.

85. Patrick McSherry, "Lee United States Naval Rifle," http://www.spanamwar
.com/lee.htm. On June 28, 1898, the *New York Times* published the results of a study
made at Guantánamo by Orlando Ducker, a pathologist who had sailed to Cuba
aboard the *Dauntless*. He had examined corpses on the battlefield of Cuzco Hill
to compare the impact of bullet wounds made by the Mauser and the Lee. Ducker
found that the shots fired from the Mauser had the effect of exploding inside the
body of the victim, making the exit wound much larger than the entrance wound;
whereas bullets fired by the Lee generally passed through the body with great velocity, but the exit wound was approximately the same size as the entrance wound.
"Modern Bullet Wounds," *New York Times*, June 28, 1898, 6.

86. Further, Mahan had suggested that future U.S. Navy war plans include the employment of the entire Marine Corps for expeditionary duty. Cosmas and Shulimson, "Continuity and Consensus," 31.

87. Ivan Musicant, *Empire by Default: The Spanish-American War and the Dawn of the American Century* (New York: Holt, 1998), 349.

88. Shulimson, "Marines in the Spanish-American War," 149.

89. Plante, "New Glory to Its Already Gallant Record," 29, and Note 1, 30; Millett, *Semper Fideles*, 134.

90. S. A. Staunton, "The Naval Campaign of 1898 in the West Indies," *Harper's New Monthly Magazine* 98 (January 1899): 191.

91. Millett, *Semper Fideles*, 134.

Chapter Three. Cubans Resist U.S. Base Acquisition

1. H. C. Taylor, "The Future of Our Navy," *Forum* 27 (March 1899): 4.

2. For extended periods of time, Guantánamo was not mentioned specifically in high-level diplomatic discussions, in part because the United States did not want to restrict its options to only one naval station, and also because it did not want to attract negative Cuban attention to any site under consideration.

3. The Philippine-American War began in February 1899 and lasted officially until 1902, even though fighting continued in the archipelago until 1909. Historian Brian Lynn estimates that at the peak of this protracted conflict, in December 1900, probably forty-two thousand U.S. troops were in the Philippine Islands. In comparison to the Spanish-American War, the Philippine insurrection (as it was formally known) was longer, bloodier, and less studied. It certainly, however, was not the "First Vietnam." Lynn makes a convincing argument that, largely because of U.S. civic action, by 1902 the Americans were more popular among Filipinos than the insurgents. Nonetheless, the Philippine insurgency helped fuel anti-imperialist sentiment in the United States, and it was also part of William Jennings Bryan's failed campaign strategy in 1900. According to Lewis Gould, McKinley skillfully countered Bryan's efforts to make the Philippines the central issue by promising that the Filipinos would have self-government "when they are ready for it." Brian McAllister Lynn, *The Philippine War, 1899–1902* (Lawrence: University Press of Kansas, 2000), 325–328; Lewis L. Gould, *The Spanish-American War and President McKinley* (Lawrence: University Press of Kansas, 1982), 125. Luzviminda Francisco, "The First Vietnam: The Philippine-American War of 1899," *Bulletin of Concerned Asian Scholars* 5, no. 4 (December 1973): 2–16.

4. Bradley M. Reynolds, "Guantánamo Bay, Cuba: The History of an American Naval Base and Its Relationship to the Formulation of United States Foreign Policy and Military Strategy toward the Caribbean, 1895–1910" (Ph.D. diss., University of Southern California, 1982), 151–152.

5. Richard D. Challener, *Admirals, Generals, and American Foreign Policy, 1898–1914* (Princeton, N.J.: Princeton University Press, 1973), 36.

6. At that time, as Mahan acknowledged, both Nicaragua and Panama were being considered as possible canal routes. *The Letters and Papers of Alfred Thayer Mahan,* vol. 2, ed. Robert Seager II and Doris D. McGuire (Annapolis, Md.: Naval Institute Press, 1975), 581–591. On March 3, 1899, President McKinley appointed the nine-member Walker Commission to investigate all possible canal routes across Central America. On February 5, 1900, the United States and Great Britain signed

the Hay-Pauncefote Treaty, giving the United States exclusive rights to build an isthmian canal. 1902, however, was the decisive year: on January 8, the U.S. House of Representatives authorized a Nicaraguan canal, but on January 18, the Walker Commission recommended the Panama route to President Roosevelt. On June 18, the U.S. Senate passed the Panama Canal bill, and on June 26, the House of Representatives also approved the Panamanian route. On June 28, President Roosevelt signed into law the Spooner Act authorizing construction of the Panama Canal. On November 18, 1903, the Hay-Bunau-Varilla Treaty between the United States and the newly independent republic of Panama empowered the United States to build the canal and to exercise "all the rights, power, and authority [within the canal zone] which the United States would possess if it were the sovereign of the territory." David McCullough, *The Path between the Seas: The Creation of the Panama Canal, 1870–1914* (New York: Simon & Schuster, 1977), 392–393. See also Dwight Carroll Miner, *The Fight for the Panama Canal Route: The Story of the Spooner Act and the May-Herran Treaty* (New York: Octagon, 1971).

7. As members of the Navy War Board, Rear Admiral Montgomery Sicard and Admiral Arent S. Crowninshield also signed this report, but Sicard was seriously ill, and Crowninshield was anxious to return to his full-time duties as chief of the Bureau of Navigation. As biographer Robert Seager notes, "the style, organization, and thought are indubitably Mahan's." Seager and McGuire, eds., *The Letters and Papers of Alfred Thayer Mahan,* vol. 2, 481–591.

8. Ibid., 588.

9. In March 1899, Bradford was promoted from commander to captain, and, as chief of the Bureau of the Equipment, he was subsequently promoted to rear admiral. Department of the Navy, *Annual Reports of the Navy Department for the Year 1899: Report of the Chief of the Bureau of Equipment,* 317–318.

10. On December 7, 1900, probably at Bradford's urging, the General Board advised Secretary Long that the United States should establish at least two permanent naval stations in Cuba, at Cienfuegos and Guantánamo. General Records of the Department of the Navy 1798–1947, General Board of the Navy, Record Group 80 (hereafter RG80), General Board (hereafter GB) no. 91, National Archives, Washington, D.C. Cited in Steven T. Ross, *American War Plans 1890–1939* (London: Frank Cass, 2002), 33.

11. See Department of the Navy, *Annual Reports of the Navy Department for the Year 1900,* charts on 448, 480–481, 519, 522; "Naval Surveys in Cuba: American Sailors Locate the Most Available Coaling Stations," *New York Times,* June 8, 1901, 9.

12. The title chief of the Bureau of Equipment understates Bradford's enormous responsibilities and expertise, which included all naval equipment ranging at minimum from battleships to torpedoes, if not from a to z. His knowledge of logistical issues, for example, was recognized at the highest levels of government, as indicated in the *Wall Street Journal* report of the cabinet meeting of April 8, 1898, prior to the Spanish-American War. "The meeting was taken up with discussing the war preparations, among them the location and strength of our fleet at various points and the amount of supplies and ammunition on hand. . . . General Schofield and Commander Bradford were consulted on these points by the President and the Cabinet." "The Cabinet Meeting," *Wall Street Journal,* April 8, 1898, 1.

13. Royal B. Bradford to the Secretary of the Navy, September 27, 1898, RG 45, PS-Bases, Cuba 1898–1910, Box 6, National Archives.

14. Royal B. Bradford, "Statement of Commander R. B. Bradford, U.S.N.,

March 30, 1898," in *Compilation of Reports of Committee on Foreign Relations, United States Senate,* vol. 7 (Washington, D.C.: Government Printing Office, 1901), 814–815.

15. *The Journal of John D. Long,* ed. Margaret Long (Rindge, N.H.: Richard R. Smith, 1956), 229.

16. Taylor was chief of the Bureau of Navigation, of which the primary responsibilities included navigational research, hydrography, and personnel management. Stockton was president of the Naval War College and a scholar of international law, and published the first codification of the law of naval warfare.

17. Royal B. Bradford, "Coaling-Stations for the Navy," *Forum* 26 (February 1899): 732–747.

18. Ibid.

19. Reynolds, "Guantánamo Bay," 165. To protect the western approach to the projected isthmian canal, Bradford considered it "absolutely essential to have a coaling-station somewhere on the western coast of South America." Once again, Bradford did not recommend a specific location, but said it could either be on an island or on the mainland. Bradford, "Coaling-Stations," 747.

20. Taylor, "Future of Our Navy," 1–6.

21. Ibid., 8.

22. C. H. Stockton, "The American Interoceanic Channel: A Study of the Commercial, Naval, and Political Conditions," *Proceedings of the United States Naval Institute* 25 (December 1899): 753–797. Captain Stockton would eventually obtain the rank of Rear Admiral and be recognized as one of the Navy's most influential strategic planners and its first expert in international law.

23. Ibid., 764.

24. Ibid., 767.

25. Ibid., 797 (the italics are mine). See also Lawrence A. Clayton, *Peru and the United States: The Condor and the Eagle* (Athens: University of Georgia Press, 1999), 84–85; Ronald Bruce St. John, *The Foreign Policy of Peru* (Boulder, Colo.: Lynne Rienner, 1992), 118–121, 140–141; Dale William Peterson, "The Diplomatic and Commercial Relations between the United States and Peru from 1883 to 1918" (Ph.D. diss., University of Minnesota, 1969), 120–148; and Seward W. Livermore, "American Strategic Diplomacy in the South Pacific 1890–1914," *Pacific Historical Review* 12, no. 1 (March 1943): 33–51.

26. The one exception was General Winfield Scott's two-month administration of Mexico prior to the signing of the Treaty of Guadalupe Hidalgo in February 1848.

27. David F. Healy, *The United States in Cuba, 1898–1902* (Madison: University of Wisconsin Press, 1963), 65–80. See also James H. Hitchman, *Leonard Wood and Cuban Independence, 1898–1902* (The Hague: Martinus Nijhoff, 1971), 17–18; Jack McCallum, *Leonard Wood: Rough Rider, Surgeon, Architect of American Imperialism* (New York: New York University Press, 2006), 134–146.

28. Brooke's accomplishments in relief and sanitation were significant. The Spaniards had destroyed public works throughout Cuba, looted and gutted buildings, and left the population mired in filth and suffering from abject poverty, disease, and starvation. Brooke fed thousands, removed the filth from streets and buildings, repaired the sewers, and refurbished government offices. His major weakness was his inability to establish and manage an effective bureaucracy. Healy, *The United States in Cuba,* 63–64. See also Philip C. Jessup, *Elihu Root,* vol. 1, *1845–1900* (Hamden, Conn.: Archon, 1964), 285–286.

29. According to James Hitchman's biography of Wood, Roosevelt's laudatory appraisal of Wood was accurate. As soon as he was in charge of Santiago, Wood hired Cubans to clean up the filth and refuse and to build new roads and bridges, compensating them first with food and then with money. He organized former Cuban soldiers into a guard force to prevent robbery and appointed the most capable Cubans he met to positions of administrative responsibility. Hitchman, *Leonard Wood and Cuban Independence,* 20–21.

30. Theodore Roosevelt, "General Leonard Wood: A Model American Military Administrator," *Outlook* 61 (January 7, 1899): 18–23.

31. Leonard Wood, "The Existing Conditions and Needs in Cuba," *North American Review* 168, no. 510 (May 1899): 593–601.

32. Theodore Roosevelt, Letter to Secretary of State John Hay, July 1, 1899, Papers of Theodore Roosevelt, series 1, subseries A (Microfilm Reel 308), Manuscript Division, Library of Congress.

33. "Criticism of Gen. Brooke," *New York Times,* August 9, 1899, 5.

34. Jessup, *Elihu Root,* 196–197; Richard Leopold, *Elihu Root and the Conservative Tradition* (Boston: Little, Brown, 1954), 15–16.

35. Jessup, *Elihu Root,* 287.

36. Healy, *The United States in Cuba,* 124.

37. Major J. E. Runcie, "American Misgovernment of Cuba," *North American Review* 170, no. 519 (February 1900): 284–297.

38. On September 4, 1899, in a letter to Root, Roosevelt compared Wood favorably to the "very best type of an English colonial administrator," saying there "is hardly a man alive now who comes up to him." On November 10, 1899, Roosevelt told Wood, "You are doing a very great work. I wish to Heaven the Administration would put you in complete control." *The Letters of Theodore Roosevelt,* vol. 2, ed. Elting E. Morison (Cambridge, Mass.: Harvard University Press, 1951), 1066–1067, 1093–1094.

39. Kathleen Dalton, *Theodore Roosevelt: A Strenuous Life* (New York: Knopf, 2002), 126; Henry F. Pringle, *Theodore Roosevelt* (New York: Harcourt, Brace, 1956), 211; Howard K. Beale, *Theodore Roosevelt and the Rise of America to World Power* (Baltimore, Md.: Johns Hopkins University Press, 1956), 26–34; Louis A. Pérez Jr., *The War of 1898: The United States and Cuba in History and Historiography* (Chapel Hill: University of North Carolina Press, 1998), 96.

40. Jessup, *Elihu Root,* 304–305.

41. Hitchman, *Leonard Wood and Cuban Independence,* 99.

42. Richard Gott, *Cuba: A New History* (New Haven, Conn.: Yale University Press, 2004), 106–107.

43. McCallum, *Leonard Wood,* 149–150, 172–173; Hitchman, *Leonard Wood and Cuban Independence,* 26.

44. My translation of the *Civil Report of the Secretary of State and Government of Cuba,* Library of the University of Havana, Rare Books Collection, 18, 77. By September 1901, yellow fever had been virtually eliminated from Havana and malaria was also under control. Wood himself said that the conquest of yellow fever was worth the cost of the War of 1898.

45. The Teller Amendment, which was enacted on April 20, 1898, in response to President McKinley's request to Congress for the right to intervene in Cuba, explicitly stated that "the United States hereby disclaims any disposition or intention to exercise sovereignty, jurisdiction, or control over said island except for pacification

thereof, and asserts its determination, when that is accomplished, to leave the government and control of the island to its people." Upon learning that Congress had authorized McKinley to intervene in Cuba, Spain immediately severed diplomatic relations with the United States and on April 24 declared war. Congress responded with its own declaration of war on April 25, which it made retroactive to April 21. For this chronology, see Julius W. Pratt, *A History of United States Foreign Policy* (New York: Prentice-Hall, 1955), 380–381. Ironically, Senator Henry Teller had earlier been a moderate expansionist who favored the annexation of Hawaii, and in 1894 had proclaimed, "I am in favor of the annexation of Cuba." Teller's earlier advocacy of Cuban annexation is a vivid example of how some U.S. expansionists could change their minds with regard to Cuba. Wood initially thought that the Cubans themselves would ask to be annexed, but he also worked tirelessly to prepare them for independence. For Teller, see *Congressional Record,* 53d Congress, 2nd sess., 506, 1578. See also Julius W. Pratt, *Expansionists of 1898: The Acquisition of Hawaii and the Spanish Islands* (New York: Peter Smith, 1951), 211.

46. Patrick David DeFroscia, "The Diplomacy of Elihu Root, 1905–1909" (Ph.D. diss., Temple University, 1976), 2.

47. Nancy Mitchell, *The Danger of Dreams: German and American Imperialism in Latin America* (Chapel Hill: University of North Carolina Press, 1997), 40. Roosevelt held similar views. On February 14, 1900, he wrote to Mahan, "I do not see why we should dig the canal if we are not to fortify it so as to insure its being used for ourselves and against our foes in time of war." *Letters of Theodore Roosevelt,* vol. 1, 1185. See also Appendix A of this book.

48. Holger H. Herwig, *Germany's Vision of Empire in Venezuela, 1871–1914* (Princeton, N.J.: Princeton University Press, 1986), 197.

49. Donald Yerxa, *Admirals and Empire: The United States Navy and the Caribbean, 1898–1945* (Columbia: University of South Carolina Press, 1991), 6–7.

50. *Selections from the Correspondence of Theodore Roosevelt and Henry Cabot Lodge, 1884–1918,* vol. 1, ed. Henry Cabot Lodge (New York: Scribner's, 1925), 484–485.

51. Long established the General Board as his senior group of naval advisers on March 30, 1900. Its members consisted of the chiefs of the Bureaus of Navigation and Equipment, the president of the Naval War College, and the chief of the Office of Naval Intelligence. Its presiding officer was the admiral of the U.S. Navy, George Dewey. Although the General Board's formal role was strictly advisory and each of its members had other important, full-time responsibilities, the board's recommendations often reflected the navy's thinking about strategy and policy. Challener, *Admirals, Generals, and American Foreign Policy,* 7, 37, 47–48.

52. Long to Wood, May 11, 1900, and Root to Wood, May 14, 1900, Leonard Wood Papers, Manuscript Division, Library of Congress.

53. Ibid. Bradley Reynolds has found that Bradford, chief of the Bureau of Equipment, had drafted the letter that Long signed and sent to Root. See Reynolds, "Guantánamo Bay, " 175–176, Footnote 67, 204.

54. Hitchman, *Leonard Wood and Cuban Independence,* 91.

55. Asa Walker, "Notes on Cuban Ports," in *Proceedings of the U.S. Naval Institute* 26, no. 2 (June 1900): 333–340.

56. Ibid. According to Richard Challener's research, the arguments in favor of establishing a U.S. naval station at Havana were that it was the most likely site for an enemy attack, or, alternatively, the most logical site for a U.S. military intervention,

should that be necessary. Challener, *Admirals, Generals, and American Foreign Policy,* 95.

57. Root to Wood, June 20, 1900, Wood Papers.

58. Rebecca J. Scott, *Degrees of Freedom: Louisiana and Cuba after Slavery* (Cambridge, Mass.: Belknap Press of Harvard University Press, 2005), 186–187.

59. Another guest was Navy Secretary John Long. Charles G. Dawes, *A Journal of the McKinley Years* (Chicago, Ill.: Lakeside, 1950), 237–238.

60. "Cuba to Rule Herself," *New York Times,* July 21, 1900, 8.

61. Reynolds, "Guantánamo Bay," 179.

62. E. L. Godkin, "Cuba's Foreign Relations," *Nation* 71 (August 2, 1900): 85–86.

63. Hitchman, *Leonard Wood and Cuban Independence,* 91–92.

64. Jessup, *Elihu Root,* 307. Acting as a propagandist, Wood sought to mollify critics of U.S. policies toward Cuba by assuring them that the constitutional convention would be "entirely a Cuban affair," and that, as military governor, he would not "attempt to influence the delegates in their discussions and consideration of their form of government." Leonard Wood, "The Cuban Convention," *Independent* (November 1, 1900): 2605–2606.

65. Ibid., 307–308. See also Hitchman, *Leonard Wood and Cuban Independence,* 100–101.

66. William McKinley, "Message from the President of the United States to the Two Houses of Congress at the Beginning of the Second Session of the Fifty-Sixth Congress, with Reports of the Heads of Departments and Selections from Accompanying Reports" (abridgment), vol. 1 (Washington, D.C.: Government Printing Office, 1901), 41–44.

67. Late in January, the chair of the Committee on Relations with Cuba, Senator Orville H. Platt, told Wood that although it would not be politically feasible to grant tariff concessions to Cuba before the Cuban Constitution was adopted, Congress might react favorably on such tariffs if the constitution were "favorably settled." Platt to Wood, January 18, 1901, Wood Papers.

68. In the same letter, Root complained about being caught between conflicting pressures exerted by Congress, the Democratic press, and the Cubans, who were "howling at us to do something." As a senior cabinet official, he certainly understood the unwieldy and time-consuming nature of U.S. constitutional procedures that seek to achieve consensus, yet he seemed unwilling to permit the Cuban legislators to arrive at their own consensus. His unspoken assumption may have been, Why don't they imitate us and get on with it, rather than reinvent the wheel? Root to Wood, January 9, 1901, Elihu Root Papers, Manuscript Division, Library of Congress.

69. Ibid.

70. Root to Hay, January 11, 1901, Root Papers.

71. Ibid.

72. In preparing his well-documented biography of Wood, James Hitchman consulted Platt's papers in the Connecticut State Library and William E. Chandler's papers in the Library of Congress. Hitchman, *Leonard Wood and Cuban Independence,* 115–117.

73. Because Root's letters of January 9, January 11, and February 9, 1901, provide important insights into Root's thinking as to how Cuba should become independent and yet remain closely tied to the United States, they are printed in their entirety at Appendix B of this book along with the bilateral agreements for naval and coaling stations.

74. The committee included Enrique Villuendas, who had been a colonel in the Liberation Army; Diego Tamayo, who had served as Cuba's secretary of state and was well known as both a conservative and a strong nationalist; Ernesto Quesada, who was described as a political moderate but had made some anti-U.S. speeches; and Juan Gualberto Gomez and Manuel Silva, both of whom opposed all U.S. control. Reynolds, "Guantánamo Bay," 186, 206–207.

75. Bangs was then humor editor for *Harpers Weekly*. He subsequently became editor of *Puck* magazine.

76. A *New York Times* story published on February 16 reported that Wood and the committee planned to discuss the future of bilateral relations and accurately predicted that "the only hitch that is expected to arise . . . is the maintenance of naval stations in Cuba." "United States and Cuba," *New York Times,* February 16, 1901, 6.

77. "The Situation in Cuba," *New York Times,* April 8, 1901, 6.

78. As Jack McCallum has written in his biography of Wood, the Cubans with whom Wood felt comfortable, and whom he portrayed to Root as being "sensible," did not represent the majority of the population, who, after four centuries of colonial rule, wanted full independence. McCallum, *Leonard Wood,* 185–189.

79. Wood to Root, February 19, 1901, Root Papers.

80. The provision for sanitation measures to prevent future epidemics almost certainly reflected the views and influence of Wood and medical authorities such as Carlos Finlay, Walter Reed, and William Gorgas.

81. See Appendix E of this book for the full text of the Platt Amendment.

82. Philip S. Foner, *The Spanish-Cuban-American War and the Birth of Imperialism,* vol. 2, *1898–1902* (New York: Monthly Review Press, 1972), 569.

83. Philip C. Jessup, Memorandum on the Platt Amendment, confidential, 711.37/142, October 13, 1930, Diplomatic and Legal Branch, National Archives.

84. Senator Platt never claimed publicly to be the author of the amendment, but in a letter to the editor of his hometown newspaper, Charles H. Clark, who was also a personal friend, Platt took some credit, saying that he had composed the original draft, basing it on the instructions Root had given Wood, and that the language had been revised in subsequent consultations with McKinley, Root, and the Republican members of the Committee on Relations with Cuba. Louis A. Coolidge, *An Old-Fashioned Senator: Orville H. Platt of Connecticut* (New York: Putnam's, 1910), 349–351.

85. U.S. Senate, 56th Cong., 2nd sess., *Congressional Record* 34, pt. 3 (February 25, 1901): 2954. Also on February 25, Root forwarded to Hay a decoded confidential message he had just received from Wood reporting that he had good evidence that the German and English consuls in Havana had been trying to persuade the Cuban delegates to reject the Platt Amendment. In his covering note to Hay, Root wrote, "I have had some intimations before that these gentlemen were acting upon the theory that it was a part of their duty to their own countries to prevent any special relations between Cuba and the United States. . . . I should be glad if proper steps could be taken to secure either a change of conduct or a change of residence on their part." Root to Hay, February 25, 1901, Root Papers.

86. Walter McDougal, "Progressive Imperialism," in *Promised Land, Crusader State: The American Encounter with the World* (New York: Houghton Mifflin, 1997), 116–121.

87. Mark Twain, "As Regards Patriotism," *Mark Twain's Weapons of Satire: Anti-Imperialist Writings on the Philippines-American War,* ed. Jim Zwick (Syracuse,

N.Y.: Syracuse University Press, 1992), 116–118. See also Robert L. Beisner, *Twelve against Empire: The Anti-Imperialists, 1898–1900* (New York: McGraw-Hill, 1968), 238–239.

88. George Ade, *The Sultan of Sulu: An Original Satire in Two Acts* (New York: R. H. Russell, 1903), 11–12.

89. Lawrence A. Clayton, "The Nicaragua Canal in the Nineteenth Century: Prelude to American Empire in the Caribbean," *Journal of Latin Studies* 19, no. 2 (November 1987): 323–352; Lawrence A. Clayton, "Canal Morgan," *Alabama Heritage* 25 (Summer 1992): 6–19. Morgan opposed the annexation of Cuba for various reasons including his own racial prejudices, but he was not anti-imperialist. Samuel Gompers, on the other hand, feared that the annexation of Cuba would lead to an influx of Cuban workers willing to accept lower wages than the members of Gompers's American Federation of Labor.

90. U.S. Senate, 56th Cong., 2nd sess., *Congressional Record* 34, pt. 3 (February 25, 1901): 3036–3042.

91. David Healy, "The Formulation of United States Policy in Cuba, 1898–1902" (Ph.D. diss., University of Wisconsin, 1960), 235–237.

92. Wood to Root, February 27, 1901, Root Papers.

93. Albert G. Robinson, *Cuba and the Intervention* (London: Longmans, Green, 1905), 244.

94. Root to Wood, March 2, 1901, Wood Papers; Jessup, *Elihu Root,* 316.

95. Wood to Root, March 2 and March 6, 1901, Root Papers; Root to Wood, March 29, 1901, Wood Papers.

96. "Report of the Committee Appointed to Confer with the Government of the United States, Giving an Account of the Results of Its Labors," Copy in Root Papers. See also Healy, "The Formation of America's Cuban Policy, 1898–1902," 253.

97. Telegrams of Wood to Root and Root to Wood, May 17, 1901, Wood Papers.

98. A copy of this is in Root to Wood, May 28, 1901, Root Papers.

99. "Accept Platt Amendment," *New York Times,* May 29, 1901, 1.

100. Root to Wood, May 28, 1901, Wood Papers; Wood to Root, June 1, 1901, Root Papers.

101. Jessup, *Elihu Root,* 323.

102. Foner, *The Spanish-Cuban-American War,* 626. In a reflective mood, Wood would later comment to Roosevelt, "There is, of course, little or no independence left Cuba under the Platt Amendment." Wood to Roosevelt, October 28, 1901, Wood Papers.

103. Reynolds, "Guantánamo Bay," 218.

104. A letter from Roosevelt to William Howard Taft, dated March 12, 1901, commended Taft for his work in the Philippines. Roosevelt wrote, "I doubt if in all the world there has been a much harder task set any one man during the past year than has been set you. In the American world the tasks of the President and Secretary Root and perhaps Leonard Wood are about the only ones I think should be put in your category." This suggests, at a minimum, that Roosevelt had been closely following the progress of the Platt Amendment issue. *Letters of Theodore Roosevelt,* vol. 3, 11–12. On March 27, Roosevelt wrote to Wood to tell him that he had recently talked with John Kendrick Bangs, "who has become one of your great admirers." Roosevelt then praised Wood's ongoing efforts, telling him that he had rendered "to the Nation a greater service than any other one man. . . . Root's work which is very great, has also covered much less time." Ibid., 30–31.

105. Frederick W. Marks, *Velvet on Iron: The Diplomacy of Theodore Roosevelt* (Lincoln: University of Nebraska Press, 1979), 47–48.

106. Dewey to Long, November 1, 1901, RG 45, File 1775–1910, PS-Bases, Box 6, "Cuba," GB no. 22; Long to General Board, November 9, 1901, Letter 290245, National Archives.

107. The answer to how the Roosevelt administration succeeded in granting tariff concessions on imports of Cuban sugar and tobacco lies outside the scope of this work and is worthy of separate study. It must be said here, however, that this was not a simple exchange of Cuban naval bases for lower tariffs. Whereas, given the Platt Amendment, a naval station could be designated by an executive order issued by Roosevelt, the granting of trade concessions required that the U.S. Senate approve a treaty. Moreover, there were powerful beet and cane sugar and tobacco interests in the United States that opposed lowering the tariffs on Cuban imports. This is why Roosevelt, Root, and Wood all lobbied Congress to grant these concessions. It must also be acknowledged, as William Allen White perceptively observed, that the Platt Amendment was widely viewed by U.S. capitalists as making Cuba "a safe field for American investment." William Allen White, "Cuban Reciprocity—a Moral Issue," *McClure's Magazine* 19, no. 5 (September 1902): 388.

108. "The Annual Message of the President," December 3, 1901. Department of State. *Papers Relating to the Foreign Relations of the United States* (Washington, D.C.: Government Printing Office, 1902), xxxi–xxxii.

109. Many of Wood's letters to Root as well as his more private thoughts recorded in his diary indicate that he doubted the ability of the Cubans to establish a strong self-government, and believed that the only realistic alternative was annexation. Shortly after he left Cuba, Wood wrote in his diary: "The general feeling among the Cubans was one of intense regret at the termination of the American Government. . . . I feel we should have stayed longer." Diary of Leonard Wood, Wood Papers.

110. Secretary Hay to U.S. Minister Herbert G. Squiers, May 19, 1901, John Hay Papers, Manuscript Division, Library of Congress.

111. General Board to the Secretary of the Navy, March 25, 1902, RG 80, General Correspondence 1897–1915, Box 488, no. 11045–7, National Archives.

112. Bradford made several visits to Cuba, and he always expressed a preference for Guantánamo, but also recommended that Havana, Bahía Honda, Cienfuegos, and Nipe Bay be considered as sites for additional coaling and naval stations. At Guantánamo, Bradford tried to negotiate for a lease of approximately two hundred eighty square miles of land. *Washington Post*, April 9, 1902, 10. See also Richard Wellington Turk, "United States Naval Policy in the Caribbean" (Ph.D. diss., Fletcher School of Law and Diplomacy, Tufts University, 1968), 101; Daniel Joseph Costello, "Planning for War: A History of the General Board of the Navy, 1900–1914" (Ph.D. diss., Fletcher School of Law and Diplomacy, Tufts University, 1969), 193–194.

113. *Letters of Theodore Roosevelt*, vol. 3, 367. In an article published on October 29, 1902, the *New York Times* accurately predicted: "There is good reason for expecting that this Government will finally recede from the demand for three coaling stations, and will be content with one, and that one will be at Guantánamo, because it commands the Windward Passage." "President Palma Disapproves the Treaty," *New York Times*, October 29, 1902, 5.

114. In June 1902, U.S. Marine Captain Dion Williams published "The Defense of Our New Naval Stations" in the *Proceedings of the United States Naval Institute*.

Williams predicted that future wars involving the United States would almost certainly be naval wars in which offshore naval stations would serve multiple purposes of coaling, providing ammunition and other supplies, and making needed repairs. To perform these essential functions and avoid capture or destruction by the enemy, these naval stations had to be well fortified and defended, Williams argued. As an avid reader of the *Proceedings,* Theodore Roosevelt almost certainly incorporated Williams's views into his own thinking on this subject. Dion Williams, "The Defense of Our New Naval Stations," in *Proceedings of the United States Naval Institute* 28, no. 2 (June 1902): 181–194.

115. *Letters of Theodore Roosevelt,* vol. 3, 369–370.

116. According to Charles Chapman's research, in November 1903 the U.S. government had asked Cuba also to lease the bays of Cienfuegos and Nipe, but Estrada Palma had succeeded in restricting the terms of the request. Charles E. Chapman, *A History of the Cuban Republic: A Study in Hispanic American Politics* (New York: Macmillan, 1927), 156–157.

117. "Cuba: Lease of Coaling or Naval Stations to the United States." Department of State, *Papers Relating to the Foreign Relations of the United States 1903* (Washington, D.C.: Government Printing Office, 1903), 350–351. See Appendix D of this book for the text of the lease.

118. Ibid.

119. Roosevelt had named Moody, a Congressman from Massachusetts, secretary of the navy because, having served on both the Appropriations and Insular Affairs Committees, he was well informed on U.S. naval needs and the concerns of overseas U.S. possessions. Republicans and Democrats liked and respected Moody, and Senator Lodge had personally commended him to Roosevelt's attention by writing, "Moody is naturally with us and he has more influence with [Joe] Cannon [speaker of the House of Representatives] than anyone." *Correspondence of Roosevelt and Lodge,* vol. 1, 511.

120. George T. Davis, "The Naval Policy of the United States, 1880–1917" (Ph.D. diss., Yale University, 1938), 278.

121. "Site for a Naval Station," *New York Times,* March 25, 1903, 5. Moody's strong endorsement of Guantánamo did not necessarily have the support of another key member of the Roosevelt administration, Root. On February 9, 1903, Root wrote to Senator W. B. Allison that he was especially interested in Fort Tyler at Key West, which, he believed, "is to be the great primary naval base for all our operations in the West Indies and the Caribbean Sea. It is the southernmost point within the continental territory of the United States at which such a base can be established, and all the naval plans for the protection of the Isthmian Canal depend on the establishment of a base at that point." Root to Allison, February 9, 1903, Root Papers. See also Lejeune Cummins, "The Origin and Development of Elihu Root's Latin American Diplomacy" (Ph.D. diss., University of California, Berkeley, 1964), 136.

122. Commander of the U.S.S. *Nashville* to the Bureau of Navigation, June 8, 1903, General Board, Subject File 406, National Archives. There were other operational delays and complications including dealing with Cuban landowners and U.S. speculators along with efforts by the Cuban Eastern Railroad Company to build a railway line and erect a terminal inside the base. These developments are well covered by Reynolds in "Guantánamo Bay," 231–244.

123. Roosevelt to Root, March 15, 1903, Root Papers.

124. It is unlikely that Roosevelt could have foreseen the extent to which this

decision would bind Cuba to the U.S. economy and also generate a massive flow of U.S. investment into Cuba. See Luis E. Aguilar, *Cuba 1933: Prologue to Revolution* (New York: Norton, 1972), 24–25.

125. "The Tariff," Address of President Roosevelt at Minneapolis, Minnesota, April 4, 1903, Papers of Theodore Roosevelt, series 5, subseries A (Microfilm Reel 418), Manuscript Division, Library of Congress.

126. *Letters of Theodore Roosevelt,* vol. 3, 474; Department of State, *Papers Relating to the Foreign Relations of the United States 1903,* 350–352. See also Jane Franklin, *Cuba and the United States: A Chronological History* (Melbourne, Australia: Ocean Press, 1997), 10.

127. According to Moody, there were no plans to do anything at Bahía Honda except to delimit the leased land and possibly to station there a small marine guard force. U.S. House Committee on Naval Affairs, "Testimony before the House Committee on Naval Affairs," 58th Cong., 2nd sess., *Congressional Record* 38, pt. 3 (December 15, 1903): 484–485.

128. It should be noted that in speeches throughout the country, at Hartford (Conn.), Indianapolis, Detroit, Chicago, and Charleston from late 1901 to 1903, Roosevelt sought to prepare the nation to accept its expanded responsibilities in Cuba, Puerto Rico, and the Philippines, and the pressing need, as he described it, "to upbuild the navy." Papers of Theodore Roosevelt, Speeches and Executive Orders, Series 5, Subseries A (Microfilm Reels 417–419), Manuscript Division, Library of Congress. See also Appendix B of this book.

129. "Marines Off for Guantánamo," *New York Times,* October 28, 1903, 6; "Navy's Winter Maneuvers," *Washington Post,* October 28, 1903.

130. "Transfer of Guantánamo," *New York Times,* November 12, 1903, 1.

131. Squiers to Hay, RG 45, Subj. File to 1901, PB-Bases, Guantánamo Bay, Cuba, Box 5, no. 11045–56, National Archives.

Chapter Four. The First Overseas U.S. Base

1. Stephen Bonsal, *The American Mediterranean* (New York: Moffat, Yard, 1912), 131.

2. According to Steven Ross, the Joint Board, established in 1903, did not engage in independent planning, but acted as the final reviewing authority for plans submitted by the respective services. Steven T. Ross, *American War Plans 1890–1939* (London: Frank Cass, 2002), x.

3. Department of the Navy, *Annual Reports of the Navy Department for the Year 1903: Report of the Secretary of the Navy* (Washington, D.C.: Government Printing Office, 1903), 15–16.

4. Harold Sprout and Margaret Sprout, *The Rise of American Naval Power, 1776–1918* (Princeton, N.J.: Princeton University Press, 1939), 261.

5. For a comprehensive discussion of the 1904 House and Senate debates, see Bradley M. Reynolds, "Guantánamo Bay, Cuba: The History of an American Naval Base and Its Relationship to the Formulation of United States Foreign Policy and Military Strategy toward the Caribbean, 1895–1910" (Ph.D. diss., University of Southern California, 1982), 264–279.

6. The objections raised by many members of Congress to funding Guantánamo indicate not only a lack of appreciation for the strategic concerns that had motivated Mahan, Roosevelt, and others but also an ignorance of the high costs of building,

equipping, and maintaining a first-class navy, particularly in an era of rapidly evolving naval and ordnance technologies.

7. Ronald Spector, *Admiral of the New Empire: The Life and Career of George Dewey* (Baton Rouge: Louisiana State University Press, 1974), 168–169. According to Jeffery Dorwart, following the outbreak of the Russo-Japanese War and especially after the attack on Port Arthur, the Office of Naval Intelligence, the Naval War College, and the General Board all began to focus more on the Pacific region with particular attention to the potential Japanese threat to U.S. possessions. Jeffery M. Dorwart, *The Office of Naval Intelligence: The Birth of America's First Intelligence Agency* (Annapolis, Md.: Naval Institute Press, 1979), 79–82. Moreover, Congress authorized $826,395 to build the base at Subic Bay and an additional $700,000 for the U.S. Army to fortify it. William Reynolds Braisted, *The United States Navy in the Pacific, 1897–1909* (Austin: University of Texas Press, 1958), 175.

8. Richard D. Challener, *Admirals, Generals, and American Foreign Policy, 1898–1914* (Princeton, N.J.: Princeton University Press, 1973), 84. Sims, who would command the Atlantic Fleet in World War I, was never a proponent for establishing forward naval bases, particularly at the expense of building larger ships. His highly technical article advocating the construction of a fleet of large modern battleships never addressed the need for coaling or naval stations. It did, however, advocate the concentration of heavy fighting ships under one command in the Atlantic region in peacetime to be dispersed thereafter in squadrons "to meet the requirements of the situation." William S. Sims, "The Inherent Tactical Qualities of All Big Gun, Large Calibre Battleships of High Speed, Large Displacement, and Gun-Power," *Proceedings of the United States Naval Institute* 32 (December 1906): 1337–1366.

9. Donald Yerxa, *Admirals and Empire: The United States Navy and the Caribbean, 1898–1945* (Columbia: University of South Carolina Press, 1991), 29. Roosevelt also absorbed this lesson. In early 1909, he would warn his successor, Taft: "Dear Will, One closing legacy. Under no circumstances divide the battleship fleet between the Atlantic and Pacific Oceans prior to the finishing of the Panama Canal." Taft honored the legacy; he did not divide the fleet. *The Letters of Theodore Roosevelt*, vol. 6, ed. Elting E. Morison (Cambridge, Mass.: Harvard University Press, 1951), 1543. Mahan believed that any division of the U.S. Fleet would be suicidal, especially when Germany was following the lead of Britain and the United States in building an "all big gun" battleship fleet. In an article published in *Collier's Weekly* in 1909, Mahan predicted that within the next three years the German Navy would have a stronger fleet than the United States. Cited in John H. Maurer, "American Naval Concentration and the German Battle Fleet, 1900–1918," *Journal of Strategic Studies* 6 (June 1983): 162.

10. In Navy Secretary Meyer's annual report for 1911, for example, he mentioned that in January the Atlantic Fleet had taken advantage of its passage from the English Channel to Guantánamo to work out a scouting or search problem with the battleship fleet acting as the "enemy" and the armored cruiser and a division of destroyers constituting the scouting force. The course and speed of the "enemy" was unknown to the scouts, who succeeded in locating and tracking the movements of the "enemy" by devising effective scouting tactics and using wireless communication. According to Meyer, "The entire fleet [then] spent two months at Guantánamo . . . during which many valuable exercises in battle tactics were worked out." Department of the Navy, *Annual Reports of the Navy Department for the Year 1911: Report of the Secretary of the Navy* (Washington, D.C.: Government Printing Office, 1911), 33–34.

11. On December 19, 1903, Moody informed the House Naval Affairs Committee that the Navy Department had prepared an estimate for the complete development of Guantánamo as a navy yard. According to Moody, the total estimated cost was $12 million.

12. Reynolds, "Guantánamo Bay," 281–282.

13. "Dewey at Guantánamo," *Washington Post,* February 28, 1904, 6.

14. General Board to the Secretary of the Navy, May 2, 1904, General Board (GB) File 406, National Archives; Dewey to the Secretary of the Navy, May 19, 1904, GB File 406, National Archives. See also "Dewey to Take Command," *New York Times,* October 13, 1904, 6; "Dewey to Stay at Home," *New York Times,* February 28, 1905, 1.

15. In the meantime, Paul Morton had replaced William Moody on July 1, 1904, as secretary of the navy. In important ways all of the secretaries of the navy who served under Theodore Roosevelt were less effective as naval spokesmen and policy-makers than their immediate predecessors. This was primarily attributable to personality clashes with senior naval officers and the reality that both congressional leaders and professional naval officers looked more to Roosevelt or to Elihu Root, who had succeeded John Hay as secretary of state, for guidance and major policy decisions. Of Roosevelt's naval secretaries, Moody served the longest, from May 1, 1902, to June 30, 1904. Each of the others, Morton, Charles Bonaparte, Victor Metcalf, and Truman Newberry, served less than two years, with Newberry in the post for slightly more than three months.

16. As indicated later in this chapter and in Chapter 5, the ambitious recommendations of the Swift Board would only be implemented decades after they were proposed. Reynolds, "Guantánamo Bay," 287–290. For public notices see, for example, "Proposals," *New York Times,* December 29, 1905, 10.

17. *Letters of Theodore Roosevelt,* vol. 4, 1080–1081.

18. Ibid., 1097, 1011.

19. Ibid., 1136.

20. The request for funding for Guantánamo in the proposed naval budget for 1906–1907 fared even worse, as did all appropriations sought by the Bureau of Yards and Docks. Congress cut $6,200,000 from the $9 million requested and deleted the entire amount designated for Guantánamo. It also cut an additional $20,000 intended for Guantánamo from the Budget of the Bureau of Steam Engineering. Reynolds, "Guantánamo Bay," 314.

21. Commander in Chief of the Atlantic Fleet to all Captains of the Fleet, February 22, 1905, GB File 406, National Archives. Southerland to the Commander in Chief of the Atlantic Fleet, March 16, 1905, ibid.

22. Cowles to the Commander in Chief of the North Atlantic Fleet, March 17, 1905, GB File 406, National Archives; Rogers to the Commander in Chief of the North Atlantic Fleet, March 19, 1905, ibid.

23. General Board to the Secretary of the Navy, April 26, 1905, General Board File 406, National Archives.

24. Rogers to the Secretary of the Navy, May 5, 1906, RG 80, General Correspondence 1897–1915, Box 489, No. 11034-294, National Archives. General Board to the Secretary of the Navy, June 20, 1906, ibid. See also Reynolds, "Guantánamo Bay," 305–319.

25. Enrique Messo (Mayor of Santiago) to Ackerman, May 18, 1907, General Correspondence 1897–1915, RG 80, General Records of the Navy, Box 489, no. 11045-376, National Archives.

26. In his annual message to Congress on December 3, 1912, President William Taft announced: "There has been under discussion with the Government of Cuba for some time the question of the release by this Government of its lease-hold rights at Bahía Honda . . . and the enlargement, in exchange therefore, of the naval station which has been established at Guantánamo Bay. As the result of the negotiations . . . an agreement has been reached . . . upon terms which are entirely fair and equitable to all parties concerned." Department of State, *Papers Relating to the Foreign Relations of the United States 1912* (Washington, D.C.: Government Printing Office, 1919), xxv, 295–297. See also Department of State, *Papers Relating to the Foreign Relations of the United States 1911* (Washington, D.C.: Government Printing Office, 1916), 110–126; Department of State, State Decimal File (SDDF), Beaupré to Knox, January 22, 1913, RG 59, 811.34537/117; State Decimal File, National Archives; Beaupré to Knox, January 28, 1913, Record Group (RG) 59, 811.34537/119, National Archives; State Decimal File, Roosevelt to Crowder, July 29, 1921, File 811.345/135, National Archives.

27. Lester D. Langley, *The Cuban Policy of the United States: A Brief History* (New York: Wiley, 1968), 144–145.

28. By 1922, U.S. Ambassador Enoch Crowder estimated U.S. investment there to be approximately $15 million. Ibid. See also Janet Delavan Frost, "Cuban-American Relations Concerning the Isle of Pines," *Hispanic American Historical Review* 11, no. 3 (August 1931): 336–350.

29. In the two treaties, negotiated by Hay and British Ambassador Sir Julian Pauncefote, Great Britain acknowledged the unilateral right of the United States to build an isthmian canal and also to police and fortify the waterway. In return, the United States promised fair and equitable treatment for all canal traffic.

30. Fisher quoted by Samuel F. Wells Jr., "British Strategic Withdrawal from the Western Hemisphere, 1904–1906," *Canadian Historical Review* 49 (December 1968): 336–356. Biographer Ruddock Mackay indicates that Fisher's views on possible war scenarios changed over time. In 1901, he told Assistant Director of Naval Intelligence Prince Louis of Battenberg that war with France, or with the Dual Alliance of France and Russia, must be considered. By 1908, he ranked war with Germany as most likely, but also raised the distant possibility that Britain might have to contend with a German-U.S. naval alliance. Ruddock F. Mackay, *Fisher of Kilverstone* (Oxford: Clarendon, 1973), 257–403.

31. Wells argues that financial pressures to reduce or eliminate costly garrisons in Canada and the West Indies and return naval squadrons to home waters were determinant, "not sentiments of friendship toward America." Wells, "British Strategic Withdrawal," 339.

32. Fisher to Beresford, personal letter, February 27, 1902, in Arthur J. Marder, ed., *Fear God and Dread Nought: The Correspondence of Admiral of the Fleet Lord Fisher of Kilverstone,* vol. 1 (London: Cape, 1953), 233–234.

33. Richard Hough, *First Sea Lord: An Authorized Biography of Admiral Fisher* (London: Allen & Unwin, 1969), 136–137. Yerxa, *Admirals and Oceans,* 8. See also Ruddock Mackay, "The Admiralty, the German Navy, and the Redistribution of the British Fleet, 1904–1905," *Mariner's Mirror* 56 (August 1970): 341–346.

34. Arthur J. Marder, *The Anatomy of British Sea Power: A History of British Naval Policy in the Pre-Dreadnought Era, 1880–1905* (Hamden, Conn.: Archon, 1964), 443–445. In his thoughtful study *A Navy Second to None,* George Davis attributed the strengthening of Anglo-American relations to initiatives taken by the

McKinley administration between 1898 and 1901 generally aimed at forcing overt European imperialists, namely Spain, Russia, and Germany, to withdraw from the Western Hemisphere. Davis writes, "The outcome was . . . a genuine cordiality toward Great Britain in the United Sates and a collaboration between the two powers, which took on the appearance of an unwritten alliance. In such circumstances naval rivalry between the two States was inconceivable and each looked upon the increased sea power of the other with approval." George T. Davis, *A Navy Second to None: The Development of Modern Naval Policy* (New York: Harcourt, Brace, 1940), 114.

35. Jan Morris, *Fisher's Face* (London: Viking, 1995), 123–124.

36. Ruddock F. Mackay, "The Admiralty, the German Navy, and the Redistribution of the British Fleet," 341–346.

37. Wells, "British Strategic Withdrawal," 356.

38. Hugh Tomas, *Cuba: The Pursuit of Freedom* (New York: Harper & Row, 1971), 473–475.

39. *Letters of Theodore Roosevelt,* vol. 5, 399–402.

40. Department of State, *Papers Relating to the Foreign Relations of the United States 1906* (Washington, D.C.: Government Printing Office, 1909), 473–476.

41. Allen Reed Millett, *The Politics of Intervention: The Military Occupation of Cuba, 1906–1909* (Columbus: Ohio State University Press, 1968), 89.

42. James Frederick Lloyd, "The Political Significance of the United States Naval Base, Guantánamo Bay, Cuba" (M.A. thesis, University of Southern California, 1966), 48.

43. Millett, *Politics of Intervention,* 101–102; William H. Taft and Robert Bacon, "Report of What Was Done under the Instructions of the President in Restoring Peace in Cuba," *Annual Reports of the War Department, 1906* (Washington, D.C.: Government Printing Office, 1906), Appendix E, 444–468. Charles E. Magoon succeeded Taft as provisional governor. Magoon was widely disliked and condemned by such prominent Cuban writers as Carlos Trelles as being venal and corrupt. On the contrary, according to historians Hugh Thomas and Charles Chapman, Magoon was personally honest and a fairly effective administrator. His most controversial action was to appoint ex-revolutionary Liberals as well as Moderates to government posts in an effort to achieve a political balance. As both Thomas and James F. Lloyd have found, Magoon tried to create a U.S. type of civil service bureaucracy without U.S. standards or U.S. laws to regulate it. As a consequence, corruption became more widespread. Hugh Thomas, *Cuba: The Pursuit of Freedom* (New York: Harper & Row, 1971), 482–485; Charles E. Chapman, *A History of the Cuban Republic: A Study in Hispanic American Politics* (New York: Macmillan, 1927), 233; Lloyd, "Political Significance of the U.S. Naval Base, Guantánamo," 47–48.

44. Pillsbury to Dewey, September 27, 1906, and Dewey to Pillsbury, October 2, 1906, Department of the Navy, GB File 406, National Archives.

45. Theodore Roosevelt most clearly expressed his views on the vital need for powerful forts to control a maritime region in a personal letter he wrote many years later to Cowles after learning that British Ambassador Lord Bryce had asked Cowles, "Against whom was the United States fortifying the Panama Canal?" An astonished Roosevelt suggested that Cowles, in turn, ask Bryce, "What is he fortifying Gibraltar against? As for saying that we could protect it [the canal] with a fleet, this is such nonsense that I cannot understand an ex-member of the British Cabinet uttering it. The one thing a fleet should never be used for is as a substitute for fortifications. A

fort is placed so as to leave the fleet footloose." Roosevelt to Cowles, October 27, 1911, Theodore Roosevelt Collection, Houghton Library, Harvard University.

46. Even though the U.S. government did not act quickly to fortify Guantánamo and to transform it into a first-class naval station as Cowles requested, it would be wrong to conclude that such well-considered advocacy fell on deaf ears. As congressional testimony, it became part of the official record. Moreover, as illustrated elsewhere in this book, copies of published articles and other recorded statements by high-ranking naval officers to acquire and develop Guantánamo were often filed to be read and used by subsequent policymakers. Statement of Rear Admiral William S. Cowles, Chief of the Bureau of Equipment before the House Committee on Naval Affairs, December 13, 1906, U.S. House Committee on Naval Affairs, 59th Cong., 2nd sess., no. 46, Document 4, 108–110.

47. Guantánamo City, previously known as Santa Catalina de Guantánamo, is an historic urban center in southeastern Cuba and is the capital of Guantánamo (formerly Oriente) Province. Because it is about fifteen kilometers north of Guantánamo Bay, after 1903 many of the Cuban workers at the naval base commuted from Guantánamo City.

48. Reynolds, "Guantánamo Bay," 342–344.

49. Robley D. Evans, *An Admiral's Log, Being Continued Recollections of Naval Life* (New York: Appleton, 1910), 332.

50. Reynolds, "Guantánamo Bay," 347.

51. *Letters of Theodore Roosevelt*, vol. 6, 950–951, 956. For the impact of the voyage of the White Fleet on naval thinking about colliers and coaling stations, see James L. Abrahamson, "The Military and American Society, 1881–1922" (Ph.D. diss., Stanford University, 1977), 317–318.

52. Evans, *An Admiral's Log*, 333, 341.

53. Stephen Bonsal, *The American Mediterranean*, 33.

54. The Jamaica disaster or "Swettenham incident" of 1907 is frequently overlooked by historians of the Caribbean and Roosevelt scholars. It was covered in considerable detail at the time by the *New York Times*, the *Washington Post*, and the Jamaica *Gleaner*, and is the subject of historical study by William N. Tilchin in "Theodore Roosevelt, Anglo-America Relations and the Jamaica Incident of 1907," *Diplomatic History* 19, no. 3 (Summer 1995): 385–405. See also William N. Tilchin, *Theodore Roosevelt and the British Empire* (New York: St. Martin's, 1997), 117–168.

55. Washington also responded quickly. On January 17, the U.S. House of Representatives unanimously passed an emergency appropriations bill authorizing the president of the United States to distribute clothing, medicines, and other necessary articles from "the stores of the naval establishment" to Jamaica's earthquake victims. Secretary of Commerce Victor Metcalf, acting on his own authority, telegraphed Admiral Evans to order the supply ship *Celtic*, which was under way to Guantánamo, to proceed to Kingston and turn over its full cargo of supplies to those in need. "Aid for Quake Sufferers," *New York Times*, January 18, 1907, 3.

56. The *Yankton* arrived from Guantánamo on the afternoon of January 18 with additional medical supplies, which apparently were not needed because the Kingston and U.S. hospitals were "fully stocked." Tilchin, *Theodore Roosevelt and the British Empire*, 130.

57. The normal steaming time from Guantánamo to Kingston was approximately

twelve hours, but it obviously took additional time to load the provisions and to assemble the relief mission.

58. "Kingston Is Thankful," *Washington Post,* January 25, 1907, 2; "Swettenham Accepts Aid," *Washington Post,* January 29, 1907, 13.

59. "Orders U.S. Tars from Kingston," *Washington Post,* January 21, 1907, 1.

60. Ernest Zebrowski Jr., *The Last Days of St. Pierre: The Volcanic Disaster That Claimed Thirty Thousand Lives* (New Brunswick, N.J.: Rutgers University Press, 2002), 6–9, 201–202. According to members of the National Geographic Society who sailed to Martinique and St. Vincent on the *Dixie*, Congress had actually voted for $200,000 in supplies to aid the suffering West Indians. "The National Geographic Society Expedition to Martinique and St. Vincent," *National Geographic* 13, no. 6 (June 1902): 183–184.

61. "Conditions the *Dixie* Found at Martinique," *New York Times,* June 4, 1902, 8.

62. 60th Cong., 2nd sess., *Congressional Record* 43, pts. 2–3 (December 12, 1908): 1123–1302, 2120, 2199–2366. See also Reynolds, "Guantánamo Bay," 371.

63. Ibid., 2433–2436; Robert M. La Follette, *La Follette's Autobiography: A Personal Narrative of Political Experiences* (Madison: University of Wisconsin Press, 1968), 168–170.

64. Knox, whose approach to foreign policymaking became known as "dollar diplomacy" because of its emphasis on securing commercial and trade agreements favorable to U.S. interests, viewed the Caribbean region and Cuba in much the same way as had Roosevelt and Root.

65. Spector, *Admiral of the New Empire,* 180; Paolo E. Coletta, *The American Naval Heritage in Brief* (Lanham, Md.: University Press of America, 1978), 169.

66. Department of the Navy, *Annual Reports of the Navy Department for the Year 1909: Report of the Secretary of the Navy,* 30.

67. As Harold and Margaret Sprout have succinctly stated, "Hard times, intersectional warfare (over tariff issues), and intraparty strife hardly produced a favorable atmosphere in which to launch a great naval program." Sprout and Sprout, *The Rise of American Naval Power,* 286.

68. *The Letters and Papers of Alfred Thayer Mahan,* vol. 3, ed. Robert Seager II and Doris D. McGuire (Annapolis, Md.: Naval Institute Press, 1975), 352–357.

69. Department of the Navy, *Annual Reports of the Navy Department for the Year 1910: Report of the Secretary of the Navy* (Washington, D.C.: Government Printing Office, 1910), 32.

70. Ibid. Meyer also recommended that Key West be retained as a supply base and for quick repairs, especially for small gunboats and torpedo craft in Caribbean waters, but he saw it as an auxiliary base subordinate to Guantánamo.

71. Taft acknowledged that the closing of domestic navy yards and the transfer of their equipment to Guantánamo would "arouse local opposition," but he considered it "axiomatic that in legislating in the interest of the Navy, and for the general protection of the country by the Navy, mere local pride or pecuniary interest in the establishment of a navy-yard or station ought to play no part." William H. Taft, "Annual Report to Congress," Department of State, *Papers Relating to the Foreign Relations of the United States 1910,* xlvi–xlvii.

72. M. A. DeWolfe Howe, *George von Lengerke Meyer: His Life and Public Service* (New York: Dodd, Mead, 1919), 481.

73. Department of State, *Papers Relating to the Foreign Relations of the United States 1911,* 112–113.

74. On January 11, 1913, Secretary Knox informed Minister Beaupré that in the English text of the new agreement, with reference to enlarging the perimeter of Guantánamo, in paragraph 11 the word "northwestern" had mistakenly been substituted for "northeastern"—an error that was not in the Spanish version. On January 21, 1913, Minister Beaupré replied that the error had been appropriately corrected and sanctioned by the initials of Sanguily and himself. Department of State, *Papers Relating to the Foreign Relations of the United States 1911*, 114–126; *Papers Relating to the Foreign Relations of the United States 1912*, 295–297; *Papers Relating to the Foreign Relations of the United States 1913*, 353.

75. Mary Ellene Chenevey McCoy, "Guantánamo Bay: The United States Naval Base and Its Relationship with Cuba" (Ph.D. diss., University of Akron, 1995), 70–71. If the treaty had been approved, it would have solved the water problem at Guantánamo by expanding the base's perimeter to the middle of the Yateras River (see Appendix C of this book for the tentative treaty). Chapman mistakenly accepted the tentative treaty of December 27, 1912, as definitive. See Chapman, *A History of the Cuban Republic*, 157.

76. For a penetrating analysis of the racial, political, and socioeconomic aspects of this rebellion, see Louis A. Pérez Jr., "Politics, Peasants, and People of Color: The 1912 'Race War' in Cuba Reconsidered," *Hispanic American Historical Review* 66, no. 3 (August 1986): 509–539.

77. Beaupré to Knox, Department of State, *Papers Relating to the Foreign Relations of the United States 1912*, 245.

78. In his cable, Knox stated explicitly that the landing of marines "has been taken as a measure for protection only, and not for the purpose of putting down the insurrection, *which is clearly the duty of Cuba*." "U.S. Army Ready to Invade Cuba," *New York Times*, June 8, 1912, 1; Department of State, Memorandum of the Solicitor for the Department of State, *Right to Protect Citizens in Foreign Countries by Landing Force*, 3rd rev. ed. (Washington, D.C.: Government Printing Office, 1934), 98–101.

79. "U.S. Army Ready to Invade Cuba," 1.

80. Yerxa, *Admirals and Empire*, 36–50. See also George W. Baker Jr., "The Caribbean Policy of Woodrow Wilson, 1913–1917" (Ph.D. diss., University of Colorado, 1961), 193–199.

81. Edward Ellsberg, "Naval Strength in Naval Bases," in *Proceedings of the United States Naval Institute* 39 (September 1913): 975–980. Ellsberg was commissioned to the U.S. Navy in 1914 and served until 1951, retiring as a rear admiral. During World War II, he became the navy's expert on undersea salvage and rescue operations. Writing was a lifelong hobby for Ellsberg. He published numerous articles and books, one of which became the basis for the movie *Hells Below*, which starred Robert Montgomery.

82. Biographer Frank Freidel records that, as a Christmas present in 1897, Franklin Roosevelt received a copy of Mahan's *Influence of Sea Power upon History*, and, for his sixteenth birthday, Mahan's newly published *The Interest of America in Sea Power, Present and Future*. According to Freidel, Roosevelt cited Mahan in a school debate on the question of whether Hawaii should be annexed. Arguing the negative position, Roosevelt asserted that because the United States already had a coaling station at Pearl Harbor, there was no need to annex the island. Frank Freidel, *Franklin D. Roosevelt: The Apprenticeship*, vol. 1 (Boston: Little, Brown, 1952), 46–47.

83. *Letters of Theodore Roosevelt*, vol. 7, 779.

84. For the text of this brief but in-depth exchange of letters between Roosevelt and Mahan, see "Roosevelt-Mahan Correspondence," in Richard W. Turk, *The Ambiguous Relationship: Theodore Roosevelt and Alfred Thayer Mahan* (Westport, Conn.: Greenwood, 1987), 166–172. See also Captain W. D. Puleston, *Mahan* (New Haven, Conn.: Yale University Press, 1939), 348.

85. Mahan's article appeared in the *North American Review* 200, no. 706 (September 1914): 406–417. In analyzing the impact Mahan had on Franklin, Freidel concluded that "the greatest exponent of sea power died without having met his greatest disciple. However, Roosevelt already had amply demonstrated his faith in Mahan's theories; a time was to come when he would put them into execution on a global scale." Freidel, *Franklin D. Roosevelt*, 233–235, 410: For Mahan's obituary, see the *New York Times,* December 2, 1914, 1, 12; see also the *Washington Post,* December 2, 1914, 8.

86. The Office of Naval Intelligence devised the first War Plan Black in 1900, which the Naval War College and the General Board repeatedly revised and updated in 1905, 1910, 1913, 1915, and 1916. See Ross, *American War Plans,* 54, 60–61, 63–65.

87. In 1917, fears of German expansion into the Caribbean prompted the United States to purchase the Danish West Indies, which were renamed the U.S. Virgin Islands.

88. Yerxa, *Admirals and Empire,* 59–64.

89. Fisherman's Point would later become the site for the McCalla Airfield.

90. *Annual Reports of the Navy Department for the Year 1913: Report of the Secretary of the Navy,* 17–18. During the early war years, there was some increase in the intensity of marine and naval training at Guantánamo as well as the introduction of more aircraft and practice in detecting submarines. It was not until 1917, however, that Guantánamo would receive congressional appropriations sufficient to build more piers and docks. Reynolds, "Guantánamo Bay," in *United States Navy and Marine Corps Bases Overseas,* ed. Paolo E. Coletta (Westport, Conn.: Greenwood Press, 1985), 149.

91. Assistant Secretary to the Navy Department, June 9, 1914, GB File 406, National Archives.

92. George A. Reeder to Josephus Daniels, April 17, 1914, Papers of Josephus Daniels, Container 519, Reel 37, Manuscript Division, Library of Congress.

93. General Board to Secretary of the Navy, Memorandum to Accompany the General Board's Letter No. 404, March 4, 1916, Serial No. 472, GB File 1900–1917, Box 17, National Archives.

94. Memorandum of the Solicitor for the Department of State, in *Right to Protect Citizens in Foreign Countries by Landing Force,* 24–25.

95. According to historian Leo Meyer, a national census taken in 1919 reported only 477,786 eligible voters. Leo Meyer, "The United States and the Cuban Revolution of 1917," *Hispanic American Historical Review* 10, no. 2 (May 1930): 140.

96. This was the height of the harvest season for sugar cane, which, because of wartime demand, was selling at a high price. Ibid., 142.

97. Meyer makes the important point that it is difficult to comprehend why the Liberals revolted *before* the elections instead of waiting for the results. He also observes that their rush to violence undermined sympathy for their cause within the Wilson administration. Meyer, "The United States and the Cuban Revolution of 1917," 144–145. See also Baker, "The Caribbean Policy of Woodrow Wilson," 359–362; Harry George Mellman, "The American Policy of Intervention in the Caribbean" (Ph.D. diss., University of Illinois, 1940), 139–143.

98. As late as February 16, 1917, Liberal Cuban leaders Raimundo Cabrera and Orestes Ferrera, who had gone to New York, wrote to Secretary Lansing that the Liberal Party would welcome the mediation of the president of the United States or any other senior U.S. official to end the crisis. There is no available record indicating that Secretary Lansing answered this request. Raimundo Cabrera, *Mis Malos Tiempos* (Havana, Cuba: El Siglo 20, 1920), 125–127. Also on February 16, 1917, a front-page story in the *New York Times* reported that reliable sources had informed the *Times* correspondent in Havana that arms and ammunition used in the revolt had been purchased in the United States by Liberal leaders, including Ferrera, and that reports of German involvement in this initiative were groundless. *New York Times,* February 16, 1917, 1.

99. Secretary Lansing to U.S. Minister William González, Department of State, *Papers Relating to the Foreign Relations of the United States 1917*, 356, 368. In Santa Clara Province, for example, the Conservatives managed to win 2,427 votes even though the padded voting list numbered only 2,401 names. On January 22, Minister González reported that the maximum honest vote in Santa Clara could not exceed 1,500 given the fact that neither party had preponderant strength. Ibid., 350.

100. Germany had declared unrestricted submarine warfare on January 31, 1917.

101. David F. Trask, *Captains and Cabinets: Anglo-American Naval Relations, 1917–1918* (Columbia: University of Missouri Press, 1972), 49.

102. Josephus Daniels, The Secret Rendezvous of the Fleet: Our Navy in the World, Draft Manuscript no. 7, Papers of Josephus Daniels, Manuscript Division, Library of Congress.

103. Ibid.

104. Ibid.

105. According to Knox's account, the *Petrel*, which had been condemned and sent to end its days in Guantánamo several years before, had a bottom that was so badly pitted that the Navy Department had issued orders that prohibited taking her into deep waters. Even though the ship had been completely overhauled, Knox steered her close to shore on the forty-mile sail to Santiago so that he could beach the ship if the bottom fell off. Dudley W. Knox, "An Adventure in Diplomacy," *Proceedings of the United States Naval Institute* 52 (February 1926): 273–287.

106. Ibid. These developments in Cuba received only scant coverage in U.S. newspapers, which were almost exclusively devoted to coverage of World War I and the preparations for U.S. entry into that conflict.

107. The U.S. troops sent to Cuba in 1917 and 1918 to protect U.S. sugar interests and for "training purposes" would be stationed there until 1922. *New York Times,* January 26, 27, 1922, 1, 9.

108. Department of State, *Papers Relating to the Foreign Relations of the United States 1917*, 368.

109. Russell H. Fitzgibbons, *Cuba and the United States, 1900–1935* (New York: Russell & Russell, 1964), 159.

110. E. David Cronon, ed., *The Cabinet Diaries of Josephus Daniels, 1913–1921* (Lincoln: University of Nebraska Press, 1963), 106.

111. George Marvin, "Keeping Cuba Libre," *World's Work* (September 1917): 553–567.

112. Robert Lansing, *The War Memoirs of Robert Lansing* (Indianapolis, Ind.:

Bobbs-Merrill, 1935), 311–312. It is worth recalling in this regard that Theodore Roosevelt's decision to sign into law the Commercial Treaty of Reciprocity in 1903, which reduced the tariff on Cuban sugar by 20 percent, had the unforeseen consequence of making Cuba almost totally dependent on the U.S. market and its price for sugar. Luis E. Aguilar, *Cuba 1933: Prologue to Revolution* (New York: Norton, 1972), 24.

113. Department of State, *Papers Relating to the Foreign Relations of the United States 1917*, 404–408.

114. As soon as war was declared, Minister González requested that Washington send an additional 1,000 marines to Guantánamo, where they would be dispatched to protect copper and iron mines and to act as an auxiliary Cuban police force. The Navy Department, however, replied that it had no marines to spare. Department of State, *Papers Relating to the Relations Policy of the United States 1917*, 401–404.

115. Yerxa, *Admirals and Empire*, 69–76.

116. Telegram from V.A., N.A., and W.I. to Vice Admiral Sims, March 18, 1918, No. 902. RG 80, General Records of the Navy, Secretary of the Navy General Correspondence 1916–1926, Box 2766, National Archives.

117. Reynolds, "Guantánamo Bay, Cuba," in *U.S. Navy and Marine Corps Bases Overseas*, ed. Coletta, 150.

118. Military personnel at Guantánamo, however, did not always have access to Guantánamo City and Caimanéra. YMCA official George Reeder described the inadequate recreational facilities at Guantánamo to Daniels and also stated, "There is no city or village within miles of it [Guantánamo] and these are inaccessible to the men, as they should be, as they are most unsightly and disreputable places."

119. The word "mordida" is most commonly used in Mexico, although its meaning is more widely understood. Lamentably, the practice of bribery, or "business as usual," is worldwide.

120. Louis A. Pérez Jr., *On Becoming Cuban: Identity, Nationality, and Culture* (Chapel Hill: University of North Carolina Press, 1999), 238–242.

121. In his memoir, Lansing claimed there was evidence the "Germans were intriguing to break down the Cuban government and that German gold was being furnished to the revolutionists for that purpose." Lansing, *War Memoirs*, 311.

122. Langley, *The Cuban Policy of the United States*, 146–147; Memorandum by the Chief of the Division of Latin American Affairs (Morgan Memo), "Conversation between President Coolidge and President Machado, April 23, 1927," Department of State, *Papers Relating to the Foreign Relations of the United States 1927*, vol. 2 (Washington, D.C.: Government Printing Office, 1942), 525–528; Louis A. Pérez Jr., *Cuba: Between Reform and Revolution* (New York: Oxford University Press, 1988), 244–245; Robert F. Smith, *The United States and Cuba: Business and Diplomacy, 1917–1960* (New York: Bookman, 1960), 120–121.

123. Jenks's book was one in a series of controversial revisionist works called "Studies in American Imperialism" edited by the outspoken historian and sociologist Harry Elmer Barnes of the New School of Social Research. Leland Hamilton Jenks, *Our Cuban Colony: A Study in Sugar* (New York: Vanguard, 1928), 175–176, 194–195. Pérez, who lists Jenks in his bibliography, would agree with his interpretation of the gradual degradation of the Platt Amendment. Pérez writes that the Platt Amendment gradually came to occupy "a central position in the Cuban political system [as] political parties in Cuba sought sanction for their actions in U.S.-Cuban treaty relations . . . [and] Cuban political leaders were powerless to arrest the expansion of

American control over the national system." Louis A. Pérez Jr., *Intervention, Revolution, and Politics in Cuba, 1913–1921* (Pittsburgh, Penn.: University of Pittsburgh Press, 1978), 142–150.

124. Torriente (1872–1957) had a varied and distinguished career as a Cuban revolutionary soldier, lawyer, diplomat, and statesman. He served as ambassador to the United States and to the League of Nations, foreign minister, secretary of state, secretary of the presidency, and, shortly before his death, as a mediator between President Fulgencio Batista and the political opposition. He is largely forgotten in Cuba today, but during his lifetime he had an impeccable reputation for honesty and competence. Thomas, *Cuba*, 609.

125. Torriente took the title of his speech from a personal remark by his friend William Jennings Bryan, who had said, "God has made us neighbors, let justice keep us friends." The Spanish original for the English translation above is: "Cuando se desea molestar a nuestro pueblo se nos dice que la Enmienda Platt . . . convierte la República Cubana en una nación protegida, semi-soberana, mediatizada. . . . Sin Enmienda Platt el Gobierno de Wáshington, cuando ha estimado necesario, ha intervenido para proteger sus intereses en varias naciones americanas; y en cambio, dicha Enmienda les ha servido para que constantemente se les critique en todo el mundo." Cosme de la Torriente, "¡Dios Nos Hizo Vecinos, Que La Justicia Nos Conserve Amigos!" in *Cuba y Los Estados Unidos* (Havana, Cuba: Imp. y Papeleria de Rambla, Bouza, 1929), 314–317.

126. Cosme de la Torriente, "The Platt Amendment," *Foreign Affairs* 8, no 3 (April 1903): 364–378.

127. Guggenheim would later describe the inconsistent U.S. applications of Article Three as follows: "There has been a laissez-faire policy and there has been a tutorial policy; there have been lectures, admonitions, and threats; there has been a policy based on a strict construction of the Platt Amendment; and there has been a policy based on a broad construction." Harry F. Guggenheim, "Amending the Platt Amendment," *Foreign Affairs* 12, no. 3 (April 1934): 449.

128. Harry F. Guggenheim, "Reconsideration of Treaty Relations between the United States and Cuba," Papers of Francis White, Box 14, Financial and Political Matters, Herbert Hoover Presidential Library.

129. Ibid. See also Guggenheim, "Amending the Platt Amendment," 456.

130. Ibid.

Chapter Five. Peace and War: Franklin D. Roosevelt

1. Hugh Thomas, *Cuba: The Pursuit of Freedom* (New York: Harper & Row, 1971), 650–655, 695. See also Bryce Wood, *The Making of the Good Neighbor Policy* (New York: Norton, 1967), 81–103. After his dismissal by the revolutionary junta headed by Sergeant Fulgencio Batista, Grau complained bitterly to visiting scholar Hubert Herring, "I fell because Washington willed it." Hubert Herring, "Another Chance for Cuba," *Current History* 39 (March 1934): 656–660.

2. Luis E. Aguilar, *Cuba 1933: Prologue to Revolution* (New York: Norton, 1972), 98.

3. On May 20, 1937, FDR promoted Welles to undersecretary of state. Benjamin Welles, *Sumner Welles: FDR's Global Strategist* (New York: St. Martin's, 1997), 155–157, 164–166, 179, 197. See also Thomas, *Cuba*, 587–588; Richard Gott, *Cuba: A New History* (New Haven, Conn.: Yale University Press, 2004), 130.

4. Welles, *Sumner Welles,* 171–172. On August 23, 1933, the *New Republic* noted the presence of warships in Havana, but informed its readers that "there were no American troops onboard and we have missed the old familiar refrain that 'the marines have landed and have the situation well in hand.'" The outspoken U.S. writer Ruby Hart Phillips, whose husband was the correspondent in Cuba for the *New York Times,* had severely criticized the U.S. failure to land the marines when Machado fell. "That is the worst blunder so far committed by the present administration in its policy toward Cuba. We want to play the role of 'Good Neighbor,' but one can hardly be a good neighbor to a bunch of incorrigible children living next door." Ruby Hart Phillips, *Cuban Sideshow* (Havana: Cuban Press, 1935), 116.

5. Jane Franklin, *Cuba and the United States: A Chronological History* (Melbourne, Australia: Ocean Press, 1997), 12–13.

6. Welles, *Sumner Welles,* 186–187.

7. Editor, *New Republic,* August 23, 1933, 29; Herring, "Another Chance for Cuba," 660.

8. FDR would later recall that, upon becoming president, he "began to visualize a wholly new attitude toward other American Republics based on an honest and sincere desire to remove from their minds all fear of American aggression—territorial or financial." Quoted by Wood, *The Making of the Good Neighbor Policy,* 130–131.

9. Cordell Hull, *The Memoirs of Cordell Hull,* vol. 1 (New York: Macmillan, 1948), 312–313.

10. Sumner Welles, *The Time for Decision* (New York: Harper, 1944), 198–199. Robert Dallek presents a different rationale for Welles's diplomacy. He argues that Welles had aligned himself too closely with the Céspedes government because he believed that this son of one of Cuba's greatest heroes, who as a respected diplomat had broad experience in Europe and Latin America, was well qualified to govern Cuba. Céspedes, however, had "inspired greater confidence in Welles than in the Cuban people." Thus, the sergeant's mutiny was as much a blow to Welles's prestige as it was an attack on Céspedes. The end result was that Welles refused to recognize the new government of Grau. Robert Dallek, *Franklin D. Roosevelt and American Foreign Policy, 1932–1945* (New York: Oxford University Press, 1979), 63.

11. The Estrada Doctrine originated in a brief public statement made by Mexican Secretary of Foreign Relations Don Genaro Estrada on September 27, 1930, that the Mexican government would no longer grant official recognition to new governments that come to power by coups d'etat or by revolution. Philip C. Jessup, "The Estrada Doctrine," *American Journal of International Law* 25, no. 4 (October 1931): 719–723. See also Dallek, *Franklin D. Roosevelt,* 199.

12. Irwin F. Gellman, *Roosevelt and Batista: Good Neighbor Diplomacy in Cuba, 1933–1945* (Albuquerque: University of New Mexico Press, 1973), 110.

13. Ibid., 120.

14. Sumner Welles Papers, L. A. Files 1919–1943, Box 177, Folder 9, Cuba, Treaty of Relations, Franklin D. Roosevelt Presidential Library.

15. Ibid. This memorandum provides a rare insight into a private conversation between FDR and one of his top aides. In the preface to the collection of FDR's papers, the editor warns that because conversations in the Oval Office were not recorded, it is often difficult for researchers to determine what the president actually said. This document is reproduced in Appendix D of this book.

16. "Cuba Gets Full Independence by New Treaty; U.S. Abrogates Platt

Amendment," *Washington Post,* May 30, 1934, 1–2; "U.S. and Cuba Sign Treaty Abrogating Platt Amendment," *New York Times,* May 30, 1934, 1, 11.

17. Department of State, *Papers Relating to the Foreign Relations of the United States 1934: The American Republics,* vol. 5 (Washington, D.C.: Government Printing Office, 1934), 183–184. This document is also reproduced in Appendix D of this book.

18. Hull, *Memoirs,* vol. 1, 343.

19. Ibid. If any dissents were made in the Cuban Congress in its consideration of the new treaty, particularly in regard to renewing the indeterminate lease of Guantánamo, effusively positive public statements by Cuba's senior diplomats quickly glossed them over. It would be worth examining any records of those deliberations in Cuba's National Archives, particularly since, as Hugh Thomas has found, "the word *plattista* continued to be an adjective of denunciation in the vocabulary of the Cuban Left." Thomas, *Cuba,* 694–695.

20. Jefferson Caffery to Cordell Hull, July 23, 1934, 811.34537/219, General Records of the Department of State, Record Group (RG) 59, State Decimal File, 1933–1944, National Archives.

21. Hull, *Memoirs,* vol. 1, 342.

22. Raymond Buell, a well-known editor and writer, served as research editor of the Foreign Policy Association from 1927 to 1933, when he became its president. An early anti-isolationist, Buell championed a global policy for the United States. Ernest Gruening, who had edited the *Nation* and the *New York Post,* became an early "New Dealer," whom Roosevelt soon appointed to high-level positions in the Department of the Interior. In 1939, Gruening became governor of the Territory of Alaska, a position he held until 1953. In 1959, Gruening was elected Alaska's first U.S. senator and served until 1969.

23. Commission on Cuban Affairs, *Problems of the New Cuba: Report of the Commission on Cuban Affairs* (New York: Foreign Policy Association, 1935), 5.

24. Ibid., 497–500.

25. "Cuba Is Warned of a Dictatorship," *New York Times,* January 27, 1935, 25; "Our Cuban Policy Is Closely Examined," *Washington Post,* January 27, 1935, 1, 5; "Objective Advice on Cuba," *Washington Post,* January 28, 1935, 6; Henry E. Armstrong, "New Light on Conditions in Cuba," *New York Times,* February 3, 1935, Book Reviews 9.

26. In an acknowledgment of the historical precedent, the Reciprocal Trade Agreement of 1934 opens by stating, "The President of the United States of America and the President of the Republic of Cuba, desirous of strengthening the traditional bonds of friendship and commerce between their respective countries . . . [are] granting reciprocal preferential treatment, in continuation of the policy adopted in the Convention of Commercial Reciprocity of 1902." Department of State, *Papers Relating to the Foreign Relations of the United States 1934: The American Republics,* vol. 5, 169–175.

27. "Reciprocal Pact with Cuba Favors Island's Sugar, Rum, and Many of Our Products," *New York Times,* August 25, 1934, 1, 4; Robert F. Smith, *The United States and Cuba: Business and Diplomacy, 1917–1960* (New York: Bookman, 1960), 160–161.

28. David Healy, "One War from Two Sides: The Cuban Assessment of U.S.-Cuban Relations," *Cercles* 5 (2002): 31–38, www.cercles.com. Roig, whose

background included extensive journalistic experience, was the founder and director
of the office of historian of the City of Havana. In 1937, he began editing a documentary series titled *Colección de documentos para la historia de Cuba,* which includes
a valuable collection of the records of the ayuntamiento (municipal government) of
Havana dating from 1550. An outspoken anti-imperialist writer whose intellectual
hero was José Martí, Roig was forced into exile during the Machado regime. For
his recurrent criticisms of "Yankee imperialism," some scholars, including Cubans,
have described Roig as a communist, but this author has not found conclusive evidence to document this claim. Vilá may have best characterized Roig—"a fearless
and passionate enemy of dictatorships and imperialism." For more information on
the scholarly achievements of Roig, see Robert F. Smith, "Twentieth-Century Cuban
Historiography," *Hispanic American Historical Review* 44, no. 1 (February 1964):
44–73; Herminio Portell Vilá, "Historia de la Enmienda Platt: Una Interpretación de
la Realidad Cubana," *Hispanic American Historical Review* 18, no. 2 (May 1938):
209–211.

29. My translation of the following passage: "Dentro de la dolorosa realidad que
representaba para Cuba esa entrega a un poder extraño de parte de su territorio, los
diplomáticos cubanos que negociaron ese convenio procedieron inteligente y patrióti-
camente, obteniendo que en lugar de venta fuese arrendamiento y . . . en vez de las
cuatro estaciones—Guantánamo, Nipe, Cienfuegos y Bahía Honda—que reclamaron
oficialmente en 8 de noviembre de 1902, a sólo dos estaciones navales, Guantánamo
y Bahía Honda." Emilio Roig de Leuchsenring, *Historia de La Enmienda Platt: Una
Interpretación de la Realidad Cubana,* vol. 1 (Havana, Cuba: Cultural, 1935), 189.

30. My translation of Roosevelt's speech: "Situada como Cuba está, no sería possible para este país permitir el abuso estratégico de la Isla por ningún poder militar
extranjero. Es por esta razón que ciertas limitaciones le han sido impuestas sobre su
política financiera, y las estaciones navales han sido concedidas por ella a los Estados Unidos. . . . Ellas están situadas para prevenir toda idea de que haya ninguna
intención de usarlas nunca en contra de Cuba o de ninguna manera que no sea la
protección de Cuba de as altos enemigos extranjeros, para la mejor seguridad de los
intereses americanos en las agues al sur de nosotros." Ibid., 221–222.

31. Ibid., 199, 225–226.

32. Vilá, "Historia de la Enmienda Platt," 209–211.

33. My translation of: "Estación naval y barcos de guerra no son otra cosa que los
perros de presa puestos por el imperialismo yanqui en Cuba para vigilar y mantener,
coaccionando primero, atacando, si fuere necesario, lo que constituye lo realmente
hondo, vital, y grave en el problema de nuestras relaciones con los Estados Unidos: la
absorción y la explotación económicas de Cuba y los cubanos, las que no han aban-
donado ni abandonarán y que se realizan, de acuerdo y connivencia con nuestros
políticos y gobernantes, lacayos de imperialismo, mediante la banca, las empresas
de servicios públicos y artículos de primera necesidad (luz, gas, teléfonos, tranvías,
petróleo, etc.), los grandes centrales azucareros, los mil quinientos millones de inver-
sions yanquis en la Isla." Roig, *Historia de La Enmienda Platt,* vol. 2, 110.

34. Brian Latell, *After Fidel: The Inside Story of Castro's Regime and Cuba's Next
Leader* (New York: Palgrave Macmillan, 2005), 175.

35. Portell Vilá quotes Wood writing to Roosevelt in 1901: "With the control we
have over Cuba, a control which will soon undoubtedly become possession . . . we
shall soon practically control the sugar trade of the world, or at least, a very large
portion of it. I believe Cuba to be a most desirable acquisition for the United States."

Herminio Portell Vilá, *Historia de Cuba en sus Relaciones con los Estados Unidos y España*, vol. 4 (Havana, Cuba: Jesus Montero, 1941), 324.

36. Ibid., 362. See also see Gonzalo de Quesada, "Cuba's Claims to the Isle of Pines," *North American Review* 190, no. 648 (November 1909): 594–604.

37. Ibid., 163. In his later work, Portell Vilá characterized Long as "inept, weak, but well-intentioned." Herminio Portell Vilá, "Historia de la Guerra de Cuba y los Estados Unidos contra España," in *Cuadernos de Historia Habanera Dirigidos por Emilio Roig de Leuchsenring*, vol. 41 (Havana, Cuba: Municipio de la Habana, 1949), 81.

38. My translation of: "El espansionismo norteamericano que se aprovechó de la guerra de Cuba para desplazarse por el Caribe hacia Panamá, atravesar el Pacífico y llegar a Filipinas, para crear una Escuadra de primera clase en enfrentarse con las potencias europeas en Agadir y en la Primera Guerra Mundial, nació con la guerra de Cuba que se transformó en el planteamiento de una nueva fase de la rivalidad internacional." Portell Vilá, "Historia de la Guerra de Cuba y los Estados Unidos contra España," 14.

39. My translation of: "La destrucción de la escuadra de Cervera no resultó de inmediato en la rendición de Santiago de Cuba." Ibid., 237, 253–254 (see also 219, 231). See also Smith, "Twentieth-Century Cuban Historiography," 44–73; Duvon C. Corbitt, "Cuban Revisionist Interpretations of Cuba's Struggle for Independence," *Hispanic American Historical Review* 43, no. 3 (August 1963): 395–404; Roscoe R. Hill, "Historia de Cuba en sus Relaciones con los Estados Unidos y España," *Hispanic American Historical Review* 21, no. 4 (November 1941): 626–627.

40. My translation of: "Para mí, Cuba podia considerarse libre desde el mismo día, que comenzado por americanos y cubanos el ataque a las fortificaciones espanolas de Santiago de Cuba, la Escuadra de Cervera fué destruida por la del Almirante Sampson. . . . Sin barcos de guerra que destruyeran a los espanoles, muy largo tiempo hubiéramos necesitado los cubanos para consequirlo, y a mi juicio tarea si no imposible casi imposible, porque un pueblo pequeño como el nuestro por sí solo no levanta una flota de guerra." Cosme de la Torriente, "Fin de la Dominación de España en Cuba," in *Discurso Leido por el Academía de la Historia de Cuba* (Havana, Cuba: El Siglo 20, 1948), 153–157.

41. Emphasis mine. Torriente does not mention the Nazi takeover of the British-dependent Channel Islands off the Normandy coast, which Germany had invaded on June 30, 1940, fifteen days after the British government had decided that they were of no strategic importance and would not be defended. Germany occupied and heavily fortified these islands until the liberation of May 9, 1945, using them as a holiday destination for German troops serving in France, for slave labor death camps, for propaganda purposes, and to shoot down British and Allied fighter aircraft that came within range. For more information, see Madeline Bunting, *The Model Occupation: The Channel Islands under German Rule, 1940–1945* (London: HarperCollins, 1995); Charles Cruikshank, *The German Occupation of the Channel Islands* (London: Oxford University Press, 1975).

42. Cosme de la Torriente, "Cuba, America, and the War," *Foreign Affairs* 19, no. 1 (October 1940): 145–155. For the revisionist thoughts of modern Cuban historians, see Chapter 8 of this book.

43. Stephens was probably thinking of both the War of 1812 and the significant British support to the Confederacy during the U.S. Civil War. This included the construction of Confederate warships in Liverpool shipyards, the most famous of

which was the *Alabama*. The diplomatic skill of U.S. Ambassador Charles Francis Adams was instrumental in persuading England not to intervene more directly in that conflict.

44. Stetson Conn and Byron Fairchild, *The Framework of Hemisphere Defense* (Washington: Department of the Army, 1960), vii. This volume is in the series United States Army in World War II, edited by Kent Roberts Greenfield.

45. Edward M. Coffman, *The Regulars: The American Army, 1898–1941* (Cambridge, Mass.: Belknap Press of Harvard University Press, 2004), 233.

46. In late March 1933, FDR also froze longevity military pay increases, suspended the traditional bonuses for reenlistment, and cut rental and subsistence allowances to 15 percent below 1928 levels. Robert K. Griffith Jr., *Men Wanted for the U.S. Army: America's Experience with an All-Volunteer Army between the World Wars* (Westport, Conn.: Greenwood, 1982), 111–116, 154.

47. Ross also finds that Congress had never appropriated the funds necessary to build the U.S. Navy up to the limits established by the Washington Naval Treaty of 1922 and that in 1935 the secretary of the navy observed that even "if fully funded, 70 naval vessels would be added to the fleet, but the Navy would still be 78 ships short of treaty strength." Steven T. Ross, *American War Plans 1890–1939* (London: Frank Cass, 2002), 163.

48. Franklin D. Roosevelt, "Address at Chicago," in *The Public Papers and Addresses of Franklin D. Roosevelt,* vol. 6, ed. Samuel L. Rosenman (New York: Macmillan, 1941), 406–410. Because the Japanese had invaded China in July 1937 and heavy fighting was under way in Shanghai, some observers believed that the president's remarks were aimed at Japan, but FDR may well have considered Nazi Germany as dangerous as militaristic Japan. According to historian Norman Graebner, U.S. Ambassador to Switzerland Hugh R. Wilson had explained Hitler's rapid rearmament of Germany to Hull on January 27, 1936, by saying, "The ability of a dictator to devote practically the entire resources of his country to armament cannot be matched by democratic countries in time of peace." On February 8, 1936, U.S. Ambassador to Germany William E. Dodd warned Hull that "the development of the [German] army . . . has brought matters back to a place where Germany is even more dangerous to the world than in 1914." Norman A. Graebner, *Roosevelt and the Search for a European Policy, 1937–1939* (Oxford: Clarendon, 1980), 3.

49. Roosevelt, "Address at Chicago," 408.

50. Roosevelt subsequently confided to his speechwriter and adviser Samuel Rosenman, "It's a terrible thing to look over your shoulder when you are trying to lead—and to find no one there." Samuel I. Rosenman, *Working with Roosevelt* (New York: Harper, 1952), 165–167.

51. Franklin D. Roosevelt, *F. D. R.: His Personal Letters, 1928–1945,* vol. 1, ed. Elliot Roosevelt (New York: Duell, Sloan, and Pearce, 1950), 716–717.

52. Ibid., vol. 2, 767.

53. Franklin D. Roosevelt, Papers as President, President's Secretary File, Box 76, State-Welles, Sumner, October 1937–April 1938, Hyde Park, N.Y. Franklin D. Roosevelt Presidential Library.

54. FDR was outraged by the attack on the *Panay.* He immediately notified Tokyo that he expected a formal apology from the emperor, full compensation for the vessel, and diplomatic assurances that similar attacks would not follow. On December 16, the president told British Ambassador Ronald Lindsay that he wanted "a systematic

exchange of secret information" between U.S. and British naval representatives, and that a blockade of Japan should be instituted after "the next grave outrage." Leahy's immediate response was "to get the Fleet ready for sea, to make an agreement with the British Navy for joint action, and to inform the Japanese that we expect to protect our nationals." To investigate the possibilities for Anglo-American naval cooperation in the Far East, Captain Royal Ingersoll was sent to London on December 26, 1937. In truth, Ingersoll's visit accomplished little. He and British planners sketched out joint plans whereby the Royal Navy would exercise defensive responsibilities in the Western Pacific and the U.S. Fleet would guard the approaches to the Western Hemisphere, but both sides recognized that Britain's growing need to protect its interests in Europe and to defend the empire could restrict or obviate any contribution it could make in the Far East. As Ingersoll later recalled, "We found that there was not a great deal that could be done." John Major, "The Navy Plans for War, 1937–1941," in *In Peace and War: Interpretations of American Naval History, 1775–1978*, ed. Kenneth J. Hagan (Westport, Conn.: Greenwood, 1978), 237–262. See also Dallek, *Franklin D. Roosevelt and American Foreign Policy*, 153–154.

55. Bradley M. Reynolds, "Guantánamo Bay, Cuba," in *United States Navy and Marine Corps Bases Overseas*, ed. Paolo E. Coletta (Westport, Conn.: Greenwood, 1985), 151; U.S. House, Committee on Naval Affairs, *Report of Subcommittee Appointed to Report on Need for Additional Naval Bases and Facilities at Guantánamo Bay, Cuba, San Juan, P.R., and St. Thomas, V. I.*, CIS-NO: 76 H900-0.205, May 18, 1939, 1461–1469.

56. Donald Yerxa, *Admirals and Empire: The United States Navy and the Caribbean, 1898–1945* (Columbia: University of South Carolina Press, 1991), 108; *New York Times*, May 27, 1938, 11; *Washington Post*, May 27, 1938, sec. X, 3.

57. Patrick Abbazia, *Mr. Roosevelt's Navy: The Private War of the U.S. Atlantic Fleet, 1939–1942* (Annapolis, Md.: Naval Institute Press, 1975), 30–31.

58. According to Abbazia, FDR privately described the Munich agreement as "shameful." Indeed, he was prepared to impound German ships in U.S. ports for Allied use. Ibid., 30.

59. Ibid., 29–31; Major, "The Navy Plans for War," 240; Yerxa, *Admirals and Empire*, 107; Ross, *American War Plans*, 166; Dallek, *Roosevelt and American Foreign Policy*, 176.

60. Reynolds, "Guantánamo Bay, Cuba," 151.

61. Franklin D. Roosevelt, Papers as President, Official File, Boxes 49–50, Folders Caribbean Cruise 1 and 2, Franklin D. Roosevelt Presidential Library.

62. Captain D. J. Callaghan, Memo of Comments on Fleet Problem 20 (no date), President's Secretary's File, Box 61, Captain Dan Callaghan folder, Franklin D. Roosevelt Presidential Library. In January 1937, Brazilian President Getúlio Vargas had proposed to FDR that the U.S. government construct a naval base in Brazil for joint use in the event of a war of aggression against the Western Hemisphere. Frank D. McCann Jr., *The Brazilian-American Alliance, 1937–1945* (Princeton, N.J.: Princeton University Press, 1973), 110.

63. For an excellent account of this war game exercise, see Abbazia's chapter "A Mirror to War: Fleet Problem XX," in *Mr. Roosevelt's Navy*, 33–50. See also Yerxa, *Admirals and Empire*, 110–111.

64. Abbazia, *Mr. Roosevelt's Navy*, 46.

65. The new law also provided for the development of Cuba's Guacanayabo Bay

as a reserve training base. This relatively unknown harbor had been used to protect the Atlantic Fleet in the early days after the U.S. entry into World War I. Yerxa, *Admirals and Empire*, 119.

66. Yerxa, *Admirals and Empire*, 120–121; U.S. Department of the Navy, *Building the Navy's Bases in World War II: History of the Bureau of Yards and Docks and the Civil Engineer Corps, 1940–1946*, vol. 2 (Washington, D.C.: Government Printing Office, 1947), 1, 12–14.

67. Jana K. Lipman, *Guantánamo: A Working-Class History between Empire and Revolution* (Berkeley: University of California Press, 2009), 109. See also T. J. English, *Havana Nocturne: How the Mob Owned Havana and Then Lost It to the Revolution* (New York: Morrow, 2008).

68. Interview with Lawrence Clayton, History Department, University of Alabama, January 14, 2009.

69. U.S. Department of the Navy, *Building the Navy's Bases*, 1, 12–14.

70. Martin Gilbert, ed., *The Churchill War Papers: Never Surrender, May 1940–December 1940*, vol. 2 (New York: Norton, 1995), 360–368.

71. Dallek, *Roosevelt and American Foreign Policy*, 243; Henry L. Stimson and McGeorge Bundy, *On Active Service in Peace and War* (New York: Harper, 1948), 318–323. As a young man, Knox had served under Theodore Roosevelt in the Rough Rider regiment.

72. David G. Haglund, *Latin America and the Transformation of U.S. Strategic Thought: 1936–1940* (Albuquerque: University of New Mexico Press, 1984), 215.

73. According to Stimson's memoir, it was FDR who, "on August 13, in a meeting with [Treasury Secretary] Morganthau, Stimson, Knox, and Welles, drafted the essential principles of the agreement." Stimson and Bundy, *On Active Service in Peace and War*, 356. An unpublished account about the destroyers-bases deal by the Attorney General Robert Jackson, who as FDR's legal adviser was intimately involved in this exchange, credits Knox with proposing the acquisition of the Caribbean bases as quid pro quo for lending the destroyers: "Knox, long before he entered the Cabinet, had been pointing out in his newspaper . . . that United States defenses urgently required naval and air bases, particularly in the Caribbean to protect the Panama Canal." It was Jackson's legal opinion that leasing the bases rather than acquiring them by cession or purchase would allow FDR to execute this transfer by executive order. "In my view, the difference between cession and leasing was vital to the President's power to act independently of Congress." Robert H. Jackson, *That Man: An Insider's Portrait of Franklin D. Roosevelt* (New York: Oxford University Press, 2003), 81–103.

74. Yerxa, *Admirals and Empire*, 120.

75. Conn and Fairchild, *Framework of Hemisphere Defense*, 61. According to diplomatic historian Warren Kimball, the British government was displeased with the U.S. news coverage and publicity surrounding the destroyers-bases agreement. At one point Churchill complained to Jackson, "Empires just don't bargain." Jackson replied, "Republics do." Warren F. Kimball, *Forged in War: Roosevelt, Churchill, and the Second World War* (New York: Morrow, 1997), 58.

76. Rear Admiral Yates Stirling Jr., Retired, "Bases 'Vital Need' of American Navy," *New York Times*, August 25, 1940, 4; "Strategy: What the Bases Mean," *Time* 36 (September 16, 1940): 18.

77. Reynolds, "Guantánamo Bay, Cuba," 151. In an erudite analysis of the importance of naval geography in *Life* magazine in November 1940, Major George

Eliot described the Caribbean Sea as the "great connecting link between the Atlantic and Pacific Oceans" and, to the United States, the "most vital sea area." Further, Eliot called Guantánamo Bay the "ideal operating base for the command of the Caribbean." George Fielding Eliot, "The World of Water: Naval Geography Shows Control of the Sea," *Life Magazine* 9 (November 25, 1940): 52–55.

78. Frank O. Hough, Verle E. Ludwig, and Henry I. Shaw Jr., *Pearl Harbor to Guadalcanal: History of U.S. Marine Corps Operations in World War II,* vol. 1 (Washington, D.C.: Historical Branch, G-3 Division, U.S. Marine Corps, 1958), 8.

79. Ibid., 10.

80. Holland M. Smith, *Coral and Brass* (New York: Scribner's, 1949), 67. A *Time* correspondent described how Smith dealt with the transport issue: "Equipment was more of a problem; there wasn't any. Holland Smith started practicing with two ancient ships' launches whose engines frequently did not work. He experimented with boat builder Andrew Jackson Higgins on a fast, high-bottomed boat that could bounce over shallow reefs and hit the land hard enough to get the men into shallow waters. He got Higgins to build a boat that could carry tanks into water shallow enough for them to roll ashore. He tried an amphibious tractor 'alligator' that Donald Roebling had invented for rescue work in the Florida Everglades. For two years the aluminum cleats always came off the alligator. But it was the forerunner of today's amphibious tank." "Old Man of the Atolls," *Time* 43 (February 21, 1944): 25–27.

81. "Navy: General Smith Does a Job," *Time* 37 (May 5, 1941): 23.

82. Smith, *Coral and Brass,* 73–80.

83. "Old Man of the Atolls," 25–27.

84. Smith, *Coral and Brass,* 80. See also Henry I. Shaw Jr., "Opening Moves: Marines Gear Up for War: Atlantic Theater," http://www.nps.gov/archive/wapa/indepth/extContent/usmc/pcn-190-003115-00/sec2a.htm; Jon T. Hoffman, "From Makin to Bougainville: Marine Raiders in the Pacific War," http://www.nps.gov/archive/wapa/indepth/extContent/usmc/pcn-190-003130-00/sec1.htm.

85. Henry L. Stimson, "Memorandum," August 15, 1947, in *On Active Service in Peace and War* (New York: Harper, 1948), 503.

86. Abbazia, *Mr. Roosevelt's Navy,* 145–148.

87. As Donald Yerxa astutely comments, in World War II as in World War I, the true value of the Caribbean was that it functioned "as the locus of several vital sea lanes of communications that funneled strategic resources to the United States and Great Britain." The key difference was that in World War II, for most of 1942, the shipping through these sea lanes was severely disrupted by the German U-boat blitz. Yerxa, *Admirals and Empire,* 130–135.

88. Ibid., 132–133; Clay Blair, *Hitler's U-Boat War: The Hunters, 1939–1942* (New York: Random House, 1996), 436–439.

89. Philip Wylie and Laurence Schwab, "The Battle of Florida," *Saturday Evening Post* 26 (March 11, 1944): 14–15, 52–58.

90. The code name for the U-boat offensive in the Caribbean was Operation Neuland. Yerxa, *Admirals and Empire,* 133–134.

91. Ibid., 134.

92. Fletcher Pratt, "Caribbean Command," *Harper's Magazine* 188, no. 1125 (February 1944): 232.

93. S. W. Roskill, *A Merchant Fleet in War, 1939–1945* (London: Collins, 1962), 175–176.

94. Dan van der Vat, *The Atlantic Campaign: World War II's Great Struggle at Sea* (New York: Harper & Row, 1988), 239–247; Yerxa, *Admirals and Empire*, 136.

95. Samuel Eliot Morison, *History of United States Naval Operations in World War II*, vol. 1, *The Battle of the Atlantic, September 1939–May 1943* (Boston: Little, Brown, 1970), 260.

96. In a memorandum dated October 15, 1942, Stimson indicated that the primary concern of the Caribbean and Southern Patrols was to guard the coastline of Brazil. He wrote, "Secretary Knox, who has just returned from South America, advises that the Brazilian Army and Navy, Admiral Jonas Ingram of the United States Navy (commanding the Caribbean sea patrols), and General Robert L. Walsh of the Army Air Force are working in the closest possible cooperation for the defense of Brazil." Henry L. Stimson, *Prelude to Invasion: An Account Based upon Official Reports by Henry L. Stimson, Secretary of War* (Washington, D.C.: Public Affairs Press, 1944), 21. After the attack on Pearl Harbor, Pan-Am Airways built fifty-five airfields and bases between the United States and South America that converged on Natal in northeast Brazil. The air base in Natal earned its nickname as "the springboard to victory" because it provided a steady flow of men, aircraft, and materiel to the Allies. In November 1942, an article in *Fortune* magazine proclaimed that the threat situation posed by the geographic proximity of northwestern Africa to the bulge of Brazil had been reversed; now it was Natal that was dangerously close to Dakar. McCann, *The Brazilian-American Alliance*, 221–222.

97. Ibid., 260–265; Yerxa, *Admirals and Empire*, 137–138.

98. Wylie and Schwab, "The Battle of Florida," 52; Yerxa, *Admirals and Empire*, 138.

99. Yerxa, *Admirals and Empire*, 140.

100. German submarine commander war diary quoted in Samuel Eliot Morison, *History of Naval Operations in World War II*, vol. 10, *The Atlantic Battle Won, May 1943–May 1945* (Boston: Little, Brown, 1968), 198.

101. "Caribbean Islands Supply Strategic Raw Materials" (Kingston, Jamaica) *Masses*, February 5, 1944, 46. See also Yerxa, *Admirals and Empire*, 142.

102. Fitzroy André Baptiste, *War, Cooperation, and Conflict: The European Possessions in the Caribbean, 1939–1945* (Westport, Conn.: Greenwood, 1988), 160–165. See also Yerxa, *Admirals and Empire*, 142.

103. Baptiste, *War, Cooperation, and Conflict*, 165–166.

104. Fletcher Pratt, "Caribbean Command," 232–241.

105. William H. Minarik, *Sailors, Subs, and Señoritas* (Boston: Brandon, 1968), 30.

106. Reynolds, "Guantánamo Bay, Cuba," 152.

107. Department of State, *Papers Relating to the Foreign Policy of the United States 1941: The American Republics*, vol. 7 (Washington, D.C.: Government Printing Office, 1941), 214–216.

108. Messersmith to Hull, December 20, 1941, 837.00/9068, RG 59. Messersmith had communicated similar sentiments in a personal letter to the exiled Belgian minister of state, Frans J. Van Cauwelaert: "So far as Cuba is concerned, her reaction has been 100 percent, and, of all of the American republics, she is lending us the most complete cooperation." Messersmith to Van Cauwelaert, December 15, 1941, George S. Messersmith Papers, Box 10, Item 1484, Special Collections Department, University of Delaware Library.

109. Gellman, *Roosevelt and Batista*, 201.

110. Messersmith to Welles, July 12, 1942, Messersmith Papers, Box 10, Item 1390.

111. Spruille Braden, "Conditions in Cuba and Our Policies in Respect Thereto," Memorandum to the Policy Committee, Department of State, July 22, 1944, Personal File, Spruille Braden Papers, Rare Book and Manuscript Library, Columbia University.

112. Department of State, *Papers Relating to the Foreign Relations of the United States 1941: The American Republics*, vol. 7, 97–115; *Papers Relating to the Foreign Relations of the United States 1942: The American Republics*, vol. 6 (Washington, D.C.: Government Printing Office, 1942), 253–293. See also Gellman, *Roosevelt and Batista*, 201.

113. Gaylord T. M. Kelshall, *The U-Boat War in the Caribbean* (Annapolis, Md.: Naval Institute Press, 1988), 297.

Chapter Six. The Cold War, Part 1: Dwight D. Eisenhower

1. Memorandum for the President, Subject: Continuation of Diplomatic Relations with Cuba, March 24, 1952, Papers of Harry S. Truman, Central Files, Confidential Files, Containment in Latin America, 29A, Box 1 of 2, Harry S. Truman Library.

2. "U.S. Accepts Government of Batista," *Washington Post*, March 28, 1952, 15.

3. "Strong Man in Cuba," *Washington Post*, March 11, 1952, 8. "Dictator with the People," *Time* 59 (April 21, 1952): 38–46.

4. As Cold War scholar John Gaddis has found, one of the most shocking things to U.S. leaders about the Korean War was the rapidity with which the defense of a small and geographically remote nation—South Korea—had become vital to U.S. security interests: "To allow an underdeveloped nation with no industrial-military capacity to fall under communist control could shake self-confidence throughout the noncommunist world." John Lewis Gaddis, *The Cold War: A New History* (New York: Penguin, 2005), 123.

5. "Cuba Turns Back Russian Couriers," *Washington Post*, March 22, 1952, 5; "Soviet Exit Marks New Cuban Policy," *Washington Post*, April 9, 1952, 12.

6. Louis A. Pérez Jr., "Cuba, 1930–1959," in *Cuba: A Short History*, ed. Leslie Bethell (New York: Cambridge University Press, 1993), 83.

7. Tad Szulc, *Fidel: A Critical Portrait* (New York: Morrow, 1986), 230.

8. Ameringer documents Prío's tolerance of violence and involvement in corruption, and he also calls attention to the administration's few but notable achievements: its support for the performing arts and for freedom of expression. Ameringer writes, "Contradictions abounded. The Auténticos spent $335,828,146 on education . . . yet illiteracy stood at 23.6 percent in 1953. . . . Moreover, the Prío administration undertook to institutionalize honest government . . . through public budgets and standardized accounting procedures." Ameringer's definitive conclusion is that when Prío went into exile, Cuban democracy left with him. "The Auténticos failed the Cuban people miserably, but they gave Cuba a period of freedom it had not experienced before or, up to now, since." Charles D. Ameringer, *The Cuban Democratic Experience: The Auténtico Years, 1944–1952* (Gainesville: University Press of Florida, 2000), 117–119, 183–185.

9. Dwight D. Eisenhower, *Waging Peace, 1956–1961* (Garden City, N.Y.: Doubleday, 1965), 515–539. See also Stephen G. Rabe, *Eisenhower and Latin America: The Foreign Policy of Anti-Communism* (Chapel Hill: University of North Carolina Press, 1988), 1–5, 169–172.

10. Anthony DePalma, *The Man Who Invented Fidel: Castro, Cuba, and Herbert L. Matthews of the* New York Times (New York: Public Affairs, 2006), 80–89.

11. It was generally known that Raúl had been a member of the youth wing of the old Cuban Communist Party. For example, on July 24, 1958, Ambassador Smith, in a dispatch from Havana, mentioned the "Communist influence and penetration in the Raúl Castro group." Dispatch from the Embassy in Cuba to the Department of State, Department of State, *Papers Relating to the Foreign Relations of the United States, 1958–1960: Cuba,* vol. 6 (Washington, D.C.: Government Printing Office, 1991), 161. When Fidel later visited the United States in April 1959, he was asked in a television interview, "Are your brother Raúl and his wife Communists?" Fidel denied the accusation with clever circumlocutions. Raúl also denied it, although less convincingly. According to Brian Latell, who has been analyzing the Castro brothers since 1964, no senior official in the Eisenhower administration gave much attention to Raúl Castro. "Fidel was the only leader of the Cuban Revolution who counted. So why obsess about his brother?" E-mail to the author, June 10, 2006.

12. Latell makes a persuasive argument that by the early 1950s, Fidel had embraced Marxism-Leninism and that he exercised strong influence over Raúl's decision to become a communist. Brian Latell, *After Fidel: The Inside Story of Castro's Regime and Cuba's Next Leader* (New York: Palgrave Macmillan, 2005), 124–128, 148–149.

13. Named in honor of Fidel Castro's failed attack on the Moncada barracks on July 26, 1953.

14. According to U.S. sources, base officials had also identified Frage as a Trotskyite, but had not fired him. Jana K. Lipman, *Guantánamo: A Working-Class History between Empire and Revolution* (Berkeley: University of California Press, 2009), 136–138.

15. Ibid., 138. See also Rigoberto Cruz Díaz's discussion of Cuban base workers who were harshly interrogated and fired for stealing documents and acting as Castro's spies, and were subsequently portrayed as victims of U.S. imperial aggression. Rigoberto Cruz Díaz, *Guantánamo Bay* (Santiago de Cuba: Editorial Oriente, 1977), 141–151.

16. Kidnapping of U.S. Citizens by Cuban Rebels, June–July 1958, Department of State, *Papers Relating to the Foreign Relations of the United States 1958–1960: Cuba,* vol. 6, 6, 117.

17. Wayne Smith's comments are recorded in *Cuba on the Brink: Castro, the Missile Crisis, and the Soviet Collapse,* ed. James G. Blight, Bruce J. Allyn, and David A. Welch (New York: Pantheon, 1993), 168. On March 14, 1958, the U.S. government had suspended the shipment of 1,950 Garand rifles to Cuba and had instructed Smith to tell Batista *not* to use U.S. weapons to maintain internal order, that is, against the rebels. Jorge I. Domínguez, *To Make a World Safe for Revolution: Cuba's Foreign Policy* (Cambridge, Mass.: Harvard University Press, 1989), 11.

18. Ibid.,12; See also Lipman, *Guantánamo,* 139. The special edition of the *Boletín Informativo del Movimiento 26 de Julio* that justified the rebels' reasons for the mass kidnappings included a photograph of a captured U.S. rocket said to contain napalm and a government plane being refueled. See Military Order No. 30—Sus

Causas, Herbert Matthews Papers, Rare Book and Manuscript Library, Columbia University. See also "Cuba Pours Troops into Rebel Areas," *New York Times,* February 13, 1958, 14.

19. Carlos Franqui, *Diary of the Cuban Revolution* (New York: Viking, 1980), 358.

20. Thomas G. Paterson, *Contesting Castro: The United States and the Triumph of the Cuban Revolution* (New York: Oxford University Press, 1994), 61.

21. Secretary Dulles's News Conference of July 1, *Department of State Bulletin* 39, no. 995 (July 21, 1958): 104–110.

22. "Reports on Arms Shipments to Cuba Called Erroneous," *Department of State Bulletin* 39, no. 996 (July 28, 1959): 153.

23. Rebel radio broadcast, July 2, 1958, quoted in Fidel Castro, *Revolutionary Struggle, 1947–1958,* ed. Rolando E. Bonachea and Nelson P. Valdés (Cambridge: Massachusetts Institute of Technology Press, 1972), 384.

24. Franqui, *Diary of the Cuban Revolution,* 364.

25. At a news conference in April 2000 Fidel said, "I knew the bullets that each type of rifle required, how many we had in reserve, and everything. . . . Look, I do not hold people in high regard if they do not take care of details." Foreign Broadcast Information Service, April 27, 2000, quoted in Latell, *After Fidel,* 66, 256.

26. Eisenhower used the NSC as his primary forum for discussing and making major foreign policy decisions. As diplomatic historian Robert Divine has written, "From the outset of his administration, Eisenhower moved to revitalize the National Security Council and thereby to ensure his continuing control over all major foreign policy decisions. . . . The weekly meetings of the NSC revealed Eisenhower's intense interest and concern for foreign policy. CIA Director Allen Dulles normally opened the sessions with an intelligence briefing. . . . Eisenhower followed the discussion closely . . . gradually joining in and expressing his views." Robert A. Divine, *Eisenhower and the Cold War* (New York: Oxford University Press, 1981), 23–24.

27. Peter Kihss, "Brother of Castro Said to Apologize," *New York Times,* July 3, 1958, 1, 7; Allen Dulles, Memorandum of Discussion, Ann Whitman File, NSC Records, Dwight D. Eisenhower Library; Kihss, "Cuba Rebel Calls Captives a Shield," *New York Times,* July 6, 1958, 1, 9.

28. Earl E. T. Smith, *The Fourth Floor: An Account of the Castro Communist Revolution* (Washington, D.C.: Selous Foundation Press, 1991), 142–145.

29. Franqui, *Diary of the Cuban Revolution,* 358. Jules Dubois, *Fidel Castro: Rebel—Liberator or Dictator?* (Indianapolis, Ind.: Bobbs-Merrill, 1959), 277. On July 15, 1958, Eisenhower had ordered U.S. marines into Lebanon to counter a Soviet-backed Muslim revolt aimed at overthrowing the pro-Western government of President Camille Chamoun.

30. Smith, *The Fourth Floor,* 147–148.

31. Ibid., 150.

32. Policy Paper on Cuba, in Department of State, *Papers Relating to the Foreign Relations of the United States, 1958–1960: Cuba,* vol. 6, 186–189.

33. *New York Times,* July 29, 1958, 12.

34. Memorandum from Snow to Herter, July 30, 1958, Department of State, *Papers Relating to the Foreign Relations of the United States, 1958–1960: Cuba,* vol. 6, 174–175.

35. Ibid., 177–179.

36. Telegram from Embassy Havana to Department of State, August 1, 1958;

Memorandum from Deputy Director, Office of Middle American Affairs, to Public Affairs Adviser, August 5, 1958, Department of State, *Papers Relating to the Foreign Relations of the United States, 1958–1960: Cuba,* vol. 6, 180–184.

37. In late October 1958, Fidel took credit for resolving the security problem at Yateras. He claimed that Smith and Batista tried to cause a clash at the aqueduct between the rebels and U.S. marines that would precipitate the intervention of the United States in Cuba's civil war. According to Fidel's rendition, the publicity campaign throughout the Americas against stationing marines at Yateras, plus the "responsible attitude of the rebel forces," produced a diplomatic outcome. Castro, *Revolutionary Struggle,* 201.

38. William F. Dougherty and José "Pepe" Bahía, "Caught between Two Flags" (unpublished manuscript, Guantánamo Bay, Cuba, 1990), 85. Quoted in Mary Ellene Chenevey McCoy, "Guantánamo Bay: The United States Naval Base and Its Relationship with Cuba" (Ph.D. diss., University of Akron, 1995), 202.

39. "Did U.S. 'Give' Cuba to Castro?" *U.S. News & World Report* 49, September 26, 1960, 106–110.

40. Telegram from Embassy Havana to Department of State, November 16, 1958; Memorandum Prepared in Bureau of Intelligence and Research, November 28, 1958; Telegrams between State Department and Havana, November 29, 1958, Department of State, *Papers Relating to the Foreign Relations of the United States, 1958–1960: Cuba,* vol. 6, 257, 272–276. On December 17, 1958, a paper titled "Short-Term Trends in Cuba of Possible Interest" prepared in the Office of Naval Intelligence was circulated within the U.S. Department of the Navy. The paper argued that "whatever government emerged in Cuba would attempt to maintain friendly relations with the United States." It concluded that Fidel Castro was "aware of the strategic importance of the U.S. Naval Base, Guantánamo, and of U.S. desire to avoid political eruptions in its own backyard." It predicted, however, that Fidel would probably demand an increase in rental for the base and possibly request a status of force agreement— which would mean that the cost of the U.S. defense effort, in both monetary and political terms, would almost certainly rise. Department of State, *Papers Relating to the Foreign Relations of the United States, 1958–1960: Cuba,* vol. 6, 297.

41. Memorandum, Discussion at the 392nd Meeting of the National Security Council, December 23, 1958, NSC Series, Box 10, Dwight D. Eisenhower, Papers as President, Ann Whitman File, Dwight D. Eisenhower Library. In the final days of the Batista government, as Raúl Castro's insurgents spread across Oriente Province, Guantánamo once again was in the center of the revolution. Rebels cut off the road to the base, forcing Cuban commuter workers to remain at Guantánamo. The base hospital, at the insurgents' request, treated wounded government troops. In the final days of the revolution, Thomas Paterson recorded that "hundreds of refugees" flocked to the gates as Guantánamo "stood as a U.S. island in a rebel ocean." Paterson, *Contesting Castro,* 200, 214.

42. Fidel entered Santiago de Cuba to seize the Moncada barracks on January 1 and then marched across Cuba, arriving in Havana on January 8.

43. Whereas Smith was a wealthy businessman who had made significant financial contributions to Eisenhower's campaigns, Philip Bonsal was a seasoned diplomat who had previously served as ambassador to Colombia and Bolivia. Bonsal, whose father, Stephen Bonsal, had been one of the U.S. correspondents covering the War of 1898 (see Chapters 3 and 4 of this book), was also knowledgeable about Cuba, having worked for the Cuban Telephone Company in the 1920s and been assigned to the

U.S. Embassy as vice consul from 1938 to 1939. Former diplomat and Cuba expert Wayne Smith has argued persuasively that because Ambassador Smith had openly supported Batista, he "must be held partly responsible for the failure of American policy during that period." Unfortunately, Ambassador Bonsal proved unsuccessful in his efforts to improve U.S. relations with Fidel's government. Wayne S. Smith, *The Closest of Enemies* (New York: Norton, 1987), 18.

44. "Warships to Avoid Cuba," *New York Times*, January 16, 1959, 3.

45. Philip W. Bonsal, *Cuba, Castro, and the United States* (Pittsburgh, Penn.: University of Pittsburgh Press, 1971), 41.

46. Fidel reportedly cashed the first rent check that he received in July 1959 for the lease of Guantánamo in the amount of $ 3,386.25. The lease payments are due annually on July 2. Even though Fidel has steadfastly refused to cash all subsequent checks, the U.S. government has argued that his endorsement of the one check signified his government's ratification of the lease and that ratification renders moot all subsequent accusations of violations of sovereignty or illegal military occupation. Martin J. Scheina, "The U.S. Presence in Guantánamo," *Strategic Review*, 6, no. 4 (Spring 1976): 81–88; see also Jack Raymond, "Pentagon Warns Cuba on Base: Says Rights Are Not Revocable," *New York Times*, October 28, 1959, 4.

47. Memorandum for the President, Subject: Evaluation of the Unofficial Visit to Washington by Prime Minister Fidel Castro of Cuba, by Christian Herter, April 23, 1959, Dulles-Herter Series, Box No. 12, Dwight D. Eisenhower, Papers as President, Ann Whitman File, Dwight D. Eisenhower Library.

48. Editorial Note, Department of State, *Papers Relating to the Foreign Relations of the United States, 1958–1960: Cuba*, vol. 6, 476. In an article written for the *Reader's Digest*, Nixon summarized his initial impressions in this way: "He looked like a revolutionary, talked like an idealistic college professor, and reacted like a communist." Richard M. Nixon, "Cuba, Castro, and John F. Kennedy: Some Reflections on U.S. Foreign Policy," *Readers Digest* 85 (November 1964): 281–284.

49. Smith later told a U.S. Senate subcommittee that he believed Matthews had played a crucial role in bringing Fidel to power. "Three front-page articles in the *Times* in early 1957 written by the editorialist Herbert Matthews served to inflate Castro to world stature and world recognition. Until that time, Castro had been just another bandit in the Oriente Mountains of Cuba." "Did U.S. 'Give' Cuba to Castro?" *U.S. News & World Report*, September 26, 1960, 106–110.

50. Herbert L. Matthews, "Why Latin America Is Vital to Us," *New York Times Sunday Magazine*, April 26, 1959, 17–22.

51. Memorandum from the Assistant Secretary of State for Inter-American Affairs' Special Assistant (Hilton) to the Assistant Secretary of State (Rubottom), Department of State, *Papers Relating to the Foreign Relations of the United States, 1958–1960: Cuba*, vol. 6, 650–651.

52. Tad Szulc, "U.S. Navy Base Gets Along," *New York Times*, November 26, 1959, 20.

53. "A Big U.S. Base under Fire," *U.S. News & World Report*, December 14, 1959, 64.

54. "Gitmo: A Superb Base, An Excuse for Dispute," *Life Magazine* 49, no. 3 (July 18, 1960): 21.

55. Memorandum of Discussion at the 432nd Meeting of the National Security Council, Washington, January 14, 1960, Ann Whitman File, NSC Records, Eisenhower Library.

56. "Navy Intends to Keep Cuba Base, Says Burke," *Washington Post,* January 23, 1960, sec. A, 5.

57. Memorandum of Discussion at the 436th Meeting of the National Security Council, Ann Whitman File, NSC Records, Eisenhower Library; "Castro Aide Defies U.S. to Invade," *Washington Post,* January 27, 1960, sec. A, 12; "Cubans Still Berate U.S., Castro Is Mum," *Washington Post,* January 31, 1960, sec. A, 7.

58. Jane Franklin, *Cuba and the United States: A Chronological History* (Melbourne, Australia: Ocean Press, 1997), 24–25.

59. Samuel E. Belk to Robert Gray, Memorandum, Subject: Cuba, Department of State, *Papers Relating to the Foreign Relations of the United States, 1958–1960: Cuba,* vol. 6, 852–854.

60. The 5412 Committee, also known as the "special group," had been established by Eisenhower in 1955 to determine which covert operations were "proper" and "in the national interest." The members of the committee included the director of the CIA, the national security advisor, the deputy secretaries at the State and Defense Departments, and the chair of the Senate Armed Services Committee. Evan Thomas, *The Very Best Men: The Early Years of the CIA* (New York: Simon & Schuster, 1995), 117.

61. The timing may have been coincidental, but both of these policy-prescriptive papers reached the White House at approximately the same time. "Paper Prepared by the 5412 Committee," Department of State, *Papers Relating to the Foreign Relations of the United States, 1958–1960: Cuba,* vol. 6, 850–851, 861–863.

62. Another perspective was provided by *New York Times* correspondent Ruby Hart Phillips, who reported that the base contributed almost $10,000,000 annually to the domestic economy and that most of the base workers were cognizant of the advantages of working at the base, where the wages were considerably higher than elsewhere in Oriente Province. Ruby Hart Phillips, "Admiral Defends Ouster of Cuban," *New York Times,* March 31, 1960, 3; Philip Bonsal to State Department, March 25, 1960, Department of State, *Papers Relating to the Foreign Relations of the United States, 1958–1960: Cuba,* vol. 6, 874–875; "Stakes at the Base," *Time* 75, no. 13 (March 28, 1960): 38; "Roa to Bonsal and Bonsal to Roa," *Department of State Bulletin* 42, no. 1088 (May 2, 1960): 706–707.

63. Louis A. Pérez Jr., *On Becoming Cuban: Identity, Nationality, and Culture* (Chapel Hill: University of North Carolina Press, 1999), 241–242.

64. "A U.S. Base in Trouble 500 Miles from Home," *U.S. News & World Report,* April 11, 1960, 83–85; Bonsal to State Department, April 23, 1960, Department of State, *Papers Relating to the Foreign Relations of the United States, 1958–1960: Cuba,* vol. 6, 898–899. According to the Cuban chronology prepared by Jane Franklin, on April 4, 1960, "a plane flying out of the U.S. naval base at Guantánamo drops incendiary material in Oriente Province." This "alleged" incident, however, was not reported in the *New York Times* or the *Washington Post* and is not mentioned in any of the documents in *Papers Relating to the Foreign Relations of the United States, 1958–1960: Cuba,* vol. 6. See Franklin, *Cuba and the United States,* 26.

65. "Castro Says Cuba Fired on U.S. Ship," *New York Times,* May 14, 1960, 1; "U.S. Statement on Cuba," *New York Times,* May 15, 1960, 2; "Provocative Actions of the Government of Cuba against the United States Which Have Served to Increase Tensions in the Caribbean Area," Herbert Matthews Papers, Rare Book and Manuscript Library, Columbia University. There were significant economic clashes between Cuba and the United States in summer and fall 1960, in particular, the expropriation

of U.S.-owned oil refineries that had refused to process Soviet oil, the U.S. suspension of Cuban sugar purchases, Castro's nationalization of all U.S.-owned businesses, banks, and industrial and agricultural enterprises in Cuba, and the imposition of the U.S. trade embargo on major exports to Cuba. See Franklin, *Cuba and the United States*, 26–31.

66. Seymour Topping, "Cuba Supported: Khrushchev Vows Aid in Any Move against Guantánamo Base," *New York Times*, July 13, 1960, 1, 3.

67. Hanson W. Baldwin, "Clouds over Guantánamo," *New York Times Sunday Magazine*, August 21, 1960, 20–23.

68. *Congressional Record*, 86th Congress, 2nd sess., September 2, 1960, 6677.

69. According to the U.S. Mission at the United Nations, Castro's speech was interrupted by such loud applause from the Cuban delegation and delegations from various communist countries that it muffled Khrushchev's objection. It was later that a member of the Soviet delegation informed the U.S. delegation what the premier had said. USUN Telegram 822, September 28, 1959, summarized in Department of State, *Papers Relating to the Foreign Relations of the United States, 1958–1960: Cuba*, vol. 6, 1072.

70. "U.S. Navy Determined to Keep Guantánamo Base Despite Castro," *San Diego Union*, October 3, 1960, 6. See also "Burke Says We'll Defend Guantánamo," *Washington Post*, September 27, 1960, sec. A, 5; Interview with Chief of Naval Operations Admiral Arleigh Burke, "We're Powerful—Why Be Fearful?" *U.S. News & World Report* 49 (October 3, 1960): 70–76; Bradley M. Reynolds, "Guantánamo Bay, Cuba," in *United States Navy and Marine Corps Bases Overseas*, ed. Paolo E. Coletta (Westport, Conn.: Greenwood, 1985), 153.

71. "Cuba Sees Threat in U.S. Action," *Washington Post*, October 29, 1960, sec. A, 4; "Defiant Castro Challenges Foes to Invade Cuba," *New York Times*, October 30, 1960, 1.

72. "U.S. Marines Land Near Base," *New York Times*, November 3, 1960, 15; "Guantánamo Defenses Tested," *New York Times*, November 6, 1960, 24.

73. Trumbull Higgins, *The Perfect Failure: Kennedy, Eisenhower, and the CIA at the Bay of Pigs* (New York: Norton, 1987), 65–66.

74. "President Dwight D. Eisenhower Reiterates U.S. Position on Guantánamo Naval Base," *Department of State Bulletin* 42, no. 1118 (November 21, 1960): 780. See also "Statement by the President Regarding the U.S. Naval Base at Guantánamo, Cuba," in *Public Papers of the Presidents of the United States: Dwight D. Eisenhower, 1960–1961* (Washington, D.C.: Government Printing Office, 1961), 822, Document No. 342.

75. "President Scores Regime in Havana," *New York Times*, January 4, 1961, 3. See also "Statement by the President on Terminating Diplomatic Relations with Cuba," in *Public Papers of the Presidents of the United States: Dwight D. Eisenhower, 1960–1961*, 891, Document No. 388.

76. Department of State, *Papers Relating to the Foreign Relations of the United States, 1961–1963: Cuba*, vol. 10 (Washington, D.C.: Government Printing Office, 1997), 2, 6–7.

Chapter Seven. The Cold War, Part 2: John F. Kennedy and Lyndon B. Johnson

1. Initially JFK had voiced a favorable view of Fidel by referring to him as the heir of the Bolivarian tradition in Latin America. Philip W. Bonsal, *Cuba, Castro,*

and the United States (Pittsburgh, Penn.: University of Pittsburgh Press, 1971), 171. JFK's perception of Fidel and other potential threats to U.S. security changed during the presidential campaign as he obtained additional access to highly classified information and received top-level briefings on world developments. John Helgerson, former deputy director of the CIA, wrote in his study of CIA briefings of presidential candidates that on November 2, 1960, Acting CIA Director General Charles Cabell gave JFK a briefing on potential hot spots that included Berlin, the Taiwan Straits, and "possible action by Cuba against Guantánamo." John Helgerson, *CIA Briefings of Presidential Candidates, 1952–1992* (Washington, D.C.: Center for Studies in Intelligence, 1996), introduction to Chapter 3, www.odci.gov. According to JFK's former colleague, Florida senator George Smathers, as early as October 1960 he and JFK had discussed the likely U.S. public reaction to an assassination attempt against Castro. The two senators had also considered provoking a Cuban assault on Guantánamo. George A. Smathers, Transcript, Oral History, John F. Kennedy Presidential Library, Boston, Massachusetts, March 31, 1964, 6B-7B.

2. "Kennedy Avoids Role in Decision," *New York Times,* January 4, 1961, 1.

3. John F. Kennedy, 1961, "Inaugural Address, January 20, 1961," in *Public Papers of the Presidents of the United States* (Washington, D.C.: Government Printing Office, 1962), 1–3.

4. Memorandum of Conversation, January 22, 1961, Department of State, *Papers Relating to the Foreign Relations of the United States 1961–1962*, vol. 10 (Washington, D.C.: Government Printing Office, 1997), 46–52.

5. Hoover Institutution, "Cuba," *Hispanic American Report* 14, no. 1 (January 1961): 32.

6. Trumbull Higgins, *The Perfect Failure: Kennedy, Eisenhower, and the CIA at the Bay of Pigs* (New York: Norton, 1987), 71.

7. Peter Wyden, *Bay of Pigs: The Untold Story* (New York: Simon & Schuster, 1979), 102; Arthur M. Schlesinger Jr., *A Thousand Days: John F. Kennedy in the White House* (Boston: Houghton Mifflin, 1965), 257; "Tenth Meeting: Memorandum for the Record" (May 4, 1961 at the Pentagon), in *Operation Zapata: The "Ultrasensitive" Report and Testimony of the Board of Inquiry on the Bay of Pigs* (Lanham, Md.: University Press of America, 1984), 222–223.

8. Aleksandr Fursenko and Timothy Naftali, *"One Hell of a Gamble": Khrushchev, Castro, and Kennedy, 1958–1964* (New York: Norton, 1997), 96–97.

9. James J. Blight and Peter Kornbluh, eds., *Politics of Illusion: The Bay of Pigs Invasion Reexamined* (Boulder, Colo.: Lynne Rienner, 1998), 89, 104; Wyden, *Bay of Pigs,* 170–172; "Memorandum No. 1," *Operation Zapata: The "Ultrasensitive" Report and Testimony of the Board of Inquiry on the Bay of Pigs* (Lanham, Md.: University Press of America, 1984), 18.

10. Report by Committee of U.S. Intelligence Board, The Military Buildup in Cuba, July 11, 1961, Department of State, *Papers Relating to the Foreign Relations of the United States 1961–1962: Cuba*, vol. 10, 621–622; Memorandum for the Record, July 26, 1961, ibid., 635.

11. The conversation between Guevara and Goodwin is noteworthy in at least two respects regarding Guantánamo. It opened with bantering that alluded to the heightened bilateral tensions by citing the Bay of Pigs and Guantánamo as the two major flashpoints in U.S.-Cuban relations. Moreover, it is persuasive evidence that Guevara, widely regarded as Cuba's most revolutionary figure, dismissed as absurd the possibility that Castro's forces would ever seriously threaten or jeopardize the

U.S. naval base. Memorandum of Conversation, July 13, 1961, Department of State, *Papers Relating to the Foreign Relations of the United States 1961–1962*, vol. 10, 624–625; Memorandum from the President's Assistant Special Counsel (Goodwin) to President Kennedy, August 22, 1961, ibid., 642–645.

12. Fursenko and Naftali, *"One Hell of a Gamble,"* 134–137.

13. According to Mary McCoy, when she was doing her research at Guantánamo, U.S. Navy officials told her the incident was closed, but one of the Cuban commuters said that Ruben López was regarded as a martyr in Cuba, and that some schools in the towns near Guantánamo Bay had been named for him. Mary Ellene Chenevey McCoy, "Guantánamo Bay: The United States Naval Base and Its Relationship with Cuba" (Ph.D. diss., University of Akron, 1995), 263. See also "Violence and Silence," *Newsweek* (May 13, 1963): 31; "The Hero and the Hush-Up," *Time* (May 10, 1963): 17–18; *New York Times*, May 2, 1963, 14; *New York Times*, May 4, 1963, 2; "Occurrence at Guantanamo," *Nation* (May 11, 1963): 386.

14. Shortly after this meeting, the JFK administration sought to isolate Cuba within the Western Hemisphere. In late January 1962 at Punta del Este, Uruguay, the OAS at U.S. prompting voted by a bare two-thirds majority to expel Cuba from the organization. On February 4, in Havana, Fidel responded to the OAS decision with the "Second Declaration of Havana," which called international attention to the widespread problems of poverty, disease, and illiteracy throughout Latin America and urged "revolutionaries to make revolution." The subsequent period from 1962 to 1967 marked the high point of Fidel's efforts to export the Cuban revolution. See Jane Franklin, *Cuba and the United States: A Chronological History* (Melbourne, Australia: Ocean Press, 1997), 48–49.

15. Roger Hilsman, *The Cuban Missile Crisis: The Struggle over Policy* (Westport, Conn.: Praeger, 1996), 12; Memorandum for the Record, Cuba 1961–1962, Department of State, *Papers Relating to the Foreign Relations of the United States 1961–1962: Cuba*, vol. 10, 696–699.

16. Memorandum for the Honorable McGeorge Bundy, John F. Kennedy National Security Files, Guantánamo Base, Box 49, John F. Kennedy Presidential Library.

17. Memorandum for the Secretary of Defense: Justification for U.S. Military Intervention in Cuba, March 13, 1962, publicly released by the National Security Archive, George Washington University Gelman Library, Washington, D.C., on April 30, 2001. It is unclear to what extent Operation Northwoods was intertwined with Operation Mongoose, but a cover letter written by Lemnitzer to McNamara on March 13, 1962, would suggest that Lemnitzer's proposals had been prepared in response to directives from Lansdale approved by McNamara. Joint Chiefs of Staff Central Files, 1962.

18. Ibid.

19. Department of State, *Papers Relating to the Foreign Relations of the United States 1961–1962: Cuba*, vol. 10, http://www.state.gov/www/about_state/history/frusken.html. (This Web site cites specific documents, but not page numbers. The document referred to is no. 314.) There is no mention anywhere in this volume of Operation Northwoods, but the following intriguing notation replaces Document No. 311: "Planning transmitted to you by my memorandum of 10 March 1962 should be returned to me for destruction as a matter of security."

20. James Bamford, *Body of Secrets* (New York: Doubleday, 2001), 82–88.

21. *Papers Relating to the Foreign Relations of the United States 1961–1962: Cuba*, vol. 10, no. 315.

22. Hoover Institution, "Cuba," *Hispanic American Report* 15, no. 3 (March 1962): 224; Hoover Institution, "Cuba," *Hispanic American Report* 15, no. 5 (May 1962): 413. Raúl Castro's formal title is Minister of the Revolutionary Armed Forces, which is the equivalent of Defense Minister.

23. According to Lars Schoultz, Cuba built a series of four fences, but the United States constructed only one fence topped by barbed wire. Put together, the United States and Cuba created "one of the largest active minefields in the world." Lars Schoultz, *National Security and United States Policy toward Latin America* (Princeton, N.J.: Princeton University Press, 1987), 164.

24. Warren Hinkle, former editor of *Ramparts* magazine, and William Turner, former FBI agent, describe a failed assassination plot that reportedly involved Cuban marksmen infiltrating Cuba through Guantánamo. Warren Hinkle and William W. Turner, *The Fish Is Red: The Story of the Secret War against Castro* (New York: HarperCollins, 1981), 104–105, 358.

25. "Castro Charges U.S. Is Preparing Attack," *New York Times*, July 27, 1962, 4.

26. "Priority Operations Schedule for Operation Mongoose," May 17, 1962, Department of State, *Papers Relating to the Foreign Relations of the United States 1961–1962: Cuba*, vol. 10, no. 338.

27. According to Jane Franklin, regular SGA members included Bundy, Gilpatric, McCone, Lemnitzer, and Deputy Undersecretary of State Alexis Johnson—augmented by RFK and Taylor. Rusk and McNamara sometimes attended SGA meetings. Richard Helms, who had replaced Richard Bissell as CIA chief of operations (then known as the deputy director for plans), also participated, as did Goodwin, along with Edward R. Murrow and Donald Wilson of the U.S. Information Agency. Franklin, *Cuba and the United States*, 46.

28. Hilsman, *Cuban Missile Crisis*, 12–13; Evan Thomas, *The Very Best Men: The Early Years of the CIA* (New York: Simon & Schuster, 1995), 270–271, 288–291; "Priority Operations Schedule for Operation Mongoose."

29. Memorandum from the Chief of Operations, Operation Mongoose (Lansdale) to the Special Group (Augmented), August 8, 1962. John F. Kennedy Library, National Security Files, Meetings and Memoranda, Special Group Augmented, Operation Mongoose, 8/62, Department of State, *Papers Relating to the Foreign Relations of the United States 1961–1962: Cuba*, vol. 10, no. 367.

30. Gus Russo, *Live by the Sword: The Secret War against Castro and JFK* (Baltimore, Md.: Bancroft, 1998), 57–60, 436–437. Russo, by his own admission, was a man with a mission. As he writes in his introduction, "My research has convinced me that John and Robert Kennedy's secret war against Cuba backfired on them—that it precipitated both President Kennedy's assassination and its coverup." Russo may be right, but in this reader's judgment, he failed to present a convincing case. The research is indeed voluminous, but Russo is not a historian. There is no indication that he checked or evaluated any of his information for accuracy or veracity.

31. Russo interviewed F. Lee Bailey on March 20 and April 11, 1993. Ibid., 60, 524 n. 38.

32. In his extensive research for *The Castro Obsession*, former Latin American editor of the *Miami Herald* Don Bohning did not find any evidence of covert actions that linked Operation Mongoose to Guantánamo. Telephone conversation with the author, April 7, 2009.

33. Taylor, who had served with great distinction in World War II and had been superintendent of West Point and U.S. Army chief of staff, was invited to the White

House in the aftermath of the Bay of Pigs to act as JFK's liaison to the JCS. His official title was military representative of the president.

34. *Papers Relating to the Foreign Relations of the United States 1961–1962: Cuba*, vol. 10, nos. 380, 384, and 386. JFK's authorization for Mongoose B Plus is contained in National Security Action Memorandum 181, which is discussed more fully in the text of this chapter.

35. McCone apparently believed that the discovery of surface-to-air missiles in Cuba was merely the first step in a Soviet effort to turn Cuba into an offensive military base that would eventually have medium-range surface-to-air missiles (SAMs) aimed at the United States and possibly Panama. Ernest May and Philip D. Zelikow, eds., *The Kennedy Tapes: Inside the White House during the Cuban Missile Crisis* (Cambridge, Mass.: Harvard University Press, 1997), 45. Rusk and Bundy soon joined McCone in pressing for more U-2 overflights of Cuba after they learned that the SAMs were SA-2s, the type that had shot down Gary Powers's U-2 over the Soviet Union in 1960.

36. *Papers Relating to the Foreign Relations of the United States 1961–1962: Cuba*, vol. 10, nos. 385 and 386.

37. Cold War antagonism between Washington and Moscow had also been exacerbated by the angry encounter between Khrushchev and Kennedy at the Vienna summit in June and by the erection of the Berlin Wall in August. For an excellent depiction of the international atmosphere that framed the Cuban missile crisis, see Donald Kagan, *On the Origins of War and the Preservation of Peace* (New York: Doubleday, 1995), 437–565.

38. John McCone, "Memorandum for the Record," in *The Literary Spy*, comp. and ed. Charles E. Lathrop (New Haven, Conn.: Yale University Press, 2004), 70–71.

39. According to Fursenko and Naftali, JFK's concerns about maintaining U.S. leadership of the free world repeatedly overrode his desire to take direct military action against Fidel. Fursenko and Naftali, *"One Hell of a Gamble,"* 149–150, 157.

40. The specific works cited by Bohning in addition to *"One Hell of a Gamble"* are Anatoli I. Gribkov and William Y. Smith, *Operation Anadyr: U.S. and Soviet Generals Recount the Cuban Missile Crisis* (Chicago, Ill.: Edition Q, 1994); Carlos Lechuga, *Cuba and the Missile Crisis* (New York: Ocean Press, 2001); and Bohning, *The Castro Obsession*, 111, 255–256.

41. Central Intelligence Agency Memoranda, John F. Kennedy National Security Files, Box 46, John F. Kennedy Presidential Library.

42. *Public Papers of the Presidents of the United States: John F. Kennedy, 1962* (Washington, D.C.: Government Printing Office, 1963), 674.

43. Gribkov and Smith, *Operation Anadyr*, 115–116. See also James G. Hershberg, "Before the Missiles of October," in *The Cuban Missile Crisis Revisited*, ed. James A. Nathan (New York: St. Martin's, 1992), 255.

44. This chapter does not purport to be yet another study of the Cuban missile crisis. It will refer only to those developments that either involved Guantánamo or arguably influenced U.S.-Cuban and Soviet relations pertaining to the future of the naval base. Department of State, *Papers Relating to the Foreign Relations of the United States 1961–1962: Cuba*, vol. 11, no. 16; Hoover Institution, "Cuba," *Hispanic American Report* 15, no. 10 (October 1962): 902.

45. Department of State, *Papers Relating to the Foreign Relations of the United States 1961–1962: Cuba*, vol. 11, no. 18.

46. Luna missiles, which NATO dubbed "FROGS," were solid-fueled missiles with a twenty- to twenty-five-mile range, to be loaded with two-kiloton warheads. Gribkov and Smith, *Operation Anadyr*, 40–41, 46.

47. Michael Dobbs, *One Minute to Midnight: Kennedy, Khrushchev, and Castro on the Brink of Nuclear War* (New York: Knopf, 2008), xiv, 124–125, 351–352.

48. Off the Record Meeting on Cuba, *Papers Relating to the Foreign Relations of the United States 1961–1962: Cuba*, vol. 11, no. 21.

49. Minutes of 505th Meeting of the National Security Council, *Papers Relating to the Foreign Relations of the United States 1961–1962: Cuba*, vol. 11, no. 34.

50. Jeff Broadwater, *Adlai Stevenson: The Odyssey of a Cold War Liberal* (New York: Twayne, 1994), 209; Robert F. Kennedy, *Thirteen Days: A Memoir of the Cuban Missile Crisis* (New York: Norton, 1969), 49–50. Arthur Schlesinger Jr.'s account of events closely parallels Broadwater's work (Schlesinger, *A Thousand Days*, 807–808, 810). See also David Detzer, *The Brink: Cuban Missile Crisis, 1962* (New York: Crowell, 1979), 155–160.

51. Broadwater, *Adlai Stevenson*, 209. O'Donnell later wrote, "I had never been much of an admirer of Stevenson up to that time, but it seemed to me, as it did to President Kennedy, that Adlai's readiness to take a stand in the Oval Office meeting in favor of a compromise offer was the kind of unselfish political courage seldom seen in Washington." Kenneth P. O'Donnell and David F. Powers, *"Johnny, We Hardly Knew Ye": Memories of John Fitzgerald Kennedy* (Boston: Little, Brown, 1972), 323.

52. Curtis A. Utz, *Cordon of Steel: The U.S. Navy and the Cuban Missile Crisis* (Washington, D.C.: Naval Historical Center, 1993), 32–33.

53. Brigadier General William R. Collins, U.S. Marine Corps, arrived on October 20 to take charge of ground forces at Guantánamo. The next day, air force military air transport service planes reinforced the base with marine battalion landing team (BLT) 2/1 aircraft. On October 22, Amphibious Squadron 8 put another marine contingent, BLT 2/2, ashore. Amphibious ships carried another marine infantry battalion from Morehead City, North Carolina. Subsequent reinforcements brought in another marine BLT and Battery C of the 3rd Marine Light Anti-Aircraft Missile Battalion equipped with Hawk missiles. Navy medical teams also arrived to augment the base hospital staff. By October 26, marine units at Guantánamo were prepared not only to defend the base from a Cuban-based assault but to support any U.S. invasion. Utz, *Cordon of Steel*, 26–27, 47; Dino A. Brugioni, *Eyeball to Eyeball: The Inside Story of the Cuban Missile Crisis* (New York: Random House, 1991), 338–339; Paul H. Nitze, *From Hiroshima to Glasnost: At the Center of Decision* (New York: Grove Weidenfeld, 1989), 227, 229. Navy Lieutenant William Pendley, who flew reconnaissance missions in his seaplane out of Leeward Point to verify the departure of missiles and missile equipment on specified high-interest Soviet ships, later recalled that he and his crew were struck by the impressive military buildup at Guantánamo. "We had flown out of Gitmo for periods in June 1961 and July 1962, and it was generally a sleepy place in-between naval exercises that were routinely conducted there." Rear Admiral William Pendley (retired), e-mail to author, May 30, 2006.

54. Dobbs notes that with hundreds of Cubans commuting to the base daily, it was "a simple matter for Cuban intelligence to infiltrate its own agents onto the forty-five-square-mile base. . . . Raúl also received regular intelligence updates from Cuban spies mingling with the workers who serviced the base." Dobbs, *One Minute to Midnight*, 48, 127.

55. Fursenko and Naftali, *"One Hell of a Gamble,"* 272.

56. According to seasoned diplomat and former U.S. ambassador to the Soviet Union Charles "Chip" Bohlen, the Kremlin was humiliated by the Cuban missile crisis. He recounts that as the missiles were being withdrawn from Cuba, high-ranking Soviet official Vasily Kuznetzov told John McCloy, "You Americans will never be able to do this to us again." Charles E. Bohlen, *Witness to History, 1929–1969* (New York: Norton, 1973), 495–496.

57. Central Intelligence Agency Memorandum, November 12, 1962, John F. Kennedy National Security Files, Box 46, John F. Kennedy Library; Memorandum from Harlan Cleveland to Secretary Rusk: Conversation with Mr. McCloy about Cuba, November 28, 1962, John F. Kennedy National Security Files, Box 46, John F. Kennedy Library.

58. Letter from Adlai E. Stevenson to Carlos Alfred Bernades, "U.S. Informs UN Security Council on Cuban Fishing Boat Incident," U.S./UN press release 4360, transmitted February 7, 1964, National Security File, Guantánamo Water Crisis, Box 3, Lyndon B. Johnson Library.

59. Report of Incursion of Four Communist Cuban Fishing Vessels, Document 1-E, National Security File, Guantánamo Water Crisis, Box 3, Lyndon B. Johnson Library.

60. Guantánamo Water Crisis, February 6–21, 1964, Chronology, Index, Document 1-B, National Security File, Guantánamo Water Crisis, Box 3, Lyndon B. Johnson Library.

61. At 12:15 P.M. McNamara had already ordered two military sea transportation service (MSTS) tankers to duty as Guantánamo water carriers, thus implementing contingency plans that had been prepared several years earlier. Ibid.

62. It is an instructive experience to listen to these audiotapes at the Lyndon B. Johnson Library. The quality of these recordings is generally excellent. At this early stage of LBJ's presidency, his manner is more informal and friendly with McNamara, whom he calls "Bob," than, for example, with Rusk, whom he addresses as "Mr. Secretary." As the excerpts in the above text suggest, however, LBJ is most comfortable and open with longtime friends and former colleagues A. W. Moursund, Mike Mansfield, and especially Richard Russell. Telephone Tapes of Water Crisis at Guantánamo, WH 6402.07 PNO 5–8 and PNO 6–9, February 6, 1964, Lyndon B. Johnson Library.

63. News Release FM GITMO, February 8, 1964, National Security File, Guantánamo Water Crisis, Box 3, Lyndon B. Johnson Library.

64. William B. Breuer, *Sea Wolf: A Biography of John D. Bulkeley, USN* (Novato, Calif.: Presidio, 1989), 187.

65. Ibid., 190–191.

66. Ibid., 194.

67. The flag riots left seventeen Panamanians and three U.S. marines dead and wounded almost four hundred people throughout the country. The fundamental question in the flag-raising was, Which nation was sovereign in the canal zone—the United States or Panama? The flag controversy dated back to the Eisenhower administration, when a similar incident by nationalistic Panamanians also led to violence and prompted Eisenhower to acknowledge that Panama deserved some "visual evidence of titular sovereignty." The unresolved question—who has ultimate sovereignty in U.S.-leased territory that includes military bases?—was virtually the same for Panama and Cuba. For a study of U.S.-Panamian relations from 1941 to

1967, see Lester D. Langley, "U.S.-Panamian Relations since 1941," *Journal of Interamerican Studies and World Affairs* 12, no. 3 (July 1970): 339–366.

68. Papers of William B. Breuer, Operational Archives Branch, Naval Historical Center, Washington, D.C.

69. "Remarks of the President at 18th Annual Dinner of the Weizmann Institute of Science," Office of the White House Press Secretary, February 6, 1964. National Security File, Guantánamo Water Crisis, Box 3, Lyndon B. Johnson Library.

70. Fidel Castro, press conference, February 6, 1964, Havana Prensa Latina, Foreign Broadcast Information Service (FBIS).

71. "Base Motives," *Washington Post*, February 7, 1964, sec. A, 16.

72. A. W. Moursand, a rancher and local judge, was one of LBJ's closest friends from the Texas Hill Country outside of Austin.

73. Telephone Tapes: WH 6402.08 PNO 2; PNO 3, Lyndon B. Johnson Library, transcription by Stephen I. Schwab.

74. Emphasis mine. According to biographer Doris Kearns Goodwin, from his entry into the Senate, LBJ had realized that Richard Russell's friendship and support were essential to his ambition to achieve a leadership role. "I knew there was only one way to get to see Russell every day," Johnson explained, "and that was to get a seat on his committee. . . . So I put in a request for the Armed Services Committee." Doris Kearns Goodwin, *Lyndon Johnson and the American Dream* (New York: Harper & Row, 1976), 103.

75. Telephone Tapes: WH 6402.08 PNO 5, Lyndon B. Johnson Library, transcription by Stephen I. Schwab.

76. On January 31, 1964, Mansfield had prepared a memorandum for LBJ on the situation in Panama in which he had argued that "our actions in Panama will produce respect, rather than fear and suspicious hostility, provided that our unquestionable power is used only with restraint." Mansfield also counseled that the United States should "avoid boxing ourselves . . . by crediting Castro and Communism too heavily for a difficulty that existed long before either had any significance in this Hemisphere." LBJ almost certainly read this memorandum—it was in his personal file—and it may have influenced his measured restraint in dealing with the water crisis that erupted the following week at Guantánamo. Mike Mansfield, Memorandum to the President: The Panama Situation, Memos to the President, vol. 1, National Security File, Lyndon B. Johnson Library.

77. Shortly after the onset of any international crisis, intelligence task forces that operate twenty-four hours a day and seven days a week are organized by the CIA, the State Department, and the Department of Defense. These task forces are in ongoing communication with each other and with the White House Situation Room to provide analysis and to levy requirements to collect additional intelligence for senior policymakers. These task forces remain in existence until the crisis has officially ended. "Possible Cuban Motivations for Fishing Boat Incident and Guantánamo Water Crisis," INR Reports, National Security File, Latin America–Cuba, Box 23, Lyndon B. Johnson Library.

78. Telephone Tapes, WH 6402.9 Citation 1932, Lyndon B. Johnson Library, transcription by Stephen I. Schwab.

79. Here Russell had the final say not only in the White House press release but what would be the official U.S. policy toward Cuba with respect to the autonomy of Guantánamo. WH 6402.9, Citation 1933. See also "President's Statement on Guantánamo Dispute," *Washington Post*, February 8, 1964, sec. E, 12.

80. Guantánamo Water Crisis, Chronology, Index, Lyndon B. Johnson Library.

81. In a 1964 interview with John Bartlow Martin, RFK recalled that he got into a violent argument with McNamara and Assistant Secretary for Latin America Thomas Mann. RFK said he thought the business about the fishing vessels was "foolish. It's like a speeding ticket." He criticized McNamara and Mann for "sounding like Barry Goldwater." According to Kennedy, this was the last time he really got involved in NSC and ExComm meetings. *Robert Kennedy in His Own Words*, ed. Edwin O. Guthman and Jeffrey Shulman (New York: Bantam, 1988), 407–409; *Washington Post*, February 8–9, 1964, sec. A, 4–5.

82. Telephone Tapes, WH 6402.11 Citations 1971 and 1972, Lyndon B. Johnson Library, transcription by Stephen I. Schwab.

83. "Soviet Involvement in Cuban Fishing Boat-Guantánamo Water Escapade," INR Reports, National Security File, Latin America–Cuba, Box 23, Lyndon B. Johnson Library.

84. Cable RUECW495, National Security File, Latin America–Cuba, Box 23, Lyndon B. Johnson Library.

85. "Guantánamo Barred to Newsmen," *Washington Post*, February 12, 1964, sec. A, 4.

86. "Cubans Claim U.S. Is Now Using Water," *Washington Post*, February 17, 1964, sec. A, 13; Breuer, *Sea Wolf*, 207–209.

87. Ibid., 211–215.

88. "Water for Guantánamo," *Science News Letter* (February 29, 1964): 131.

89. Telephone Tapes, WH 6404.2 Citation no. 2833, Lyndon B. Johnson Library, transcription by Stephen I. Schwab.

90. Robert S. McNamara, Memorandum for the President: Guantánamo Base, August 28, 1964, National Security File, Latin America–Cuba, Box 23, Lyndon B. Johnson Library.

91. It was in handling the simultaneous crises in Panama and Cuba that LBJ believed he had asserted his authority over foreign policy matters. Historian Robert Dallek characterizes LBJ as exercising a largely peripheral role in the JFK administration and being a "shadow figure" during the Cuban missile crisis. Robert Dallek, *Flawed Giant: Lyndon Johnson and His Times, 1961–1973* (New York: Oxford University Press, 1998), 18–19.

92. *Public Papers of the Presidents of the United States: Lyndon B. Johnson, 1963–1964*, vol. 1 (Washington, D.C.: Government Printing Office, 1965), 304–305.

93. Ibid., 365–372, 417, 566.

94. Fidel would persist in harassing the base; the most notable subsequent incident occurred on the night of June 28, 1964, when the Cubans installed blinding searchlights just outside the perimeter fence. True to form, Bulkeley retaliated the following day by having the Seebees mold a circular concrete slab on the hillside facing the front gate, on which they painted the world's largest Marine Corps emblem in iridescent red, gold, and white colors. That evening, when the Cubans discovered that they could not aim their floodlights at the sentries without illuminating the emblem, they turned off the lights. Breuer, *Sea Wolf*, 224–227.

Chapter 8. Guantánamo Endures

1. I argue in this book that Guantánamo became truly autonomous of Cuba when LBJ fired the Cuban commuters and installed the desalination plant in 1964

after the Castro regime tampered with the base's water supply. See Chapter 7 of this book.

2. According to British historian John Major, World War II had stimulated a shift in U.S. strategic focus from the Atlantic and Caribbean to Europe and the seas around it, and the onset of the Cold War had confirmed this shift with the new threat posed by the Soviet Union and "the inability of Britain and France to contain it." Further, technological developments, including nuclear weapons and long-range missiles, had rendered the Panama Canal indefensible. Finally, the United States could no longer shrug off the challenges of Panamanian nationalism as easily as it had in the past. John Major, "Wasting Asset: The U.S. Reassessment of the Panama Canal, 1945–1949," *Journal of Strategic Studies* (May 1980): 123–146.

3. The dimensions of the canal locks are 1,100 feet long and 110 feet wide. A Nimitz-class carrier is 1,092 feet long and 252 feet wide. Approximately 10 percent of the world's commercial vessels cannot use the canal, nor can major oil tankers. Lars Schoultz, *National Security and United States Policy toward Latin America* (Princeton, N.J.: Princeton University Press, 1987), 193, 215–216.

4. David Binder, "Naval and Civilian Aides See Guantánamo Base as Declining Asset," *New York Times,* August 30, 1977, 4. See also Donald Yerxa, *Admirals and Empire: The United States Navy and the Caribbean, 1898–1945* (Columbia: University of South Carolina Press, 1991), 158–159.

5. In May 1975, Senator George S. McGovern reported his recent trip to Cuba and his conversations with Fidel to the U.S. Senate Committee on Foreign Relations. According to McGovern, when he mentioned Guantánamo, Fidel replied, "If you ask the average Cuban, he will probably tell you that a foreign nation should not have a military base on our soil. But I will tell you that it is a secondary issue. We are not pressing the matter now." McGovern then privately reflected that "the possibility that Guantánamo could become a Soviet base is a major concern of American strategists." According to Cuba expert Brian Latell, Cuban-Soviet strategic military issues remained neuralgic for all occupants of the White House until the Soviet Union began to collapse in 1989. All of JFK's successors feared they could not live up to his "success" in the Cuban missile crisis. U.S. Senate Committee on Foreign Relations, Cuban Realities: May 1975, 94th Cong., 1st sess., 1975, Committee Print, 14–15; e-mail exchange with Brian Latell, March 15, 2007.

6. Binder, "Naval and Civilian Aides See Guantánamo Base as Declining Asset," 4.

7. Wayne S. Smith, *Selected Essays on Cuba,* Occasional Paper no. 9 (Baltimore, Md.: School of Advanced International Studies, Johns Hopkins University, 1986), 20–22.

8. Robert A. Pastor, *Whirlpool: U.S. Foreign Policy toward Latin America and the Caribbean* (Princeton, N.J.: Princeton University Press, 1992), 51.

9. "Raúl Castro Raises Issue of Guantánamo Base," *New York Times,* April 6, 1977, 4; "Castro Sets Terms for Better Ties," *New York Times,* April 9, 1977, 3.

10. According to Hugh Thomas's authoritative account, in 1933 Rodríguez had joined the communist movement when he was a compromise candidate for mayor of Cienfuegos. In 1934 he went to Havana, where he worked with an antigovernment strike committee. His entry into Batista's government in 1942 "marked the high tide of communist collaboration with the Batista regime." Hugh Thomas, *Cuba: The Pursuit of Freedom* (New York: Harper & Row, 1971), 733. Telephone conversation with former assistant secretary of state Ambassador Viron P. Vaky, December

5, 2004; e-mail exchange with former national security adviser for Latin America Robert Pastor, December 6, 2004.

11. Pastor saw a threat to U.S.-Cuban relations in Cuban-Soviet interventionism throughout Africa, and he also argued that Castro valued his role in Africa more than he did the normalization of relations with the United States. Pastor, *Whirlpool,* 52–53. See also Hedrick Smith, "U.S. Sees Cuba's African Buildup Blocking Efforts to Improve Ties," *New York Times,* November 17, 1977, 49.

12. "Castro Assails Carter on Human Rights," *Washington Post,* July 27, 1978, sec. A, 20.

13. For news reports on the Soviet MIG-23s in Cuba and the subsequent Gulf EX79 exercise, see "U.S. Sends Spy Planes to Study MIGs in Cuba," *Washington Post,* November 18, 1978, sec. A, 3; "U.S. Watches Soviet Moves in Caribbean," *Christian Science Monitor,* November 17, 1978, 3; "U.S. and British Flex Muscles in Cuban Theater," *Christian Science Monitor,* November 24, 1978, 7.

14. A noteworthy example was President Richard Nixon's three-month protest from October 1970 to January 1971 of Moscow's plan to build a nuclear-powered submarine base at Cienfuegos, Cuba. Deciding not to risk another major confrontation in Cuba, the Soviets canceled the project. See "Remarks on Cuba Base Reflect Worry about Soviets," *Washington Post,* October 1, 1970, sec. A, 15; also see "President Terms Cuba Off-Limits for Soviet Subs," *New York Times,* January 5, 1971, 1.

15. David D. Newsom, *The Soviet Brigade in Cuba: A Study in Political Diplomacy* (Bloomington: Indiana University Press, 1987), viii, 18–22, 50–59; "1,800 Marines Land at Guantánamo in Show of U.S. Might," *New York Times,* October 18, 1979. See also Stansfield Turner, "The Stupidity of Intelligence," *Washington Monthly* 18 (February 1986): 29–33; Pastor, *Whirlpool,* 56–57.

16. "War Games at Guantánamo through Cuban Eyes," *New York Times,* May 1, 1984, sec. A, 2; "Guantánamo Bay: U.S. Navy's 82-Year-Old Caribbean Toehold," *Christian Science Monitor,* December 3, 1985, 3.

17. According to correspondent David Binder, in 1979 there was a contingent of 420 marines, 1,850 navy, and 20 coast guard and air force personnel assigned to Guantánamo. "Once a Declining Asset, Guantánamo Gets New Life," *New York Times,* October 7, 1979, sec. E, 2.

18. "Navy Puts 94 Bases on Hit List," *Washington Post,* April 25, 1990, sec. A, 25.

19. "Haitians Caught in Legal Limbo," *Miami Herald,* November 5, 1991, sec. A, 1; "Haitian Repatriations Halted," *Miami Herald,* November 20, 1991, sec. A, 1. See also Brandt Goldstein, *Storming the Court: How a Band of Yale Law Students Sued the President—and Won* (New York: Scribner's, 2005), 12–13.

20. The U.S. government's reluctance to grant asylum to Haitian refugees was certainly based on prejudice, but it was not merely a partisan matter. In 1979, at the same time President Carter was extending an open welcome to Vietnamese and Cuban refugees, both the State Department and INS were treating Haitian "boat people" as "economic refugees" or mere job seekers not entitled to asylum. "8,000 Haitians Need Political Asylum Now," *New York Times,* October 25, 1979, sec. A, 19; "President Says U.S. Offers 'Open Arms' to Cuban Refugees," *New York Times,* May 6, 1980, sec. A, 1.

21. As Gary Maris found in his doctoral study of the international legal aspects of U.S.-Cuban relations, Guantánamo's legal status is anomalous in that the U.S. government has consistently refused to concede any aspect of its leasehold to the Cubans, but, at the same time, "the retention by Cuba of sovereignty over the area

has never been denied by the United States and remains a basic part of the legal relationship involved." Gary Maris, "Some Aspects of International Law in U.S.-Cuban Relations, 1898–1964" (Ph.D. diss., Duke University, 1965), 329. See also the Introduction and Chapter 3 of this book.

22. *Haitian Refugee Center v. Baker*, 112 S.Ct. 1245 (1992).

23. Koh had firsthand experience with seeking political asylum. When he was a child, his father, Kwang Lim Koh, was a South Korean diplomat assigned to Washington, D.C., when a military coup overthrew the democratically elected South Korean government he had served. Goldstein, *Storming the Court*, 24, 30–31.

24. Goldstein, *Storming the Court*, 143, 195–196, 208–209. Marine Corps Col. Larry Zinser, who was in charge of Guantánamo's refugee camp, sought repeatedly and unsuccessfully to have medical evacuations to the United States for the sickest refugees. Zinser then complained to the press, saying he was "upset" that the INS had rejected his requests. He eventually asked the Yale legal team to bring in a physician expert in treating AIDS. Derrick Z. Jackson, "Ready to Be a Martyr," *Boston Globe*, February 14, 1993, Sec. A, 7.

25. This portrayal of living conditions may be contrasted with the report prepared by the U.S. Atlantic Command, which, in connection with Camp Bulkeley, mentions "packets of health and comfort items" as well as an ample supply of toys for the children and dresses for the Haitian women. See Captain William R. McClintock and Captain Alexander G. Monroe, "Operation GTMO, 1 October 1991–1 July 1993," *USACOM Special Historical Study* (Norfolk, Va.: U.S. Atlantic Command), 19–20. See also Goldstein, *Storming the Court*, 122–123.

26. Harold Hongju Koh, "The 'Haiti Paradigm' in United States Human Rights Policy," *Yale Law Journal* 103, no. 8 (June 1994): 2391–2435.

27. Donald Rumsfeld and General Richard Myers, Department of Defense News Briefing, December 27, 2001, Avalon Project at Yale Law School, http://www.yale.edu/lawweb/avalon/sept_11/dod_brief137.htm.

28. Karen Greenberg, *The Least Worst Place: Guantánamo's First 100 Days* (New York: Oxford University Press, 2009), 16–19.

29. Ibid., 185–197. See also Karen J. Greenberg, "When Gitmo Was Relatively Good," *Washington Post*, January 25, 2009, B1.

30. Greenberg, *The Least Worst Place*, 212.

31. Goldstein, *Storming the Court*, 309–310.

32. Letter from Michael Ratner, *New York Times*, May 19, 2004, sec. A, 24.

33. James R. Van de Velde, "Camp Chaos: U.S. Counterterrorism Operations at Guantánamo Bay, Cuba," *International Journal of Intelligence and Counter-Intelligence* 18, no. 3 (Fall 2005): 538–548. A trainer of interrogators I interviewed when I visited Guantánamo in May 2007 explained that the original guidance for interrogators at Guantánamo specified that they were to interview each suspected terrorist every day. The interrogators were so shorthanded that they could only comply with this instruction by spending about thirty minutes with each suspect. The result was that the transcripts were highly repetitive and much of the information was of little or no value.

34. *Rasul v. Bush*, 124 S. Ct. 2686 (2004).

35. Jay Alan Bauer, "Detainees under Review: Striking the Right Constitutional Balance between the Executive's War Powers and Judicial Review," *Alabama Law Review* 57, no. 4 (Summer 2006): 1081–1104.

36. Emphasis mine; www.law.georgetown.edu/faculty/nkk/documents/Military Commissions.pdf.

37. Antonio de la Torre, "Cuba Would Return Escaped Prisoners to Guantánamo," *Reuters,* January 19, 2002.

38. Michael J. Strauss, *The Leasing of Guantanamo Bay* (Westport, Conn.: Praeger, 2009), 170.

39. In 1993 and 1994 the numbers of Cubans fleeing the island to seek asylum in the United States increased dramatically. A *New York Times* article of January 2, 1994, reported that 3,656 Cuban refugees had reached Florida by boat in 1993—the largest exodus since the Mariél boatlift of 1980. The *Times* attributed this increase largely to Cuba's economic problems following the collapse of the Soviet Union and the loss of Soviet subsidies. Clinton's executive decision to send Cuban refugees to Guantánamo, however, occurred in mid-August 1994, when the U.S. Coast Guard began rescuing Cuban rafters numbering almost four thousand in the Florida straits. "Record Number of Cubans Float to Florida Coast in '93," *New York Times,* January 2, 1994, 12; "137 Cubans Land in Florida; Largest Boatload since 1980," *New York Times,* July 2, 1994, 6; "U.S. Will Expand Patrols to Stop Cuban Refugees," *New York Times,* August 23, 1994, sec. A, 1, 16.

40. Statement by the Government of Cuba to the National and International Public Opinion, released by the Foreign Ministry of Cuba, January 11, 2002, 1–4.

41. Joint Statement, Office of the White House Press Secretary, May 2, 1995.

42. Author's interview with U.S. negotiator, Washington, D.C., August 10, 2006. Actually, the background to this particular request was that an aircraft had skidded off the runway while landing at Guantánamo.

43. Greenberg, *The Least Worst Place,* 11–12; Carol Rosenberg, "Disaster Drill Illustrates New Approach to Cuba," *Miami Herald,* July 20, 2009, A1.

44. Statement by the Government of Cuba.

45. It is important to keep in mind that the United States currently has more than seven hundred overseas military bases, and, as political scientist Bartholomew Sparrow has observed, "The presence of these foreign bases, in combination with the United States' navy, airpower, ground forces, and intelligence and technical capabilities, has allowed the United States to command the open seas throughout the last half of the twentieth century and has given the U.S. military the capability to operate and potentially intervene almost anywhere in the world." Bartholomew H. Sparrow, *The Insular Cases and the Emergence of American Empire* (Lawrence: University Press of Kansas, 2006), 233.

46. George Friedman, "Beneath the U.S. Obsession with Cuba," *Stratfor Global Intelligence* (April 13, 2009), http://www.stratfor.com/weekly/20090413 _beneath_u_s_obsession_cuba.

47. Elmore Leonard, *Cuba Libre* (New York: HarperTorch, 2002), 383–384.

48. Torre, "Cuba Would Return Escaped Prisoners to Guantánamo."

49. My translation of "De toda la historia de las bases situadas hoy en el mundo, el caso más trágico es el de Cuba: una base a la fuerza en nuestro territorio inconfundible, que está a buena distancia de las costas de los Estados Unidos, contra Cuba y contra el pueblo, impuesto por la fuerza y como una amenaza y una preocupación para nuestro pueblo." República de Cuba, Ministerio de Relaciones Exteriores, *Historia de Una Usurpacion: La base naval de Estados Unidos en la bahía de Guantánamo* (Havana, Cuba: Ministerio de Relaciones, 1979), 72.

50. The Statement by the Government of Cuba cited earlier affirms its intention to avoid making its claim to Guantánamo "a major issue [or] even a specially important issue, among the multiple and grave differences" that exist between Cuba and the United States. See this entire document in Appendix F of this book.

51. My translation of "Han visto ya a Guantánamo, jamás renunciarán a po-seerla." José Sánchez Guerra y Wilfredo Campos Cremé, *La Batalla de Guantánamo 1898* (Havana, Cuba: Verde Olivo, 2000), 142.

Appendix A: Imperial Germany and the Caribbean

1. "A Footnote: Kaiser's Plan to Invade U.S.," *New York Times,* April 24, 1971, 1.

2. In 1899, the uneasy truce over Samoa was disrupted by civil war among the Samoans. This crisis was also resolved diplomatically, but the fact that both the United States and England had opposed German efforts to dominate these islands enhanced the influence of naval militarists, especially Admiral von Tirpitz, who were pressing for the enlargement of Germany's battleship fleet. In July 1898, the respective flotillas of Admirals George Dewey and Otto von Diederichs clashed in Manila Bay when a German warship entering U.S. blockaded waters failed to show its colors and received a warning shot across the bow. Holger H. Herwig, *Politics of Frustration: The United States in German Naval Planning, 1889–1941* (Boston: Little, Brown, 1976), 14–39.

3. Herwig, *Germany's Vision of Empire,* 153. See also Thomas Schoonover, *Uncle Sam's War of 1898 and the Origins of Globalization* (Lexington: University Press of Kentucky, 2003), 74–75.

4. Commander J . . . . , "Sketches from the Spanish-American War" (Washington, D.C.: Office of Naval Intelligence, 1899), 5–6.

5. Alfred Vaghts, "Hopes and Fears of an American-German War, 1870–1915," *Political Science Quarterly* 55, no. 1 (March 1940): 53–76. From 1901 to 1903, according to Marks, Germany had a naval squadron permanently assigned to Caribbean and South American waters. Kaiser William II not only threatened to occupy Venezuelan ports but ordered soundings off the coast of Marguerita Island and Santo Domingo, and expressed serious interest in purchasing the Danish Virgin Islands. Frederick W. Marks, *Velvet on Iron: The Diplomacy of Theodore Roosevelt* (Lincoln: University of Nebraska Press, 1979), 6–7.

6. Steven T. Ross, *American War Plans, 1890–1939* (London: Frank Cass, 2002), x, 59.

7. Nancy Mitchell, "The Height of the German Challenge: The Venezuela Blockade, 1902–1903," *Diplomatic History* 20, no. 2 (Spring 1996): 206–207.

8. Nancy Mitchell, *The Danger of Dreams: German and American Imperialism in Latin America* (Chapel Hill: University of North Carolina Press, 1997), 225–228. It must be acknowledged, however, that such negative interpretations of late nineteenth- and early twentieth-century U.S. expansionist policies resonate with many students of Cuban history simply because U.S. policymakers did not share their fears or concerns regarding German "saber-rattling" with Havana. How to share sensitive information or to discuss threat perceptions even among close allies is fraught with such difficult questions as how much information can be exchanged without placing valuable, perhaps irreplaceable sources of such information at risk. Given this reality, it may be more understandable why policymakers such as Root, Wood, McKinley, and Roosevelt were unwilling to take Cuban leaders—whom they regrettably regarded as their intellectual and cultural inferiors—into their full confidence.

9. Paul W. Schroeder, "World War I as Galloping Gertie: A Reply to Joachim Remak," *Journal of Modern History* 44, no. 3 (September 1972): 319–345.

10. Marks, *Velvet on Iron,* 9.

BIBLIOGRAPHY

Manuscript Collections

Braden, Spruille. Spruille Braden Papers, Rare Book and Manuscript Library, Columbia University, New York, New York.

Breuer, William B. Papers of William B. Breuer. *Sea Wolf* Source Materials. Operational Archives Branch, Naval Historical Center, Washington, D.C.

Daniels, Josephus. Papers of Josephus Daniels, Manuscript Division, Library of Congress.

Hay, John. Papers of John Hay, Manuscript Division, Library of Congress.

Knox, Dudley. Papers of Dudley Knox, Manuscript Division, Library of Congress.

Lawrence, Alma. R. "Memorandum for Rear Admiral E. E. Duvall, U.S.N." December 10, 1952. OP-296/fes. Operational Archives Branch, Naval Historical Center, U.S. Navy Yard, Washington, D.C.

Matthews, Herbert. Herbert Matthews Papers. Rare Book and Manuscript Library, Columbia University, New York, New York.

McCalla, Bowman. *Bowman McCalla Memoirs*. U.S. Navy Library, U.S. Navy Yard, Washington, D.C.

Messersmith, George S. George S. Messersmith Papers. Special Collections Department, University of Delaware Library, Newark, Delaware.

Roosevelt, Theodore. Papers of Theodore Roosevelt. Series 1, Subseries A (Microfilm Reel 308), Manuscript Division, Library of Congress.

———. Papers of Theodore Roosevelt, Series 5, Subseries A (Microfilm Reels 417–424), Manuscript Division, Library of Congress.

Root, Elihu. Papers of Elihu Root. Manuscript Division, Library of Congress.

Schlesinger, Arthur M., Jr. Papers of Arthur M. Schlesinger Jr., John F. Kennedy Presidential Library, Boston, Massachusetts.

Welles, Sumner. Papers of Sumner Welles. Franklin D. Roosevelt Presidential Library, Hyde Park, New York.

White, Francis. Papers of Francis White. Herbert Hoover Presidential Library, West Branch, Iowa.

Wood, Leonard. Papers of Leonard Wood. Manuscript Division, Library of Congress.

Archival Collections

Acheson-Truman Memorandum. Papers of Harry S. Truman, Central File, Confidential Files, Containment in Latin America, 29A, Box 1 of 2, Harry S. Truman Library, Independence, Missouri.

Bradford, Royal B. Royal Bradford to the Secretary of the Navy, September 27, 1898, Record Group 45, PS-Bases, Cuba 1898–1910, Box 6, National Archives, Washington, D.C.

Cuba, Republic of. Secretary of State. Civil Report of the Secretary of State and Government of Cuba. Rare Books Collection, Library of the University of Havana, Havana, Cuba.

Dulles-Herter Series, Dwight D. Eisenhower Library, Abilene, Kansas.

John F. Kennedy National Security Files, Boxes 35–64, John F. Kennedy Presidential Library, Boston, Massachusetts.

Memorandum for the Secretary of Defense: Justification for U.S. Military Intervention in Cuba. http://www.gwu.edu/~nsaarchiv/news/20010430/northwoods .pdf. National Security Archive, George Washington University Gelman Library, Washington, D.C.

National Security Files, Lyndon B. Johnson Library, Austin, Texas.

Roosevelt, Franklin D. Papers as President. President's Secretary File. Box 76, State— Sumner Welles, October 1937–April 1938. Franklin D. Roosevelt Presidential Library, Hyde Park, New York.

Roosevelt, Theodore. Theodore Roosevelt Collection. Letters of Theodore Roosevelt to William Sheffield Cowles. BMS AM 1834 (788–820). Houghton Library, Harvard University, Boston, Massachusetts.

———. Letters of Theodore Roosevelt to Corinne Roosevelt and Douglas Robinson. BMS AM 1540 (63–127), Houghton Library, Harvard University, Boston, Massachusetts.

Smathers, George A. George A. Smathers Transcript, Oral History, John F. Kennedy Presidential Library, Boston, Massachusetts.

Telephone Tapes of Water Crisis at Guantánamo, Lyndon B. Johnson Library, Austin, Texas.

U.S. Department of State. File 811.345/135. General Records of the Department of State, State Decimal File, 1921. National Archives of the United States, Washington, D.C.

———. Record Group 59, General Records of the Department of State, State Decimal File, 1933–1944. National Archives of the United States, Washington, D.C.

U.S. Department of the Navy. General Board, Subject File 1900–1947, National Archives of the United States, Washington, D.C.

———. Secretary of the Navy. Record Group 45, Collection of the Office of Naval Records and Library, 1911–1927, National Archives of the United States, Washington, D.C.

———. Secretary of the Navy. Record Group 80, General Records of the Department of the Navy, Secretary of the Navy General Correspondence, 1916–1926, National Archives of the United States, Washington, D.C.

Whitman, Ann File. National Security Council Records, Dwight D. Eisenhower Library, Abilene, Kansas.

Government Publications

Congressional Record. 51st Cong., 1st sess., vol. 21. Washington, D.C.: Government Printing Office, 1890.

Congressional Record. 56th Cong., 2nd sess., vol. 34, pt. 3. Washington, D.C.: Government Printing Office, 1901.

Congressional Record 8, pt. 3. Testimony before the House Committee on Naval Affairs. December 15, 1903. 58th Cong., 2nd sess.

Congressional Record. 60th Cong., 2nd sess., vol. 43, pt. 2. Washington, D.C.: Government Printing Office, 1908.

Cuba, República de, Ministerio de Relaciones Exteriores. *Historia de Una Usurpacion:*

La base naval de Estados Unidos en la bahía de Guantánamo. 1979. Havana, Cuba: Ministerio de Relaciones Exteriores.

McClintock, Captain William R., and Captain Alexander C. Monroe. "Operation GTMO, 1 October 1991–1 July 1993," *USACOM Special Historical Study.* Norfolk, VA: U.S. Atlantic Command.

McKinley, William. *Message from the President of the United States to the Two Houses of Congress at the Beginning of the Second Session of the Fifty-Sixth Congress, with Reports of the Heads of Departments and Selections from Accompanying Reports (The Abridgment).* Vols. 1–2. Washington, D.C.: Government Printing Office, 1901.

Public Papers of the Presidents of the United States, John F. Kennedy, 1961. Washington, D.C.: Government Printing Office, 1962.

Public Papers of the Presidents of the United States, Lyndon B. Johnson, 1963–1964, Book 1. Washington, D.C.: Government Printing Office, 1965.

United Nations. *Vienna Convention on the Law of Treaties, 1969,* United Nations Treaty Series, vol. 1155, 2005.

U.S. Central Intelligence Agency. *CIA Documents on the Cuban Missile Crisis.* Edited by Mary S. McAuliffe. CIA History Staff, Center for Studies in Intelligence, 1992.

U.S. Department of Defense. Memorandum for the Secretary of Defense: Justification for US Military Intervention in Cuba, March 13, 1962, publicly released by the National Security Archive on April 30, 2001. Washington, D.C.: George Washington University Gelman Library, 2001.

U.S. Department of the Navy, *Annual Reports of the Navy Department.* Washington, D.C.: Government Printing Office, 1881–1944.

———. *Annual Report of the Navy Department for the Year 1898: Report of the Chief of the Bureau of Navigation.* Washington, D.C.: Government Printing Office, 1898.

———. *Annual Reports of the Navy Department for the Year 1898:* "Appendix to the Report of the Chief of the Bureau of Navigation." Washington, D.C.: Government Printing Office, 1898.

———. *Annual Report of the Navy Department for the Year 1899: Report of the Chief of the Bureau of Equipment.* Washington, D.C.: Government Printing Office, 1899.

———. *Annual Reports of the Navy Department for the Year 1903: Report of the Secretary of the Navy,* by William H. Moody. Washington, D.C.: Government Printing Office, 1903.

———. *Annual Reports of the Navy Department for the Year 1909: Report of the Secretary of the Navy,* by George von Lengerke Meyer. Washington, D.C.: Government Printing Office, 1909.

———. *Annual Reports of the Navy Department for the Year 1911: Report of the Secretary of the Navy,* by George von Lengerke Meyer. Washington, D.C.: Government Printing Office, 1911.

———. *Building the Navy's Bases in World War II: History of the Bureau of Yards and Docks and the Civil Engineer Corps, 1940–1946.* Vol. 2. Washington, D.C.: Government Printing Office, 1947.

———. Fleet Marine Force Reference Publication (FMFRP 12–32). "Foreword," *Naval Strategy.* Washington, D.C.: Department of the Navy, 1991.

U.S. Department of State. *Department of State Bulletin* 39, no. 995 (July 21, 1958).

——. *Department of State Bulletin* 39, no. 996 (July 28, 1959).

——. *Department of State Bulletin* 42, no. 1088 (May 2, 1960).

——. *Department of State Bulletin* 42, no. 1118 (November 21, 1960).

——. "Memorandum of the Solicitor for the Department of State." In *Right to Protect Citizens in Foreign Countries by Landing Force*. 3rd rev. ed. Washington, D.C.: Government Printing Office, 1934.

——. *Papers Relating to the Foreign Relations of the United States, 1901*. Washington, D.C.: Government Printing Office, 1902.

——. *Papers Relating to the Foreign Relations of the United States, 1902*. Washington, D.C.: Government Printing Office, 1903.

——. *Papers Relating to the Foreign Relations of the United States, 1903*. Washington, D.C.: Government Printing Office, 1904.

——. *Papers Relating to the Foreign Relations of the United States, 1906*. Washington, D.C.: Government Printing Office, 1909.

——. *Papers Relating to the Foreign Relations of the United States, 1910*. Washington, D.C.: Government Printing Office, 1916.

——. *Papers Relating to the Foreign Relations of the United States, 1911*. Washington, D.C.: Government Printing Office, 1918.

——. *Papers Relating to the Foreign Relations of the United States, 1912*. Washington, D.C.: Government Printing Office, 1919.

——. *Papers Relating to the Foreign Relations of the United States, 1934: The American Republics*. Vol. 5. Washington, D.C.: Government Printing Office, 1934.

——. *Papers Relating to the Foreign Relations of the United States, 1941: The American Republics*. Vol. 7. Washington, D.C.: Government Printing Office, 1962.

——. *Papers Relating to the Foreign Relations of the United States, 1942: The American Republics*. Vol. 6. Washington, D.C.: Government Printing Office, 1963.

——. *Papers Relating to the Foreign Relations of the United States, 1941: The American Republics*. Vol. 7. Washington, D.C.: Government Printing Office, 1962.

——. *Papers Relating to the Foreign Relations of the United States, 1958–1960: Cuba*, vol. 6. Washington, D.C.: Department of State, 1991.

——. *Papers Relating to the Foreign Relations of the United States, 1961–1963: Cuba*, vol. 10. Washington, D.C.: Department of State, 1997.

——. "Cuba, 1961–1962." *Papers Relating to the Foreign Relations of the United States, 1961–1963: Cuba*, vol. 10, nos. 314, 315, 338, 367, 380, 384, 386. http://www.state.gov/www/about_state/history/frusken.html.

——. "Cuban Missile Crisis and Aftermath," *Papers Relating to the Foreign Relations of the United States, 1961–1963: Cuba*, vol. 11, nos. 16, 18, 21, 34. http://www.state.gov/www/about_state/history/frusken.html.

U.S. House. Committee on Foreign Affairs. "Statement of Commander Bradford, U.S.N., March 30, 1898." *Compilation of Reports of Committee on Foreign Relations*, vol. 7. Washington, D.C.: Government Printing Office, 1901.

——. Committee on Naval Affairs. *Report of Subcommittee Appointed to Report on Need for Additional Naval Bases and Facilities at Guantánamo Bay, Cuba, San Juan, P.R., and St. Thomas, V.I.* May 18, 1939. CIS-NO: 76 H900-0.205.

———. *Statement of Rear Admiral William S. Cowles, Chief of the Bureau of Equipment, before the House Committee on Naval Affairs.* December 13, 1906. 59th Cong., 2nd sess., No. 46, Document 4.

U.S. Senate. Committee on Foreign Relations. *Cuban Realities: May 1975.* A report by Senator George S. McGovern. 94th Cong., 1st sess. Washington, D.C.: Government Printing Office, 1975.

———. *Senate Executive Document* No. 43. 51st Cong., 1st sess. Washington, D.C.: Government Printing Office, 1890.

Collected Works, Memoirs, and Contemporary Accounts

Adams, Henry. "The Session." *North American Review* 111 (July 1870): 29–62.

Alger, R. A. *The Spanish-American War.* New York: Harper, 1901.

Bancroft, Frederick. "Seward's Ideas of Territorial Expansion." *North American Review* 167 (July, 1898): 79–89.

Billman, Howbert. "Marines at Cusco Hill." In *The Chicago Record's War Stories by Staff Correspondents in the Field.* Chicago, Ill.: *Chicago Record*, 1898.

Bohlen, Charles E. *Witness to History, 1929–1969.* New York: Norton, 1973.

Bonsal, Philip W. *Cuba, Castro, and the United States.* Pittsburgh, Penn.: University of Pittsburgh Press, 1971.

Bonsal, Stephen. *The American Mediterranean.* New York: Moffat, Yard, 1912.

Bradford, Royal B. "Coaling-Stations for the Navy." *Forum* 26 (February 1899): 732–747.

———. "Statement of Commander R. B. Bradford, U.S.N., March 30, 1898." In *Compilation of Reports of Committee on Foreign Relations, United States Senate.* Vol. 7. Washington, D.C.: Government Printing Office, 1901.

Brugioni, Dino A. *Eyeball to Eyeball: The Inside Story of the Cuban Missile Crisis.* New York: Random House, 1991.

Cabrera, Raimundo. *Mis Malos Tiempos.* Havana, Cuba: El Siglo 20, 1920.

Castro, Fidel. *Revolutionary Struggle, 1947–1958.* Edited by Rolando E. Bonachea and Nelson P. Valdés. Cambridge: MIT Press, 1972.

Churchill, Winston. *The Churchill War Papers: Never Surrender, March 1940–December 1940.* 2 Vols. Edited by Martin Gilbert. New York: Norton, 1995.

———. *My Early Life: A Roving Commission.* London: Leo Cooper, 1989.

Commission on Cuban Affairs. *Problems of the New Cuba: Report of the Commission on Cuban Affairs.* New York: Foreign Policy Association, 1935.

Coolidge, Louis A. *An Old-Fashioned Senator: Orville H. Platt of Connecticut.* New York: Putnam's, 1910.

Crane, Stephen. *The War Dispatches of Stephen Crane.* Edited by R. W. Stallman and E. R. Hagemann. New York: New York University Press, 1964.

Cronon, E. David., ed. *The Cabinet Diaries of Josephus Daniels, 1913–1921.* Lincoln: University of Nebraska Press, 1963.

Dawes, Charles G. *A Journal of the McKinley Years.* Chicago: Lakeside, 1950.

Eisenhower, Dwight D. *Waging Peace, 1956–1961.* Garden City, N.Y.: Doubleday, 1965.

Ellsberg, Edward. "Naval Strength in Naval Bases." *Proceedings of the United States Naval Institute* 39 (September 1913).

Etzold, Thomas H. "Is Mahan Still Valid?" In *Proceedings of the United States Naval Institute* 106 (August 1980): 38–43.

Evans, Robley D. *An Admiral's Log, Being Continued Recollections of Naval Life.* New York: Appleton, 1910.

Fisher, John Arbuthnot. *Fear God and Dread Nought: The Correspondence of Admiral of the Fleet Lord Fisher of Kilverstone.* Edited by Arthur J. Marder. Vol. 1 of 3. London: Jonathan Cape, 1953.

Godkin, E. L. "Cuba's Foreign Relations." *Nation* 71 (August 2, 1900): 85–86.

Gribkov, Anatoli I., and William Y. Smith. *Operation Anadyr: U.S. and Soviet Generals Recount the Cuban Missile Crisis.* Chicago, Ill.: Edition Q, 1994.

Guggenheim, Harry F. "Amending the Platt Amendment." *Foreign Affairs* 12, no. 3 (April 1934): 448–457.

Harrison, Benjamin, and James G. Blaine. *The Correspondence between Benjamin Harrison and James G. Blaine 1882–1893.* Collected and edited by Albert T. Volwiler. Philadelphia, Penn.: American Philosophical Society, 1940.

Herbert, Hilary A. "The Lessons of the Naval Review." *North American Review* 156 (June 1893): 641–647.

Herring, Hubert. "Another Chance for Cuba." *Current History* 39 (March 1934): 656–660.

Hilsman, Roger. *The Cuban Missile Crisis: The Struggle over Policy.* Westport, Conn.: Praeger, 1996.

Howe, M.A. DeWolfe. *George von Lengerke Meyer: His Life and Public Service.* New York: Dodd, Mead, 1919.

Hull, Cordell. *The Memoirs of Cordell Hull.* Vol. 1. New York: Macmillan, 1948.

Hunt, William. *The Life of William H. Hunt.* Brattleboro, Vt.: E. L. Hildreth, 1922.

Kennan, George. *Campaigning in Cuba.* New York: Century, 1899.

Kennedy, Robert F. *Thirteen Days: A Memoir of the Cuban Missile Crisis.* New York: Norton, 1969.

———. *Robert Kennedy: In His Own Words.* Edited by Edwin O. Guthman and Jeffrey Shulman. New York: Bantam, 1988.

Koh, Harold Hongju. "The 'Haiti Paradigm' in United States Human Rights Policy." *Yale Law Journal* 103, no. 8 (June 1994): 2391–2435.

Kohlsaat, H. H. *From McKinley to Harding.* New York: Scribner's, 1923.

Knox, Dudley W. "An Adventure in Diplomacy." *Proceedings of the United States Naval Institute* 52 (February 1926): 273–287.

La Follette, Robert M. *La Follette's Autobiography: A Personal Narrative of Political Experiences.* Madison: University of Wisconsin Press, 1968.

Lansing, Robert. *The War Memoirs of Robert Lansing.* Indianapolis, Ind.: Bobbs-Merrill, 1935.

Lodge, Henry Cabot, ed. *Selections from the Correspondence of Theodore Roosevelt and Henry Cabot Lodge, 1884–1918.* Vol. I. New York: Scribner's, 1925.

———. "Our Blundering Foreign Policy." *Forum* (March 1895): 8–17.

———. "Our Duty to Cuba." *Forum* (May 1896): 278–288.

Long, Margaret, ed. *Journal of John D. Long.* Rindge, N.H.: Richard R. Smith, 1956.

Mahan, Alfred Thayer. "The Isthmus and Sea Power." *Atlantic Monthly* 72 (October 1893): 459–472.

———. *The Influence of Sea Power upon History 1660–1783.* Boston: Little, Brown, 1890.

———. *Letters and Papers of Alfred Thayer Mahan,* eds. Robert Seager II and Doris D. McGuire. Vols. 1–3. Annapolis, Md.: Naval Institute Press, 1975.

————. "The Panama Canal and the Distribution of the Fleet." *North American Review* 200, no. 706 (September 1914): 406–417.

Marvin, George. "Keeping Cuba Libre." *World's Work* (September 1917): 553–567.

McIntosh, K.C. "Guantánamo Bay." *American Mercury* (January 10, 1927): 106–112.

McNeal, Herbert P. "How the Navy Won Guantánamo Bay." *Proceedings of the United States Naval Institute* 79 (June 1953): 616–619.

Menocal, General Mario G. "Cuba's Part in the World War." *Current History* 9, no. 2 (November 1918): 315–318.

Minarik, William H. *Sailors, Subs, and Señoritas* (Boston: Brandon, 1968), 30.

Müller y Tejeiro, José. "Battles and Capitulation of Santiago de Cuba." *Notes on the Spanish War, War Notes, no. 1.* Washington, D.C.: U.S. Department of the Navy, Office of Naval Intelligence, 1899.

Newsom, David D. *The Soviet Brigade in Cuba: A Study in Political Diplomacy.* Bloomington: Indiana University Press, 1987.

Nitze, Paul H. *From Hiroshima to Glasnost: At the Center of Decision.* New York: Grove Weidenfeld, 1989.

O'Donnell, Kenneth P., and David F. Powers. *"Johnny, We Hardly Knew Ye": Memories of John Fitzgerald Kennedy.* Boston: Little, Brown, 1972.

Paine, Ralph D. *Roads of Adventure.* Boston: Houghton Mifflin, 1925.

Pastor, Robert A. *Whirlpool: U.S. Foreign Policy toward Latin America and the Caribbean.* Princeton: Princeton University Press, 1992.

Phillips, Ruby Hart. *Cuban Sideshow.* Havana: Cuban Press, 1935.

Pratt, Fletcher. "Caribbean Command." *Harper's Magazine* 188, no. 1125 (February 1944): 232.

Quesada, Gonzalo de. "Cuba's Claims to the Isle of Pines." *North American Review* 648, no. 190 (November 1909): 594–605.

"Replacement of Cuban Commuters with Jamaican Contract Workers." Operational Archives Branch, Naval Historical Center, U.S. Navy Yard, Washington, D.C.

Robinson, Albert G. *Cuba and the Intervention.* London: Longmans, Green, 1905.

Roosevelt, Franklin. *F.D.R.: His Personal Letters, 1928–1945.* Vol. 1. Edited by Elliott Roosevelt. New York: Duell, Sloan, and Pearce, 1950.

————. *The Public Papers and Addresses of Franklin D. Roosevelt.* Vol. 6. New York: Macmillan, 1941.

Roosevelt, Theodore. *Letters from Theodore Roosevelt to Anna Roosevelt Cowles, 1870–1918.* New York: Scribner's, 1924.

————. *The Letters of Theodore Roosevelt.* Edited by Elting E. Morison. Vols. 1–8. Cambridge, Mass.: Harvard University Press, 1951.

————. *The Naval War of 1812.* With an introduction by H. W. Brands. New York: Da Capo, 1999.

————. "General Leonard Wood: A Model American Military Administrator." *Outlook* 61 (January 7, 1899): 18–23.

————. "The Influence of Sea Power upon the French Revolution and Empire, 1793–1812." *Atlantic Monthly* 71 (April 1893): 556–559.

————. "The Influence of Sea Power upon History." *Atlantic Monthly* 66 (October 1890): 563–567.

————. Letter of the Assistant Secretary of the Navy to the Department, Transmitting the Proposed Personnel Bill, U.S. Senate, 55th Congress, 2nd Session, Document no. 97, December 9, 1897, 1–13.

Runcie, J. E. "American Misgovernment of Cuba." *North American Review* 170, no. 519 (February 1900): 284–297.

Sampson, William T. "The Atlantic Fleet in the Spanish War." *Century Illustrated Magazine* 57 no. 6 (April 1899): 886–914.

Schlesinger, Arthur M., Jr. *A Thousand Days: John F. Kennedy in the White House.* Boston: Houghton Mifflin, 1965.

Sherman, Forrest. "The British Occupation of Guantánamo Bay." *Proceedings of the United States Naval Institute* 57 (April 1931): 509–512.

Sims, William S. "The Inherent Tactical Qualities of All Big Gun, Large Calibre Battleships of High Speed, Large Displacement, and Gun-Power." *Proceedings of the United States Naval Institute* 32 (December 1906).

Smith, Earl E. T. *The Fourth Floor: An Account of the Castro Communist Revolution.* Washington: Selous Foundation Press, 1991.

Smith, Holland M. *Coral and Brass.* New York: Scribner's, 1949.

Smith, Wayne S. *The Closest of Enemies.* New York: Norton, 1987.

———. *Selected Essays on Cuba.* Occasional Paper No. 9. Washington: School of Advanced International Studies, Johns Hopkins University, 1986.

Smollett, Tobias. *The Adventures of Roderick Random.* New York: New American Library, 1964.

Staunton, S. A. "The Naval Campaign of 1898 in the West Indies." *Harper's New Monthly Magazine* 98 (January 1899): 175–193.

Stimson, Henry L. *Prelude to Invasion: An Account Based upon Official Reports by Henry L Stimson, Secretary of War.* Washington, D.C.: Public Affairs Press, 1944.

Stimson, Henry L., and McGeorge Bundy. *On Active Service in Peace and War.* New York: Harper, 1948.

Stockton, C. H. "The American Interoceanic Channel: A Study of the Commercial, Naval, and Political Conditions." *Proceedings of the United States Naval Institute* 25 (December 1899).

Taylor, H. C. "The Future of Our Navy." *Forum* 27 (March 1899): 1–6.

Torriente y Peraza, Cosme de la. *Cuba y Los Estados Unidos.* Havana, Cuba: Imp. y Papelería de Rambla, Bouza, 1929.

———. *Cuarenta Años de mi Vida (1898–1938).* Havana, Cuba: El Siglo 20, 1939.

———. "Cuba, America, and the War." *Foreign Affairs* 19, no. 1 (October 1940): 145–155.

———. "Fin de la Dominación de España en Cuba." In *Discurso Leido por el Academía de la Historia de Cuba.* Havana, Cuba: El Siglo 20, 1948, 153–157.

———. "The Platt Amendment." *Foreign Affairs* 8, no. 3 (April 1903): 364–378.

Turner, Stansfield. "The Stupidity of Intelligence." *Washington Monthly* 18 (February 1986): 29–33.

Twain, Mark. *Mark Twain's Weapons of Satire: Anti-Imperialist Writings on the Philippines-American War.* Edited by Jim Zwick. Syracuse, N.Y.: Syracuse University Press, 1992.

Van de Velde, James R. "Camp Chaos: U.S. Counterterrorism Operations at Guantánamo Bay, Cuba." *International Journal of Intelligence and Counter-Intelligence* 18, no. 3 (Fall 2005): 538–548.

Walker, Asa. "Notes on Cuban Ports." *Proceedings of the United States Naval Institute* 26, no. 2 (June 1900).

Welles, Sumner. *The Time for Decision.* New York: Harper, 1944.

White, William Allen. "Cuban Reciprocity—A Moral Issue." *McClure's Magazine* 19, no. 5 (September 1902): 387–394.

Williams, Dion. "The Defense of Our New Naval Stations." *Proceedings of the United States Naval Institute* 28, no. 2 (June 1902).

Wood, Leonard. "The Cuban Convention." *Independent* (November 1, 1900): 2605–2606.

———. "The Existing Conditions and Needs in Cuba." *North American Review* 168, no. 510 (May 1899): 593–601.

Wylie, Philip, and Laurence Schwab. "The Battle of Florida." *Saturday Evening Post* 26 (March 11, 1944): 14–15, 52–58.

Books: Secondary Sources

Abbazia, Patrick. *Mr. Roosevelt's Navy: The Private War of the U.S. Atlantic Fleet, 1939–1942.* Annapolis, Md.: Naval Institute Press, 1975.

Aguilar, Luis E. *Cuba 1933: Prologue to Revolution.* New York: Norton, 1972.

Ameringer, Charles D. *The Cuban Democratic Experience: The Auténtico Years, 1944–1952.* Gainesville: University Press of Florida, 2000.

Arevalo, Juan José. *The Shark and the Sardines.* New York: Lyle Stuart, 1961.

Bailyn, Bernard. *Atlantic History: Concept and Contours.* Cambridge, Mass.: Harvard University Press, 2005.

Bamford, James. *Body of Secrets.* New York: Doubleday, 2001.

Baptiste, Fitzroy André. *War, Cooperation, and Conflict: The European Possessions in the Caribbean, 1939–1945.* Westport, Conn.: Greenwood, 1988.

Beale, Howard K. *Theodore Roosevelt and the Rise of America to World Power.* Baltimore, Md.: Johns Hopkins University Press, 1956.

Beeler, John F. *British Naval Policy in the Gladstone-Disraeli Era, 1866–1880.* Palo Alto, Calif.: Stanford University Press, 1997.

Beisner, Robert L. *Twelve against Empire: The Anti-Imperialists, 1898–1900.* New York: McGraw-Hill, 1968.

Bemis, Samuel Flagg. *John Quincy Adams and the Foundations of American Foreign Policy.* New York: Norton Library, 1973.

Bender, Lynn Darrell. *The Politics of Hostility: Castro's Revolution and United States Policy.* Hato Rey, Puerto Rico: Inter-American University Press, 1975.

Blair, Clay. *Hitler's U-Boat War: The Hunters, 1939–1942.* New York: Random House, 1996.

Blight, James G., and Peter Kornbluh, eds. *Politics of Illusion: The Bay of Pigs Invasion Reexamined.* Boulder, Colo.: Lynne Rienner, 1998.

Blight, James G., Bruce J. Allyn, and David A. Welch, eds. *Cuba on the Brink: Castro, the Missile Crisis, and the Soviet Collapse.* New York: Pantheon, 1993.

Bohning, Don. *The Castro Obsession: U.S. Covert Operations against Cuba, 1959–1965.* Washington, D.C.: Potomac, 2005.

Bouvier, Virginia M. *Whose America? The War of 1898 and the Battles to Define the Nation.* Westport, Conn.: Praeger, 2001.

Braisted, William Reynolds. *The United States Navy in the Pacific, 1897–1909.* Austin: University of Texas Press, 1958.

Breuer, William B. *Sea Wolf: Biography of John D. Bulkeley, USN.* Novato, Calif.: Presidio, 1989.

Broadwater, Jeff. *Adlai Stevenson: The Odyssey of a Cold War Liberal.* New York: Twayne, 1994.

Brown, Charles H. *The Correspondents' War: Journalists in the Spanish-American War.* New York: Scribner's, 1967.

Buell, Thomas B. *Master of Sea Power: A Biography of Fleet Admiral Ernest J. King.* Annapolis, Md.: Naval Institute Press, 1995.

Bunting, Madeline. *The Model Occupation: The Channel Islands under German Rule, 1940–1945.* London: HarperCollins, 1995.

Chadwick, French Ensor. *Relations of the United States and Spain: The Spanish-American War,* Vols. 1 and 2. New York: Scribner's, 1911.

Challener, Richard D. *Admirals, Generals, and American Foreign Policy, 1898–1914.* Princeton, N.J.: Princeton University Press, 1973.

Chapman, Charles E. *A History of the Cuban Republic: A Study in Hispanic American Politics.* New York: Macmillan, 1927.

Clayton, Lawrence A. *Peru and the United States: The Condor and the Eagle.* Athens: University of Georgia Press, 1999.

Coffman, Edward M. *The Regulars: The American Army, 1898–1941.* Cambridge, Mass.: Belknap Press of Harvard University Press, 2004.

Coletta, Paolo E. *Bowman Hendry McCalla: A Fighting Sailor.* Lanham, Md.: University Press of America, 1979.

———. *French Ensor Chadwick: Scholarly Warrior.* Lanham, Md.: University Press of America, 1980.

Coletta, Paolo E., ed. *American Secretaries of the Navy.* Vols. 1 and 2. Annapolis, Md.: Naval Institute Press, 1980.

———. *Threshold to American Internationalism.* Jericho, N.Y.: Exposition, 1970.

Conn, Stetson, and Byron Fairchild. *The Framework of Hemisphere Defense.* Washington, D.C.: U.S. Department of the Army, 1960.

Cooling, Benjamin Franklin. *Gray Steel and Blue Water Navy: The Formative Years of America's Military-Industrial Complex.* Hamden, Conn.: Archon, 1979.

Cosmas, Graham A. *An Army for Empire: The United States Army in the Spanish-American War.* College Station: Texas A&M University Press, 1994.

———. "Joint Operations in the Spanish-American War." In *Crucible of Empire: The Spanish American War and Its Aftermath.* Edited by James C. Bradford. Annapolis, Md.: Naval Institute Press, 1993.

Cruikshank, Charles. *The German Occupation of the Channel Islands.* London: Oxford University Press, 1975.

Cruz Díaz, Rigoberto. *Guantánamo Bay.* Santiago de Cuba: Editorial Oriente, 1977.

Dallek, Robert. *Franklin D. Roosevelt and American Foreign Policy, 1932–1945.* New York: Oxford University Press, 1979.

———. *Flawed Giant: Lyndon Johnson and His Times, 1961–1973.* New York: Oxford University Press, 1998.

Dalton, Kathleen. *Theodore Roosevelt: A Strenuous Life.* New York: Knopf, 2002.

Davis, George T. *A Navy Second to None: The Development of Modern Naval Policy.* New York: Harcourt, Brace, 1940.

DePalma, Anthony. *The Man Who Invented Fidel: Castro, Cuba, and Herbert L. Matthews of the New York Times.* New York: Public Affairs, 2006.

Detzer, David. *The Brink: Cuban Missile Crisis, 1962.* New York: Crowell, 1979.

Divine, Robert A. *Eisenhower and the Cold War.* New York: Oxford University Press, 1981.

Dobbs, Michael. *One Minute to Midnight: Kennedy, Khrushchev, and Castro on the Brink of Nuclear War.* New York: Knopf, 2008.

Domínguez, Jorge I. *To Make a World Safe for Revolution: Cuba's Foreign Policy.* Cambridge, Mass.: Harvard University Press, 1989.

Dorwart, Jeffery A. *The Office of Naval Intelligence: The Birth of America's First Intelligence Agency.* Annapolis, Md.: Naval Institute Press, 1979.

Dubois, Jules. *Fidel Castro: Rebel—Liberator or Dictator?* Indianapolis, Ind.: Bobbs-Merrill, 1959.

English, T. J. *Havana Nocturne: How the Mob Owned Cuba—and Then Lost It to the Revolution.* New York: Morrow, 2008.

Fesperman, Dan. *The Prisoner of Guantánamo.* New York: Knopf, 2006.

Fitzgibbons, Russell H. *Cuba and the United States, 1900–1935.* New York: Russell & Russell, 1964.

Foner, Philip S. *The Spanish-Cuban-American War and the Birth of Imperialism.* Vol. 2, *1898–1902.* New York: Monthly Review Press, 1972.

Franklin, Jane. *Cuba and the United States: A Chronological History.* Melbourne, Australia: Ocean Press, 1997.

Franqui, Carlos. *Diary of the Cuban Revolution.* New York: Viking, 1980.

Freidel, Frank Burt. *The Splendid Little War.* Boston: Little, Brown, 1958.

———. *Franklin D. Roosevelt.* Vol. 1, *The Apprenticeship.* Boston: Little, Brown, 1952.

Fursenko, Aleksandr, and Timothy Naftali. *"One Hell of a Gamble": Khrushchev, Castro, and Kennedy, 1958–1964.* New York: Norton, 1997.

Gaddis, John Lewis. *The Cold War: A New History.* New York: Penguin, 2005.

Garraty, John A. *Henry Cabot Lodge: A Biography.* New York: Knopf, 1953.

Gellman, Irwin F. *Roosevelt and Batista: Good Neighbor Diplomacy in Cuba, 1933–1945.* Albuquerque: University of New Mexico Press, 1973.

Geyer, Georgie Anne. *Guerrilla Prince: The Untold Story of Fidel Castro.* Boston: Little, Brown, 1991.

Goldstein, Brandt. *Storming the Court: How a Band of Yale Law Students Sued the President—and Won.* New York: Scribner's, 2005.

Goodwin, Doris Kearns. *Lyndon Johnson and the American Dream.* New York: Harper & Row, 1976.

Gott, Richard. *Cuba: A New History.* New Haven, Conn.: Yale University Press, 2004.

Gould, Lewis L. *The Presidency of William McKinley.* Lawrence: University Press of Kansas, 1980.

———. *The Spanish-American War and President McKinley.* Lawrence: University Press of Kansas, 1982.

Graebner, Norman A. *Roosevelt and the Search for a European Policy 1937–1939.* Oxford: Clarendon, 1980.

Greenberg, Karen. *The Least Worst Place: Guantánamo's First 100 Days.* New York: Oxford University Press, 2009.

Griffith, Robert K., Jr. *Men Wanted for the U.S. Army: America's Experience with an All-Volunteer Army between the World Wars.* Westport, Conn.: Greenwood, 1982.

Hackemer, Kurt. *The U.S. Navy and the Origins of the Military-Industrial Complex, 1847–1883.* Annapolis, Md.: Naval Institute Press, 2001.

Haglund, David G. *Latin America and the Transformation of U.S. Strategic Thought: 1936–1940*. Albuquerque: University of New Mexico Press, 1984.

Hansen, Jonathan M. *The Lost Promise of Patriotism: Debating American Identity, 1890–1920*. Chicago, Ill.: University of Chicago Press, 2003.

Healy, David F. *The United States in Cuba, 1898–1902*. Madison: University of Wisconsin Press, 1963.

Heinl, Robert D., Jr. *Soldiers of the Sea: The United States Marine Corps, 1775–1962*. Annapolis, Md.: U.S. Naval Institute, 1962.

Helgerson, John. *CIA Briefings of Presidential Candidates, 1952–1992*. Washington, D.C.: Center for Studies in Intelligence, 1996. Available at www.odci.gov.

Herrick, Walter R., Jr. *The American Naval Revolution*. Baton Rouge: Louisiana State University, 1966.

Hershberg, James G. "Before the Missiles of October." In *The Cuban Missile Crisis Revisited*. Edited by James A. Nathan. New York: St. Martin's, 1992.

Herwig, Holger H. *Politics of Frustration: The United States in German Naval Planning, 1889–1941*. Boston: Little, Brown, 1976.

———. *Germany's Vision of Empire in Venezuela, 1871–1914*. Princeton, N.J.: Princeton University Press, 1986.

Higgins, Trumbull. *The Perfect Failure: Kennedy, Eisenhower, and the CIA at the Bay of Pigs*. New York: Norton, 1987.

Hinkle, Warren, and William W. Turner. *The Fish Is Red: The Story of the Secret War against Castro*. New York: HarperCollins, 1981.

Hitchman, James H. *Leonard Wood and Cuban Independence, 1898–1902*. The Hague: Martinus Nijhoff, 1971.

Hough, Frank O., Verle E. Ludwig, and Henry I. Shaw Jr. *Pearl Harbor to Guadalcanal: History of U.S. Marine Corps Operations in World War II*. Vol. I. Washington, D.C.: Historical Branch, G-3 Division, Headquarters, U.S. Marine Corps, 1958.

Hough, Richard. *First Sea Lord: An Authorized Biography of Admiral Fisher*. London: Allen & Unwin, 1969.

Jackson, Robert H. *That Man: An Insider's Portrait of Franklin D. Roosevelt*. New York: Oxford University Press, 2003.

Jenks, Leland Hamilton. *Our Cuban Colony: A Study in Sugar*. New York: Vanguard, 1928.

Jessup, Philip C. *Elihu Root*. Vol. 1, *1845–1900*. Hamden, Conn.: Archon, 1964.

Johnson, Willis Fletcher. *The History of Cuba*. Vol. 2. New York: B. F. Buck, 1920.

Jones, Howard. *The Bay of Pigs*. New York: Oxford University Press, 2008.

Kagan, Donald. *On the Origins of War and the Preservation of Peace*. New York: Doubleday, 1995.

Kelshall, Gaylord T. M. *The U-Boat War in the Caribbean*. Annapolis, Md.: Naval Institute Press, 1988.

Kimball, Warren F. *Forged in War: Roosevelt, Churchill, and the Second World War*. New York: Morrow, 1997.

LaFeber, Walter. *The New Empire: An Interpretation of American Expansion, 1860–1898*. 2nd ed. Ithaca, N.Y.: Cornell University Press, 1965.

Langley, Lester D. *The Cuban Policy of the United States: A Brief History*. New York: John Wiley and Sons, 1968.

Latell, Brian. *After Fidel: The Inside Story of Castro's Regime and Cuba's Next Leader*. New York: Palgrave Macmillan, 2005.

Lathrop, Charles E., comp. and ed. *Literary Spy.* New Haven, Conn.: Yale University Press. 2004.

Leonard, Elmore. *Cuba Libre.* New York: Harper, 2002.

Leopold, Richard. *Elihu Root and the Conservative Tradition.* Boston: Little, Brown, 1954.

Lipman, Jana A. *Guantánamo: A Working-Class History between Empire and Revolution.* Berkeley: University of California Press, 2009.

Livezey, William E. *Mahan on Sea Power.* Norman: University of Oklahoma Press, 1981.

Lynn, Brian McAllister. *The Philippine War, 1899–1902.* Lawrence: University Press of Kansas, 2000.

MacKay, Ruddock. *Fisher of Kilverstone.* Oxford: Clarendon, 1973.

Major, John. "The Navy Plans for War, 1937–1941." In *In Peace and War: Interpretations of American Naval History, 1775–1978.* Edited by Kenneth J. Hagan. Westport, Conn.: Greenwood, 1978.

Marder, Arthur J. *The Anatomy of British Sea Power: A History of British Naval Policy in the Pre-Dreadnought Era, 1880–1905.* Hamden, Conn.: Archon, 1964.

Margulis, Joseph. *Guantánamo and the Abuse of Presidential Power.* New York: Simon & Schuster, 2006.

Marks, Frederick W. *Velvet on Iron: The Diplomacy of Theodore Roosevelt.* Lincoln: University of Nebraska Press, 1979.

May, Ernest R., and Philip D. Zelikow, eds. *The Kennedy Tapes: Inside the White House during the Cuban Missile Crisis.* Cambridge, Mass.: Harvard University Press, 1997.

McCallum, Jack. *Leonard Wood: Rough Rider, Surgeon, Architect of American Imperialism.* New York: New York University Press, 2006.

McCann, Frank D., Jr. *The Brazilian American Alliance, 1937–1945.* Princeton, N.J.: Princeton University Press, 1973.

McCone, John. "Memorandum for the Record." In *The Literary Spy.* Compiled and edited by Charles E. Lathrop. New Haven, Conn.: Yale University Press, 2004, 70–71.

McCullough, David. *The Path between the Seas: The Creation of the Panama Canal, 1870–1914.* New York: Simon & Schuster, 1977.

McDougall, Walter A. *Promised Land, Crusader State: The American Encounter with the World since 1776.* Boston: Houghton Mifflin, 1997.

McSherry, Patrick. "Lee United States Naval Rifle." http://www.spanamwar.com/lee.htm.

Miller, Tom. *Trading with the Enemy: A Yankee Travels through Castro's Cuba.* New York: Atheneum, 1992.

Millett, Allan. *Semper Fideles: The History of the United States Marine Corps.* New York: Macmillan, 1980.

———. *The Politics of Intervention: The Military Occupation of Cuba, 1906–1909.* Columbus: Ohio State University Press, 1968.

Millis, Walter. *The Martial Spirit.* Cambridge, Mass.: Riverside, 1931.

Miner, Dwight Carroll. *The Fight for the Panama Route: The Story of the Spooner Act and the May-Herran Treaty.* New York: Octagon, 1971.

Miranda Bravo, Olga. *Vecinos Indeseables: La Base Yanqui de Guantánamo.* Havana, Cuba: Editorial de Ciencias Sociales, 1998.

Mitchell, Nancy. *The Danger of Dreams: German and American Imperialism in Latin America.* Chapel Hill: University of North Carolina Press, 1997.

Morison, Samuel Eliot. *The Atlantic Battle Won, May 1943–May 1945: History of Naval Operations in World War II*. Vol. 10. Boston: Little, Brown, 1968.

———. *The Battle of the Atlantic, September 1939–May 1943: History of United States Naval Operations in World War II*. Vol. 1. Boston: Little, Brown, 1970.

Morris, Jan. *Fisher's Face*. London: Viking, 1995.

Murphy, M. E. *The History of Guantánamo Bay 1494–1964*. Guantánamo, Cuba: U.S. Naval Base. http://www.nsgtmo.navy.mil/history/gtmohistory murphyvo11ch1.htm.

Musicant, Ivan. *Empire by Default: The Spanish-American War and the Dawn of the American Century*. New York: Holt, 1998.

Nevins, Allan. *Grover Cleveland: A Study in Courage*. New York: Dodd, Mead, 1966.

Offner, John L. *An Unwanted War: The Diplomacy of the United States and Spain over Cuba, 1895–1898*. Chapel Hill: University of North Carolina Press, 1992.

Operation Zapata: The "Ultrasensitive" Report and Testimony of the Board of Inquiry on the Bay of Pigs. Frederick, Md.: University Press of America, 1984.

O'Toole, G. J. A. *The Spanish War: An American Epic—1898*. New York: W.W. Norton, 1984.

Paterson, Thomas G. *Contesting Castro: The United States and the Triumph of the Cuban Revolution*. New York: Oxford University Press, 1994.

Pérez, Louis A., Jr. "Cuba, 1930–1959." In *Cuba: A Short History*. Edited by Leslie Bethell. New York: Cambridge University Press, 1993.

———. *Cuba: Between Reform and Revolution*. New York: Oxford University Press, 1988.

———. *Intervention, Revolution, and Politics in Cuba, 1913–1921*. Pittsburgh, Penn.: University of Pittsburgh Press, 1978.

———. *On Becoming Cuban: Identity, Nationality, and Culture*. Chapel Hill: University of North Carolina Press, 1999.

———. *The War of 1898: The United States and Cuba in History and Historiography*. Chapel Hill: University of North Carolina Press, 1998.

Perkins, Bradford. *The Great Rapprochement: England and the United States, 1895–1914*. New York: Atheneum, 1968.

Pletcher, David M. *The Diplomacy of Trade and Investment: American Economic Expansion in the Hemisphere, 1865–1900*. Columbia: University of Missouri Press, 1998.

Plischke, Elmer. *U.S. Department of State: A Reference History*. Westport, Conn.: Greenwood, 1999.

Porch, Douglas. *Wars of Empire*. London: Cassell, 2000.

Portell Vilá, Herminio. *Historia de Cuba en sus Relaciones Con los Estados Unidos y España*. Vol. 4. Havana, Cuba: Jesus Montero, 1941.

———. *Historia de la Guerra de Cuba y los Estados Unidos contra España*. In *Cuadernos de Historia Habanera*. Dirigidos por Emilio Roig de Leuchsenring. Vol. 41. Havana, Cuba: Municipio de la Habana, 1949.

———. *A History of United States Foreign Policy*. New York: Prentice-Hall, 1955.

———. *Theodore Roosevelt en la Historia de Cuba*. Havana, Cuba: Habanera, 1950.

Pratt, Julius W. *Expansionists of 1898: The Acquisition of Hawaii and the Spanish Islands*. New York: Peter Smith, 1951.

Pringle, Henry F. *Theodore Roosevelt*. New York: Harcourt, Brace, 1956.

Puleston, W. D. *Mahan*. New Haven, Conn.: Yale University Press, 1939.

Rabe, Stephen G. *Eisenhower and Latin America: The Foreign Policy of Anti-Communism*. Chapel Hill: University of North Carolina Press, 1988.

Reynolds, Clark. *Command of the Sea: The History and Strategy of Maritime Empires*. New York: Morrow, 1974.

Roig de Leuchsenring, Emilio. *Historia de La Enmienda Platt: Una Interpretación de la Realidad Cubana*. Vols. 1 and 2. Havana, Cuba: Cultural, 1935.

Rosenman, Samuel I. *Working with Roosevelt*. New York: Harper, 1952.

Roskill, Captain S. W. *A Merchant Fleet in War, 1939–1945*. London: Collins, 1962.

Ross, Steven T. *American War Plans: 1890–1939*. London: Frank Cass, 2002.

———. *U.S. War Plans: 1938–1945*. Boulder, Colo.: Lynne Rienner, 2002.

Russo, Gus. *Live by the Sword: The Secret War against Castro and JFK*. Baltimore, Md.: Bancroft, 1998.

Sanchez Guerra, José, and Wilfredo Campos Cremé. *La Batalla de Guantánamo, 1898*. Havana, Cuba: Verde Olivo, 2000.

Sargent, Herbert H. *Campaign of Santiago de Cuba*. Vols. 1–3. Chicago, Ill.: McClurg, 1907.

Schoultz, Lars. *National Security and United States Policy toward Latin America*. Princeton, N.J.: Princeton University Press, 1987.

Schriftgiesser, Karl. *The Gentleman from Massachusetts: Henry Cabot Lodge*. Boston: Little, Brown, 1944.

Scott, Rebecca J. *Degrees of Freedom: Louisiana and Cuba after Slavery*. Cambridge, Mass.: Belknap Press of Harvard University Press, 2005.

Seager, Robert II. *Alfred Thayer Mahan: The Man and His Letters*. Annapolis, Md.: Naval Institute Press, 1977.

Seeger, Pete. *Where Have All the Flowers Gone: A Singer's Stories, Songs, Seeds, Robberies*. Edited by Peter Blood. Bethlehem, N.H.: Sing Out Corporation, 1993.

Shulimson, Jack. *The Marine Corps' Search for a Mission, 1880–1898*. Lawrence: University Press of Kansas, 1993.

———. "Marines in the Spanish-American War." In *Crucible of Empire: The Spanish-American War and Its Aftermath*. Edited by James C. Bradford. Annapolis, Md.: Naval Institute Press, 1993.

Shulman, Mark Russell. *Navalism and the Emergence of American Sea Power, 1882–1893*. Annapolis, Md.: Naval Institute Press, 1995.

Smith, Robert F. *The United States and Cuba: Business and Diplomacy, 1917–1960*. New York: Bookman, 1960.

Sparrow, Bartholomew H. *The Insular Cases and the Emergence of American Empire*. Lawrence: University Press of Kansas, 2006.

Spector, Ronald. *Admiral of the New Empire: The Life and Career of George Dewey*. Baton Rouge: Louisiana State University Press, 1974.

Sprout, Harold, and Margaret Sprout. *The Rise of American Naval Power, 1776–1918*. Princeton, N.J.: Princeton University Press, 1939.

St. John, Ronald Bruce. *The Foreign Policy of Peru*. Boulder, Colo.: Lynne Rienner, 1992.

Strauss, Michael J. *The Leasing of Guantanamo Bay*. Westport, Conn.: Praeger, 2009.

Szulc, Tad. *Fidel: A Critical Portrait*. New York: Morrow, 1986.

Thomas, Evan. *The Very Best Men: The Early Years of the CIA.* New York: Simon & Schuster, 1995.

Thomas, Hugh. *Cuba: The Pursuit of Freedom.* New York: Harper & Row, 1971.

Tilchin, William N. *Theodore Roosevelt and the British Empire.* New York: St. Martin's, 1997.

Trask, David F. *Captains and Cabinets: Anglo-American Naval Relations, 1917–1918.* Columbia: University of Missouri Press, 1972.

———. *The War with Spain in 1898.* New York: Macmillan, 1981.

Turk, Richard W. *The Ambiguous Relationship: Theodore Roosevelt and Alfred Thayer Mahan.* Westport, Conn.: Greenwood, 1987.

Utz, Curtis A. *Cordon of Steel: The U.S. Navy and the Cuban Missile Crisis.* Washington, D.C.: Naval Historical Center, 1993.

Van der Vat, Dan. *The Atlantic Campaign: World War II's Great Struggle at Sea.* New York: Harper & Row, 1988.

Welles, Benjamin. *Sumner Welles: FDR's Global Strategist.* New York: St. Martin's, 1997.

Widenor, William C. *Henry Cabot Lodge and the Search for an American Foreign Policy.* Berkeley: University of California Press, 1980.

Wood, Bryce. *The Making of the Good Neighbor Policy.* New York: Norton, 1967.

Wyden, Peter. *Bay of Pigs: The Untold Story.* New York: Simon & Schuster, 1979.

Yerxa, Donald. *Admirals and Empire: The United States Navy and the Caribbean, 1898–1945.* Columbia: University of South Carolina Press, 1991.

Zebrowski, Ernest, Jr. *The Last Days of St. Pierre: The Volcanic Disaster That Claimed Thirty Thousand Lives.* New Brunswick, N.J.: Rutgers University Press, 2002.

Zimmermann, Warren. *First Great Triumph: How Five Americans Made Their Country a World Power.* New York: Farrar, Straus & Giroux, 2002.

Media: Newspapers, Newsletters, News Magazines, and Radio Transcripts

American Mercury, January 10, 1927.

Boston Globe, February 14, 1993.

Bulletin of Concerned Asian Scholars, December 1973.

Christian Science Monitor, November 17, 24, 1978; December 3, 1985.

Harper's New Monthly Magazine, January 18, 1899.

Life, November 25, 1940.

Marine Corps Gazette, December 1929.

Miami Herald, November 5, 20, 1991.

Nation, August 2, 1900.

New Republic, August 23, 1933.

New York Herald, January 31, 1890.

New York Times, May 1898–May 2004.

Newsweek, May 13, 1963.

Puck, 1881, 1901, 1902, 1903.

Reuters, January 9, 19, 2002.

Science News Letter, February 29, 1964.

Time, May 5, 1941; February 21, 1944; April 21, 1952; March 28, 1960; May 10, 1963.

U.S. News & World Report. December 14, 1959; April 11,1960; September 26 1960; October 3, 1960.

Wall Street Journal, January 1898–December 1903; February 1958–February 1964.

Washington Post, 1900–1988.

Articles and Periodical Literature

Bauer, Jay. "Detainees under Review: Striking the Right Constitutional Balance between the Executive's War Powers and Judiciary Review." *Alabama Law Review* 57, no. 4 (Summer 2006): 1081–1104.

"Caribbean Islands Supply Strategic Raw Materials." (Kingston, Jamaica) *Masses,* February 5, 1944, 46.

Clayton, Lawrence A. "Canal Morgan." *Alabama Heritage* 25 (Summer 1992): 6–19.

———. "The Nicaragua Canal in the Nineteenth Century: Prelude to American Empire in the Caribbean." *Journal of Latin Studies* 19, no. 2 (November 1987): 323–352.

Corbitt, Duvon C. "Cuban Revisionist Interpretations of Cuba's Struggle for Independence." *Hispanic American Historical Review* 43, no. 3 (August 1963): 395–404.

Cosmas, Graham A., and Jack Shulimson. "Continuity and Consensus: The Evolution of the Marine Advance Base Force, 1900–1922." *Proceedings of the Citadel Conference on War and Diplomacy* (1977): 31–36.

"Cuba." In *Hispanic American Report* 14, no. 1 (January 1961): 32.

"Dictator with the People." *Time* 59 (April 21, 1952): 38–46.

Eliot, George Fielding. "The World of Water: Naval Geography Shows Control of the Sea." *Life Magazine* 9 (November 25, 1940): 52–55.

Field, James A. "AHR Forum—American Imperialism: The Worst Chapter in Almost Any Book." *American Historical Review* 83, no. 3 (June 1978): 644–683.

Francisco, Luzviminda. "The First Vietnam: The Philippine American War of 1899." *Bulletin of Concerned Asian Scholars* 5, no. 4 (December 1973): 2–16.

Frost, Janet Delavan. "Cuban-American Relations Concerning the Isle of Pines." *Hispanic American Historical Review* 11, no. 3 (August 1931): 336–350.

"Gitmo—A Superb Base, an Excuse for Dispute." *Life Magazine* 49, no. 3 (July 18, 1960): 21.

Greenberg, Karen. "When Gitmo Was Relatively Good." *Washington Post,* January 25, 2009, B1.

Healy, David. "One War from Two Sides: The Cuban Assessment of U.S.-Cuban Relations." *Cercles* 5 (2002): 31–38. Available at www.cercles.com.

"The Hero and the Hush-Up." *Time* 81 (May 10, 1963): 17–18.

Heinl, Robert D., Jr. "How We Got Guantánamo." *American Heritage* 13, no. 2 (February 1962): 19–21, 94–97.

Hill, Roscoe R. "Historia de Cuba en sus Relaciones con los Estados Unidos y España." *Hispanic American Historical Review* 21, no. 4 (November 1941): 626–627.

Hoffman, Jon T. "From Makin to Bougainville: Marine Raiders in the Pacific War." http://www.nps.gov/archive/wapa/indepth/extContent/usmc/pcn-190 -003130-0/sec1.htm.

Langer, William L. "Farewell to Empire." *Foreign Affairs* 41, no. 1 (October 1962): 115–130.

Langley, Lester D. "U.S.-Panamanian Relations since 1941." *Journal of Interamerican Studies and World Affairs* 12, no. 3 (July 1970): 339–366.

Lazar, Joseph. "International Legal Status of Guantanamo Bay." *American Journal of International Law* 62, no. 3 (July 1968): 730–740.

———. "'Cession in Lease' of the Guantanamo Bay Naval Station and Cuba's 'Ultimate Sovereignty,'" *American Journal of International Law* 63, no. 1 (January 1969): 116–118.

Livermore, Seward W. "American Strategy Diplomacy in the South Pacific, 1890–1914." *Pacific Historical Review* 12, no. 1 (March 1943): 33–51.

Mackay, Ruddock. "The Admiralty, the German Navy, and the Redistribution of the British Fleet, 1904–1905." *Mariner's Mirror* 56 (August 1970): 341–346.

Major, John. "Wasting Asset: The U.S. Reassessment of the Panama Canal, 1945–1949." *Journal of Strategic Studies* (May 1980): 123–146.

Maurer, John H. "American Naval Concentration and the German Battle Fleet, 1900–1918." *Journal of Strategic Studies* 6 (June 1983): 147–181.

McClellan, Edwin North. "The American Marines of 1740–1742." *Marine Corps Gazette* 14 (December 1929): 286–297.

Meyer, Leo J. "The United States and the Caribbean Revolution of 1917." *Hispanic American Historical Review* 10, no. 2 (May 1930): 138–166.

Mitchell, Nancy. "The Height of the German Challenge: The Venezuela Blockade, 1902–1903." *Diplomatic History* 20, no. 2 (Spring 1996): 185–209.

"The National Geographic Society Expedition to Martinique and St. Vincent." *National Geographic* 13, no. 6 (June 1902): 183–184.

"Navy: General Smith Does a Job." *Time* 37 (May 5, 1941): 23.

Nowell, Charles E. "The Defense of Cartagena." *Hispanic American Historical Review* 42, no. 4 (November 1962): 477–501.

"Occurrence at Guantánamo." *Nation* (May 11, 1963): 386.

"Old Man of the Atolls." *Time* 43 (February 21, 1944): 25–27.

Pérez, Louis A., Jr. "Politics, Peasants, and People of Color: The 1912 'Race War' in Cuba Reconsidered." *Hispanic American Historical Review* 66, no. 3 (August 1986): 509–539.

———. "Supervision of a Protectorate: The United States and the Cuban Army, 1898–1908." *Hispanic American Historical Review* 52, no. 2 (May 1972): 250–271.

Plante, Trevor K. "New Glory to Its Already Gallant Record: The First Marine Battalion in the Spanish-American War." *Prologue* 30, no. 1 (Spring 1998): 21–31.

Portell Vilá, Herminio. "Historia de la Enmienda Platt: Una Interpretación de la Realidad Cubana." *Hispanic American Historical Review* 18, no. 2 (May 1938): 209–211.

Reynolds, Bradley. "Guantánamo Bay, Cuba." In *United States Navy and Marine Corps Bases Overseas*. Edited by Paolo E. Coletta. Westport, Conn.: Greenwood Press, 1985: 146–157.

Rosenberg, Carol. "Disaster Drill Illustrates New Approach to Cuba." *Miami Herald* (July 20, 2009): A1.

Scheina, Martin J. "The U.S. Presence in Guantánamo." *Strategic Review* 4 (Spring 1976): 81–88.

Schroeder, Paul W. "World War I as Galloping Gertie: A Reply to Joachim Remak." *Journal of Modern History* 44, no. 3 (September 1972): 319–345.

Shaw, Henry, I., Jr. "Opening Moves: Marines Gear Up for War: Atlantic Theater." http://www.nps.gov/archive/wapa/indepth/extContent/usmc/pcn-190-003115 -oo/sec2a.htm.

Smith, Robert F. "Twentieth-Century Cuban Historiography." *Hispanic American Historical Review* 44, no. 1 (February 1964): 44–73.

Thomas, Hugh. "The U.S. and Castro." *American Heritage Magazine* 29, no. 6 (October–November 1978): 26–35.

Tilchin, William N. "Theodore Roosevelt, Anglo-America Relations, and the Jamaica Incident of 1907." *Diplomatic History* 19, no. 3 (Summer 1995): 385–405.

Vaghts, Alfred. "Hopes and Fears of an American-German War, 1870–1915 [Part] II." *Political Science Quarterly* 55, no. 1 (March 1940): 53–76.

"Violence and Silence." *Newsweek* (May 13, 1963): 31.

"Water for Guantánamo." *Science News Letter* (February 29, 1964): 131.

Wells, Samuel F., Jr. "British Strategic Withdrawal from the Western Hemisphere, 1904–1906." *Canadian Historical Review* 49, no. 4 (December 1968): 335–356.

Unpublished Materials

Abrahamson, James L. "The Military and American Society, 1881–1922." Ph.D. diss., Stanford University, 1977.

Baker, George W., Jr. "The Caribbean Policy of Woodrow Wilson, 1913–1917." Ph.D. diss., University of Colorado, 1961.

Brown, April LaSchaun. "Between Nationalism and Hegemony: The United States and the Cuban Revolution." Ph.D. diss., University of Arkansas, 2006.

Costello, Daniel Joseph. "Planning for War: A History of the General Board of the Navy, 1900–1914." Ph.D. diss., Fletcher School of Law and Diplomacy, Tufts University, 1969.

Cummins, Lejeune. "The Origin and Development of Elihu Root's Latin American Diplomacy." Ph.D. diss., University of California, Berkeley, 1964.

Davis, George T. "The Naval Policy of the United States, 1880–1917." Ph.D. diss., Yale University, 1938.

DeFroscia, Patrick David. "The Diplomacy of Elihu Root." Ph.D. diss., Temple University, 1976.

Healy, David Frank. "The Formulation of United States Policy in Cuba, 1898–1902." Ph.D. diss., University of Wisconsin, 1960.

Herrick, Walter Russell, Jr. "General Tracy's Navy: A Study of the Development of American Sea Power, 1889–1893." Ph.D. diss., University of Virginia, 1962.

Lane, Jack C. "Leonard Wood and the Shaping of American Defense Policy." Ph.D. diss., University of Georgia, 1963.

Lloyd, James Frederick. "The Political Significance of the United States Naval Base, Guantánamo Bay, Cuba." M.A. thesis, University of Southern California, 1966.

Maris, Gary Leroy. "Some Aspects of International Law in U.S.-Cuban Relations: 1898–1964." Ph.D. diss., Duke University, 1965.

McCoy, Mary Ellene Chenevey. "Guantánamo Bay: The United States Naval Base and Its Relationship with Cuba." Ph.D. diss., University of Akron, 1995.

Mellman, Harry George. "The American Policy of Intervention in the Caribbean." Ph.D. diss., University of Illinois, 1940.

Mercogliano, Salvatore Robert. "Sealift: The Evolution of American Military Sea Transportation." Ph.D. diss., University of Alabama, 2004.

Peterson, Dale William. "The Diplomatic and Commercial Relations between the United States and Peru from 1883 to 1918." Ph.D. diss., University of Minnesota, 1969.

Reynolds, Bradley M. "Guantánamo Bay, Cuba: The History of an American Naval Base and Its Relationship to the Formulation of United States Foreign Policy and Military Strategy toward the Caribbean, 1895–1910." Ph.D. diss., University of Southern California, 1982.

Seager, Robert, II. "The Progressives and American Foreign Policy, 1898–1917: An Analysis of the Attitudes of the Leaders of the Progressive Movement toward External Affairs." Vols. 1–2. Ph.D. diss., Ohio State University, 1956.

Turk, Richard Wellington. "United States Naval Policy in the Caribbean." Ph.D. diss., Fletcher School of Law and Diplomacy, Tufts University, 1968.

Interviews

Bohning, Don. Former Latin American correspondent for the *Miami Herald*. Telephone interview by author, April 7, 2009.

Clayton, Lawrence. Professor of History, University of Alabama. Interview by author, January 14, 2009.

Latell, Brian. Former senior Cuban analyst of the Central Intelligence Agency. Telephone interview by author, March 9, 2006; e-mail exchanges, June 10, 2006, and March 15, 2007.

Pastor, Robert. Former national security adviser for Latin America. E-mail exchange with author, December 6, 2004.

Pendley, William, Rear Admiral (retired). Telephone interview by author, May 30, 2006.

Vaky, Viron P. Ambassador and former assistant secretary of state for the Western Hemisphere. Telephone interview by author, December 5, 2004.

INDEX